LORD DUNMORE
Reduced from old engraving in Wisconsin Historical Society's Library

DOCUMENTARY HISTORY
OF
DUNMORE'S WAR

1774

Compiled from the Draper Manuscripts in the
Library of the Wisconsin Historical Society
and Published at the Charge of the
Wisconsin Society of the
Sons of the American Revolution

Edited by
Reuben Gold Thwaites, LL.D.
and
Louise Phelps Kellogg, Ph.D.

HERITAGE BOOKS
2007

HERITAGE BOOKS
AN IMPRINT OF HERITAGE BOOKS, INC.

Books, CDs, and more—Worldwide

For our listing of thousands of titles see our website
at
www.HeritageBooks.com

A Facsimile Reprint
Published 2007 by
HERITAGE BOOKS, INC.
Publishing Division
65 East Main Street
Westminster, Maryland 21157-5026

Copyright © 1905 Reuben Gold Thwaites, LL.D.
and Louise Phelps Kellogg, Ph.D.

— Publisher's Notice —
In reprints such as this, it is often not possible to remove blemishes from the original. We feel the contents of this book warrant its reissue despite these blemishes and hope you will agree and read it with pleasure.

International Standard Book Number: 978-1-55613-226-1

ACKNOWLEDGMENT

At a meeting of the Executive Committee of the Wisconsin Historical Society, held on October 15, 1903, Vice President (now President) William Ward Wight made the following announcement:

> The Sons of the American Revolution, Wisconsin Society, offers to publish for the State Historical Society of Wisconsin such MSS. belonging to the latter society as would be appropriate for the former society to assist in circulating; it being understood that the Historical Society should edit the publication, and that the expense to the Sons of the American Revolution should not exceed $500.

Whereupon the Committee unanimously adopted the following resolution:

> *Resolved,* That the secretary be requested to convey to the Wisconsin Society, Sons of the American Revolution, the Wisconsin Historical Society's grateful appreciation and acceptance of the generous offer made through Mr. William Ward Wight, to supply the funds for the publication of a book under the direction of this Society.

After due consideration, it was agreed between the representatives of the Sons of the American Revolution and the Wisconsin Historical Society, that the projected volume should be devoted to a selection of papers appertaining to Dunmore's War (1774), from the Draper Manuscript Collection, now the property of the Society. A combination of circumstances prevented an earlier appearance of the book; but the delay has in some measure contributed to its betterment.

The members of the Society, and students of Western history in general, certainly owe a debt of gratitude to the Sons of the American Revolution for financing this publication of documents bearing upon that stirring and picturesque trans-Alleghany campaign—a colonial war which was participated in by a body of typical American borderers, who a year later were utilizing their military experience in the fateful struggle with the mother land.

The volume is also significant, in that it is the first considerable publication directly from the Draper Manuscript Collection, and exhibits the character and scope of that remarkable store of material for the original study of the beginnings of the Middle West.

R. G. T.

CONTENTS

ACKNOWLEDGMENT. *R. G. T.* v

INTRODUCTION. *The Editors.* ix

CLASSIFICATION OF DOCUMENTS

Western Surveys, Indian Depredations, and Defense of the Frontier, 1-9, 19-32, 52-61, 63-67, 69-78, 88-91, 138-142, 151, 161-163, 192-195, 202-205, 208-212, 216-222, 224-235, 238-252, 278, 279
Yellow Creek Massacre, 9-19
The Borderers "Forting", 33-67, 78-80, 94-97, 99-101, 103-106
Preparations for the Ohio Expedition, 68, 80-88, 91-93, 97, 98, 101-103, 106-110, 136-138, 142-150, 163-176, 179, 180, 199-202
Hanson's Journal, April 7-August 9, 110-133
Sinking Creek Massacre, 134-136
McDonald's Expedition, 151-156
Lewis's Column, on march to Camp Union, 156-161, 176-179
At Camp Union, 181-192, 195-199, 205-208, 222-224, 260, 261
Lewis's Column, Camp Union to Point Pleasant, 212-215
Point Pleasant, before the Battle, 236-238
Fleming's Account of the Battle of Point Pleasant, 253-257
Christian's Account, 261-266
Floyd's Account, 266-269
Shelby's Account, 269-277
Preston's Account, 291-295
Other Reports of the Battle, 257-259, 279-281
Fleming's Journal, August 27-September 29, 281-291
Close of the Campaign, 297-312, 395, 396
Fleming's Orderly Book, September 4-November 22, 313-360
Newell's Journal, October 17-October 27, 361-367
Dunmore's Official Report, 368-395
Muster Rolls of Companies defending the Frontier, 85, 94, 229, 234, 396-404
Muster Rolls of the Expedition, 106, 200, 405-412
Returns of the Troops, 189, 280, 288, 289, 296, 297, 301, 315, 317, 330-332, 344, 355, 363, 366, 367, 413-420
List of other Participants, 421-425
Biographies of Field Officers, 425-433
Contemporary Verse, 361, 362, 433-439

INDEX 441

ILLUSTRATIONS

                                                     Page

PORTRAIT OF LORD DUNMORE. From old engraving in the Society's Library   *Frontispiece*

HEADWATERS OF THE CLINCH AND THE HOLSTON. Map by Daniel Smith, in the Draper MSS. . . . 30

COMMISSION OF CAPT. GEORGE ROGERS CLARK, MAY 2, 1774. From original in Draper MSS. . . . 156

SITE OF THE BATTLE OF POINT PLEASANT. Map in the Draper MSS. 254

"THE FORM OF THE MARCH." Map by Col. William Fleming, from the Draper MSS. (text cut) . . 283

MAP OF THE VILLAGE OF POINT PLEASANT, AS SURVEYED IN JUNE, 1819. From original in Draper MSS. . 290

INTRODUCTION

Most histories of trans-Alleghany pioneering ascribe the origin of the Dunmore War of 1774 to an isolated set of occurrences upon the upper Ohio, happening in the spring of that year. But its roots went far deeper than this. It was the culmination of a long series of mutual grievances and outrages between the frontiersmen of Virginia and Pennsylvania and the savages of the Ohio Valley. The crushing of New France by Great Britain brought but partial rest to the English borderers. The pioneers of the British colonies relentlessly pushed westward; aboriginal hunting grounds were converted first into their own game walks and then into farms, and in the process the tribesmen were often harshly treated. Savage resentment and reprisal were to be expected—blazing into the swift flame of Pontiac's conspiracy (1763), and only half smothered by the severity of Bouquet's retaliatory expedition. The frontier was the line of contact for two irreconcilable races; real peace could not be had, until one or the other was vanquished beyond question.

The policy of the English government had been to limit settlement by the Alleghanies ;[1] but pressure was

---
[1] See Proclamation of King George, Oct. 7, 1763, in *Wis. Hist. Colls.*, xi, pp. 46-52; and Quebec Act, 1774, *Ibid*, pp. 53-60.

exercised by influential persons interested in American development, and by 1768 native title to lands between the mountains and the south bank of the Ohio was quieted by the treaty of Fort Stanwix, re-inforced by that of Lochaber (1770) with the Southern Indians, whose boundary was then fixed at Kentucky River.

The backwoodsmen of Pennsylvania and Virginia were a special class, formed chiefly of Scotch-Irish and German settlers, whom Lord Dunmore, then governor of Virginia, thus characterized in a report to the colonial secretary in London: "They acquire no attachment to Place: but wandering about Seems engrafted in their nature; and it is a weakness incident to it, that they Should forever imagine the Lands further off, are Still better than those upon which they are already settled."[2] Into the vast transmontane region which had been acquired at Stanwix and Lochaber, these men feverishly pressed, eager for fresh hunting grounds and virgin farms. Collision between them and the aborigines, many of whom denied the validity of the cessions, was inevitable.

North of the Ohio, a readjustment of tribes had recently taken place. The Delawares, first encountered by whites in the river valleys of eastern Pennsylvania, had gradually been dispossessed, and forced westward, until they reached the fertile valleys of the Muskingum and the Tuscarawas, in the eastern part of the present Ohio. Thither a peaceful remnant had brought Moravian missionaries, who built the towns of Beautiful Spring (Schönbrunn), Tents of Grace (Gnadenhütten), and Peace (Salem), where they gathered

---

[2] See p. 371, *post*.

their converts about them. These Christian villages probably were the most important element in restraining the Delaware tribe from yielding to the importunities of their neighbors to take up the hatchet against the Virginians. White Eyes, their principal chief, kept his people loyal to their peace pledge, and aided Lord Dunmore with information and advice that was as valuable as disinterested. Neighbors to the Delawares, dwelt the fierce Shawnee. Their history is involved in much obscurity, but their first home appears to have been to the south and west. In the first decades of the eighteenth century, their migration northward was being urged by French officials. From the middle of the century they were securely seated upon the Scioto, which became a centre of marauding parties launched against the Virginia frontier. Originally somewhat mild and peaceful under French control, their growth in numbers and influence made them the terror of the English border. Back of the Shawnee lay the tribes that had engaged in Pontiac's uprising—the Wyandot, the Ottawa, and the great confederacy of the Miami.

Throughout 1773 the dread of another Indian uprising lay heavy upon the hearts of Virginians, and the unprovoked massacre of young Boone and Russell, in Powell's Valley, in October, was considered a harbinger of evil. Through the long winter days, tales of raid and captivity on the Virginia borders, in 1755 and 1763, were rehearsed at every hearthstone —the attack on Draper's Meadows, when Colonel Patton was shot down, and the wives and children of Draper and Ingles carried to the Scioto villages; and the raid led by the Shawnee war-chief Cornstalk, who, under the guise of friendship, massacred the unsuspecting settlers on the Greenbrier. Rifles were taken down from their chimney pegs, and carefully cleaned and re-fitted, long hunting-knives were sharpened— the bordermen were determined not to be taken unaware, when the opening of spring made the valleys and their streams passable for both white and savage forays.

In the Indian towns, likewise, there was muttering and alarm. Itinerant traders straggling into the white settlements, reported that the savages were sullen, and at Detroit were exchanging their peltry for powder, ball, and tomahawks. George Croghan, Pennsylvania's deputy Indian agent at Fort Pitt, sent for some Shawnee chiefs, whom he detained as quasi-hostages from December, 1773, until the following April. In January, they were fired upon in their huts, by a party posing as Virginia militia, assembled by Dr. John Connolly, who had been sent by Lord Dunmore to maintain the authority of that province at the Forks of the Ohio. No one was injured, but the apprehensions of the natives were allayed with difficulty. By March, the people of southwest Virginia were abandoning their farms and retreating northeastward to more thickly settled neighborhoods. The panic was now so general that danger existed lest the Clinch and Holston valleys might be wholly abandoned. March 24th, a Williamsburg paper printed an address to the governor, urging a speedy declaration of war as "necessary, nay, inevitable." With such a quiver of expectancy in the air, it is idle to inquire who struck the first blow, or where Dunmore's War was begun.

As early in the spring as practicable, surveyors continued the work of the previous year, exploring and locating lands in Kentucky. At the request of Washington and other prominent Eastern men, Col. William Preston, official surveyor for Augusta County, dispatched several parties to lay out tracts for colonial officers entitled to land grants for military services. One of Preston's parties advanced down the Kanawha River and as far along the Ohio as the little Guyandotte, where Floyd writes of the indignities inflicted upon several persons by neighboring Shawnee. These latter claimed to have received instructions from Croghan to kill all Virginians, and to whip and rob any Pennsylvanians found trespassing upon their territory. Thomas Hogg, who had been surveying on the Kanawha, was reported missing, and it was feared he had been killed by hostiles. April 16th, a canoe belonging to one Butler, a prominent Pennsylvania trader, was fired upon near the mouth of the Little Beaver, and two of its Indian occupants killed. Incited by these events, and the numerous rumors flying about, Connolly, probably acting on his own initiative, issued on the twenty-first of April, a somewhat incendiary circular, asserting that a state of war already existed, and calling on the borderers to arm themselves in their own defense. The panic became contagious. There was a rapid retreat across the Monongahela—more than a thousand are said to have passed over in one day.

Connolly's circular reached the neighborhood of the modern Wheeling on the twenty-fourth or the twenty-fifth of the month. Stirring events had, shortly before, taken place in this neighborhood. A number of young men were waiting here for the spring freshet to carry them down to Kentucky; among these, George

Rogers Clark, a youthful Virginian who was destined to play a prominent part in Western history. From a letter by Clark, written twenty-four years after, we learn that a plan to march against the Indians, in any direction, was enthusiastically embraced by the waiting emigrants. For leader there was proposed Capt. Michael Cresap, a Maryland prospector, with experience in Indian warfare, who was settling near by. But to the surprise of all, Cresap sought to dissuade them from the enterprise, and pleaded for peace. A few days later, however, on the arrival of Connolly's circular, war was declared in the usual barbarous fashion of the frontier: "The war post was planted, a Council called and the Ceremonies used by the Indians on so important an Occasion acted, and war was formally declared. . . . The same evening, two scalps were brought to Camp."[3] Cresap having been selected as the white leader, the disturbance which followed was, despite his declination of the office, popularly styled "Cresap's War." Accordingly the Indians laid to Cresap's charge the wilful murder of Chief Logan's family at the mouth of Yellow Creek, on the morning of the thirtieth of April—a disgraceful deed in which that worthy took no part.

Despite the threatening aspect of affairs, the tribesmen appear to have been slow in taking the war-path. Isolated parties went out with hostile intent, as the long catalogue of ravages show; but as late as July 21st, the ill-treated Logan stated in a letter to the whites, "The Indians are not angry, only myself."

---

[3] Clark's letter, in Mayer, *Logan and Cresap*, pp. 149–154; Jacob, *Life of Cresap*, pp. 154–158; Perkins, *Western Annals*, p. 143.

INTRODUCTION

The Pennsylvanians hoped that peace might still be preserved. The deputy Indian agents of that province summoned the chief to Fort Pitt, and with the aid of the peacefully-inclined Delawares attempted to readjust the terms of the treaty. While negotiations were pending, the Shawnee protected a body of white traders then operating in their country, and sent them under escort to Fort Pitt, where the native guard was treacherously fired upon by irresponsible Indian haters.

But from the borders of southwest Virginia, alarming reports continued to pour into Williamsburg, the Virginia capital. The enemy had penetrated to within thirty miles of Botetourt courthouse, and all settlers upon the Holston and Clinch were gathered within fortified stockades. Impelled by this serious condition, Lord Dunmore took the initiative, issued a circular letter (June 10) calling out the militia of the western counties, and prepared for aggressive measures. The responsible local military official was the county-lieutenant; upon him devolved the commissioning of officers, the raising and provisioning of troops, the location of forts, and measures for defense and offense. When this officer, as in the case of Col. William Preston of Fincastle, was also sheriff and county surveyor, practically all public business passed through his hands. The preservation, therefore, of the Preston Papers, in the Draper Manuscript Collection, enables us to present an epitome of the times—especially in matters relating to Fincastle, then the most western Virginia county, embracing all of the present state of Kentucky and much of what is now West Virginia.

Colonel Preston's first care was for the surveyors who had been sent out to Kentucky. Should they linger in that exposed quarter, their lives were in imminent danger. Capt. William Russell, who lived upon Clinch River—the border of southwestern settlement—secured Daniel Boone and Michael Stoner, two seasoned woodsmen, to go as runners through Kentucky, and warn the surveyors and any outlying settlers or hunters of their impending peril. In a successful circuit of over sixty days, the two messengers ventured as far as the Falls of the Ohio (the modern Louisville), their timely warnings saving all the surveyors exept Hancock Taylor and his companions. They also notified a company of pioneers under James Harrod, who were building cabins near the site of Harrodsburg, but who returned to the settlements in time to join the troops destined for Point Pleasant. The next care was for the distressed inhabitants of the frontier. Dependent for sustenance upon their crops, they were collected within numerous small stockade forts, garrisoned by those men and youths of the neighborhood who were not serving elsewhere in the militia. From these log strongholds they could in favorable seasons make sorties to care for their corn and the cattle running loose upon the range. From each centre of defense thus established, scouts were despatched along the trails toward the Indian "tracks," and news of Indian "sign" was quickly spread from fort to fort. Notwithstanding these precautions, bands of stealthy savage marauders continued to slip in, and during July and August there were frequent reports of plunderings, burnings, captures, and massacres at their hands.

Meanwhile, the governor had continued his preparations. In July he left Williamsburg to visit the frontier, and sent orders to Col. Angus McDonald to move down the Ohio, build a fort at Wheeling, and advance against the nearest Shawnee town on the Muskingum. This expedition, however, but stirred the hornets' nest. The Indians were now thoroughly aroused, frequent war-parties were despatched against the frontier, ravages multiplied, and the need of sterner measures became apparent.

On the twenty-fourth, his lordship wrote from Winchester to Col. Andrew Lewis, of Botetourt, commander-in-chief of the southwestern militia, to the effect that he was on his way to Fort Pitt with as large a force as he could gather in that region; he desired Lewis "to raise a respectable body in your quarter, and join me either at the mouth of the Great Kanawha or Wheeling, or such other point on the Ohio as may be most convenient for you to meet me." Lewis, an experienced Indian fighter, had served throughout the French and Indian War side by side with Washington, and knew all the bordermen with whom he had to deal. Already, upon the receipt of previous orders from the governor (sent July 12) he had hastened expresses to his brother Charles, county-lieutenant for Augusta—embracing the central valley of Virginia, and its neighborhood west and north—and to his friend Preston, in Fincastle, to prepare for an expedition to the Indian towns, as the surest method of "reducing our inveterate enemies to reason." Thereupon the county-lieutenants summoned their men to arms. "The opportunity we have so long wished for," wrote Preston, "is now before us." The appeal did not fall upon unheeding ears. The men of the frontier responded with alacrity. A generous rivalry arose among the officers, as to who should have the largest and best-equipped company. Five weeks were spent in enlisting, securing provisions, and marching to the appointed rendezvous. Settlers in the neighborhood of Staunton gathered under the command of Charles Lewis, a brave and dashing officer, the idol of the army. Fourteen companies, captained by their natural leaders, arrived first at the appointed rendezvous—Camp Union (Lewisburg, W. Va.), on the Big Levels of the Greenbrier; their camp-fires furnished a beacon for the tardier troops from Botetourt and Fincastle. Every man in one company of Augusta troops was said to measure above six feet in his moccasins. Col. Andrew Lewis being in general command, placed his particular division under the charge of Col. William Fleming, a skilful surgeon, and a man of culture, whose popularity with his men was unbounded. Under Fleming, seven captains led out the Botetourt troops, three hundred and fifty strong. Upon Fleming's arrival at Camp Union, he found not only the Augusta contingent, but companies of men from Holston, under Captains Shelby and Russell. The Holston men were the advance guard of civilization, on the farthest border yet pushed out into the Western wilderness, out of which the states of Kentucky and Tennessee were in due time to be carved. The remaining Fincastle men, under the command of Col. William Christian, arrived at the rendezvous September 6th, the evening before the march of the advance. To their chagrin, this tardiness resulted in their being assigned to the rear rank.

in charge of the baggage and supplies. Before the troops left the Levels, they were joined by two independent companies from neighboring eastern counties —Col. Thomas Buford bringing in a contingent of Bedford men, and Col. John Field an independent command from Culpeper.

With McDonald's men as the nucleus, the governor had raised a force from the northwestern counties of Virginia and the neighborhood of Pittsburg, embodying quite twelve hundred men. While these were gathering at Fort Dunmore—the new stockade on the site of Fort Pitt—the governor was treating with what Indian chiefs he could assemble there, and planning for an advance in the direction of the recalcitrant tribes. By the thirtieth of September his column was at Wheeling, moving down the Ohio in two divisions, one by land, the other by river. At the mouth of Hockhocking they halted, erected a stockade styled Fort Gower, and awaited news of Lewis's brigade.

That officer was meanwhile advancing over the rugged paths of the Kanawha route. By the twenty-seventh of September he had reached the mouth of Elk River, where is now the capital of West Virginia. Here the little army tarried a few days to build canoes for the easier transportation of supplies, and to reconnoitre for Indian parties, supposed to be hovering on their flanks. It was, therefore, the sixth of October before the main body of the army reached the Ohio River, and, eleven hundred strong, encamped at Point Pleasant, the triangle formed by the conjunction of the Great Kanawha and the Ohio.

Rage and resentment animated the savages, as their scouts brought word of the two brigades, both of Dunmore and Lewis, apparently bent on their destruction. They thought that by assailing these isolated columns, they might crush each in turn. Disregarding the advice of Cornstalk, who counselled peace, it was determined to surprise Lewis's division at dawn, and then if successful to advance against his lordship and prevent the union of the two wings. Silently, under cover of the forest, there were gathered a thousand painted savages—Shawnee for the most part, re-inforced by Mingo, Delaware, Wyandot, and Ottawa braves—who crossed the Ohio on rafts during the night of the ninth of October, and before daybreak stood ready to assault the sleeping camp at Point Pleasant.

It is not proposed here to narrate in detail the events of the memorable battle, and the death of the gallant Charles Lewis and his fellow officers; that is more effectively done by the actors themselves, in the contemporary documents published for the first time in the present volume. One movement, perhaps unduly magnified by secondary writers, receives scant notice in these documents—that is, the attempt of Shelby, Matthews, Arbuckle, and Stuart to flank the Indian line by a march along the east bank of Crooked Creek.[4] The Indians apparently interpreted this as the reinforcement of Christian, who did not, in fact, arrive until midnight; thus the aborigines made a rapid retreat, half an hour before sunset, and withdrew with their dead and wounded across the Ohio.

At first, the whites could not believe that their stubborn enemy had fled. But it appears that the braves

---

[4] See Stuart's "Narrative," in *Va. Hist. Colls.*, i.

INTRODUCTION

were disheartened. At the council of the tribesmen, held to decide their action, Cornstalk caustically proposed that all their women and children should be killed, and the warriors go forth to battle until they too were slain. Receiving no response, the chief exclaimed, "Then, I will go and make peace." Forthwith, Matthew Eliot, a white man with the Indian army, was sent to intercept Lord Dunmore's advance, and if still possible to accept terms which the governor had previously offered.

Meanwhile, Dunmore had left his position on Hockhocking, and was crossing the country to the Indian villages. He had heard rumors of an attack upon Lewis; but knowing that the latter had with him eleven hundred men, and that Christian was advancing with about three hundred more, he thought the southern army might readily cope with the hostiles, and sent word to its commander to meet him at the native towns. Indeed, the governor's forces had not marched far, when an express overtook them with news of the victory at Point Pleasant, which occasioned great joy in his camp. Dunmore was, therefore, not unprepared for the Indian deputation requesting peace. When, on the night of October 16th, Eliot came to his tent, the governor replied that he would listen to their proposals, but should not withdraw from the Indian country until satisfactory terms were made. The next day he moved to within eight miles of the chief Indian village, where he halted and formed Camp Charlotte. Here, negotiations with the humbled chiefs were at once opened.

On the same day, Lewis, having buried his dead and refreshed his men, crossed the Ohio in accordance with his lordship's original orders, and started for the Indian towns. A guard for the camp and the wounded was left at Point Pleasant, under command of Colonel Fleming, with Captains Lockridge, Slaughter, and Herbert, to whom instructions were given for the building of a small stockade fort. Flushed with victory, and eager for revenge because of their losses sustained in the battle, Lewis and his men pushed rapidly on, hoping to strike the discomfited enemy at the Scioto villages. Great was their chagrin at receiving word from Lord Dunmore that a treaty of peace was nearly completed, and ordering the southern wing at once to return to Point Pleasant. This unpalatable command was not immediately obeyed; whereupon the Indian deputies, kept informed of every detail by their runners, hastily left Camp Charlotte and hurried back to defend their threatened habitations. Dunmore, fearing that the war would break out afresh, set off in person for Lewis's camp. After courteously thanking the assembled officers for their services, he peremptorily ordered a retreat, and was reluctantly obeyed.

Negotiations were thereupon resumed with the chiefs, who now, for the most part returned to Camp Charlotte. But Dunmore noted the absence of the Mingo deputies. Hearing that Logan had just returned to his village with several prisoners and scalps, from a foray against southwestern Virginia, the governor sent John Gibson, a well known trader, to bring the warring chief to camp. Logan was surly and refused, saying that he was a warrior, not a councillor. Upon further urging, he delivered to Gibson his now classical speech, to serve as an apology to his lordship. The Mingo tribesmen still proving recalcitrant, Maj.

INTRODUCTION xxiii

William Crawford was ordered out against their towns, which he effectually destroyed, thus conducting the only aggressive movement of Lord Dunmore's wing of the Virginia army. The treaty signed at Camp Charlotte was designed as but preliminary to a larger and more important council to be held at Fort Pitt the following spring. On their part, the Indians agreed to return all prisoners; to make good the stolen horses from their own herds; to regard the Ohio as a boundary between them and the whites, even for hunting excursions, and to permit boats to pass thereon unmolested; finally, to accept trade stipulations to be later formulated. They gave hostages as an assurance of the fulfilment of these terms.

Dunmore intended to go out to Fort Pitt, the following spring, and complete the peace negotiations. As an evidence of good faith, he issued a proclamation on January 23rd, 1775, reciting the submission of both the Northern Indians and the Cherokee, and calling upon all citizens to protect the natives and preserve the peace. But in the confusion incident to the revolutionary movements of the Virginians, Dunmore was unable to leave for the frontier; whereupon he commissioned Connolly as his agent to treat with the tribesmen. The night before the intended council at Fort Pitt, the Virginia deputy was arrested by the Pennsylvania authorities, to the great confusion of the Indian envoys.

In June following, the Virginia assembly took up the matter on their own behalf, and appointed a commission of five persons, consisting of Thomas and John Walker, Andrew Lewis, James Wood, and Adam

Stephen, to arrange the proposed treaty at Fort Pitt. Captain Wood went to notify the tribesmen, but found the Mingo still hostile and sullen, and the Delawares suspicious, although the Shawnee were inclined to peace. The chiefs met at the appointed time and place, regardless of the opposition raised by the British commandant at Detroit. The American continental congress had meanwhile appointed Lewis Morris and James Wilson to attend on its behalf. Negotiations lasted from the twelfth of September to the twenty-first of October, resulting in an agreement that kept the Northwest Indians quiet throughout the two first years of the Revolutionary War.

A study of contemporary documents will convince any fair-minded student of history that Lord Dunmore acted in this episode with disinterested discretion; although it has been common to ascribe to him treacherous motives—a desire to stir up the Western tribes to harry the borderers and thereby distract them from their seditious attitude, and to encompass the destruction of Lewis's wing by leaving it unsupported at Point Pleasant. When colonial difficulties had reached a crisis in 1775, and Dunmore's zeal for the royal cause had won him hatred throughout the province, all his previous acts were suspected, and the succeeding generation of border historians persuaded themselves of his intended treachery—an accusation which has, with variations, been repeated unto the present day. It should be observed, however, that the officers of the army, on their return halt at Fort Gower, passed resolutions of sympathy for the cause of American independence, and at the same time of respect for their commander, "who, we are confident, underwent the fatigue of this singular campaign from no other motive than the true interest of this country."[5] We see no reason for doubting the truth of this contemporary endorsement, made by those best qualified to judge.

The affair at Point Pleasant has often been styled "the first battle of the American Revolution." This is an over-statement; but it was distinctly an American victory. Not only were there no regular troops or officers in the campaign, but the initiative was distinctly colonial; and the English home authorities evinced their disapproval of the governor's martial enterprise. Moreover, the training and experience obtained in this contest, were of great advantage in the organization of the continental forces from the Southern provinces. The men in the armies of both Lewis and Dunmore were in large part participants in the Revolution. Lewis was the general who drove Lord Dunmore from Virginia. At least ten of his captains were officers in the Revolutionary army, not including those serving in George Rogers Clark's Illinois regiment, which was in great measure recruited from the men of Point Pleasant. In the governor's brigade was also Daniel Morgan, hero of Quebec (1775) and the Cowpens (1781), who first led out his riflemen to join McDonald, then united with Dunmore, and served under Crawford in his Mingo expedition. Morgan writes of the influence of these early associations upon his later career: "We as an army victorious formed ourselves into a society pledging our word of honor to each other to assist our brethren of Boston in case hostilities should commence." In less than eight months, Captain Morgan

---

[5] *Amer. Archives,* 4th series, i, pp. 962, 963.

led his rifle corps, composed of many of the same expert marksmen who had served under his command in 1774, into Washington's camp at Cambridge. The two commanding officers at the battle of King's Mountain (Oct. 7, 1780), Gen. William Campbell and Gen. Isaac Shelby, both had captaincies under Colonel Lewis. Christian, one of Lewis's division commanders, drove back the threatened Cherokee invasion of 1776, at the head of an expedition whose officers and men had also fought under Lewis. Among the leaders in Dunmore's War, at least four afterwards served (1788) as members of the Virginia convention that ratified the constitution of the United States. Several were in due time to become United States senators and governors of states. In fact, most of the men who were prominent in the West during the first decades of its history, were in the war of 1774, either upon the expedition or guarding the frontier.

Thus, Lord Dunmore's War was in a sense a focal point in Western history. Here were gathered in either wing of the army the men who by dint of daring enterprise had made their way to the frontier, and had carried American institutions across the Appalachian barrier. Here, in a pitched battle, they met and subdued nearly an equal number of the most redoubtable of their savage foes. From Point Pleasant and Camp Charlotte they scattered far and wide, to fight the coming battle for independence—some on the shores of the Atlantic, some in the forests of the Southwest, others on the prairies of the Illinois. The victory at Point Pleasant opened an ever lengthening pathway to Western settlement. Thenceforward new vigor was in-

INTRODUCTION xxvii

fused into the two chief forces of the future century—American expansion and American nationalism.

The documents printed in this volume have been selected from the mass of manuscript historical material accumulated by the late Dr. Lyman Copeland Draper, during nearly fifty years of zealous interest in the beginnings of the Middle West.[6] That indefatigable collector not only obtained these papers from the relatives and descendants of the men who participated in the great events of trans-Alleghany pioneering, but he himself visited in person many of the survivors, or their children, and took from their lips personal anecdotes and recollections that might otherwise have perished. The Draper Manuscripts might readily have furnished two volumes of this size, upon the Dunmore War; but a limit had necessarily to be set, and we have given but the essential and most interesting of the material in hand. References, however, have been made in footnotes and elsewhere, to scores of other documents in this collection, bearing upon the theme, making it possible for readers who so desire to prosecute a still closer study.

Acknowledgments are due to J. T. McAllister, Esq., of Hot Springs, Virginia, for aid in completing, so far as now seems practicable, a list of participants in the battle of Point Pleasant; also for securing from the heirs of Col. William Preston a careful transcript of the important letter by Col. William Christian (p. 261), giving what is practically an official report of the battle of Point Pleasant, and thus admirably supplementing

---

[6] See Thwaites, "Lyman Copeland Draper: A Memoir," in *Wis. Hist. Colls.*, i (reprint), pp. ix–xxix.

the papers in the Draper Manuscripts. The proof-reading, always a difficult task in a volume of this character, has been skilfully supervised by Miss Annie A. Nunns of the Society's staff.

R. G. T.
L. P. K.

DUNMORE'S WAR

WESTERN SURVEYS; INDIAN DEPREDATIONS

[Dr. Hugh Mercer to Col. William Preston. 3QQ1.]

SIR—When I had the pleasure of seeing you in Williamsburgh, we had some conversation as to the Time you intended to begin the officers Surveys and the necessary assistance each claimant should furnish. You could not then fully determine, but may by this time have considered the Matter—as Mr Taylor furnishes an opportunity I should be extreamly glad to have your Sentiments on these particulars—and also to know whereabout on the Ohio you would chuse to begin—whether your deputies take different parts of the Country, or whether the whole is kept together to render the Party more formidable. I intend to go to Pittsburgh early in the Spring & would willingly proceed from thence to meet you or your deputies at any place assigned; It would be very satisfactory to know, if any certain intelligence is received with regard [to] it, what Indians they were who killed Mr Russel—whether the Massacre is supposed to be owing to the Indians Jelousy of our settling near them, or to a private Quarrel.¹ If I mistake not I gave you my Warrant of Survey & the Plot of Land which Mr Taylor surveyed for me on the Ohio. It is very probable I may make choice of part of that tract & would willingly secure it, without being obliged to keep the whole—but cannot determine on the Quantity till I see it.

I am with Esteem Sir Your Obed^t Humble Servt

HUGH MERCER.²

Wed. 8th Jany 1774

INDIAN ALARMS; FRONTIERSMEN REMOVING

[Capt. Daniel Smith to Col. William Preston. 3QQ15.]

CASTLE'S WOODS³ March 22^d. 1774.

D^r SIR—Yours by Mr. Boles came to hand 18th Inst I was at home, because I had called a muster the next day, the badness of the weather prevented the people from meeting. So next day I came down here, and

---

¹ Upon Boone's first migration toward Kentucky, in the autumn of 1773, his eldest son, James, and Henry Russell, a young son of Capt. William Russell, were set upon and killed by a roving party of Indians, only a short distance from the main camp in Powell's Valley, Va. This untoward incident led to the temporary abandonment of the advance into Kentucky.—ED.

² Dr. Hugh Mercer was a Scotchman, born in 1720, who served with the Pretender (1745) and shortly after emigrated to America, settling first in Pennsylvania. After being wounded at Braddock's Defeat, and serving with Forbes (1758), he removed to Fredericksburg, Virginia. Embracing the colonial cause, he commanded a Virginia regiment in the Revolution, being killed at the battle of Princeton, 1777.—ED.

³ A well-known locality on Clinch River in Russell County, the home of William Russell and a fort for the protection of the inhabitants of the upper Clinch.—ED.

Survey'd Mr Lynch's Millseat Yesterday. The people on this River are much more fearful of the Indians than I expected to find them. The late Reports alarm'd them so much that 4 families in my neighborhood mov'd over to Holston before I heard of their Setting off, they went in Such haste that they left all their Stock and greatest part of their Household Furniture. When they got to Holston they heard news that mitigated their fears a little, and they ventur'd back again to take care of their Effects, then I saw them and p[r]evail'd on them to Stay. The badness of the Weather and the troublesome Office you conferr'd on me lately hath prevented me from making any more than seven surveys yet, nay, from making any proper beginning yet, I fear you'll say I'm lazy, but hope to make you think otherwise in four Weeks. This day I leave this neighbourhood to go towards the Rye Coves.[4] Please to make my Compliments acceptable to your Lady. I am in Haste, so conclude with assuring you that I am

Dr Sir, Your respectful humble Servt

DAN SMITH.[5]

Money is so scarce on this River that I fear I shall make a very sorry collection—not one penny recd yet.

To Col. William Preston. at Smithfield.

---

[4] Rye Coves was one of the most westerly settlements of the day, on a western affluent of the Clinch, in the present Scott County, Va.—ED.

[5] Daniel Smith was born in Stafford County, Virginia, 1748. Early settling upon Western waters, he was appointed deputy surveyor of Augusta County in 1773. He aided in defending the frontier during the Revolution, and in 1775 assisted in drawing up the resolutions for liberty. At the close of the war, he emigrated to the Cumberland settlement,

SCOUTS SENT OUT

[Instructions by Capt. William Russell to scouts. 3QQ18.]

Instructions given to Richard Stanton, Edward Sharpe, Epraim Drake, and William Harrel, Runners; Gentlemen. Agreeable to Instruction from Colo William Preston, I have appointed by your mutual consent, you the aforesd four Persons as Runners to scout, and Reconnoitre, to the Westward of this sittlement. First you are to proceed to the head of Powels Vally,[6] where you are particularly, on, and near the Warriours path[7] to look for Indian Signs, and should you make any such discovery, you are then to find as near as you can their Number, the rout they are taking, and

---

where he was prominent in its affairs, serving as secretary of the territory, 1790-96; U. S. senator from Tennessee, 1798-99, 1805-09. He died at his home in Sumner County in 1818. See Thwaites, *Early Western Travels* (Cleveland, 1904), iii, pp. 255, 256, for account of this pioneer.—ED

[6] Powell's Valley is the most westerly of the several long narrow valleys found in southwestern Virginia and northeastern Tennessee, made by the sources of the Tennessee River. It was first explored in 1750 by Walker, one of whose party, Ambrose Powell, cut his name upon a tree in this valley, whence was derived the name. The first cabin was erected therein by Joseph Martin in 1768. It was in Powell's Valley that Boone's party were turned back from Kentucky settlement by the Indian outbreak of 1773. By 1777, the settlement in the valley could muster nearly a thousand men; but during Indian ravages, it was highly exposed, the road from Cumberland Gap passing directly through the valley.—ED.

[7] The Warriors' Path was a well-known trace along which the Northern Indians came through eastern Kentucky. See map of Kentucky by Filson (1784), where it is outlined directly from the mouth of Scioto to Cumberland Gap. A branch diverged by way of the Blue Licks.—ED.

SCOUTS SENT OUT

as nearly as possible their Intentions, and upon a supposition only of your Company that any such party discovered, intend Warr Immediately upon our Inhabitants, you must give the most speedy Acct thereof to me, or in my absance to the next Officer convenient that the same may be reported to the County Lieutennant; but in case you make no such discovery, you are in Powels Vally to find the boundary Line between us and the Cherrokees, which line (if possible, you must follow to the Water course it Terminates on, and then to follow such River, if Cumberland, as low as the Hunters Road, if Louisa thro' the small Mountains, till you come to such old Incampments of the Hunters, as may fully satisfy you, that you may return an Acct upon Oath, that the same may be reported to the Assembly touching the certainty of such boundary River between the Cherrokees and Virginia:[8] this being perform'd you are to return with the utmost expedition, that such Report, may be laid before the

---

[8] By the treaty of Fort Stanwix (1768), the Six Nations (Iroquois) ceded all the southern and western land to the king of Great Britain. Thereupon the Cherokee complained that their claims had not been properly recognized, and at the treaty of Lochaber (1770), Stuart, the English Indian agent, recognized the right of this tribe to all lands west of a line "from six miles above the Big Island in Holston in a direct course to the mouth of Great Kanawha." The following year, Col. John Donelson was appointed commissioner by the Virginia authorities to meet with Cherokee envoys and run the line. Instead of following it to the Great Kanawha, it was surveyed to the head of a river supposed to be the Kentucky (or Louisa), but by some thought to empty into Cumberland River. This line, being accepted by the Cherokee, it was important to ascertain its real limits, since officers' warrants for the grants of the French and Indian War were waiting to be located; and it was a question whether any below the Kentucky could legally be received.—ED.

Assembly in order to recommend you, to the consideration of the House, who I doubt not, in the least, will reward You adequate to your services. And tho' we are at present apprehensive the Cherrokees, and northward Indians intend War, Yet should you by accident, fall in with any of their Parties; You are to avoide acting toward them, in a Hostile manner; unless in cases of the last extreemity; because the least Hostility committed by You, at this Time when the Indians appear ripe for War; wod not only blast our fairest hopes of Settleing the Ohio Country; and be Attended with a train of Concomitant Evils; but doubtless, involve the Government in a Blooddy War. Relying greatly on your Fidelity, after wishing you an agreeable Journey, and safe return; Remain Gentlemen your most Obedt Humb. Servt

W RUSSELL[9] Capt

---

[9] Gen. William Russell was born in Culpeper County about 1748, his father being high-sheriff of the region. By 1770 he had removed to Clinch River, where he soon became one of the Western leaders, being justice of Fincastle County upon its organization (1772). After the Point Pleasant campaign, in which he commanded a company, he took a leading part in the Revolutionary movement, signing the Fincastle resolutions of 1775, and being chosen delegate to the Virginia assembly in 1776. At the outbreak of the war, he was chosen colonel of colonial troops, serving efficiently during the entire period, taking part in the capture of Stony Point, and being part of the army surrendered at Charleston. After effecting an exchange he was in the army until 1783, retiring brigadier-general by brevet. The same year he married the widow of Gen. William Campbell, sister of Patrick Henry, and removed to Saltville, where he developed the works. Madam Russell's house stood here until recently. General Russell died in 1794; his son of the same name became a prominent Kentucky pioneer, and general in the War of 1812-15.—ED.

TROUBLE ON THE OHIO

[John Floyd to Col. William Preston. 3QQ19.]

LITTLE GIANDOT, 26th April 1774.[10]

DEAR SIR—Inclosed you hav three Warrants the Gent^m. desire to send you we are to survey the Land without Entering. last night Thos. Glen Lawrence Darnell & William Nash came to our camp who were Orderd off the River by a Party of Indians who only saw them across the River. The Shawneese took Darnell & 6 Others prison[er]s[11] a few Weeks ago & held a Counsel Over them three Days; after which they took everything they had & sent them off: telling them at the same time it was their directions from the Superintendent Geo Crohon[12] to kill all the Virginians they could find on the River & rob & whip the Pennsylvanians. this they told them in English. The whites & Indians the 15th Instant had a skirmish at

---

[10] For the route of the party of surveyors from Fincastle to this river—a small affluent of the Ohio in Cabell County, West Virginia—see journal of Thomas Hanson, *post.*—ED.

[11] Lawrence Darnell had come out from Pittsburg the previous year, with nine companions, and had surveyed in Kentucky, where Lawrence Creek, in Mason County, was named in his honor. See Jacob, *Life of Cresap* (Cincinnati, 1866), pp. 54, 55, for further account of this robbery.—ED.

[12] George Croghan emigrated from Ireland and engaged in the Pennsylvania Indian trade. His first employment in the public service was in 1747; and in 1756 he was chosen deputy Indian agent by Sir William Johnson, in which capacity he continued until 1778. His home at this time was about four miles above Pittsburg. For further details, see "Croghan's Journals," in Thwaites, *Early Western Travels,* i.—ED.

the mouth of Beaver Creek 45 mile below Pittsburg One white Man killd another wounded & One other yit missing the Wounded man got in to Fort Pitt where Dr. Wood Dressed his Wounds. this I have from the second hand & I think may be depended on.[13] the Other news I wrote you that 3 or 4 Indians down the River were thought to be killed is not so, I have since seen One of the men that should have been in the ingagemt. & the Indians only Robd them; he says no lives were lost. I wrote you fully a few days ago & inclosed Colo Washingtons Plot.[14] which Letter I imagine you will Receive with this, Our Men are almost daily Retreating. If any Men are sent down to see which River is the Line to the Ohio pray direct them to let us know [as soon] as they can. I am in doubt about it & dont [MS. torn] what to do: I find all the best of the Country to lie [MS. torn] as Mr Dandridge has concluded to Retire Since I began this

---

[13] These were the men in Butler's canoe: see Jacob, *Cresap*, pp. 55, 133, 134; *Amer. Archives*, 4th series, i, p. 468. Meanwhile reports that the surveying party, led by Floyd, had been stopped brought about the first outbreaks of the whites against the Indians, higher up on the Ohio River. See Butterfield, *Washington–Crawford Letters* (Cincinnati, 1877), pp. 47, 48.—ED.

[14] George Washington was much interested in Western lands, and since the close of the French and Indian War (1763) had been endeavoring to secure patents for the 200,000 acres promised to colonial soldiers and officers who took part therein. In 1770 he had made a surveying trip as low as the Kanawha in the interest of these claims, many of which he had purchased from other officers or their heirs. The surveying trip of Floyd was undertaken largely with a view to locating these lands. See Col. William Preston's advertisement, in Maryland *Gazette*, Mar. 10, 1774; *Washington–Crawford Letters*, pp. 47, 48, note.—ED.

Letter I need only add that I wish you health & Success & am D Sir yours affectionately

JACK FLOYD[15]

I dont know how it may happen but I have never rued yet I am in great haste. J. F.

Col⁰. William Preston.
By favr of Mr. Dandridge.

OUTBREAK OF WAR

[Reminiscences of Judge Henry Jolly. 6NN22-24.][16]

* * * * * * * *

In the Spring of the year 1774 a party of Indians encamped on the Northwest of the Ohio, near the

---

[15] John Floyd was born in Virginia in 1750, and when about twenty-two years of age removed to Fincastle County, and engaged in school-teaching, living in the home of Col. William Preston. In 1774 he was appointed deputy sheriff, and in the spring of the same year led a surveying party into Kentucky. Upon his return he joined the Point Pleasant expedition, but arrived too late to engage in the battle. The following year he returned to Kentucky as surveyor for the Transylvania Company and remained at St. Asaph's till the summer of 1776. Returning to Virginia, he embarked on a privateering enterprise, was captured, and spent a year in Dartmouth prison, England. Having effected an escape to France, Franklin aided him to return to America, where he married Jane Buchanan, a niece of Colonel Preston, and in 1779 set out for his final emigration to Kentucky. There he built a station on Beargrass Creek; but was shot and mortally wounded by Indians in 1783. His son John became governor of Virginia.—ED.

[16] The following was sent to Dr. Draper in 1849, by S. P. Hildreth, who had had an interview with Judge Jolly. The latter was sixteen years of age at the time of these occurrences, and recollected them well. There has been much controversy over these incidents; for the statements of other contemporaries, see Sappington, in Jefferson's *Notes on Vir-*

mouth of Yellow Creek.[17] a party of whites called Greathouse's party, lay on the opposite side of the river, the Indians came over to the white party—I think five men, one woman and an infant babe, the whites Gave thim rum, which three of them drank, and in a short time became very drunk. the other two men and the woman refused, the Sober Indians were chalenged to shoot at a mark, to which they agreed, and as soon as the[y] emptied their Guns, the whites shot them down, the woman Attempted to escape by flight, but was also shot down, She lived long enough however to beg mercy for her babe, telling them that it was a Kin to themselves, they had a man in the Cabbin, prepared with a tomahawk for the purpose of killing the three drunk Indians, which was immediately done. the party of men women &c moved off for the Interior Settlements, and came to Catfis[h] camp on the evening of the next day, where they tarried untill the next day,[18] I very well recollect my mother, feeding and dressing the Babe, Chirping to the little innocent, and it smiling, however they took

---

ginia (ed. of 1825), pp. 336-339 Tomlinson, in Jacob's *Cresap*, pp. 133-137; George Rogers Clark's letter, *ibid*, pp. 154-158; *Washington-Crawford Letters*, pp. 86, 87; and *N. Y. Colon. Docs.*, viii, pp. 463-465.—ED.

[17] The massacre at Yellow Creek occurred April 30, 1774; see Valentine Crawford's statement in *Washington-Crawford Letters*, p. 86. Yellow Creek is an affluent of the Ohio, on the right or Ohio side, about fifty miles below Pittsburg.—ED.

[18] Now Washington, Pennsylvania; there they met Crawford and Neville returning to Pittsburg from Virginia, the former of whom took possession of the child. So L. C. D. in Draper MSS., 14J275; Crawford, May 8, 1774, in *Washington-Crawford Letters*, pp. 48, 49; and *N. Y. Colon. Docs.*, viii, p. 464.—ED.

OUTBREAK OF WAR

it away, and talked of sending it to its supposed father, Col. Geo. [John] Gibson of Carlisle (Pa.) who was then [and] had been for several years a trader amongst the Indians[19] The remainder of the party, at the mouth of Yellow Creek, finding that their friends on the opposite side of the river was Massacred, the[y] attempted to escape by descending the ohio, and in order to avoid being discovered by the whites, passed on the west side of Wheeling Island, and landed at pipe creek, a small stream that empites into the ohio[20] a few miles below Graves creek, where they were overtaken by Cresap with a party of men from Wheeling, the[y] took one Indian scalp, and had one white man badly wounded, (Big Tarrence)[21] they I believe carried him in a

---

[19] Col. John (not George) Gibson was born at Lancaster in 1740. After receiving a good education, he entered the army under General Forbes (1758), and at the close of the war engaged in Indian trade. At the outbreak of Pontiac's War (1763) he was captured, but saved from the stake by being adopted by a squaw. The following year he was set at liberty by Bouquet's expedition, and continued his dealings with the Indians. Logan's sister, who was killed at Yellow Creek, was his Indian wife. After Dunmore's War, he embarked in the Revolutionary cause, commanded the 13th Virginia, and after 1778 was stationed at Fort Pitt. He held several public offices in the latter years of his life, being judge of Allegheny County, Pa., and secretary of Indiana territory. He died in western Pennsylvania in 1822.—ED.

[20] The affair at Pipe Creek occurred April 27, three days before that at Yellow Creek. The Indians killed were Shawnee, not Mingo. Consult Clark's letter, as cited above, and *N. Y. Colon. Docs.*, viii, p. 463.—ED.

[21] "A man of Cresap's party named Morrison was shot in the hip, and brought to Dr. Charles Wheeler's, in the neighborhood of Edward White's, and remained under Dr. Wheeler's care until he recovered, some two or three months later. It was not until after this, and Morrison's recovery, that the people abandoned the settlement (four miles west of Red-

litter from Wheeling to redstone.[22] I saw the party on the return from their victorious campaign.[23]

The Indians had for some time before this event thought themselves intruded upon by the long Knife,

---

stone). Dr. Wheeler probably went to Brownsville, as some others did. Morrison taught school subsequently, but was ever after a cripple from his wounds; bones affected."—Information given to Dr. Draper in 1846 by Capt. Jacob White: Draper MSS., 3S, book 5, pp. 1, 2.—ED.

[22] The first overt acts of the war have usually been attributed to Michael Cresap, although it has abundantly been proven that he was not concerned in the massacre of Logan's relatives, as attributed to him in the famous speech of that chief. In extenuation of the attacks upon Indians made by the Cresap party, account should be taken of Lord Dunmore's proclamation, issued April 25, 1774 (*Amer. Archives,* 4th series, i, p. 283) calling upon Virginia militia to protect the settlers from Indians, and of Cresap's claims that Dunmore's agent at Pittsburg, Dr. John Connolly, had sent out a circular letter to the inhabitants, and that what he did was by Connolly's orders. (*Amer. Archives,* 4th series, i, pp. 287, 484: Clark's letter, "The reception of this [Connolly's] letter was the epoch of open hostilities with the Indians.")

Michael Cresap was the son of Col. Thomas Cresap, a well-known Maryland pioneer. Born in 1742, the younger Cresap early set up as a trader, and had a store at Redstone in 1772. He came to the Ohio and made improvements on land claimed by Washington. Commissioned captain by Dunmore in June, 1774, he served throughout the campaign. The spring of the next year, he enlisted a rifle company of Maryland troops, and joined Washington at Cambridge; but died in October, 1775, in New York city, where he received the honors of war and was buried in Trinity churchyard. For recent details of this family, see Ohio Arch. and Hist. Soc. *Publications,* x, pp. 146–164.

Redstone was the site of the storehouse built by the Ohio Company in 1752. In 1758 Fort Burd was erected at this place. It is now known as Brownsville, and was long an important point of embarkation for Western pioneers descending the Ohio.—ED.

[23] That portion of this narrative which relates to Capt. M. Cresap agrees with the evidence of Col. Eb. Zane, published in Jefferson's *Notes.*—L. C. D.

OUTBREAK OF WAR 13

as they Called the Virginians at that time,[24] and many of them were for war—however the[y] calld a Council, in which Logan acted a Conspicuous part, he admited their Ground of complaint, but at the same time reminded them of some aggressions on the part of the Indians, and that by a war, they could but harrass and distress the frontier Settlements for a short time, that the long Knife would come like the trees in the woods, and that ultimately, they would be drove from their good land that they now possessed; he therefore strongly recommended peace, to him they all agreed, Grounded the hatchet, every thing wore a tranquil appearance, when behold, in came the fugitives from Yellow creek; Logan's father,[25] Brother and sister murdered; what is to be done now; Logan has lost three of his nearest and dearest relations, the consequence is that this same Logan, who a few days before was so pacific, raises the hatchet, with a declaration, that he will not Ground it, untill he has taken ten for one, which I believe he completely fulfilled, by taking thirty scalps and prisoners in the sumer of 74. the above has often been told to me by sundry persons who was at the Indian town, at the time of the Council alluded to, and also when the remains of the party came in from Yellow creek; thomas Nicholson[26] has

---

[24] On the origin of this term see Thwaites, *Daniel Boone* (New York, 1902), p. III, note.—ED.

[25] Logan's father was the famous Oneida chief Shickalamy, who died at his village at the forks of the Susquehanna in 1749. See Thwaites, *Early Western Travels*, i, p. 235. For the life of Logan, see *post*.—ED.

[26] Thomas Nicholson was a well-known scout and interpreter who guided McDonald's expedition, and later served under Dunmore. With his brother Joseph, who accompanied

told me the above and much more, another person (whose name I cannot recollect) told me that he was at the towns when the Yellow Creek Indians came in, that there was a very Great lamentation by all the Indians of that places, some friendly Indian advised him to leave the Indian Settlement, which he did

Could any person of common rationality, believe for a moment, that the Indians came to Yellow creek with hostile intention, or that they had any suspicion of the whites, having any hostile Intentions against them, would five men have crossed the river, three of them in a Short time dead drunk, the other two discharging their Guns, puting themselves entirely at they mercy of the whites, or would they have brought over a Squaw, with an infant paupoos, if they had not reposed the utmost Confidence in the friendship of the whites, every person who is acquainted with Indians Knows better, and it was the belief of the Inhabitants who were capable of reasoning on the Subject, that all the depredations Commited on the frontiers was by Logan and his party, as a retaliation, for the murder of Logans friends at Yellow creek—I mean all the depredations commited in the year 1774. It was well Known that Michael Cresap had no hand in the Massacre at Yellow Creek.

Washington in 1770, he led Crawford's unfortunate expedition to the Sandusky towns, in 1782. At the close of the war he retired to Pittsburg.—ED.

OUTBREAK OF WAR

[Information given to Dr. Draper by Michael Cresap, Jr., in the autumn of 1845. 2SS, book 5, pp. 33-35.]

Jos. Tomlinson said, that one of the Squaws was in the habit of crossing to Bakers to get milk, & Mrs. Baker was kind in giving her some for her 2 children. this squaw was Logan's sister, & the father of her children was John Gibson. One day she said that the Indians were angry & w^d be over next day by a certain hour, & advised Mrs. Baker to move to Cat Fish's camp: the next day several Indians came at the appointed time with their faces painted black; the men at the time were not in [the] house; the Indians went into Bakers, & without permission took liquor & drank, & also took what rifles there were there, & one put on Nathaniel Tomlinson's military coat. After a little, Daniel Greathouse, Danl. (?) Sappinton, & Nathl. Tomlinson, George Cox, & one other came in. Tomlinson wanted his regimental coat, which the Indian did not feel disposed to yield to its owner; & Tomlinson declared he would kill him, if he did not, & the probability is the Indians were indulged with more liquor. Cox was opposed to this summary course, said it would breed an Indian war, & that he would have no hand in it; & had not gone far in the woods [when he] heard firing at the house. Greathouse, Tomlinson & Sappington were all that were concerned in the affair. Baker had no hand in it, nor was he probably present.

[Recollections of Bazaleel Wells, "who emigrated to this country in 1779," related to Dr. Draper in 1845. 2S, book 2, pp. 5, 6.]

Logan's family &c.—Cresap's party had killed an Indian at mouth of Capteen, the day before the affair at Baker's—& also one killd. in canoe above Wheeling. Greathouse & his party from Cross Creek, thinking the war now broke out, went to Bakers, concealed themselves, & engaged Baker to get the Indians drunk —one of whom got drunk, took down a military coat & put it on, swaggering around swearing "I am white man," when John Sappington shot him. Then the Inds. dropped down in canoes to see wht. was done when Greathouse's party shot in & killed at least one. Then killed others in camp, Logan's sister etc.

[Recollections of George Edgington of West Liberty, Pa., related to Dr. Draper in 1845. 2S, book 3, p. 34.]

Dunmore's War.—On the Town Fork of Yellow Creek, where the Indian town was, a small one; and they concluded to move Elsewhere down the river, stopped at Baker's, drank. Mrs. Baker told Danl. Greathouse that a squaw told her (in a drunken fit) that the Indians intended to murder Baker's family before leaving. Greathouse went & raised a party of abt. 30 men, George Cox, Edward King & others & went to Baker's; there an Indian [Logan's brother.— L. C. D.] was drinking & strutting around in a military coat, some one shot him, & King then stabbed him while in the agonies of death, saying "Many a deer have I served in this way." Then killed another Indian there; & two squaws—the two latter shot by Dan!. Greathouse & John Sappington. One of the squaws had a child, which was saved & sent to Col. Gibson as its father. Twelve Indians were killed in all. Greathouse died of the measles the following year.

[Recollections of Capt. Michael Myers,[27] Newburgh, Ohio, given to Dr. Draper February 25 and 26, 1850. 4S132-134.]

In the Spring of 1774, M[r]. Myers was residing on Pigeon Creek,[28] in now Washington Co. Pa. & was called out to guard the frontier, with others, to the Greathouse Settlement at Baker's Bottom.

Two men came there, who wished to cross the Ohio to Yellow Creek, & desired a pilot, & engaged M[r]. Myers to go over with them. They swam over their horse beside the canoe, & went two or 3 miles up on the western side or bank of Yellow Creek. Their object was to examine land. It was near night, & concluded to stop, spanseled out the horse, & prepared to camp. The horse feeding, rambled over a rise of ground about 300 yards distant; & soon after, hearing the bell on the horse rattling rather violently, Myers and the men picked up their guns & went to see what it meant: and when within 40 yards, Myers discov-

---

[27] Captain Myers was born in Westmoreland Co., V[a]., about 1753. He is a man of great respectability, for many years a justice of the peace.—L. C. D.
[28] An affluent of the Monongahela, below Brownsville.—ED

ered an Indian in the act of unspanselling the horse, who was rather restive (running round towards the camp of his white masters) not seeming to like his new visitor. The Indian's gun was lying on the ground near by. Myers drew up & shot the Indian who fell over, as if dead. It was now near sun-down. Presently—in a few minutes—Myers discovered another Indian approach with a gun in his hand, who had been attracted thither by the report of Myers' shot; & when about 30 yards from Myers, looking down the hill at the dead fallen or wounded Indian, as if in astonishment, Myers having reloaded immediately after his former shot, now fired, & this second Indian also fell, whether dead or not, Myers did not wait to see.[29] The Indian camp was only about a hundred yards off, with a large number of deer & bear skins presented to view. By this time the two white men had got their horse & ran off; & when Myers reached the river, the men were partly over in the boat with their horse swimming beside, & would not consent to return. Myers hurried up the river to a spot where he could ford it, & thus got over.[30]

Next morning an Indian came to inquire who shot the two Indians the day before; and some of the party stationed there (about 30, Mr. Myers thinks) killed

---

[29] If this evidence may be taken, then we have the prompting cause of the Indians' design to destroy Baker's family, as divulged by the squaw. * * * I doubt not the Indians at Yellow Creek heard of it (the Cresap attack) during the 30th of April, * * * and hence while in their cups, they might well be angry.—L. C. D.

[30] Mr. N. B. Craig adds, he learned from Mr. Sloane of Newburgh, that the spot indicated by Myers where he shot the two Indians, is about 2 miles up Yellow Creek at a place known as the Diamond Rocks.—L. C. D.

this Indian. Myers, however, did not participate in this murder. The same day, or the next, as Myers thinks, a large "dug-out" came over a few rods below the mouth of Yellow Creek. Greathouse's party, and Myers with the rest, some 30 or 40, were posted along the Southern bank of the river behind trees & bushes, & logs, & as the Indian canoe came within 5 or 6 rods (Myers says he thinks nearer) of shore, they fired upon the Indians as directed by their Captain (Greathouse). the Indians had guns with them, [he] thinks all of them were shot (& erroneously supposes there were some 30 of them.)[31]

The remainder of this Indian party, who did not attempt to come over, went down the river to Wheeling & there got attacked.

Sappington lived a little below Greathouse's; Geo. Cox was a large man and well known to Myers.

Mr. Myers was not out with McDonald, Dunmore nor Lewis in 1774.

SCOUTS RETURN; VIRGINIA BOUNDARY

[Capt. William Russell to Col. William Preston. 3QQ23.]

DEAR COLO.—Upon my return from Williamsburg, finding the upper Settlers on Clinch River had totally

---

[31] I am at a loss what confidence Myers's statement is deserving; on the whole, I rather think I should not like fully to adopt it. * * * I do not think Myers means to deceive, but from his old age, and long familiarity with the Yellow Creek affair, he has, I suspect, blended some subsequent incident with it. It seems to me that he was one of Greathouse's party and aided in firing upon the canoes.—L. C. D.

Evacuated their Plantations; I thought it my Duty, agreeable to your Instructions, to employ four Men, as Runners, in the service of the Country; in hopes thereby to prevail on the remainder of the Inhabitants to desist from so Ruinous an undertaking: Accordingly, I dispatched them, giving them such Instructions, as I thought wood most likely direct them, to intercept the March of any parties of Indians that might be comeing in, to annoy the Inhabitants, of either Holston or Clinch Rivers. As it may be found conveniant, to take with you those Instructions to Williamsburg, I have inclosed for your satisfaction a Copy.[32] The Runners return'd the 6th of this Instant haveing faithfully (I believe) performed the Service, both as Scouts, and in regard to the boundary Line; and made the Report upon Oath; which I have also inclosed that it may be laid before the Assembly Immediately. As the Report is upon Oath, I think it will Admit of no doubt hereafter, that it is Louisa River,[33] which [is] the boundary Line between the Cherrokees, and Virginia Terminateson; as it may make a wide difference respecting the Entrys made, below the Louisa, and above; the Information at this Time, may be extreemly usefull especially: as the dispute may be Immediately Adjusted before the Governor, Council, and House of Burgeses, and thereby know whether Patents may be obtained by the Officers below with the same Legallity, as above if not, it will afford such Gentlemen time, and Opportunity e'er it

---

[32] See *ante*, p. 4.—ED.
[33] The Kentucky River, first called Louisa by Dr. Thomas Walker in 1750. For note on the boundary line, see *ante*, p. 5.—ED.

be too late, to remove their Entrys, at the expence of a Surveyors fee Extraordinary: from so considerable an advantage I hope such Interested Gentlemen will, exert themselves, to have the Runners pay Levyd for them Immediately, otherways the poor fellows must suffer by the Service. None but Men greatly to be depended on, wood have perform'd this Service to satisfaction; therefore I thought It most prudent to engage Persons of some Veracity, who, were oblige to hire others to work their Plantations till their return. I hope you will have great Time to go to the Assembly, your selfe, which I sinceerly hope may be conveniant for You; as your Personal appearance will (at this favourable Juncture) Enable You to have things set in Order, of the greates Importance to all the Claiments on Ohio. I wood Sir with the greates pleasure have waited on you, with the Report; but as my Wife has been Extreemly Indisposed, ever since my return from Wms.burg, I flatter my selfe, thro' your goodness, the excuse will pardon me.

If Mr John May[34] has not gone to Williamsburg before You, request your good Office to serve me, in applying for my Warrant with Mr. May, and should You think it necessary, I was favoured with Colo. Byrds[35] kind promise to wait on the Governor for me,

---

[34] Of a prominent Virginia family, John May became a Kentucky pioneer, taking up the land on which May's Lick and Maysville were located, in Mason County of that state. He was killed by Indians (1790) while descending the Ohio River.—ED.

[35] Col. William Byrd of Westover, third of the name, was born in 1728, served in the French and Indian War, and died in 1777.—ED.

to obtain it. The Messenger is waiting to convey this to Capt. Campbells, to be forwarded; therefore hope you'l excuse haste: after Tendering my Compliments to your Lady:

Subscribe my selfe D^r. Colo. your Real Friend, and most Obedt. Humb. Servt.

W. RUSSELL.

May the 7th. 1774.

NEWS OF THE SURVEYORS

[Letter of Alexander Spottswood Dandridge to Col. William Preston. 3QQ26.]

May ye 15th. 1774

D^r SIR—I make no doubt but you'l be much Surprised at the News of my Speedy return from the Ohio,[36] the cause of which was the meeting of one Lawrence Darnold an experienced woodsman of good reputation & extreemly well acquainted with the Lands upon the Ohio him I thought a proper person to entrust the locating of my Lands to & having so done & being mindfull of my business in Hanover, with three other Gentlemen from Frederick County I parted with my Company which had increased to the Number of thirty three on the twenty seventh day of April on the little Giandott about thirty miles below the mouth of New River[37] & made the best of my way home. Nothing worth mentioning happened to us

---

[36] See letter of Floyd, *ante*, p. 7.—ED.
[37] The Kanawha was frequently called New River, from its principal tributary.—ED.

upon our Journey to the Ohio saving overtaking Hancock Taylor & Seven others about 20 miles from the New River where we dug canoes and went together in the greatest friendship & harmony[38] I left the whole company under great apprehensions of danger from the Indians, for the causes of which Apprehensions I [refer you] to Mr Floyd's letter of which I was the beare[r] According to your instructions Mr Floyd Surveyed for Colo. Washington 2000 Acres of Land & Sent a platt of the Same in a letter to you by Thos. Hogg who after receiving the same upon the Ohio has with two other men never been heard of. I am Sorry it is not at this time in my power to wait for your return & in person give you an Account of our adventures but expect to be this way again in a Short time on my return to Hanover. in the meanwhile please to enter for me 1000 acres of Land upon Lawrence's Creek abt. five miles from the Ohio beginning at a large lime stone Spring & thence down the Said Creek I had almost forgot to inform you that it is the desire of the Surveyors that you'd Send for their horses from Green Briar they are at the house of Jas. Davis on Muddy Creek in the Care of Jas. Campbell who expects 20/ for taken care of them. I'll reserve

---

[38] Hancock Taylor was brother of Richard, a pioneer settler of Kentucky, father of the president Zachary Taylor. In 1769 he accompanied a party of explorers to the Falls of the Ohio, and thence they floated to New Orleans, returning by sea. In 1773 Taylor surveyed in Kentucky, accompanying the McAfees and Captain Bullitt. He was the leader of one division of the surveying party sent out in the spring of 1774 by Colonel Preston, but was shot by the Indians and died upon Taylor's Fork of Silver Creek, Madison County.—ED.

the rest of the News untill I see you & in the mean time Sign myself

yr. mot. Obd. Humble Servt.
ALEX. SPOTSd. DANDRIDGE[39]

[Extract from a letter of Col. William Preston to Col. George Washington, dated Fincastle, May 27th, 1774. 15S79.]

Agreeable to my promise, I directed Mr. Floyd, an assistant to survey your land on Cole river[40] on his way to the Ohio, which he did, & in a few days afterwards sent me the plat by Mr. Thomas Hogg: Mr. Spotswood Dandridge, who left the surveyors on the Ohio after Hogg parted with them, wrote me that Mr. Hogg and two other men with him had never since been heard of. I have had no opportunity of writing to Mr. Floyd since; though I suppose he will send me the courses by the first person that comes up, & so I shall make out the certificate & send it down. This I directed him to do when we parted to prevent accidents. But I am really afraid the Indians will

---

[39] Alexander Spottswood, son of Nathaniel West Dandridge, grandson of the governor of Virginia who first crossed the Blue Ridge (1714), and a near relative of Martha Dandridge Washington, was born Aug. 1, 1753, in Hanover County, Virginia. He received the best education possible at the time, and was a young man of great promise and popularity. He went out to Kentucky with Henderson in 1775, when the Transylvania Company made the Boonesborough settlement. On the outbreak of the Revolution he joined the colonial army and was aide-de-camp to Washington. About 1780, he married the daughter of Col. Adam Stephen in Jefferson County, Va., where he died in 1785.—ED.

[40] Coal River is a western tributary of the Kanawha, flowing into the latter a few miles below Charleston.—ED.

hinder them from doing any business of value this season, as the company being only 33, & daily decreasing, were under the greatest apprehension of danger when Mr Dandridge parted with them.

PAY FOR SCOUTS

[Col. William Preston to Capt. Samuel McDowell.[41] 3QQ27.]

DEAR SIR—I take the Liberty of inclosing to you a Certificate to lay before the Committee of Claims for an Allowance.

The Reason of this Service was, when Capt. Russell returned to Clinch in April he found that many Families had deserted their Plant[at]ions under Apprehensions of Danger from the Indians. Upon which he sent out the scouts, having Instructions to do so if he saw it necessary, and the[y] continued no longer on Duty than was necessary to perform the Rout he directed them. This eased the Minds of the People who

---

[41] Samuel McDowell was the eldest son of John, one of the earliest settlers of the Valley of Virginia. Born in Pennsylvania in 1735, he removed to Augusta County when but two years of age. Five years later his father was killed by Indians. The younger McDowell served in Braddock's campaign, was a member of the Virginia assembly in 1773, and led a company in Lord Dunmore's War. He represented Augusta in the state convention of 1776, and commanded a regiment that fought under Greene at Guilford Court House (1781), and in the campaign against Cornwallis. At the close of the Revolution he removed to Kentucky (1783), and became one of the most prominent citizens of that commonwealth, serving as judge of the first district court, president of seven conventions agitating for statehood, and member of the constitutional convention of 1792. He died near Danville in 1817.—ED.

returned to their Habitations again. Beside their going down the Louisa was rendering a very necessary service to the Country as it had been greatly disputed whether that River or Cumberland was the Line between Virginia and the Cherrokees. The Hunters or Settlers can now have no Excuse or Plead Ignorance in going over the Louisa or Infringing on the Indians Claim.

I hope you will use your Interest to have their Pay allowed, and the rather as I verily beleive it to be Just. They have made no Charge for Provisions Therefore it is to be presumed they found themselves which ought also to be considered.

I only got the Writ for the Election last Night & have appointed the 10th. of June for the Election of a Burgess in the Room of Mr. Doack.

I wish you Health and am sir
     Your most hble Servt.
May 27th. 1774   Wm Preston.
To Capt. Samuel McDowell in Williamsburg

DANGER OF INDIAN INROADS

[Rev. John Brown to Col. William Preston. 3QQ29.]

My Dr. Br.—After a fataguing Journey with a View to pay you a Visit at Smithfields, I had the mortification to be disappointed.

 * * * * * * * *

I can asure I am no ways satisfied with your situation; you lay too much in the way of the Indians. New River has been the Course they came formerly to War & probably will come you had need to be upon your watch & take every prudent method to prevent a surprize, you have a great number under your Care whose dependance for protection (under God) is upon you; a loving Wife and a number of helpless Children I think it wou'd not be amiss if any apparent danger come to remove them to some place of greater safty. but in these thing I am only a Tyro. I envy this letter because it has the place that I expected to have had in person but I hope you will accept it with my Wife's love to you & sister Preston together with your dr. Children & believe me to be your affectionat Br. whilest I am

JOHN BROWN[42]

May 28th 1774 From Mr Howards

P. S. The Brakenbridge Boys are well & Jamy will make a good scholar.[43]

---

[42] The Rev. John Brown was born in Ireland, came to America while still a youth, and was graduated from Princeton in 1749. In 1753 he was called to the charge of the New Providence and Timber Ridge Presbyterian congregations, Augusta County, Va., and remained pastor of the former for forty-four years. He married Margaret, sister of Col. William Preston, with whom he was on terms of affectionate intimacy. His sons John and James became prominent Kentuckians. In 1796-97, Dr. Brown resigned his pastorate, and joined his sons in Kentucky, where he died in 1803.—ED.

[43] Col. Robert Breckenridge of Botetourt County married Lettice, sister of Col. William Preston, and had four sons, William, John (ancestor of the Kentucky branch), James, and Preston. The reference is doubtless to the two younger sons, whose father had died in 1772, and of whom Colonel Preston acted as guardian. James was born in 1763, and after serving in the Revolution was graduated from William and Mary in 1785. He settled in Botetourt County, where he practiced law, representing his district in the state assembly and in congress (1809-17). He died at Fincastle, 1846.—ED.

DELAWARES FRIENDLY; SHAWNEE ON WARPATH

[Contemporary newspaper extracts. 2JJ58-60.]

Extract of a letter dated Pittsburg, May 30[44]

I arrived here last Wednesday with Messrs. Duncan & Wilson,[45] guarded by a party of Delawares,[46] who treated us with great deal of kindness, & gave us great reason to think they mean nothing but peace & friendship from all their actions. The Shawanese have raised 20 warriors to strike the Virginians, who sat off last Monday. I fear all the traders are killed at the Shawanese towns, as there was a party of Mingoes gathered for that purpose.[47] I am of opinion it will

---

[44] Printed in the *Maryland Journal*, Saturday, June 18, 1774.—ED.

[45] Col. George Wilson, a Scotch-Irishman who was born in Augusta County, Virginia, had removed to Westmoreland County, Pa., after the French and Indian War, in which he had served under Braddock. During the bounaary controversy he sided with the Pennsylvania proprietors, and was a magistrate for that colony. In 1776, he was commissioned lieutenant-colonel of the 8th Pennsylvania and died in service in New Jersey (1777).—ED.

[46] The Delawares were the original inhabitants of Pennsylvania, but by this time the larger part of the tribe had removed to the Ohio towns on the Muskingum River. They were hostiles during the French and Indian and Pontiac's wars; but they kept the treaty made with Bouquet (1764), and, largely through the efforts of the Moravian missionaries, took no part in the Shawnee outbreak of 1774.—ED.

[47] The Mingo are usually spoken of as the "Iroquois of the Ohio," although there is reason to believe that they were originally the kindred tribe known to the Dutch as Minquas, to the French as Andastes, and to the English as Susquehannocks or Conestogas. See Shea, in *Historical Magazine*, ii, pp. 294-301. The tribe were conquered by the Iroquois about 1675, and the remnant incorporated in their league. The Mingo of the eighteenth century were a mongrel race, chiefly wanderers from the New York Iroquois stock.—ED.

be a general Indian war, though Col. Croghan thinks the matter will be settled in a short time.

Extract of a letter from Bedford, May 30

I suppose you have heard of the Indians being killed at Whaling; since that time Indian White Eyes,[48] Mr. Duncan and Mr. Saunderson, who were sent down the river from Fort Pitt, in order to accomodate matters with the Shawanese, are returned, but had hard work to get back; the Delawares, who at present seem to be friends, had enough to do to save their lives; the poor traders among the Shawanese, no person can tell whether they are dead or alive.[49] White-Eyes on his return to Fort Pitt, said the Shawanese were for war, & that forty odd of them were at present out, intending a stroke (as it is supposed) at some part of Virginia. The Delawares say they will not go to war, but there is no dependance in them; we expect every day to hear of their striking in some quarter. It is lamentable to see the multitudes of poor people that are hourly running down the country; such of them as stay, are building forts; God knows

---

[48] "Indians being killed at Whaling" refers to murders by the Cresap band, see *ante*, pp. 11, 12. White Eyes, whose Indian name was Koquethagechton, was a Delaware chief of great bravery and virtue, who proved a friend to the whites, and restrained his tribe from hostilities during this war. For his services to Dunmore in making peace, see *post*. After the outbreak of the Revolution, he endeavored to maintain neutrality, but finding it impossible embraced the American cause (1778). His death the same year was a loss to the frontier.—ED.

[49] For further account of this embassy sent by Croghan to the Shawnee, see letter of St. Clair in *Pennsylvania Archives*, 1st series, iv, pp. 501–504. The trader here called Saunderson is mentioned as Anderson in the *Archives* See also account of Duncan's danger and escape, in St. Clair's letter.—ED.

how it will turn out with them. We intend, as soon as we hear of any damage being done, to erect fortifications here. The Shawanese themselves say, that they have nothing against Pennsylvania, but only Virginia; but we may depend, as soon as they strike Virginia, they will also fall on us.

SETTLEMENTS TO BE DEFENDED

[Capt. Daniel Smith to Col. William Preston. 3QQ149.]

INDIAN CREEK[50] 30th May, 1774.

SIR—Your Letter of the 24th Inst. came to hand yesterday In consequence of which I appointed a muster 12th. June, which I thought as soon as the men could get notice as they live much dispers'd. I shall very carefully observe the Directions you gave me, and exert myself in keeping the people from abandoning their settlements, and trying to make them punctually obey orders, In which case the amendment in the Invasion Law, I judge will be very helpfull. There is a very great scarcity of Powder and Lead in this part of the Country, a Circumstance as alarming as any that occurs to me now. For should there be an immediate invasion, I believe that one half the people Could not raise five Charges of Powder, Altho' I have threatned to fine several, who on hearing these threats have assured me they knew not where to buy

---

[50] Indian Creek is an affluent of Maiden Spring Creek or the South Fork of Clinch River. See Smith's MS. map, in this volume.—ED

HEADWATERS OF THE CLINCH AND THE HOLSTON
Reduced facsimile from original by Daniel Smith, in the Draper MSS.—4XX62.

it. Would it not be prudent to cause a more immediate supply than what is expected from Col. Lewis's orders? I mention this because Major Philips[51] informs me that Capt. Arthur Campbell has by him a large quantity reserved against a time of need, and I have engaged Mr. Watsion to go by his house and enquire its goodness &c. and make report to you. I shall write you by every opportunity how matters stand, and shall be obliged to you for frequent Instructions.

I am Sir With much respect Your very humble Servt.

DAN SMITH.

Capt. Russell's Letter is gone to him by a safe hand. Should he go to Court or see you shortly, please to engage him to call on me.

INHABITANTS FLEEING; SURVEYORS IN DANGER

[Abraham Hites to Col. William Preston. 3QQ35.]

HAMPSHIRE[52] June 3d. 1774

DEAR SIR—There is two Expresses just arrived from Pitsburgh to Col. Hites my Father[53] who is from

[51] Probably the Captain Philips who was ambuscaded in this locality in 1763. See Thwaites, *Withers's Border Warfare* (Cincinnati, 1895), p. 97, note.—ED.

[52] Hampshire County was erected in 1753, out of Frederick County, and included the lower part of the Valley of Virginia. This division of the Hite family lived near Moorefield, on the South Branch of the Potomac, in the present Hardy County.—ED.

[53] Col. Abraham Hite was fourth son of Joist Hite, an early settler of the Virginia Valley (1732). He married Rebecca Van Meter, and was a man of wealth and influence, frequently sent to the House of Burgesses. He joined his sons in Kentucky, where he died.—ED.

Home at Baltamore; the Purport of which are, that an Indian War is commenced, and the out Inhabitants are all Forting[54] [or] fleeing in; the Distress which the Inhabitants are in your own Imaginetion will easily paint to you.

There is likewise a Lad, who is just come in that says he was at the Mouth of the big Connawas about six weeks since, that my Brother[55] & the other surveyors were there with about thirty Men besides, But then were in great doubt what to do, wheether to proceed down the River, as this Lad had been stoped by them [the Indians] and they declared none should [go] down, or else make a halt there to know the Issue, they had not then heard of any thing done above them, so that their situation, I doubt, is attend'd with the greatest Hazard.

I am, dear & respectable Sir, in hast, your asurred Frend &c.

ABRAHAM HITES Junr.[56]

P. S. This comes with an Express to Col. Lewis.

Col. Preston.

---

[54] Meaning that they are building blockhouses, for refuge from Indian attacks.—ED.

[55] Capt. Isaac Hite, who was with Floyd's surveying party. See Hanson's *Journal,* post. He had been out with Bullitt in 1773, and in 1775 led a party to Kentucky, which made one of the first settlements near Boonesborough. He took an active part in the early events of the Kentucky settlement, being member of the Transylvania legislature, signing the protest to the Virginia assembly (1775), and taking part in the first Kentucky court (1781). Later he removed to Jefferson County, which became his permanent home.—ED.

[56] Abraham Hite, jr., also joined the Kentucky pioneer movement, going out with Harrod in 1773, and with his brother in 1775. He likewise settled in Jefferson County, which he represented in the state senate in 1800-03.—ED.

PLANS FOR DEFENSE AND ATTACK

[Circular letter of Lord Dunmore, sent to the county-lieutenants. 3QQ39.]

WILLIAMSBURG 10th June 1774

SIR—The intelligence which I have received from Fort Pitt, of the Motions and disposition of the Indians, giving me now good grounds to believe that hopes of a pacification can be no longer entertained,[57] and that these People will by no means be diverted from their design of falling upon the back parts of this Country and Committing all the outrages and devastations which will be in their power to effect, it is necessary (the Assembly not having thought proper to pay attention to this Momentous business though they were Sufficiently apprised of it[58]) that we Should have recourse to the only means which are left in our power to extricate ourselves out of so Calamitous a Situation.

You are therefore upon the receipt of this letter immediately to give orders that the Militia of your County be forthwith embodied, and held in readiness either to defend that part of the Country or to march to the Assistance of any other, as occasion may require,

---

[57] For the attempts at pacification made by the Indian agents Croghan and McKee, see *Amer. Archives,* 4th series, i, pp. 475–483. These councils and messages were successful in regard to the Delawares and Iroquois, but not for the Shawnee and Mingo.—ED.

[58] This was the Virginia assembly dissolved by the governor for passing resolutions of sympathy with Boston, and for appointing the day the Boston Port Bill took effect (June 1), as one of fasting and prayer. See *Amer. Archives,* 4th series, i, p. 350.—ED.

and in General to exert those few powers, which the Act of Assembly, in this Case, authorizes, in the best manner, according to your abilities, that may answer the present exigence; leaving it to your own Zeal and discretion to provide extraordinary means for any extraordinary occasions that may arise, as, if you Should find, by following the Enemy into their own Country and beyond the limits prescribed in the Act of Assembly and can prevail on your Men to agree to it, that it would be an opportunity of Stricking Such a Stroke as might prove decisive, I cannot but Suppose the Necessity of it would Justify you with your Country, and the benefit accruing from it ensure you their applause, and therefore oblige the Assembly to indemnify you; but this however I can only recommend to your own Judgment to do as you shall think best, as people will be more apt to determine the merit of such a Measure by the event than by the reasons which induced you to adopt it, and it exceeds the Authority which I have to vest you with.

I also recommend to your own Judgment, whether you Should not employ your men to erect Small Forts in Such places as would Serve best to protect the adjacent Settlers, to Secure all important papers, and likewise to Cover the retreat of the Militia in Case the Number of the Indians should unfortunately make that Step at any time Necessary; it has been represented to me that a Fort at the Conflux of the Great Kanhaway and the Ohio would Answer Several good purposes of this kind, which however I must leave to be Considered by you, and the other Commanding Officers of the Militia, whose knowledge of the Country will make them proper Judges of its expediency.

PLAN OF CAMPAIGN

You ought to keep up a constant Correspondence with all the Lieutenants and Commanding Officers of the adjoining Counties, so as that you may be able to assist each other in the most effectual and expedetious Manner, and, if to answer any good purpose to join your respective Corps of Militia into one body.

And you are to report to me from time to time all your proceedings.

That the Country may be convinced of my resolution not to neglect any thing in my power to Serve it, I shall, at my own risque endeavour to furnish you with powder and ball; and as expedetiously as possible.

I am Sir Your most Obedient humble Servant

DUNMORE[59]

P. S. If a Communication was kept open between the Mouth of the Great Kanahaway and Fort Pitt now called Fort Dunmore,[60] it might effectually protect the Settlers in that part of the Country and awe the Indians. D.

Colº. William Preston.

---

[59] The letter is written by a clerical hand, but signed by Dunmore.—ED.

[60] Fort Pitt was evacuated by order of Gen. Gage, in October, 1772. When Connolly came out as Dunmore's agent in January, 1774, he restored the fort and re-named it for his chief.—ED.

RAVAGES OF INDIAN INVADERS

[Extract of a letter from Fort Pitt, dated June 12, 1774.[61] 2JJ, book 3. p. 60.]

We have great reason to be no longer in suspense concerning a war with the Indians, as they have already been guilty of several massacres; on Saturday, the 4th inst. were killed & scalped by them one Benjamin Spear, his wife & six children, on Duncard Creek;[62] and the Monday following one Henry Wall, within sight of a fort that is built on Muddy Creek; one Keener, near the same place;[63] and one Procter, near Grave Creek; there was also one Campbell, lately from Lancaster county, killed & scalped at New Comer's-Town by the Mingoes.[64]

---

[61] This was published in the *Pennsylvania Gazette*, June 22, 1774.—ED.

[62] For a further account of this attack, see *Amer. Archives*, 4th series, i, p. 405. Dunkard Creek is a branch of Monongahela River, in Greene County, Pa., so named because of its early settlers, who were of the German sect of that name. See Thwaites, *Withers's Border Warfare*, pp. 75-77.—ED.

[63] Muddy Creek is in Pennsylvania, a Western tributary of Monongahela in the present Greene (then part of Westmoreland) County. See the *Washington-Crawford Letters*, p. 93. This is to be distinguished from the Muddy Creek of Greenbrier. The leader of the party ravaging in Pennsylvania was undoubtedly the chief Logan, who desisted only when he had taken thirteen scalps, supposed to equal the number of Indians killed at Yellow Creek.—ED.

[64] Grave Creek, in Marshall County, West Va., with the town of Moundsville at its mouth, takes its name from the "Big Grave"—a pre-historic Indian mound in the vicinity. Newcomerstown, or Gekelemupechunk, was the capital of the Delaware tribe on the Muskingum. It was north of Tuscarawas Creek, a short distance from the present Ohio town of that name. In 1771, when visited by the Moravian missionary Zeisberger, it contained a hundred log houses;

INDIAN FORAYS

[Extract from a letter dated Pittsburg, June 13, 1774. 2JJ61.][65]

This morning we received certain accounts from a place called Ten Mile Creek, above Red Stone, that the Indians killed & scalped one Francis McClure, who formerly lived at Weilin [Wheeling] Creek, down the river, & shot one Samuel Kinkade through the arm, but he got away.[66]

FRONTIER MOVEMENTS

[Synopsis of letter of Lord Dunmore to Capt. John Connolly, in *Amer. Archives,* 4th series, i, p. 473.]

WILLIAMSBURG, June 20, 1774.

Entirely approves of plan of building fort at Wheeling, and of marching to Shawnee towns, if he has sufficient force. Hopes he will prevail on well-affected Delawares and Mingo to remove from the Shawnee. Necessary for Connolly to remain at Fort Dunmore, Capt. William Crawford, a prudent, resolute officer,

---

but in 1775 the majority of its inhabitants had removed to the present site of Coshocton.

For another mention of these attacks, see *Penna. Archives,* iv, p. 513.—ED.

[65] This was printed in the *Pennsylvania Gazette,* June 29, 1774.—ED.

[66] This was a militia company sent out in pursuit of Logan's raiding-party, commanded by Captain McClure, with Kinkead as lieutenant. Ten Mile Creek is in Greene County, Pa., a western affluent of the Monongahela. For further reports see *American Archives,* i, pp. 435, 471; *Penna. Archives,* iv, pp. 517, 519. In the latter account St. Clair says that Connolly abandoned an intended expedition down the Ohio, to the Indian towns, because of this accident.—ED.

may be sent to co-operate with Lewis, or to strike a stroke himself. Recommends making prisoners of Indian women and children, and that no terms be given unless six hostages are furnished.

CHEROKEE INDIAN KILLED

[Letter of Maj. Arthur Campbell to Col. William Preston. 3QQ40.][67]

SIR — Since the rash action of killing a Cherokee on Wattaugo,[68] the lower settlement on this, and Clynch Rivers, is greatly alarmed. some preparing to move off: and indeed from the behaviour of the Squa & Indian fellow, that was in Company with the one that was killed; we may expect a reprisal will be made shortly, if there is not some Men sent to cover the Inhabitants, until the matter can be made up with the Chiefs. I imagine a Letter from Colo. Lewis (as he is an old acquaintance and it is a relation of old Outassatus[69] that is killed called Billey) would be of service

---

[67] Letter undated, about June 20, 1774.—L. C. D.
[68] An eastern affluent of the Holston. Watauga River, whose upper waters pierce Yellow Mountains and form a pass from North Carolina, was the site of one of the earliest settlements on the upper Tennessee, Robertson building a cabin thereon in 1770.—ED.
[69] Colonel Lewis had had long experience in frontier warfare, and had accompanied Colonel Byrd on his expedition against the Cherokee in 1761.
Campbell probably refers here to the great Cherokee chief usually called Oconastota. He had visited England in 1730 when quite a youth. In 1738 he was chosen head-chief of the tribe, with his seat at Chota, on Tellico River. He led the attacks upon the English forts during the French and Indian War; but after making peace, remained the friend

at this time; at least might prolong an invasion until we are better prepared. One Crabtree is generally suspected to be the Principal, in the late dispatching of Cherokee Billey. However let the consequence of the affair be what it will, I am persuaded it would be easier to find 200 Men to screen him from the Law, than ten to bring him to Justice; Crabtrees different robberies, the Murder of Russell, Boons; & Drakes Sons is in every ones mouth.

I am Sir
        your mo. Obedient Servt.
           ARTHUR CAMPBELL[70]

---

of the English, who used his attachment for them to persuade him to harry the border during the American Revolution. He made the treaty with the Transylvania Company (1775); but about 1778 was deposed in favor of a more peaceable chief. He is said to have been still living in 1809, a victim of strong drink, and a sad example of fallen greatness.—ED.

[70] Arthur Campbell was born in Augusta County in 1743, son of David, one of the earliest Scotch-Irish settlers of this region. When a boy of fifteen he was captured ne r Dickenson's Fort by Northwestern Indians, carried to their towns on Lake Erie, and after three years' captivity succeeded in escaping to the British army. His return to Virginia was hailed with great joy, and the state allowed him for his services as guide 1000 acres, which were surveyed in 1774 on Beargrass Creek, near Louisville, Ky. See Hanson's *Journal, post.* In 1665 his father purchased the "Royal Oak" estate on the Middle Fork of Holston, in what is now Smyth County. Here young Campbell built the first mill in the vicinity (1770), and upon the erection of Fincastle County (1772) was chosen justice of the peace, and soon thereafter major of the militia. As one of the most prominent men of southwest Virginia, he took part in all stirring border events. In 1775 he represented his county in the Virginia assembly; in 1776 was chosen county lieutenant for the newly-erected Washington County—an office held for over thirty years. In 1780, he conducted a brilliant campaign against the Cherokee, but resigned the leadership in the King's Mountain expedition (1780) to his cousin, Gen.

[Maj. Arthur Campbell to Col. William Preston. 3QQ41.]

ROYAL OAK[71] June 22ᵈ. 1774

SIR—Yesterday I received your Letter with the two inclosed. This morning I had a favourable oppertunity to send them to Wattago; and from thence I have reason to expect a speedy conveyance to the nation As I had some acquaintance with Mr. Cameron, I took the liberty to write to him, on the same subject:[72] mentioning briefly the late murder on Wattago; and what degree of detestation it is held in, by the sober minded, in this Country; I also enlarged fully on the provocations we received last Fall; taking the liberty at the same time to blame his conduct, for giving Orders, for robberies, on the Indian Lands whereby, perhaps the profligate part of the nation, is both our Judges, and executioners.

Nothwithstanding these earnest endeavours, to prevent a calamity, that may be very destructive to us; It appears that Crabtree, and a few mislead followers,

---

William Campbell. The following year, he became involved in a movement for a new state, and joined Sevier in the Franklin episode. For this he was removed from office by Gov. Patrick Henry, but reinstated by the legislature, and endorsed by the suffrages of the people. A man of much ability, with marked literary tastes, and a natural leader of men, his imperious and hasty temper made him many enemies. In the latter years of his life he joined his sons in Kentucky, and died near Middlesborough in 1811.—ED.

[71] The home of Arthur Campbell, near the present Marion, Va.—ED.

[72] Alexander Cameron was a Scotchman who had married a Cherokee wife. Living in the middle towns of that tribe, he had acquired a large influence over them. He was deputy commissioner of Indian affairs for the southern district, and during the Revolution incited attacks upon the borders, in favor of the British.—ED.

will frustrate all we can do. Last Week he returned from an adventure over, at Nola-Chuckee, to one Browns[73] (a Smith that Works for the Cherokees) as he was informed, before he left Holston, that there was 2 or 3 Indians there a hunting However our Hero, was disappointed in his expectations; for instead of finding, two, or three, defenceless wretches he was informed of 37 Warriors being in the Neighbourhood, who were apprized of his intentions; and would not fail to examine Strangers, strictly; upon this intelligence, he departed the place, with precipitation, and came up to his Fathers at the Big Lick.[74] Yet still restless he went down the River a few days ago to make another attempt.

Since the alarm on Copper Creek,[75] I think, the most of people seem to disapprove Crabtrees' conduct: They were ready enough then; to ascribe that supposed Murder, to his doings; however inconsistant they were before in avowing, they would screen him from Justice.

I shall esteem it my Duty to transmit to you an account of any true alarm, that may happen; and please favour me with the like account, if the War has actually broke out to the Northward.

---

[73] Nolichucky River is an eastern affluent of the Holston, in northeastern Tennessee. The first cabin built on this stream was that of Jacob Brown, who in 1771 crossed the mountains to this valley. He had a considerable influence with the Indians, from whom he made a large purchase of lands in 1772.—ED.

[74] Big Lick was on the North Fork of Holston, in the present Washington County, Virginia, on the road to the Clinch River settlements. See Smith's MS. map.—ED.

[75] Copper Creek is an eastern tributary of the Clinch, in southwestern Virginia.—ED.

I am very uneasy about my Friend Floyd, as my night tho't of him seems to presage his fate: I hope he is only in Danger
I am Sir Your Obedient Humble Servt
                                        ARTHUR CAMPBELL

PLAN FOR FORT AT MOUTH OF KANAWHA

[Col. William Christian to Col. William Preston. 3QQ42.]

DUNKARD-BOTTOM [76] Wednesday morning 22[d]. June 74

SIR—I received your letter yesterday with the extract from Connellys letter in which he observes that a party of Shawnese were gone out against the Inhabitants;[77] that in intelligence from the Shawnese must have been near a month ago and of course if true they must have made the stroke by this time. As that is not the case it seems more probable to me that the

---

[76] Colonel Christian's home in the present Pulaski County, on the west side of New River. A fort was built at this place in 1755.—ED.

[77] Dr. John Connolly was born in Lancaster County, Pa., about 1750. He was well connected, and married a daughter of Samuel Semple, a noted Pittsburg lawyer. In 1774 Lord Dunmore chose Connolly as his agent. The latter is accused of fomenting the boundary dispute between Virginia and Pennsylvania, and of bringing on the border troubles with the Indians. At the rupture between England and the colonies, Connolly adhered to the former. He was arrested in Maryland (early in 1775) and relieved of treasonable correspondence. After that he was kept a prisoner until 1781, when escaping to Canada he plotted a descent upon Pittsburg, and the next year led a force which destroyed Hannastown. Later (1788-89), he was concerned in English intrigues to capture New Orleans, and visited Kentucky with that purpose; but was recognized, and expelled from the country.—ED.

Enemy would wait the resolutions of the grand council which was to be held; And I confess I still think the Surveyors safe until some of them comes in, they would not all be killed if fallen on. I had thoughts of writing to Capt Thompson, or Capt. W. Campble[78] whose Company he is in to encourage Crabtree to go in search of the Surveyors, and if he did that business well, it might serve to atone for his guilt in killing the Cherokee but I was afraid to do it without having your consent. When the News of the peoples being killed at Copper creek proved false several of the militia were assembled to go over there, and it was said they were sorry, exceedingly so, that it did prove false. So desirous are some of them for an Indian War; tho I cant help fearing that it is the most worthless and the men least to be depended on.

I have not a beast to ride but a little leazy trotting mare or I would have waited on you to day my self, and being also uncertain where I should find you; whether on the way or at home. I observe in yours that the Governor expresses a desire that a Fort might

---

[78] Capt. James Thompson was a native of Augusta County, being a grandson of its first settler, Col. James Patton. He early removed to the Holston, being in 1772 appointed justice of the peace and captain of militia for the newly-erected county of Fincastle. He remained to watch the frontier during the Point Pleasant campaign; but acted as guard to Colonel Christian in the Cherokee expedition of 1776.

William Campbell was a cousin of Arthur, being born in Augusta County, in 1745. In 1767 he removed to the Holston, and in 1774 was chosen captain of a militia company, and in 1777 lieutenant-colonel of Washington County. In that capacity he commanded the troops at the battle of King's Mountain, later served at Guilford, and died (1781) in Lafayette's army before Yorktown. For further details see Draper, *King's Mountain and its Heroes* (Cincinnati, 1881), pp. 378-402.—ED.

be built at the mouth of New river, how that could be done without particular orders as there should be a large body of men & a method of finding provisions to support them when there I dont well know: But I will take the liberty to mention some thoughts of my own which I think would answer a good purpose for some time. You seem to signify that you dont think yourself warrantable in ordering out the Militia unless we are actually invaded, that may be so, but I think you could safely encourage men to rise and go out without expresly ordering them to do so. From what I have heard I think one 100 might be got in a few days who would find their own provisions (& Each man a horse) sufficient to serve 2 or 3 weeks. If you approve of the Scheme & write what you think proper for their encouragement, I will get all the Captains who you think could best spare the men out of their companies to call those together whom they have drafted, & see if they are willing to go & take their chance of pay; All this can be done this week as I suppose Herbert, Crockett, Trigg, & Robertson[79] would

---

[79] These were the captains of militia for Fincastle County. William Herbert later went on the expedition in command of a company from New River. He died in 1776. Walter Crockett belonged to a family that early settled on the headwaters of the South Fork of Holston. He was a county magistrate and at the Battle of King's Mountain in 1780. Stephen Trigg was a prominent Fincastle man, delegate to the Virginia assembly in 1774, signed the articles of association in 1775, and guarded the border in Revolutionary days. In 1779 he went out to Kentucky as land commissioner, erected a station in Lincoln County, represented Kentucky County in 1780, and was killed leading his men to a charge at the Battle of Blue Licks (1782). James Robertson was not the pioneer of Tennessee, but belonged to the Augusta family of that name, and was magistrate of Botetourt County in 1770, and of Montgomery 1780.—ED.

FORT AT KANAWHA 45

be enough, if you thought, Cloyd & Taylor[80] had better not spare any. Perhaps 50 would be enough—I could find ammunition as far as 80 [lbs] powder & 80 of lead, which I would run the risque of being paid for. Then if you approved of it I would march down the War path on this side of New river, as far as the mouth, and if any Indians are coming in, we would be very apt to meet them, if any small Companies were coming & see our Sign they would not proceed but immediately run home.

If we could take a months provision we could stay some time about the Ohio which I think would much alarm the Shawnese, indeed we could not want Fish is so plenty there. Perhaps our going might paye the way & encourage others to follow, so that something could be done towards the Fort as his Lordship desired. My time trouble & expense I will freely give as well as find ammunition. Indeed I would also pay for a sufficient Quantity of Meat for a month or five weeks if that would do. If you go upwards today or to morrow pray tell the boy where I can meet you, & I will.

I really think I could get the men to go, if you encourage it & thinks well of it.

If you like this or thinks of any Scheme, You'll please to Command me & I shall not loose a moment

---

[80] Capt. Joseph Cloyd was one of a family settled near Draper's Meadows, on the upper waters of New River, who were nearly all massacred by Indians in 1764. Joseph, who escaped, became prominent in Fincastle affairs, was field officer, and served in the Revolution as major of militia, rescuing Colonel Preston at a critical moment in Greene's campaign.

John Taylor settled on Clinch in 1777. In 1782, he was major commandant for that district.—ED.

in putting it in Execution. I sent the boy to my Fathers for the musket, they had taken her to pieces & oiled her, he did not bring her but I'll send her to fields, (?) this week, I would have sent to you in the night last night but feared frightening Mrs. Preston. Farewell   WILLIAM CHRISTIAN[81]

To Col⁰. William Preston By Tim

[Col. William Christian to Col. William Preston. 3QQ43.]

NEW DUBLIN[82] Wednesday 11: OClock

DEAR SIR—I came up a while ago with design to meet you at Sawyers's today but my Horse has such a sore back and sore feet that I cant well proceed.

I had no other business but to get your opinion and Orders about the trip I proposed, in case it was approved off, and thought necessary by you. So that I think my presence needless, as you can issue all orders to the Captains you think proper above here tomorrow, or say nothing about it as you judge most prudent; Whatever you do will please me.

I have not talked to any men about going, but from the willingness to go against the Indians, that has appeared by the Mens behaviour in turning out voluntarily; I conclude one hundred, might be got who would take their chance of pay, I have no design in it but to serve the Inhabitants, & perhaps cover the retreat of the Surveyors Could I save one life I should

---

[81] For life of Col. William Christian, see *post*.—ED.

[82] Near the mouth of Peak Creek, on New River, in Montgomery County. See Hale, *Trans-Allegheny Pioneers* (Cincinnati, 1886), pp. 326, 327.—ED.

think my self recompensed. Tho I cant help having some distant thoughts, but you can contrive something about the desired Fort. In one week a small one could be erected, the only difficulty that occurs to me is to Occupy it afterwards If a War ensues no doubt but it would be approved of.

If I am well I shall be at Michael prices on saturday as I promised Capt Taylor I would go there; Perhaps I may see you on your way home in the evening.

I am Sir Your Humble Servant

WILLIAM CHRISTIAN

To Col⁰. William Preston pʳ. Mʳ. Brander

CHEROKEE INCLINED TO PEACE

[Maj. Arthur Campbell to Col. William Preston. 3QQ44.]

SIR—I Received yours of the 20th. Inst., and immediately afterwards got my Brother John,[83] to set out down the River, to the settlement adjoining the Indian Line, that he might see to the sending out the Spy, and your Orders in other respects more effectually executed, than could be done by Letter.

I have recommended it to the Spy, that goes from Holston, to go as far as the Ford on Broad River:[84] and to be particularly attentive, to observe the path, as

---

[83] Capt. John Campbell, a younger brother of Arthur, lived near the latter at Royal Oak. He served as a lieutenant in the Point Pleasant campaign, and as captain at the Battle of Long Island Flats (1776). He was county-clerk for Washington for many years (1779-1815).—ED.

[84] The French Broad, a large eastern affluent of Holston below the Nolichucky.—ED.

the[y] go along, at least, twice a Day, and to travel some distance, up, and down, the River, after they arrive at the Ford. If this piece of Duty is well executed, I have reason to expect we will have timeous [timely] notice, to be prepared to met a large Body, if an Enemy approaches.

From the expressions of the Little Carpenter,[85] when last on Wattago; and the behaviour of some Indians, that has since been on Nola-Chuckee; I think the Cherokees would willingly avoid a War with us; except some repeated affront from Crabtree, provokes them to it; and rather so, as I am informed, their Magazine of Powder is chiefly damaged, by being Stored up in Bags, in a Cave, or some such place, under Ground. However, it may be prudent for us, to be on our guard, as it may be, the Seventy that was to meet at the Grand-Council, may return with some Shawanese in Company, who may choose to take some Scalps with them, by way of a Declaration of War.

I have wrote to Capt. Shelby[86] to send me notice im-

---

[85] Little Carpenter was a "half king"—chief of a large village—of the Overhill Cherokee, who was especially favorable to the whites, aiding Henderson and Hart on their expedition to effect the Watauga purchase.—ED.

[86] Evan Shelby was born in Wales in 1720; early in life he emigrated to Maryland, and was actively employed upon the frontier, going out under Braddock as a scout, and commanding a company under Forbes (1758). At the close of the French and Indian War he engaged in Indian trade, and in 1771 removed to Holston, where he settled near the border line between Virginia and Tennessee. After the Point Pleasant campaign, in which he distinguished himself, he went out second in command to Christian, in the Cherokee expedition (1776), and led a successful raid upon the Chickamauga towns (1779). Virginia appointed him general of militia; therefore during the troubles connected with the state of Franklin, the old frontiersmen refused to join the

mediately of any alarm that may happen; and I will then, without delay, transmit the same to you by Express.

I expect a few weeks will clear up our Doubts, by whom we are to be attacked; I shall be very uneasy until the Ammunition arrives from Rocky Ridge.

I am Sir Your most Obedient Servt

ARTHUR CAMPBELL

June 23^d 1774

FORTS BEING BUILT; BOONE SENT TO WARN SURVEYORS

[Capt. William Russell to Col. William Preston. 3QQ46.]

D^R. COL^o.—Your favourable Advices Dated the 20th of this Instent, were presented me Yesterday Morning and as that Day was an appointed Time for the meeting of my Company, I had an opportunity, to lay before the People, so much of your Instructions as was necessary for their Satisfaction.

* * * * * * * *

The rest of my Company Yesterday, Voted two Forts to be Immediately built, I think, in as convenient Places, as we can get; and We shall begin Instantly to Erect them. I am sorry to hear there is no other Powder to be had; but that sort of M^r. Triggs; however being satisfy'd, that yours, and Col^o. Christians good

---

movement for a new community. His home at King's Meadows (now Bristol, Tenn.) was finally adjudged to be on the North Carolina side of the line, and there he died in 1794, leaving many descendants, of whom the most noted was Gov. Isaac Shelby.—ED.

Endeavoures, will not be wanting, to Expedite a sufficient Quantity, of the first that comes to Hand, for our Safety: shall in the Interim take the greatest care of what is sent, and Use my Interest; to make the People easy.

I believe, not all I could have said would have diverted the People from flying had not your Office provided a Remedy: by satisfying the People, I might call for any Number of Men from Holston, whenever the Service, might require.

At first Sight it appeared Strange to me, to hear of the ruinous, and Distressed Situation, the People of Red Stone,[87] and about Fort Pit were in; but when I consider a Combination of, all the Northern Indians, together with the Cherrokees; the Murders they will be capable to perpetrate, attended with a general Devastation of the Frontiers; it really appears shocking to Humanity: and I am too much afraid such a Confederacy will be form'd. I am Sensible good Sir. of your Uncommon concern for the Security of Capt. Floyd and the Gentlemen with him, and I sincerely Sympathize with You, least, they should fall a Prey, to such Inhuman, Blood thirsty Devils, as I have so lately suffered by; but may God of his Infinite Mercy, Shield him, and Company, from the present appending Danger, and could we (thro' Providence) be a means of preserving such Valuable Members, by sending out Scouts, such a procedure wood Undoubtedly be, of the most lasting, and secret Satisfaction to us; and the Country in general. I have Engaged to start Immediately, on the occasion, two of the best Hands I could

---

[87] For Red Stone Old Fort, the site of the present Brownsville, Pa., see *ante*, p. 12.—ED.

think of Danl. Boone, and Michl. Stoner;[88] who have Engaged to search the Country, as low as the falls, and to return by way of Gaspers Lick, on Cumberland,[89] and thro' Cumberland Gap: so that by the assiduity of these Men, if it is not too late, I hope the Gentlemen will be apprised of the eminent Danger they are Daily in. The Report prevailing among You, of the Family being kill'd on Copper Creek, is altogether groundless, as is that of three Cherrokees on the Head of Clinch. As my Company is sittled very remote, I shall esteem it a favour if you wood appoint a second Lieutennant, or Ensign, or send me a blank Commission for that purpose. having nothing more to trouble You with, at this Time, after desireing to render my best Compliments to your Lady, beg leave to subscribe my selfe Dr. Colo. yours most Affectionately.

W. RUSSELL

CLYNCH Sunday June the 26th. 1774

---

[88] Boone said he was sent out by Lord Dunmore, and relates his instructions, also those of Col. Andrew Lewis, at whose house he stopped before setting forth.—Draper MSS., 6C 103-105. For the career of this pioneer, see Thwaites, *Daniel Boone* (New York, 1902).

Michael Stoner first visited Kentucky in 1767, when he came down the Ohio from Pittsburg, proceeded to the Illinois region, and as far south as the site of Nashville. In 1775 he went out with Boone to the Transylvania settlement, aided in the defense of Boonesborough in 1777, where he was wounded, and finally established a station called by his name, in Bourbon County, on a branch of the Licking.—ED.

[89] Probably Mansco's Lick, named for Kasper Mansco (Mansker), who as one of the party of the "Long Hunters" visited this region in 1769. In 1772 he discovered the lick, and three years later, on a hunting excursion, visited it again. In 1779 he led out a settlement to this point, soon after the founding of Nashville by Robertson. Mansco's Lick is in the northeastern part of Davidson C unty. On the adventures of this pioneer see Roosevelt, *Winning of the West*, i, pp. 147-152.—ED.

RANGING PARTY ORDERED OUT

[Col. William Preston to Col. William Christian. 3QQ47.]

FORT CHISWELL[90] June 27th. 1774

SIR — The present defenceless Situation of the Frontier Inhabitants of the County of Fincastle make it absolutely necessary [to] Raise & keep on foot a Number of Men, to Protect the Frontiers & annoy the Enemy, the Neighbouring [counties] not more expos'd than this have raised men, & Lord Dunmores Orders Justifies the measure, 1 have given Orders to Six Captains to raise twenty men out of each of their Companys either as Volunteers or by a Draught: which with what men can be engag'd from other Companies, will make up the party one Hundred & fifty men besides Officers.

You are to take the Command of this party, Captains Crocket & Campbell will go with you & each will have fifty men beside the Necessary Officers. the remaining fifty will be under your Immediate Command as a Company, & as one subaltern will be enough, I am in hopes Ensign William Buchanan will answer that purpose.

You will endeavour to procure ammunition & Provisions for this Service. I expect a good many of the Soldiers will take their Horses to carry the provisions,

---

[90] Fort Chiswell was built (1758) at the lead-mines in the present county of Wythe, by Col. William Byrd, and named in honor of the owner of the mines, Col. John Chiswell. At this time Fincastle county-seat was located at this place. The fort was about two miles south of the present town of Max Meadows.—ED.

for which they ought to be made an allowance this allowance & the value of provisions or whatever else may be Necessary for this Service you will please to have Settled by two honest men on Oath; & beside giveing Certificates to the Owners you will be pleasd. to keep a fair & Just account of every article you receive to prevent Confusion in adjusting those accounts hearafter.

I have appointed the Soldiers to meet you at the Town House on Holston[91] early next week, from whence you are to begin your march to Clinch & from thence over Cumberland Mountain by any Gap or pass you think proper that Leades to the head branches of the Kentucky & there Range together or in seperate parties & at such places as you Judge most likely to discover & repulse the Enemy on their Approach to our Settlements, it is believd. there is a large party of Cherokees on their way to or from the Shawneese Towns, if you should fall in with this Company & knows them I must leave it to your own Prudence in what Manner to treat them, tho it is generally Said that these Indians are about [to] Join our Enemies, yet as this Report is not reduced to a Certainty, I cannot give any Particular orders herein, You will Probably be able to Judge by the Manner of their approach, or other Circumstances that cannot now be foreseen, what Indians they are & then you will act Accordingly but upon the whole I would earnestly Recommend the utmost caution and Discretion in this very nice & Important part of your duty Should this party of Chero-

---

[91] In the present Smyth County, on the Middle Fork of Holston.—Ed.

kees which is generally said to be about Seventy in number, come in a Hostile manner there is no doubt but they will be Accompanyd. by a number of Shawnesse or other Enemy Indians which may render them formidable to your party

I would therefore Recommend Your keeping out some active Men on the right & left, in the front & Rear even to the distance of a mile on Your march and at Camp to keep out a proper Number of Centinals, to prevent a Surprize which is two often attended with fatal Consequences, this above all things ought ever to be Guarded against, nor Should this Part of the duty be Neglected or even Relaxed on any occasion whatsoever.

But this with every other part of your Duty while out I must leave to yourself, only Recommending it to you to Consult your Officers when there is Occasion, who I hope will not only be very alert & obedient in their Duty; but that they will keep Good order & Discipline in their Companies & be unanimous & Friendly amongst themselves that every Intention of Sending out the Party may be fully answered.

If, on your Tour there is any Possibility of giving the Surveyors Notice of their danger (if they have not already fatally felt it) it would be rendering an Essential Service to the Country, as many lives thereby may be sav'd.

Should any thing extraordinary happen, you are if possible to give me Notice thereof.

You will keep up good order & Discipline amongst the Officers & men, who are hereby Required & Commanded to Obey you, according to the Militia Laws now in force,

As it is expected you will have none but choice officers & men on this little Expedition: therefore the Eyes of the Country will be upon you: So that I have no doubt but every person in his station will exert himself to answer the wishes & expectations of his Country, and serve it as much as in his power lies

That Heaven may give you Success & Safety it is the Sincere [wish]
of Sir your most Humble Servant

Wm Preston

If you find it usefull I dare Say you will Endeavour to Stay out a month or Six weeks

Col⁰. William Christian

[Col. William Christian to Col. William Preston. 3QQ48.]

Sawyers.[92] Monday Evening

Sir—I intend to go home to night if I can possibly get over Peek creek[93] but as there is no Canoe I doubt I cant. I want to look for waggons, I find there is a parcel of Men who would be Spared very well along the river in Triggs Company. If I cant get them to go freely, I propose to summon them (if you approve of it) as far as seven or eight. If you dont I beg you

---

[92] Col. John Sawyers was born in Virginia in 1745, and died in Knox County, Tenn., in 1831. He removed West at an early day, and went out on the Point Pleasant campaign, in Shelby's Company. See muster-roll, *post*. He served on the Cherokee (1776) and Chickamauga (1779), expeditions, and commanded a company under Shelby at King's Mountain (1780). He was major, next colonel, of militia, and represented his district in the state assembly.—Ed.

[93] Peak Creek is a western tributary of New River, discharging near the present Newbern, Pulaski County.—Ed.

56   DUNMORE'S WAR

will leave a line at Mr Thompsons—Upon second thought I Suppose you need not be at the trouble, as I will send a man to your house on Saturday or Sunday, for Your Orders I reckon the longer the better as you may Get some intelligence from some part of the Frontiers. If you would please to have the orders ready the messenger could return the same day I think it best for me not to start until monday morning early & then evory thing will be before me. I can go to Davis or A. Campbells[94] that night, as I wont have any luggage myself.

I am Sir Your hble Servant

Wm CHRISTIAN.

ATTACK ON GREENBRIER

[Col. William Christian to Capt. Joseph Cloyd. 3QQ49.]

SIR—News is this minute come that Capt Dickison[95] has had a battle, with the Indians at green Bryer, that one man is killed & two wounded the rest fled to a house where they are beseiged. As that is the case I make no doubt but more parties are out. I therefore think it your indispensable duty to send a messenger to Walkers Creek, blue Stone[96] &c. to warn the people

---

[94] Davis's Bottom was on the Middle Fork of Holston, above Royal Oak, the home of Arthur Campbell.—ED.

[95] For Captain Dickinson, who was wounded at Point Pleasant, see *post*. A further account of this battle is in *Amer. Archives*, 4th series, i, p. 536.—ED.

[96] Walker's Creek and Blue Stone River are western tributaries of New River. The former, in Giles County, Va., was named for Dr. Thomas Walker, probably on his western trip

of their danger, that they may gather together for a few days, & be on their guard untill we hear more. indeed I think the high waters may have hindered them from making more attacks at the same time, as soon as they fall we may expect it.

You are also this day to warn all the men to whom you gave notice at your muster to be ready to meet you at M^r. Thompsons tomorrow morning—there to receive further orders—entreat your men to take each a horse, all the ammunition & provisions they possibly can to the place as it is uncertain how long they may be wanted.

I expect Colo. Preston will pass there tomorrow on his way home & then you will know what more to do. You will no doubt advise all the people to agree upon proper places to Erect Forts & to proceed to work immediately—& by no means to think of moving off

I am y^r. hble Servt.

Wm Christian

June 29. 1774
To Capt Joseph Cloyd

CHEROKEE BEGIN HOSTILITIES

[Maj. Arthur Campbell to Col. William Preston. 3QQ50.]

Dear Sir—The hour that I so much dreaded (as to the peace of this Country) is now I am apprehensive

---

in 1748. Blue Stone River, in Mercer County, West Va., is supposed to have first been visited by Christopher Gist in 1751. The settlements upon this stream were recent and much exposed.—Ed.

near at hand; The Cherokees has at length commenced hostilities.

The[y] have murdered their Traders, and the Messengers that went from Wattago And I expect the Principal part of this Country will meet with the same fate soon, if not speedily succored, there is forty Shawanese in the Cherokee Towns I hope your known tenderness and humanity will excite you to make a vigorous effort to defend the Inhabitants; I am certain the[y] will all below Stalnacres[97] fly before the Enemy; as the scarcity of Ammunition is the general cry. I hope the Pittsylvania and Bedford Militia will be drawn out on this occasion.[98] For could we be able to face them about the lower settlement on this River the War might not be so calamitous. In consequence of your former Orders I have requested of Capt. Crockett & Doack one half of their Men to meet against next Tuesday or sooner at the Town House. You can direct matters down lower as may be best.

I am Sir Your most Obedient

ARTHUR CAMPBELL

July 1st. 1774
[To Colonel Preston]

---

[97] Samuel Stalnaker was a Cherokee trader whom Dr. Thomas Walker met in 1750 on the Middle Fork of Holston, and assisted in raising his cabin. "Stalnaker's" is marked on Hutchins's map as being in 1755 the farthest western settlement of Virginia. That same year Indians attacked the outlying cabin of this pioneer, killed his wife and son, and took him prisoner. He soon escaped, and was at a council of war held in this neighborhood in 1756.—ED.

[98] Pittsylvania (formed in 1767) and Bedford (formed in 1753) were the two adjacent southwest counties east of Blue Ridge.—ED.

CHEROKEE HOSTILE 59

[Col. William Preston to Col. William Christian; undated, but written about July 3. 3QQ51.]

Sir—I have Just now rec^d. a letter by Express from Capt. Arthur Campbell on Holston, Informing me that he has Intiligence from the Cherokee Nation that the Traders are all Murdered & that they have also murdered the two men who went from Watawgo in Behalf of the People to endeavor to Compromise the affair of killing the Cherokee at the Races; that there [are] forty Shawnesse in the Cherokee Nation, who it is believed will Join the Cherokees & fall upon the People of Holston immediately.

In consequence of these alarming Accounts it will be necessary to take every Measure in our Power for the Defence of the Country. Therefore you are to give Orders to Capt Herbert and Capt. Madison[99] to draught fifty Men out of their Companies. Cap^{ts} Crockett & Doack thirty Men Cap^{ts} Arther Campbell, William Campbell & James Thompson forty Men besides those already Draught for the Defence of the Settlements on Clinch

You are also to give immediate Notice to the Captains of the three lower Companies on Holston to have Eighty Men in Readiness on the shortest notice to Join the Draught above mentioned if there be a neces-

---

[99] Capt. Thomas Madison was a brother of James, president of William and Mary College, and of George, later governor of Kentucky. They were descended from John, an early settler of Augusta, and distant relatives of President Madison. Captain Madison was born in Augusta in 1746; he did not join the expedition of 1774, but was commissary and paymaster of that of 1776 against the Cherokee. He married Susanna, youngest sister of Patrick Henry.—Ed.

sity. These Men are to Assemble at the Town House as soon as Possible. You are to Order a L.t & Ensign with thirty Men to range at the heads of Sandy Creek & Clinch for the Defense of the Inhabitants on that Quarter.[1] And the Remainder of the Draughts are to March down Holston for the Defence of that part of the Country, if you find they are realy in Danger.

You will be pleased to Send at least seventy five Men out of the first Draught under proper Officers from the Town House immediately to Clinch, for the Protection of the People on that Quarter; and you will march the remainder Down Holston to the lower Road to Clinch or even to the Road through Mockison Gap[2] & then you can Judge from the accounts you receive whether it will be most for the Defence of the Country; to March to Clinch or proceed down holston; and which ever appears most proper you will be pleased to take.

If you proceed down the River you will take both your own Party and the new Draft under your Command & you may call out such other officers as you Choose to be over the men. If you should proceed to Clinch with your Party, and find there is a Necessity of sending any men down the River, then you may put them under the Command of such Officers as you think proper.

Upon the whole, as you will be upon the Spot you will be best able to Judge what Steps may be most for

---

[1] The heads of Sandy and Clinch rivers approach each other in Tazewell, Buchanan, and Dickenson counties, Va.—ED.

[2] There were several passes over Clinch Mountain to the valley of that river. Of these, Mocassin Gap, where the creek of that name breaks through to join the Holston, is best known.—ED.

the Protection of the Country. and those Steps you will no Doubt take, but at the Same time I would have you endeavour all in your Power not to Incur any Expence to the Country but what is absolutely Necessary for the Protection of the People, as also not to Order any Forces down Holston untill your In[te]ligence is well attested.

If you find it Necessary to Augment the number of Scouts, I think it ought to be done, & these should not only be good Woodsmen but Men of Property and Veracity, as such may easily be procured there.

You will be pleased to write to me as often as opportunity offers, and if any thing Extraordinary happens to send an Express.

If you find it necessary to take any other Measures for the Defence of the Frontiers than what I have above directed, you will be [free] to adopt them & suit your Conduct to the Danger of the Country.

I am S^r.

W^m. PRESTON

To Col^o. W^m. Christian

PLANS OF GOVERNOR

[Lord Dunmore to Col. William Preston. 3QQ53.]

WILLIAMSBURG 3^d July 1774

SIR—I have received your letters dated the 27th of May and 22^d. of June.

I am in hopes the Steps you have taken will prevent any Considerable damage from being done by the Savages on your frontier, and, that if they should attempt making a Stroke, that the joint forces of the frontier Counties will be able to repel and effectually Chastize those restless and inveterate Enemys of Virginia.

By the last Account from Fort Dunmore, dated the 7th. of June Captⁿ. Connolly informs me of Several Murders Committed by the Indians in that quarter, and that he intended in a few days to March towards the Enemys Country at the head of a Considerable Body of Men, and that he Should halt at the Mouth of Wheelin to build a Small Fort there, and an other on the opposite Side of the Ohio, for a reposetory of Stores, and if possible keep the Enemy engaged in their own Country, by small parties continually detached from Wheelin to their Towns; but in this he expected to be Supported by you and Col^o. Andrew Lewis, as I had informed him of my having recommended building a Fort at the Mouth of the Great Kanhaway or some where near it.

This plan I much approved of, and ordered Captⁿ. Connolly to inform the Commanding Officers on the frontiers of his notions, and keep a Constant Correspondance with them and Co-operate with them in Such Measures as they may think most expedient and effectuall.[3]

I am Still convinced of the Necessity and Security it would be to that part of the Country to have a Fort erected at or near the mouth of the Great Kanhaway; and if a Body of Men could be Marched into the Enemys Country that it would put a Speedy and

---

[3] See *Washington–Crawford Letters,* pp. 95, 96, on the officers consulted.—ED.

effectual end to the War, and Secure you a lasting peace.

I can give no farther instructions respecting the Locating of the Officers and Soldiers Lands than the Order of Council in December last to which I refer you.

I shall not fail to take proper Notice of the Murder Committed at Watawgo, tho I think it would answer no good end my writing to the Indians at this time, but that [it] will be more proper an effectual to do it through the Superintendant of that district or his deputy.

Inclosed is the two Majors Commissions, and am Sir Your most Obedient humble Servant

DUNMORE

To Colo. William Preston

DISTRESS ON THE FRONTIER

[Col. William Christian to Col. William Preston. 3QQ54.]

NEW DUBLIN Thursday 4 July 1774

DEAR SIR—The people on New river up to Mouth [of] reed creek[4] I understand are gone & going of [f] to day to Fort at Bells meadows.[5] Smiths, Ninian Cloyds, & Crouchs families are there. Smiths Wife & children are really distressed, as the woman is helpless & unwell Could it be possible to let them

---

[4] Reed Creek is a western tributary of New River, and its waters interlace with the upper Holston. It was named for James Reed, who settled in the vicinity as early as 1753.—ED.

[5] Named probably for James Bell, an early settler who was captured by the Indians in 1756.—ED.

come home, I know you will but how to relieve them I dont know 6 men out of this Compy that went to Clinch are not returned, & I hear Draper[6] got 15 with him. I expect the 6 at Clinch next week.

Crouch has a large crop of oats now falling.

Little James Skeggs,[7] I am well satisfied saw an Indian last Thursday between Ninian Cloyds & Peter Poors, or some person dressed like one, & some other signs, tho it might be horsethieves or runaways

I am told just now that there is a report come that Some people were killed at muddy creek last week, but I never depend on reports unless well attested, there being so many false ones.

There came 50lb Powder yesterday, being all that Donald sent on account of the barrel I bespoke for the Expidition the complaints are so great here for Powder that I dont know how to keep it, I have put the people of[f] by telling them that it came for the Expidition & that I cant undertake to touch it unless I have your orders, & that I believe you cannot break on it at any rate unless the neighbourhood is really attacked.

---

[6] John Draper, born in 1730, was one of the pioneer settlers of Draper's Meadows, where the massacre occurred in 1755. His wife and sister were captured and only restored after many hardships. In 1765 Draper sold out his interest in Draper's Meadows, and removed west to Draper's Valley, on the dividing line between Pulaski and Wythe counties. His descendants have lived here in recent years. In 1774 he was a lieutenant in one of the Fincastle companies, his commission being yet preserved in the family. Draper lived to be ninety-four years of age, dying at his home in 1824. See Hale, *Trans-Allegheny Pioneers*, pp. 105, 106.—ED.

[7] Probably of the family of Henry Skaggs, one of the famous "Long Hunters" of Kentucky, who settled in the new state in 1775.—ED.

Colo. Byrd & Mr Madison are set off for Vausses[8] the first talks of proceeding down the Country whether he will or not I dont know yet I will let you know when I come back this day week.

On enquiry I find Ingram & Waggoners people are at home & I believe the Montgomerys [and] Pattons.[9] So that I cant think the people on the river in the least danger if they would stay at home but I'm afraid to over persuade them, as they will return of their own accord in some days. My people are at home, I believe that is all on this side the river down to peppers,[10] but they have had several races up here as the reports come & so goes home in a day or two.

If I hear anything more I shall send for my family & meet them at Flemings they begin to be distressed with the hot weather & water, the great want of rain below is alarming. If no more news I propose setting of in the afternoon my self. Daniel Trigg will remain here till I come back & will obey any orders you think necessary

[8] Vause's (Vaux) Fort was one of the western defenses in the French and Indian War. It was built about 1755 on the upper waters of Roanoke, in the present Montgomery County, not far from the town of Lafayette. June 25, 1756, it was attacked by Indians and all the garrison and settlers captured or killed. The next year it was rebuilt as a government fortification by Capt. Peter Hogg, and visited by Washington on his tour of inspection of western defenses.—ED.

[9] The Montgomerys were a prominent Holston family, located on the South Fork, near the North Carolina boundary line. Capt. James was a magistrate of Washington County. The Pattons were not descendants of Col. James, who left only daughters as heirs.—ED.

[10] The Peppers were a pioneer family of southwest Virginia, two of whose members were captured at Fort Vause in 1756. They operated a ferry above Ingles's, on New River. See Thwaites, *Early Western Travels*, iii, p. 48, note 59.—ED.

I am sorry to be away at this time, but I will make it short & take care to go away no more, But stay and assist all I can.

I am Sir with respect Yours ever

Wm CHRISTIAN.

To Colo William Preston

WAR INSTIGATED BY VIRGINIANS

[Letter from Carlisle, Pennsylvania, dated July 4, 1774. 2JJ63-65.] [11]

Our last accounts from Fort Pitt are very good in one sense. The traders are all arrived safe with their goods at that place, being escorted & protected by some Shawnese Indians, who were sent to Col. Croghan's, as it was imagined they would not be safe at the fort, the Virginians having a party of militia under arms at that place. Conolly, their captain, as soon as he heard of the Indians being at Croghan's, sent forty of his men to take them prisoners, notwithstanding their kindness to our people; but the traders giving them notice of the design, they immediately went off. Conolly's party followed and overtook them, fired upon and wounded one of them; the other two took the wounded Indian off, & made their escape, and a day or two afterwards met a party of Indians, escorting another of the traders with his effects from the Lakes. The escorting party of Indians no sooner saw the wounded man, but they immediately ordered the skins to be unloaded, and held

---

[11] Copied from *Pennsylvania Gazette*, July 13, 1774.—ED.

a council what was best to be done. But the traders, who had arrived at Fort Pitt, fearing some bad consequences might happen from the conduct of the party, which Conolly had sent out, immediately followed the Indians, & came up with them the day after they had met with the other party, and advised them to return to their own country; at the same time telling them that Pennsylvania had no part in the mischief already done, and that the Virginians entirely were in fault.[12]

We hear from Virginia, that a large body of men are going out against the Indians by order of government, the rendezvous to be at the mouth of the great Kanhawa river, and there to build forts, & fortify themselves.

We are informed that young Cressop, who first began the quarrel with the Indians, and murdered a number of them in a cowardly manner, has received a letter of thanks from Lord Dunmore. From hence it appears that the scheming party in Virginia are making a tool of their Governor, to execute the plans formed by them for their private emolument, who, being mostly land-jobbers, would wish to have those lands, which were meant to be given to the officers in general.[13]

---

[12] See further account by Richard Butler in *Penna. Archives*, iv, pp. 569, 570.—ED.

[13] As part of the boundary controversy between Pennsylvania and Virginia, the partisans of the former accused those of the latter with inciting the Indians on their own behalf. See similar accusations in *Amer. Archives*, 4th series, i, pp. 547-549, 674.—ED.

PREPARATIONS FOR ADVANCE

[Receipt of Capt. William Harrod[14] to Abraham Van Meter. 4NN7.]

July 4th. 1774 Then Recd. of Abraham Vanmeetre Three Steers & one Cow; one Steer & the Cow mark'd a Crop & half penny in ye Near Ear half penny in the of[f] Ear, one Steer unmark'd, the other Mark'd, half Crop in the Near Ear, & Slit in the of[f] Ear Being Apprais'd by Jacob Vanmeetre & Edmd. Polke according to Order of Capt John Connoly Commander at fort Dunmore Being for the Use of Governmt. of Virginia & Apprais'd To Sixteen Pounds Ten Shillings Recd. Pr me.

[WILLIAM HARROD]

---

[14] William Harrod, elder brother of James, founder of Harrodsburg, Kentucky, was born at Big Cove, Bedford County, Pa., in 1737. He was in the army of General Forbes (1758), and about 1772 settled on Ten Mile Creek, a tributary of the Monongahela. He was commissioned captain by Lord Dunmore (Draper MSS., 4NN5), and acted as commissary during the summer and autumn of 1774. He was with his brother James at Harrodsburg in 1775 and again in 1777; but seems to have retained his permanent home in western Pennsylvania, where a commission of captain of militia was issued to him in 1776. In 1778 he recruited a company for the Illinois expedition, joined George Rogers Clark at the Falls of Ohio, and acted efficiently throughout that campaign. The next year he brought a company from the Falls of Ohio to participate in Bowman's expedition, and in 1780 was still a militia captain in that neighborhood. He died in 1801.—ED.

SCOUTING IN SOUTHWEST VIRGINIA

[Capt. Daniel Smith to Col. William Preston. 3QQ57.]

SIR—The constant Rumor of the Indians being just ready to fall on the Inhabitants hath scared away almost the whole settlement at the head of the north fork of Clinch and Bluestone. I am sorry to find that the people are so scary and that there are so many propagators of false reports in the country, not that I think there is no danger of an Indian War, I would only [MS. torn] reports which ought to stir us up to common Defence, by passing thro' the mouths of imprudent people, do more damage, than their not coming at all, by causing timorous people to run away. This the people at the head of the river did before I got the least notice of their intention to start. The Men have said they will return again after carrying their wives and children to a place of Safety; If they do 'twill be rather more than I expect. They alledge as an excuse for their going away that there was no Scout down Sandy creek. This was only an excuse, tho' they spoke the truth, and it was no fault of mine. Mr. Maxwell (who is gone down to Botetourt to see his family, and whose return is not expected shortly) and myself had agreed to muster our men in separate companies, for the convenience of the inhabitants and withal because it would conduce more to their safety in general as we thought; especially as we agreed to send each other word by express in case of an invasion, or any other important news that might require the men to be join'd. As he lived most convenient to the head of Sandy Creek I consulted him with regard to scouts that should go down that water course. His brother Thomas[15] was one pitched upon. On their return from their first trip, altho they brought no account of Indians as your letter of the 20th ult. came to hand about that time I sent two scouts down a river or [MS. torn] called Louisa,[16] and at the recommendation of Mr. Th. Maxwell appointed one Israel Harmon to act with him down Sandy Creek, for it was natural for me, as I reposed much confidence in Mr. James Maxwell to pay regard to what his Brother Thomas advised. I am now to inform you that Mr Thomas Maxwell proved Highly unworthy the confidence I reposed in him, so much that I think his behaviour requires that he should be called to an account at the next court martial, as I've just been inform'd there really is a Militia law yet subsisting; for instead of going down Sandy Creek as I strictly charged him to do he went to the head of the river, reported the danger they were in, and Assisted Jacob Harmon[17] to move into the New River Settlement. It was at least a Week afterwards before I knew there was no Scout down Sandy Creek. As soon as I got such information I rode to the head of the river, learn'd the truth of the account, and employed two men to go down that stream that may be relied on, which took me two days constant employ. I don't think my time lost

---

[15] Thomas Maxwell settled on Blue Stone, in Tazewell County, in 1772. He was in Capt. Isaac Shelby's company at the battle of King's Mountain (1781), and was killed by Indians in 1787.—Ed.

[16] The north branch of the West Fork of Sandy River.—Ed.

[17] Jacob Harmon, who settled on Blue Stone in 1771, probably was of the family of Adam, one of the early pioneers of New River who rescued Mrs. Ingles on her journey to the settlement (1755).—Ed.

as I prevail'd on some to stay at the same time that would have gone.

As the Spirits of the men that yet are left in my Company Are not in a very high flow, I do think that a Company of men station'd on the river if there was not over 20 [MS. torn] would greatly encourage the settlers, if they did nothing but Assist to build forts in this busy time of laying by Corn. I really shall be greatly pleased if you should be of the same Opinion. I may observe to you that they may be in readiness to march against any enemy the Scouts shall discover, or join any Company that may require Assistance.

You have inclosed a sketch of this river, and the heads of some of the adjacent waters. Had I expected I ever should have been called on for such a thing, I should have taken better observations, that it might have been done with greater accuracy. As you seem to want it now I let you have the same notion of the courses of the Waters and distances of places which I have.[18] It was done in a hurry, therefore I hope you will excuse its not being done in a fairer manner. The north fork of Holston is made too big, for 'tis a smaller river than Clinch. Should it want an amendment, or you any information on the subject that is in my power to give, you know you need only signify so much.

I am Dr Sir with greatest esteem Your very humble Serv.

DAN SMITH

8th July 1774

---

[18] See manuscript map reproduced in this volume, found in Draper MSS., 4XX62.—ED.

Powder and lead are yet very scarce articles with us. I wish that may come to hand shortly which I hear you've sent for

To Col William Preston in Fincastle   To the care of Capt. Arthur Campbell

---

CHEROKEE PEACEFUL; RANGING PLANS

[Maj. Arthur Campbell to Col. William Preston. 3QQ58.]

HOLSTON July 9th 1774

SIR—About the latter end of last Week the Wattago Messengers returned safe from the Cherokee Towns. They say that upon their first arrival it appeared as if they Indians intended to take immediate satisfaction for the loss of their Man, on Wattago; But thro the interposition of some of their chiefs they were dissuaded from such a rash step.

The consternation this appearance give the Traders; was the foundation of the late report, as some of them set out for Carolina in time of the hurry. A few days before the Messengers set out on their return, the Great Warriour had all the Principal Chiefs convened, when the Murder of Capt Russells son &c the robberies of the Hunters together with the late affair on Wattago was debated; They deny'd having any share, as they knew of, in the murder, and as to the robberies, they had Mr. Camerons authority for it. They confessed the Raven with four others had gone to the Shawanese early in the Spring, without the approbation of the Nation; and that they expected he was killed as the Shawanese had killed one of their men lately in sight of their Town.

From these Mens account, I would willingly believe that peace may yet be preserved with the Cherokees, if some fresh provocation, dont put them out of all temper. Crabtree is become a very insolent person; but I believe his timidity, on dangerous attempts, will mostly get the better of his ferocity.

About the time the above account came to Camp, Col. Christian received a Letter from Capt Doack informing him of some Indian signs being Seen near his Fathers. upon consultation it was judged impracticable to attempt a long March, out of the Inhabitants, until more Ammunition arrived. Therefore it was considered as best for the present to divide the party to cover the Frontier. One Company under Capt. Crockett, was to range about the head of Clinch & Blue Stone, another to be sent to Castle Wood, and the other to range at and near Mockison Gap & the Island. The new draughts was on this disposition discharged and I returned home.

I am Sir your most Humble Servant

ARTHUR CAMPBELL

[To Colonel Preston]

NEWS FROM AUGUSTA AND FORT PITT

[Col. Charles Lewis to Col. William Preston. 3QQ59.]

DE[A]R SIR—I Received your Letter of the 19th of June and will take all oportunity to a Quente you of Every thinge that hapens here worth your Notise. no Dout but you have herd of ye engagement that Capt Dickenson is had with ye Indians he had one man killed and his Lieutenant Wounded. a fewe Days ago ye Indians fired at W^m M^cfarlon Neere ye Warm Springs[19] and wounded him slitly. Y^e inhabitents of our Fruntier is in ye Greates Confuson they are all gethred in forts. I have ordered out Several Compneys of Militia which I am in hop[e]s will put a stope to thir indended Hostilities. I hear that ye Assembly is to Meet ye 11th of Next Month when I hope they will fall on som Method to but [put] an End to ye War. Since I begane to Rite to you I have Re^d by way of Ex[p]ress from fort Pitt that ye Indians is Suing for P[e]ace as to further perticlers I will Refer you to my Brother home [whom] I have sent Capt Connlly['s] letter with ye Indians speech.[20]

I am Dr Sir your Humb^b Servent

CHA^S LEWIS[21]

July 9th 1774

---

[19] The Warm Springs in the present Bath County, then in Augusta, was a noted landmark of the region; the town is now the county seat.—ED.

[20] Andrew Lewis lived at this time in Botetourt County, on Roanoke River, near Salem. Charles Lewis was probably at the Lewis homestead, two miles east of Staunton. Connolly issued a proclamation June 18, advising the inhabitants to prepare for war. See *Amer. Archives*, 4th series, i, p. 475. Meanwhile, McKee was negotiating with Delaware Indians, who said that all chiefs except the Mingo were favorably inclined to peace.—*Ibid*, pp. 545, 546. Letters from the frontiers, however, proved that attacking parties were still carrying on their bloody work. See *Ibid*, pp. 521, 526, and our own preceding manuscripts.—ED.

[21] Col. Charles Lewis, youngest son of the Augusta pioneer, John Lewis, was born (1733) after the arrival of the family in Virginia. He was especially noted as a gallant Indian fighter and frontiersman; tradition relating that in one of his escapes he exhibited great daring. See Waddell, *Annals of Augusta County* (2nd ed. Staunton, 1902), p. 127. He was captain of a company under his brother, Maj. Andrew Lewis, and Col. George Washington, which advanced for the defense of the frontier after Braddock's defeat. A copy of

PATROLLING THE FRONTIER

[Col. William Christian to Col. William Preston. 3QQ60.]

Andrew Colvins.[22] July 9. (Saturday morning) 1774

Sir—On my way up Reed Creek I met some news about the Cherokees which made me think it best to stop all the last ordered draughts, on Tuesday evening I met Wm Falling one of the two men who went from Wataga & then I was fully satisfied, nothing was to be feared.

* * * * * * * *

Capt Cample marched on the lower settlement in Holston near the Island[23] with odds of 40 men, and

---

the journal written by Charles Lewis during this campaign, is in Draper MSS., 18U. Charles Lewis was first lieutenant in Captain Preston's ranging company in West Augusta (1757-59), and during Pontiac's War (1763) pursued, overtook, and defeated a native raiding party on the South Fork of the Potomac. He is known to have been out with Bouquet in 1764, but based his claims for land upon his services as a ranger—Draper MSS., 2QQ153. These lands were located in Kentucky, and were part of his heirs' inheritance. As county-lieutenant for Augusta, he led its troops to the Point Pleasant campaign, where he was killed in the battle. His words, when he fell, are said to have been, "Push on, boys. Don't mind me."—Draper MSS., 1R75. Charles Lewis was popular, and beloved by all the Western army; his loss was a general affliction. He left five small children, whose descendants still live in the Valley of Virginia.—Ed.

[22] Capt. Andrew Colvill early settled near Wolf Hills (Abingdon), on Holston. He commanded at Fort Black in 1776, and through several years ranged for the protection of the frontiers, distinguishing himself at the Battle of King's Mountain (1780).—Ed.

[23] Long Island, now in Sullivan County, Tenn., at the junction of the two forks of Holston, was then thought to be in Fincastle County, Va. It was the centre of a considerable settlement, the site of a fort, and the rendezvous for Christian's Cherokee expedition (1776).—Ed.

will meet me to morrow on Clinch, he goes thro Moccison Gap, I cross over by the head of moccison, the two gaps may be 30 miles apart.

On thursday last Mr Doaks letter to Crockett was shown to me at Cedar Creek[24] about 9 miles on this Side of Stalnakers, I thought it best to send Crockett of[f] with 40 men to the head of Sandy creek, that the reed creek and head of Holston people might know where to send to him in case any attack should be made, that he might way lay or follow the enemy. Breckinridge told me that he thought there was no chance of Mr Doaks getting more than about 10 men together on the last orders. I wrote to him, that I thought he might as well disband or range a few days in the inhabitants with them until more news, or orders from you. Yesterday I heard a report that 50 Indians were seen at Sandy creek but as it came thro several hands it may not be true, And this morning I recd. an Account that on the 6 Instant, you got word that Robertson &c had discovered an Indian Camp on Paint Creek, that Capt. Cloyd had stopt at Culbersons[25] to wait for more men. The report goes here that there was 300 Indians.

I am at a loss to know what to do, but I am thinking to send Capt Campble towards Cumberland Gap, or to the lower settlement on Clinch, and of stoppi[ng] some days, about half way betwixt him & Crocket that I may march either way in case of need—in all there will be 130 men. I got but 25^{lb} powder from

---

[24] For this creek, see Smith's MS. map. It is a branch of Clinch.—ED.
[25] Culbertson's Bottom was on a creek of that name, an eastern affluent of New River, fifty miles below Ingles's Ferry.—ED.

Brander, more will be wanted soon,—I cant go thro Moccison gap I doubt untill more arrives—Indeed I am afraid to go thro least a body should come up Sandy creek. And moreover perhaps you might want me to hurry down, blue stone or Walkers creek if any large numb[er] of the enemy, comes in that way. as I doubt you will be hard put to to get any body of men together, the great road being almost the Fronteer from Arthur Campbells to new river.

It appears to me that the three lower Companies could better spare men than any part of the County, especially Shelbeys and Cocks, those two might send out 50. The people here seems to think themselves in the greatest security. The news of the enemys being on Sandy creek, made the Moccison & Copper Creek people come of[f] yesterday. I found it was out of my power to go over before this day. If any Ammunition is come, the bearer can carry some powder in a Cagg, or should you choose to send any Quantity to Capt Campbles, to be lodged there I can send there for it. The bearer is one of the drafts, and I thought might as well be employed as an express it will be the cheapest way—And I really wanted further orders from you, as I thought you might alter the disposition of some of the parties I propose placing as above, in consequence of Events down New river. I ordered Crocket to be always ready at an hours warning to march either towards New river if you called on him or down Clinch if I sent to him.—when I get over if I find any truth in the report of the enemys being on Sandy creek, I will hasten up that way to Join Crocket, & send in messengers to the Inhabitants to wait the news of some attack that I may waylay or follow the enemy—or if I can find their track I will follow them in to the Inhabitants. Boone has been gone 10 or 12 days, in search of the surveyors I had some thought of sending Drake alone, and engaging to give the pay of two Scouts, he is very willing to go.[26] but I conclude to stop him about 10 or 12 days more, indeed he must wait to be a witness against Crabtree.

* * * * * * * *

As soon as I go to Clinch, I will send again if anything more happens.

I am Sir your most hble Servt.

WILLIAM CHRISTIAN

FRONTIER FORTS BEING BUILT

[Capt. Robert Doack to Col. William Preston. 3QQ61.]

SIR—Agreeable to your Order I Drafted men & was in Readiness to March to the heads of Sandy Creek & Clinch, When some tracts were Seen in this Neighbourhood Supposd. to be Indians which Colo.

---

[26] Joseph Drake early settled on the frontiers of West Virginia, and was one of the leaders of the "Long Hunters" (1770–71). He served as a private in Bouquet's Ohio expedition (1764); married (1773) Margaret, daughter of Col. John Buchanan; and served the next year in Christian's regiment on the Point Pleasant campaign. Among the early adventurers he visited Kentucky in the spring of 1775, and in June aided to pilot a party to explore the region of Green River; and the same year he settled on a tract of land six miles below Abingdon, Virginia. He removed to Kentucky in March, 1778, and was killed by Indians in sight of Boonesborough, in August following. He was a rough, fearless man, well-fitted for frontier life and hardships.—L. C. D. (Draper MSS., 3B251).

FRONTIER FORTS 79

Christian hearing Sent Capt. Crockett to where I was, Ordered & Directed me to range near the Inhabitants. we were informd, that Sixteen Indians Were Seen on Walkers Creek which I went down with 25 men but not finding any Signs & hearing the News Contradicted Dischargd. them. The people were all in Garison from Fort Chiswell to the Head of Holston & in great Confusion. They are fled from the Rich Valley[27] & Walkers Creek. Some are Building forts they have Began to Build at My Fathers James Davis', & Gaspar Kinders.[28] I think they are not Strong enough for three forts but might do for two. If you thought proper to Order that a Sergeants Command might be Stationed at each of those places on Mischief being Done Or at any two of them—I think it would keep this part of the Country from leaving it & would enable them to save their Crops this I humbly Conceive would be a protection & encouragement & on an alarm when people fled to the forts with their Familys those men would always be Ready to follow the Enemy. I have two Scouts in the Valley and Walkers Creek by Colo. Christians Orders Shall I Continue them or call them. I sent you some platts by my wife who I Suppose was Afraid to leave the great Road & would Send them from Craigs. I am Ready at all times to go wherever you Command let the

---

[27] Rich Valley is between Walker's Mountain and the North Fork of Holston, in Washington County.—ED.

[28] Probably these forts were at David Doack's mill, on Clinch River, and at James Davis's (or Davis's Fancy), on the headwaters of the Middle Fork of Holston, which this pioneer had purchased in 1748, and where his descendants still reside. Kinders was probably a German settler at the modern Kinderhook, on the west side of the North Fork of Holston, in Poor Valley.—ED.

party be ever so small As I would rather at this time wish to be Serviceable than to look for high pay. I have Sent you a list of my Company which at this time is very Scarce of Ammunition. If any is Come up for the Country pray let us have Our proportion of it. Should it not be made use of in Defending the Inhabitants I will take Care that it shall not be wasted & Such Orders as you give About it Shall be Obey^d.

I am D^r. Sir with great Esteem your Most Obedient & very humble Servant

ROBERT DOACK

July 12th. 1774

To Col^o William Preston Fincastle Favoured by M^r. Davis

EXPEDITION TO OHIO TOWNS PLANNED

[Col. William Christian to Col. William Preston. 3QQ63.]

CAPT. RUSSELL'S FORT,[29] July 12th 1774

SIR—I arrived at this place on Sunday last, and on Monday Capt. Campbell joined me with his Company, after marching through Mockison Gap about thirty Miles below this place, and coming up Clinch River. There are now here ninety nine Men, Officers included; and with Capt. Crockett forty. I wrote to you by Hamilton the Cause of my sending him to the Heads of Clinch & Sandy Creek. The inclosed Letter [is] from Capt. Doack to Crockett; the Messengers Report that Capt. Doack could not possibly raise the thirty men

---

[29] At Castle Woods, on Clinch—likewise called Cowan's Fort, from David Cowan, on whose land it was built. Russell later named it Fort Preston; see *post*.—ED.

You had ordered; & the Report of the Discovery that should have been made down New-River, made Me think it my Duty to cover the Inhabitants that lie exposed to the Sandy Creek Pass, untill your further Pleasure should be known. That step, and the Cherokee affair have delayed the first proposed Trip. When I got here, I found that Boon & Stoner had set off Yesterday two Weeks, in search of the Surveyors: They were to go down the Kantucky, to Your salt Lick; from thence across the Country to the Falls of Ohio; & from there home by way of Gaspers Lick, on Cumberland River. If they find Them on the Kantucky, they will be back in a few Days; if not 'till they go to the Falls, it will probably be ten Days from this Time before they return. Captain Russell thinks they have passed the Falls some Days ago, as Boone would loose no Time, if he could not find the People: this makes Me think it unnecessary to send Drake, as I before proposed, until Boone's Rout is known

Tomorrow the Pack-Horses will be sent over for the Flour that was left at Mr. Cummins's.[30] There is no Beef to be had in this Neighbourhood; I have heard there is some about 12 Miles off. Benjamin

---

[30] Probably Rev. Charles Cummings, the well-known Presbyterian clergyman of the Wolf Hills (Abingdon) Sinking Spring church. A Scotch-Irishman from Pennsylvania, he first preached at North Mountain church, Augusta County (1766-72). Receiving a call to the Holston, he built the first church in that valley, and served without interruption until his death (1812). He was a strong upholder of the Revolutionary cause, is supposed to have drafted the Fincastle resolutions of 1775, and served for several years on the committee of safety. He was also a fighting parson, and accompanied Christian on his Cherokee expedition (1776), and organized a company for the relief of Fort Watauga when besieged by Indians in 1776.—ED.

Logan on Hols[t]on,[81] wanted to drive over forty Beeves but I would not encourage him when he spoke to me. We are very ill provided with Kettles. I know where to get about 1500 of flour, more than we have; and I am told about fifteen Bushels of Corn may be had on Clinch. Neither Corn or Flour are to be had on Hols[t]on River. I am advised by the Officers to have the Flour brought over & to collect the Corn as soon as I can; but not to have the Beeves drove over, until I receive an Answer from You.

We have these two Days been consulting what is best to be done: the Result of which is, that I should let you know, it is the Opinion of the Officers here, that 150 or 200 Men are sufficient to March to the Ohio, at the mouth of Sciota; & then if nothing extraordinary happened, that we might go over & attack the lower Shawnese Town, which is not above 45 Miles

---

[81] Benjamin Logan was born of Scotch–Irish parents in Augusta County, Virginia, in 1743. His father died when he was but fourteen years of age, whereupon young Logan took upon himself the care and support of his mother and the younger children. In 1764 he went out as a sergeant with Bouquet; and about 1771 removed to the Holston, where he raised hemp, on which there was a royal bounty. In the Point Pleasant campaign he was a lieutenant; and the following year (1775) removed to Kentucky, where he built Logan's Station, ten miles from Boonesborough. His family was brought out the next year, and in the autumn the fort was besieged by a large body of Indians. Logan went to the Holston settlements for ammunition, and returned on foot in ten days. In 1779, he was second in command of Bowman's expedition, and brought a relief party to Blue Licks (1782), but too late for the battle. He was a noted Indian fighter, and in 1793 allied himself with the proposed Kentucky enterprise against the Spaniards at New Orleans. The same year he removed to Shelby County, where he died in 1802. Logan was a tall, spare man, with thin visage, and a wiry frame. He was a typical Westerner, with the faults and virtues of his race.—ED.

from that Place: A good Pilot can be had, who can lead us thro' the Woods either by Night or Day. It is thought by the Gentlemen, that is not best to say any thing publickly of attacking the Towns, but only to propose going to Ohio & returning up New-River, as it is doubted among us whether the Soldiers would be willing to cross the river: tho the majority are of Opinion they would after going so near the Enemy's Country; & if nothing of this kind can be effected, our marching up the New River might be of considerable Service. Capt. Russell informs me it is only 120 Miles to the Ohio, from this Place, which makes it not more than 165 Miles to the lower Town from here.

In order to raise the Men, Capt. Russell can get 30 on Clinch; the three lower Companies on Hols[t]on 75; Out of these, & the 140 now on Duty, it is proposed to get 200 to march from here, out of which 150 of the best Men are to cross the River at the Mouth of Sciota, & might in all probability reach the Town undiscovered, by travelling thro the Woods below Sciota, where an Enemy would not be expected. It is also proposed, that the tired & lame Men should erect a small house on the bank of the Ohio, to assist the Men when crossing, on their return in case of a Defeat.

I am advised to delay marching to the Heads of the Kentucky according to your first Orders & from seeking for the Surveyors; for should they be alive it is very probable they are now on their return; & we do not know which way they will come. If an Attack should be made on New-River, I flatter myself you will give me the speediest Notice thereof, that I may endeavour to way-lay the Enemy on their return home about the Banks of the Ohio. The Gentlemen here assert to me that this place is nearer the Mouth of the New-River, than where you live; I am convinced it is to the Mouth of the Sciota: for such an attempt I could take choice Men enough from here out of those now on Duty, without calling away Capt. Crockett's, who I am afraid to send for as I think Hols[t]on can better spare Men than New-River.

Should you be of Opinion that our Scheme of going to the Town[s] is impracticable, I yet hope you will allow me to go [to] the Ohio with the Men I now have. I confess I want to delay some time to see whether Boone returns, & by that time every thing could be well fix'd, & have nothing to stop us but a Defeat: As to this your Orders shall determine me.

I shall send Capt. Campbell with a Party, to range 20 odd miles down the River, toward Cumberland Gap; and Lieut. Edmiston[32] about 15 Miles up, as I think it will be better to keep the Men moving slowly, than have them remain at Camp.

I think I shall in a few Days ride over to Arthur

---

[32] Lieut. William Edmiston (Edmondston) was born in Maryland (1734), but early emigrated to Virginia, where he owned the tract in Augusta on which Liberty Hall was situated. He was a private in the French and Indian War, and on the Cherokee campaign of 1760. This experience led to his appointment as ensign, and later as lieutenant (1763), of Augusta militia. One of the earliest settlers on the Middle Fork of Holston, along with the Campbells, he long served second in command to William Campbell, and acted in that capacity at the battle of King's Mountain. Upon the death of his chief, he took his place as colonel of the Washington militia (1782). He was an ardent Whig, signed the Association in 1775, and was one of the committee of safety (1776). He died at his home in Washington County in 1822. Prominent in all the affairs of southwestern Virginia, his relatives and descendants were among the most influential of the region. Eight members of this family were in service at King's Mountain, where three were killed and one badly wounded.—ED.

EXPEDITION TO OHIO

Campbell's to meet your Orders: should they be for the Ohio Scheme, I can then set about fixing, & sending over the Necessarys & Men; at any rate as I hinted above the Gentn. think a Trip to the Kantucky had better be postponed, 'till you consider the Proposals of going to the Ohio; & to the Towns if thought practicable when at the River.

There are four Forts erecting on Clinch in Capt. Russell's Company; one at Moore's, four miles below this, another at Blackmore's 16 Miles lower down, & one at Smiths 12 Miles above this Place.[33] I am about to Station 10 Men at Blackmore's & 10 here; Capt. Russell thinks this will do, as the other Forts are very strong & well supplyed with Men.[34]

Colo Christian 1774

The number of men to be ordered at several places on the Frontiers of Fincastle

at Blackmores back of Moccison gap	30
at Moores—Capt Thompson	10
at Russells	10
at J. Smiths	10
at D. Smiths	10
at head Sandy creek	30
at Cove & Walkers creek	15
	115

It is recommended by the officers that Colo. Preston should allow 5 horses to every Company of 50 men to carry their Baggage & Blankets & such like.

---

[33] Blackmore's Fort was the lowest on Clinch, at the mouth of Stony Creek, in Scott County. The Blackmores removed to Cumberland settlement in Tennessee in 1779. Moore's (Fort Byrd) was at the home of William Moore, who was wounded at King's Mountain, but lived to an old age, dying in this vicinity in 1826. The fort at Daniel Smith's was named Fort Christian.—Ed.

[34] Endorsed by Colonel Preston: "Col. Christians letter delivered by himself but not finished."—Ed.

GOVERNOR'S INSTRUCTIONS TO COLONEL LEWIS

[Lord Dunmore to Col. Andrew Lewis. 46J7.]

Sir—I have Just now receiv'd yours of the 5th Inst. and am Sorry to find there is so great a probability of your being engaged in a war with the Indians; especially as you are not I doubt so well provided for it as I could wish. All I can now say is to repeat what I have before said which is to advise you by no means to wait any longer for them to Attack you, but to raise all the Men you think willing & Able, & go down immediately to the mouth of the great Kanhaway & there build a Fort, and if you think you have forse enough (that are willing to follow you) to proceed derectly to their Towns & if possible destroy their Towns & Magazines and distress them in every other way that is possible. and if you can keep a Communication open between you, Wheeling Fort,[35] & Fort Dunmore I am well persuaded you will prevent them from crossing the Ohio any more & Consequently from Giving any further Uneasiness to the Inhabitants on the Waters of the Ohio. I am now so far on my way up to the blue Ridge from whence there is alrea[dy] march'd a large body of Men to Join you, thinking you would be ere this at the Mouth of the Great Kanhaway.[36]

---

[35] The fort at Wheeling—named Fincastle, for one of Dunmore's titles—was built early in June by Maj. William Crawford, whom Connolly sent down the river for this purpose. See *Penna. Archives*, iv, pp. 519, 552; and *Washington-Crawford Letters*, p. 95. During the Revolution the name was changed to Fort Henry, in honor of Gov. Patrick Henry.—Ed.

[36] Dunmore left Williamsburg July 10 on this visit to the Western frontier. See *Amer. Archives*, 4th series, i, p. 536;

INSTRUCTIONS TO LEWIS

and I shall immediately on my going up see if more men fit for that Service are to be had [and] send them down, if I should think it Necessary. I make no doubt that Colo. Preston will do all in his power to Assist you & I flatter myself that from your Joint efforts you will be able to give a pritty good Act. of them & wishing you all Success I am
   Sir your most Obt. & very Hbl. Servt
            DUNMORE.
ROSEGILL[37] July 12th 1774

SOUTHWEST VIRGINIA BACKWARD

[Portion of a letter of Col. Andrew Lewis to Col. William Preston. 3QQ62.][38]

* * * * * * * *

[The go]venor from what he wrote us has taken it for granted that we would fit out an Expedition & has acted accordingly I make no doubt but he will be as much Surprised at our backwardness, as he may call it, as we are at ye precipetet steps in ye other quar-

---

and the following from *Pennsylvania Gazette* of July 27. "Williamsburg, July 14.—Last Sunday morning his Excellency our Governor left this city, in order to take a view of the situation of the frontiers of this Colony. It seems his Lordship intends to settle matters amicably with the Indians if possible, and purposes to have confcrances with the different nations, to find out the cause of the late disturbances." Dunmore refers in his letter to the men who composed Maj. Angus McDonald's expedition, which left Pittsburg the latter part of July.—ED.

[37] Rosegill, in Middlesex County, was the home of Ralph Wormsley, one of the councillors for the colony.—ED.

[38] Unfortunately the manuscript of the first portion of this letter is too mutilated to be readable.—ED.

ter. Don[t] faile to come and let us do something. I would, as matters stand, use great risque rather than a misscarrage should happen.

I am Your Humble Servt.

Andw. Lewis

SITUATION ON CLINCH RIVER

[Capt. William Russell to Col. William Preston. 3QQ64.]

Dr. Colo.— Since I wrote you last, the Inhabitants of this River have, altered the Plan for two Forts only, on this River below Elk Garden, and have erected three, one in Cassel Wood, which I call Fort Preston, a second ten Miles above, which I call Ft. Christian, the third five Miles below the first, which I call Fort Byrd, and there are four Familys at John Blackmores near the mouth of Stoney Creek,[39] that will never be able to stand it, without a Comm^d. of Men, therefore request you, if you think it can be done, to Order them a supply sufficient to enable them, to continue the small fortification they have erected. I am in hopes, from this time, in about two, or three Weeks M^r. Boone will produce, the Gentⁿ. surveyors here, as I can't believe they are all Kill'd: Boone has Instructions to take different routs, till he comes to the Falls of Ohio, and if no discovery there, to return Home thro' Cumberland Gap, which will give them opportunity to discover, if they are about the upper Entrys on Salt Lick River,[40]

---

[39] Elk Garden was upon a branch of Clinch, Cedar Creek. See Smith's MS. map, in this volume. For the other forts, see *ante*, p. 85.—Ed.

[40] An early name for Licking River, Kentucky.—L. C. D.

CLINCH RIVER

or have Advanced towards Cumb: River, to make what few surveys, were to be there: in which Tower (if they are alive) it is indisputable, but Boone must find them. I have kept the other Scouts out continually on Duty some to watch the Head of Kentuckey, and between that and Sandy Creek; and the others about Cumberland Gap, and down Clynch River, and as they are Men that may be depended on, I hope the Enimy cannot come upon us, without being discovered, before they make a stroak, if so, there is a probability of Rewarding them well for their trouble between this and Ohio. Colo. Christian, and Gentlemen under him, Arrived here Sundy last. I am sorry to find Sir. I can't be Indulged to serve my Country with a Captns. Command, as early as others; who, are but new Hands: when I accepted of the Commission, War then threatened, and together with a desire of shewing, I had not the least Objections, of serving under You; my only Inducement was my Country; which was your Intentions; I must beleive, at the Time you was pleased, to honour me with it; but Sir. I can't help thinking, the Result of your Council at Ft. Chiswell, is a Procedure which, intirely disables me, from attempting to comply with your late, Orders; as these Companys are sent, without any Orders for me to join them, upon an Alarm; and they to reconnoitre the very Warriour Paths, most convenient to me; whence it follows, that upon any Acct. from my scouts; to prevent greater Expence to the Country: It wood I think, be my duty to inform Colo. Christian of it, reather then take any Steps to Inlarge the Expence, by calling out more Men; when this Command, might be sufficient to pursue any Party, that wood ever come at once; upon our Frontier. I hope good Sir. you'l Pardon me, and am persuaded your Courtesy cannot help considering the Inhabitants of this River, who are liable to a Stroke from the Northward Indians, before those on Holston, and when ever that is the case, it's certain we in general, poor as we are, must be ruined, and tho' the pay of the Country as soldiers cannot be thought Adequate to such risques yet it might in a small measure, encourage the People, to stand their Ground: indeed was there to be no War, a month, or two in Service, wood never make us whole, for the trouble we have been at, in building Fortifycations; which we might have avoided, by taking our Family's down the Country, And have left the People on Holston in our present situation, and was that to be the case, I am persuaded theres not a Man on the River, but what wood think, such an Indulgence was his due. Was I to keep a Commission, in hopes of Benefiting my Country, or selfe, and my only hopes was, from a set of Gentlemen; who, were all desireous to serve as well as my selfe; I am assured against such powerful Connexions, as are upon Holston, and New River Waters, It wood be useless for me to mention, one Word about it. And to be plain, unless a singular favour, of your own Authority; Places me in the service, it would be more to the Interest of my helpless Family, and the Cr[ed]it of my selfe, to be without such Commission. I am satisfied the Gentlemen Officers appointed to the present Detachment, are worthy Men, and were the Men as Zealous to serve their Country, as the Officers; they might Distroy some of the Enimy in a Week or two. The Ammunition is so bad, that the Inhabitants in the Different Forts seam easy about it, whether they have it by them or not to make Defence, and they are Intirely without, and we have only fifty wt of Lead with the Podder; I have sent over a Man for some of the other Kind, as Capt. A. Campbell wrote me, it wood be up last Week. I hope by this Time, you have had some Acct. from Ft. Pitt, whether it is like to be peace, or War, and till I have the pleasure to hear from You remain Dr. Colo. your most Obedt. Humbl. Servt.

W Russell

Fort Preston July the 13th 1774

N. B. pray excuse haste, my Hands are so sore at Work about the Fort, I can scarce Write.

VOLUNTEERS FOR EXPEDITION CALLED OUT

[Circular letter of Col. William Preston. 3QQ139.]

Smithfield 20th July 1774

Dear Sir—Inclosed you have a Copy of Lord Dunmore's Letter to Colo. Lewis of the 12th. Instant, In Consequence of which, the Colo. has Called upon me to Attend on the Expedition, with at least, two Hundred & fifty Men, or more if the[y] can Possibly be raised; This Demand if Possible must be Complyed with, as it is not Altogether our Quota; & indeed it appears reasonable, we should turn out cheerfully On the present Ocasion in Defence of our Lives and Properties, which have been so long exposed to the Savages; in which they have had too great Sucess in taking away. We may Perhaps never have so fair an Opportunity of reducing our old Inveterate Enemies to Reason, if this should by any means be neglected. The Earl of Dunmore is Deeply ingaged in it. The House of Burgesses will without all Doubt enable his Lordship to reward every Vollunteer in a handsome manner, over and above his Pay; as the plunder of the County will be valluable, & it is said the Shawnese have a great Stock of Horses. Beside it will be the only Method of Settling a lasting Peace with all the Indians Tribes Arround us, who on former Occasions have been Urged by the Shawnese to ingage in a War with Virginia   This useless People may now a[t] last be Obblidged to abandon their Count[r]y   Theire Towns may be plundered & Burned,   Their Cornfields Distroyed; & they Distressed in such a manner as will prevent them from giving us any future Trouble;   Therefore I hope the men will Readily & cheerfully engage in the Expedition as They will not only be conducted by their own Officers but they will be Assisted by a great Number of Officers & S[o]ldiers raised behind the Mountains whose Bravery they cannot be Doubtfull of, while they Act from the same Motive of Self Defence. The whole will be under the Command of an Officer whose Experience, Steadiness & conduct on former Occasions, has Induced his Country to Call him forth at an Advanced Age to Command the present Expedition. The nec[ess]ary Provisions will be procured without loss of time, Amunition will also be provided. Every man Inter[e]sted & that I think, is every man in the County will I hop[e] exert himself to the Utmost to Forward this Expedition; on the Success of which so much Depends   I would Willingly hope for the Honour as well as the interest of the County of Fincastle, that we shall not be behind our

Neighbours in furnishing men, Provisions or any other ne[ce]ssaries the County can Spare The Oppertunty we hav So long wished for, is now before us, The Eyes of this & the Neighbouring Colonies are upon us. The Governor of Virginia calls for us, Our County is ready to pay, & support us; & all the Countries [counties] behind the great Mountains are willing to Join in Assisting us. Our Cause is good; & theirfore we have the greatest Reason, to hope & expect that Heaven will bless us with Success in the Defence of ourselves, & families against a parcel of Murdering Savages Interest Duty, Honour, Selfpreservation, and every thing, which a man ought to hold Dear or Valuable in Life ought to Rouze us up at present; & Induce us to Join unanimously as one man to go [on] the Expedition. The Len[g]th of the Journey, or the badness of the Road ought not to be Objected to, as we cannot expect any Rest from these Indians, until it is Travelled for this purpose; & their cannot be a finer Season than what is now before us & I am fully poswaded our young Active Woodsmen will Heartily engage in this Service, which will be of so short a Continuance; & from the well known Justice, & Generosity of our Assembly; I have not a single[41]

---

[41] This letter is a rough copy, made by some inept scribe, of the circular letter which Preston undoubtedly sent out to the captains of militia, and through them to the people in general. The copy terminates abruptly.—ED.

ROBERTSON TO COMMAND AT CULBERTSON'S

[Maj. James Robertson to Col. William Preston. 3QQ66.]

Tuesday night July 19th 1774

Sir—Since I Rec^d. your Letter I have been Continually on Horse Back amongst the People. I will get 18 or 20 men Ready to Start Thursday Evening or friday morning, for My Soul I Could not get them to March Sooner and to Leave them behind I never Expected to See them untill the new Draft again and Scarc then. I am in Hopes there will be no Great Danger untill we get there.

I am Sir Your Servant

JAMES ROBERTSON

To Col. William Preston

Wednesday morning 20th July 1774

Sir—Since I Rec^d. your letter I have not had an Hours Rest I am Sure. I have with A Great Deal of Both good words and Bad ones Prevail'd on the following Persons to march with me Thursday: Samuel Lister, John Lister, Blackburn Atkins, Samuel Keith, Edmond Vancee, Jeremiah Pate, Rubⁿ. Skaggs, John Shillin, W^m. Ratliff, James Hill, Zach. Skaggs, Thomas Luallen, Jonathen Davise, Willm. Lessly Ad^g, Skaggs, Shorgan Bryans, Samuel McGeehey, William Robinson, John Craig

The following Persons has promised to follow me in less then 8 days: John Shain, Thomas Alley, Jesse Elkins, John Elswick There is three or four more I

Can Pick up I believe I thought to Got them marchd to day but it was not in my power Some had Grain to put up and to Leave them would [n]ot do for I would Scarcely Ever See them again. I am your Servt.

JAMES ROBERTSON

N. B. This last news I Expect is no more than Some of the Usual Alarms. But if they are about I am in hopes we will be there time Enough for them. Pray Sir if Possible Procure me a Quire of Paper as I cannot get one Sheet.

To Col. William Preston. To be forwarded by M^r. Petter Stiffay In Haste.

[Instructions of Colonel Preston to Major Robertson. 3QQ138.]

SIR—You are to march immediately down the River with what Men you have, & when you go to Culberson's Bottom take the Command of the Officers and Men there. If there are more Officers than are allowed by Law for the proportion of Men, they are to be discharged, or take their chance for their Pay when the Accounts come to be settled. You are to use your utmost Endeavours to prevent the Enemy from comeing by that important Pass, & to Protect the Settlers at that Place as well as at Rich Creek. You are with your Men & the Inhabitants at the Bottom to construct a small Stockhade Fort for the Protection of the Inhabitants, and the Reception of a Company. I will not engage that the Men shall be paid, but on your keeping a just account of their Labour, I shall use my endeavours for that Purpose. This Fort when built must be a place for the Company to resort, in order to be supplied with Provisions when they are ranging. I need not tell you how necessary it is to be constantly on your Guard to prevent a surprize, upon this depends the Lives of many of your Company & many of the Inhabitants as also your own and the Company's Reputation as Soldiers. The detestable practice of wantonly firing Guns without any cause is also to be avoided, as it not only wastes Ammunition which is so very scarce, but gives the Enemy notice where you are, so that they will either take the advantage of your Imprudence and surprize you, or Pass by the Company & ravage the Country. You are to keep up a strict Discipline amongst the Men & see that every Officer under your Command punctually and faithfully perform their duty and if any are Mutinous disobedient or neglegent thereof, you are to keep an Account & return such to me when you come that they may at least lose their Pay; and be otherwise punished as the Invasion Law directs. But as the Officers & Soldiers are out with a view to serve & protect their Country & share the benefit of such Protection; I hope they will behave in the best manner & not subject you to the disagreeable Necessity of Reporting any bad Conduct, or me to the Task of having any Punished, either by loss of Pay or otherwise. But you are by no means to secrete or overlook Breeches of Duty, as you may also depend in this case of being proceeded against as the Law directs, & not being called upon active duty for the future. You will endeavour to have the Men provided for on the cheapest and easiest Terms you Possibly can. You are also to have the Care of any Scouts on that Quarter, this is a most important duty, & must be carefully looked into. You are to write to me as opportunity offers, or by Express if there is Occasion. In every part of your duty you are to behave yourself as a good an[d] faithful Officer ought to do. I wish you Safety and Success & am Sir Your humble Servt

WM. PRESTON

July 22d 1774

To Major James Robertson who is to take command of a Company

EXPEDITION TO OHIO ORDERED

[Lord Dunmore to Col. Andrew Lewis. 3QQ141.[42]]

SIR—I received your's and Colo. Charles Lewis Letters. the general Confederacy of Different Indian Nations their repeated Hostilities (there were six Men Murdered on Dunkard Creek on the 18th instant)[43] the Discovery of Indians & universal Alarm throughout all the frontiers of the Colony & the unhappy situation of the Divided People settled over the Alagany Mountain's makes it necessary for [me to] go in Person to Fort Dunmore to put Matters under the best Regulation to Support that Country for a Barrier [and] give the Enemies a Blow that will Breake the Confederacy & render their plans abortive I in-

---

[42] This letter is a copy made for Colonel Preston by some illiterate person.—ED.
[43] On the massacre at Dunkard Creek, see *Amer. Archives,* 4th series, i, p. 678; *Penna. Archives,* iv, p. 550; and Crumrine, *Washington County* (Phila., 1882), p. 69.—ED.

tend to take as [many] men from this quarter as I Can get in order in some [so] short time & Desire you to raise a respectable Boddy of Men and join me either at the mouth of the greate Kanaway or Waiten as is most Convenient for you. the Indians having Spies on the Frontiers the[y] may Bring all the Force of the Shawnees against you in your march to the Mouth of the Kenawey so I would have you Consider in What Time You Could get them and other things ready so to meet me at eny Place at Ohio in as Short time as you Can let me know the Same by the return of the express and forward the Letter to Colo. Wm. Preston with the greatest Dispatch as I want his Assistance as well as that of your Brother, Charles Lewis. the Expense of the Numerous scouting Parties in the Different Counties forming an Expensive Frontere Will soon exceed the Expences of an Expedition Against their Towns which will be more effectiaul & we may as well depend on the House of burgess providing for the Expedition as for a greater Expence of Acting on the Defensive at eny rate we know the Old Law [is] Still in force as far as it goes we are sure of being reimbersed I wish you would Acquaint Colo. Preston of Contents of this Letter that those he Sends Out may joine you and Pray be as explicit as you Can as to the time & place of Meeting I need not inform You how necessary Dispatch is.

 I am Sir Your Most Obt. & very Hbl. Ser
           DUNMORE

WINCHESTER July 24th 1774
Colo. Lewies

DEFENSE OF NEW RIVER

[Maj. James Robertson to Col. William Preston. 3QQ67, 68.]

FORT DUNMORE[44] 26th July 1774

SIR—I have met at this Place Six or Seven men that Left Culberson's and has Perswaded them all Back but one (William Atkins) Tomorrow I Expect they will Set off all hands as they Declare they will, unless I Can Stop them this Evening this morning I met with Seven men Just making Ready to Leave this Fort that had Given up their Crops Intirely as they were some on Blue Stone though Every one Lived a Great Distance from here. they have Engaged to be Ready at a Call at any time Hary Tomson Sets of[f] to morrow they tell me and his Party all Goes off with him, Onless you Send Some men down the Case will be Bad So that I must stay with not more then Six men unless I kill part and tye the Other I Expect we will have a war amongst our Selves without that of the Indians. these men tells me they are fresh Signs of Indians Seen Every Morning about the plantation at Forbes, Sir Both men and Amunition will be much wanted about this Place verry Soon as I Expect A Large Body of Indians Emediately. I Shall Stand by the Place Agreeable to my Orders if Death Should be my Fate I am Sir yours

JAMES ROBERTSON

N. B. the men I got to day I Station Here as the

---

[44] Not the fort at Pittsburg; evidently a local blockhouse on New River.—ED.

Setlers here was under the Necessity of moving I have made them up Ten Soldiers and they Seem Satisfy'd

To Col. W^m. Preston Pr Robt. Cravat

FORT BYRD[45] 28th July 1774

D^R. S_{IR}—we will have our Fort Genteely finished this week. we have 25 private at this Place I have ten at old Billey wood's. I would be glad to have Some more men and Amun[i]tion if it was not So good, it would do to keep the fort. there is Signs of the Indians Seen here Every morning and I Expect they will give us a Salute when they Assemble their party altogether if I had Some more men I Could turn out with a party which I would be Extreamly fond of. I have Sent out the Scouts this morning and to Continue out three days unless they See much signs of Indians.

I am D^r. Sir your H^{bl}. Servant

JAMES ROBERTSON

N. B. there is a good many of the men in this place will go with me to the Shany's [Shawnee] towns Tom Masdin is Sick and wants to go home. Harry Thomson Set off yesterday with Some men. I Could not Prevail on him to Stay a few days, untill the men would Come out, as he Said his Business was So Urgent at Court. Sir as I [am] on Duty here and has no Chance to Raise A Company for the present Exp^{dn}.

---

[45] Not the one of that name on Clinch, see *ante,* p. 85; probably the fort at Culbertson's, which Robertson was ordered out to build. Col. William Byrd was popular with the frontiersmen, and no doubt more than one stockade received his name.—E_D.

Please to give my Comlmts. to Old Will In[g]les[46] & with a Litle of your own assistance I hope you Can Engage us Some men

I am yrs. J R

To Col William Preston p^r. Thos. Masdin

PROVISIONING THE EXPEDITION

[Capt. John Connolly to Capt. William Harrod. 4NN8.]

FORT DUNMORE July 16th 1774

SIR—As Capt. Pentecost[47] has engaged to furnish all the Militia on Service with Provisions, you will

---

[46] William Ingles was born in Ireland in 1729; at an early age he emigrated with his father to Pennsylvania, and in 1744 started on an exploring trip to southwest Virginia, where in 1748, with John Draper, he made the earliest settlement on western waters at Draper's Meadows (Smithfield). Two years later he married Mary Draper, who was captured by Indians during his absence from home in 1755. She afterwards made her famous escape, and remarkable journey home, from the Ohio towns to the settlements. See Hale, *Trans-Allegheny Pioneers*, pp. 29-98; Waddell, *Augusta County*, pp. 110-115. Ingles was occupied during all the Indian wars in defense of the frontier. In 1756, he went as lieutenant on the Sandy Creek expedition; from 1758-60 he was ranging or defending the fort at Ingles's Ferry. In 1763, he overtook a raiding party, rescued several prisoners, and regained much booty. On the Point Pleasant campaign he acted as commissary, with the rank of major. Upon the organization of Montgomery County (1777), he was made colonel of militia; but his loyalty to the American cause was considered somewhat doubtful, and in 1780 a court was convened to try him for complicity in a Loyalist plot. The evidence proved inconclusive, but he was held to a large bond. Two years later (1782), he died at his home at Ingles's Ferry, where his descendants still reside, the principal people of the neighborhood.—ED.

[47] Dorsey Pentecost was a Virginian, who settled in the present Westmoreland County, Pa., in 1769. He served as magistrate for Pennsylvania, but in the boundary dispute

please to let Him have the Cattle you have bought for Whalin, for to be sent down there with all possible expedition. The Men who you have had in pay you are to discharge immediately, & give them a certificate for their Services done.

They had better enter into some Companies that are on actual Service of Government to the end that they may be completed

I am Sir Yours &c:

JNO. CONNOLLY

Capt. W^m. Harrod Ten Mile

[Capt. Dorsey Pentecost to Capt. William Harrod. 4NN9.]

July 20th 1774

D^R S_{IR}—I am appointed conductor of stores and provisions and Contractor for the Army and Capt. Connolly Tells me you have purchased up a percel of Cattle for the use of the Militia in actual Service, if you have Convey them to the mouth of Wheeling as Quick as Possible, & Take an acct. of our Expences, what you gave for them and when you deliver them have them appraised and Take cear of all the accs. as I may be able to Settle with you, Capt. Connolly desire you may discharge what men you have Except you can raise a Company. I am D. Sir y^{rs}.

D^{OR} PENTECOST

---

sided with Virginia, and was one of Connolly's ablest lieutenants. In 1777 he removed to Youghiogheny River, and for several years was judge for Washington County. In 1778 he aided as county lieutenant in gathering troops for Clark's Illinois expedition. He died in 1802 at his home on Chartier's Creek.—E_D.

GREENBRIER AND NEW RIVER

[Receipt of Capt. William Crawford to Capt. William Harrod. 4NN9.]

August the 2ᵈ. 1774

Received of Capt. Wᵐ. Herrad Twenty Five Beeves for the use of the militia at Fort Fincastle I say Recᵈ.

Wᴍ. CRAWFORD[48]

ATTACKS ON GREENBRIER; DEFENSE OF NEW RIVER

[Maj. James Robertson to Col. William Preston. 3QQ69.]

CULBERSONS 1ˢᵗ August 1774

SIR—About three hours agoe John Draper Came here with thirteen men, which makes our Number 33 or thereabouts this minet I got flying news of the Indians Shooting at one of Arbuckles Centery's on mudy Creek.[49] they Say Likewise that they Atacted

---

[48] William Crawford was born about 1722, in Virginia, whence he removed to the frontier in early manhood. He learned surveying from Washington, and in 1755 was an ensign of Virginia troops serving throughout the French and Indian War and that of Pontiac (1763). In 1765 he removed to the Youghiogheny and was one of the earliest and most influential settlers, accompanying Washington down the Ohio in 1770. In Lord Dunmore's War, he made three expeditions toward the Indian territory, in the second of which he built Fort Fincastle. He was major in Dunmore's division, and commanded a side expedition which destroyed the Mingo towns—see *post*. He was colonel of a Virginia regiment in the Revolution, and in 1782 led an expedition against the Wyandot at Sandusky, when he was captured, and tortured to death at the stake. See Butterfield, *Expedition against Sandusky* (Cincinnati, 1873).—ED.

[49] Capt. Matthew Arbuckle was one of the most experienced woodsmen and Indian fighters of his time. He was born about 1742, and removed while young to the upper James. In 1765, with one or two companions, he explored the Kanawha

one Kelley's yesterday about half a mile from that Fort where they Tomhak'd Kelley and Cut him Vastly, but the men from the fort heard the Noise and Ran to their Assistance and drove the Indans. off before they Either Kill'd or Sculp'd Kelley they took his Daughter Prisoner its Said;[50] but the Certainty of any of the newes I Canot Assert   I am in hopes they will be able to defend themselves at no great Risque there, as John Stewart has A Company they tell me in the Levils of Greenbrier not more then Six miles from Arbuckles fort[51] I keep the Scouts out Continualy and has Seen no fresh Signs this four or five days.   I

Valley to the Ohio—the first white man to pass this way except as an Indian prisoner. On this campaign he was chosen captain of a company of scouts, and as guide for Lewis's division of the army. In 1776 he was sent to command Fort Randolph, erected at the mouth of the Kanawha, and defended this important frontier post for three years, being in charge when Cornstalk was killed. He was an able and efficient officer, much trusted by General Hand, the head of the division at Fort Pitt. Captain Arbuckle was killed on his way home from Staunton to Greenbrier (1781), by a falling tree in a great storm. His son, of the same name, was a general in the regular army.—Ed.

[50] For full details of this disaster, see Stuart's "Narrative," in *Virginia Historical Collections*, i, pp. 37-68; and *Magazine of American History*, i, pp. 668, 740. The captive was Kelly's niece.—Ed.

[51] Capt. John Stuart (his autograph signature reads at different times both Stuart and Stewart) was born in Scotland, 1749, and twenty years later made the first settlement on Greenbrier, where the town of Frankfort now is. He had a private fort on his own estate, called Fort Spring. In 1770 he was a magistrate of Botetourt County, and later first clerk of Greenbrier. He commanded a company under Col. Charles Lewis for the Point Pleasant campaign, and in his old age (1820) wrote a narrative thereof (see preceding note). He died at his Greenbrier home in 1823.

The "Levils of Greenbrier" was the present site of Lewisburg (organized as a town in 1782), where Camp Union stood, the rendezvous of Lewis's army.—Ed.

Set out tomorow with about Twenty men and will take a Trip Nigh to the Glades, and Return as Quick as possible again Least there Should be use for us nearer Our fort, as John Draper Came down Yesterday he Surely Seen the Tracks of five or Six Indians he says on Wolf Creek,[52] and they made in towards the Setlement, it would be well for the people to be on their Guard or Indeed some party sent that way to Range about. as to my Going in Sir its Impossible Unless we Give up this place Intirely for the men Swairs the minet I set off they Will Start Likewise. and Indeed I cannot leave the Compy. as I See, for there is no one that Can keep any Accts. or do any thing towards Geting Provisions for the Compy. Which is Realy Vastly hard to get I was in hopes there would been some flower fr[om] M. Thomsons for us before now the Place must Undoubtedly Bre[ak] up Unless we Get Some Amunition there has not been three Loads of the Powder that I got from you made use of but that Quaintyty to Pretend to keep A Fort and Range About in Such A Place is Equail almost to none. I Should be Sorry to Urge but there is no Possibility of Defending our Selves or doing any good Without Amunition. we have finished our fort and I think not a dispiseable one. I have been about Raiseing a House for to hold Provisions and Amunition but I am Afraid the Place wont be Over Stocked with Either, in haste, as the one Cant be Possibley got, and the Other People Seems Easey About furnishing us with. Sir I Abide by Your Directions and Waits for any Orders from you which

---

[52] Wolf Creek is a southwestern affluent of New River.—ED.

Shall be Obey'd with as much Exactness as in my power Lys Sir I heartyly wish you & your Famyley Safety and am your Obdt. Servant

JAMES ROBERTSON

N. B. I am afraid Ill be far behinn about my Comy. for the Shany Exp^{dn}. as I am confined here

Holton Monoy	Jo^s. Turner	
W^m. Neal	Jno. Corder	10
Jno. Alsup	Michael Stump	
W^m. Day	Ab Mounts	
Alex^r. Mares	Jno. Denton	
Peter Dingus	Jo^s. Mares	14
John Smith	Ja^s. Adair	15
Thos. Shannon	Jno. Shannon	16

To Col. William **Preston** To be forwarded by M^r. W^m. Thompson In Haste

---

OFFICERS FOR HOLSTON

[Col. William Preston to Capt. Evan Shelby. 5XX4.]

DEAR SIR—I wrote to you last night begging your acceptance of a Commission in our Militia. Since which time Capt. Bledsoe[53] Resigned alleging he did

---

[53] Anthony Bledsoe was born in Culpeper County in 1733. In early life he left home and pushed to the frontier, being a merchant at Fort Chiswell as early as 1766. He removed in 1774 to the neighborhood of the Shelbys. He was active in all public affairs, being magistrate of Botetourt, Fincastle, and Washington counties. In 1777–78 he was member of the assembly for Washington. In 1784 he removed to Cumberland, and settled at Bledsoe's Lick, immediately becoming prominent in that country, representing his district in the North Carolina assembly from 1785 until killed either by Indians or white enemies (1788). In military affairs Bledsoe was most useful. He went on the Point Pleasant campaign (see letters, *post*) as commissary for Christian's division, with rank of major. In 1776 he held high rank

not get the Rank he ought to have done. I have appointed Mr. W^m. Cocke a Captain[54] Therefore the lower part of the old Company will fall to you. The Division may be made by You and Capt Cocke; & I have filled a Lieutenants Commission for your Brother who I hope will accept thereof, as Mr. Logan will be in Cockes Company.

I hope my Dear Captain Shelby you will Excuse my giving you so much Trouble but the apology I made

---

under Christian, and commanded the forces at Long Island until July, 1777. He went out against the Chickamaugas in 1779; and only remained at home from King's Mountain upon the representation that it was his duty to protect the frontier. A prominent, able officer and representative, his death was a great loss to the young community of which he made part. Many of his autograph letters are in the Draper MSS.—E<small>D</small>.

[54] William Cocke was one of the remarkable men of this region, serving in the legislatures of four states, and in the federal senate, as well as on many military campaigns. He was born (1748) in Amelia County, son of a well-known colonial family (for his antecedents, see sketch in *American Historical Magazine*, Nashville, July, 1896). He studied law before removing to Holston, where he settled in 1769. He was an orator of brilliancy and power, and popular with his community. After his service in Lord Dunmore's War, he went out to Kentucky with the party that settled Boonesborough, but returned to the Watauga, and participated in the Cherokee campaign, in which he was accused of cowardice, and suspended from his office. In 1777, however, he was sent to the Virginia assembly, and in 1780 led a company at King's Mountain. Upon the formation of the State of Franklin, he embraced the new movement with enthusiasm, and was sent to Washington in its behalf. After that failure, he was made brigadier-general of militia for Tennessee, and in 1796 one of the first of its federal senators—an office to which he was re-elected in 1799. In 1809 he was circuit judge for Tennessee, and later a member of its legislature. In 1812 he removed to Columbus, Miss., and upon the outbreak of the War of 1812-15 volunteered as a private soldier. Appointed Cherokee Indian agent in 1814, he died at Columbus, Miss., in 1828.—E<small>D</small>.

last night in my Letter is all I can make now. Therefore hopes it will Suffice.

I am with great Respect Dr Sir your most Obedt. Servt

W^M. PRESTON

Wednesday Evening 2nd [Aug]ust 1774

To Capt Shelby on Holston

HARROD'S PARTY GO OUT ON EXPEDITION

[Maj. Arthur Campbell to Col. William Preston. 3QQ70.]

SIR—I have just now met the Bearer M^r. Harod, and has communicated to him what was agreed upon, about his affairs Yesterday; He Wishes that the Name of the Command of his own Men, may be given him, and that he may be esteemed, and consulted, as their Chief officer, on future Occasions;[55] I told him that all that was intended, was that he was

---

[55] In March, 1774, James Harrod, born in Pennsylvania in 1742, then resident upon Ten Mile Creek, in Washington County, Pa., advertised that he would lead a party to take up lands in Kentucky—a region he had explored the preceding year. About thirty young men thereupon collected at Grave Creek, upon the Ohio, and in canoes floated down to the mouth of the Kentucky, thence up that river and the Licking, where they began improvements on the site of Harrodsburg. Nearly forty cabins had been raised and much corn planted, when Boone and Stoner warned the party of the danger of Indian assaults. The entire party set out for the Holston settlements; and Harrod, finding recruiting going on, persuaded most of his party to enlist. They were in Christian's brigade, and so too late for the battle at the Point. In 1775 Harrod returned to Kentucky; and thenceforward lived permanently at Harrodsburg, much respected by the community until his death in 1793. He died in the woods, and his family believed that he had been murdered.—ED.

to be joined, to Capt. Russell only in making Returns, to the General officer, and the pay Roll; he has wrote back to Mr. Cowan (who Acts as his Lieutenant)[56] to bring the Men to my House, or whatever place I appoint on Holston, for Rendezvous. It may be well to encourage such a Man as Capt. Harod. with his party, on the present occasion: as far as may be consistant with the discipline, that may be necessary on the Expedition, as he seems very forward to go against the Enemy; Please write me back by him about this affair that I may inform Capt. Russell.

I am Sir your most Humble Servt.

ARTHUR CAMPBELL

McCAULS[57] Augt. 3d. 1774

RANGING AND ENLISTING

[Maj. James Robertson to Col. William Preston. 3QQ71.]

Saturday 6th August 1774 CULBERSONS

SIR—I suppose you heard of the Indians Killing Kelley on mudy Creek, we heard Some Flying accts of it, but not the perticulars I have been Out and Sent Party's Out Every Other day Since I came down John Draper Sets off to day with about Twenty men to the Clover Bottom on Blue Stone, and if no Signs there he Will Take Round by the Glades and Into the

---

[56] John Cowan was with Harrod in 1774 and again in 1775. He settled at Harrodsburg, and was a prominent Indian fighter.—ED.

[57] James McCall was a pioneer who lived on Reed Creek as early as 1750, when Dr. Walker passed that way. One of the same name acted as scout in the Cherokee campaign of 1776.—ED.

Garison by the mouth of Blue Stone the Scouts is Constantly out but Wheither or no they are to be trusted with Such A Weighty Afair or not I Cannot tell. Sir I would be Glad you Could Send a few hands down to Joyn John Draper and his Party which is only thirteen as, the most of the men that Came with me and mastins party that Came with him wants to be Releiv'd Against the last of Next week as Several of them is Determined to go with me to the Shanesse towns, Sir you must know the Great Necessity I have to be in, to try to make up my Compy. and make Ready as well as these men that goes with me. I would been in Sooner but by no means Could Leave the men for several Reasons, and the Day I Set off I Am Sure they will all be Along, and Against we get in it will be three weeks and Some A month, as Long as one party I believe Can Well Stay. Sir I am Your Hble. Servant

JAMES ROBERTSON

N. B. we have not Seen the Signs of any Indians Since I Came here. Pray Sir Send down Some flower and Powder and Lead if Possible, Let it be Good or Bad

Col. William Preston   Pr. John Shillin.

HANSON'S JOURNAL, APRIL 7—AUGUST 9

[Extract from a Journal kept on the River Ohio in the year 1774. 14J58-84.[58]]

April 7th. 8th. We left Col. Wm Preston's in Fincastle County at one o'clock in high spirits, escorted

---

[58] This journal was copied in 1855 for Lyman C. Draper from the original in the possession of Mrs. Louisa Johnston

by the Colⁿ. three miles, eight of us being in company, viz Mr. John Floyd assistant surveyor, Mr. Douglas,[59] Do. Mr. Hite, Mr. Dandridge, Thos Hanson, James Nocks [Knox.[60]—L. C. D.] Roderick Mc Cra & Mordecai Batson. We travelled fifteen miles to John Mc. Guffin's at Sinking Creek.[61]

9th. We rose early in the morning, and crossed Rich Creek mountain & travelled 27 miles to Robt. Carliles and were entertained very well according to the People's ability

---

Trigg of Abingdon, Virginia, by Prof. George F. Holmes of the University of Virginia. In May, 1890, W. D. Hixson compared with this his copy, also taken from the original, and made a few corrections. See also notes in Roosevelt, *Winning of the West*, i, pp. 159-164.—ED.

[59] For Floyd see *ante*, p. 9. James Douglas had visited Kentucky the year before (1773), having led an exploring party down the Ohio, and visited the Big Bone Lick, where he built a tent, using the giant bones as poles. As will appear later, the outbreak of the war and the massacre of three men near Harrodsburg caused Douglas's party to escape. They went in a big perogue down the Ohio and Mississippi to New Orleans, thence via Pensacola and Charleston to Williamsburgh, where Douglas arrived in Dec., 1774 (autograph letter in Draper MSS., 3QQ137). The next spring this pioneer went out to Harrodsburg, whence he was a delegate to the Transylvania Convention (1775). He finally settled in Bourbon County, Ky., where he died in 1793.—ED.

[60] James Knox was an Irishman, who emigrated to America when but fourteen years of age, and began a career as hunter and trapper. He was a leader of the "Long Hunters" of 1769, and scout in Lord Dunmore's War. At its close he enlisted a company of men for Morgan's rifle corps, and served with distinction at Saratoga and Stillwater, retiring with the rank of major. He settled in Kentucky, where he acquired land and distinction, was colonel of militia, member of the state legislature, and married the widow of Gen. Benjamin Logan. He died at his home in Shelby County in Dec., 1822. See Draper MSS., 3D251, 252.—ED.

[61] Sinking Creek is so called because at low water it sinks below ground, and empties into New River, below the surface of the latter, at the base of Anvil Cliff.—ED.

10th. We travelled to Mr. Hardy's, 27 miles the land mountanious with some good bottoms or pieces of Low Grounds,

11th. We travelled to Mr. Kelly's old house 15 miles over a Mountain, and bought a brass kettle for 18 shillings.

12th. We traveled about 30 miles over a Ridge and Hills—& stopped at a Laurel Branch.

13th. We traveled about 27 miles—crossing Gauly Mountain, & overtook Mr. Hancock Taylor, assistant surveyor & his Companey of seven men and Himself.

14th. We arrived at Mr. Kelly's below the falls of New River[62]—24 miles where we expected to have got a canoe, but were disappointed, Taylor likewise stopped to make a Canoe, and Mr. Floyd hearing there was one at Elk River unfinished hired a man at 3s per day to go & finish it.

15th. We proceeded 14 miles down the river passing by the burning springs—which is one of the wonders of the world.[63] Put a blaze of pine within 3 or

---

[62] The expedition passed up the east side of New River, crossing Sinking Creek, then Rich Creek—a branch not far from Grey Sulphur Springs. Laurel Branch is an affluent of Greenbrier, which latter river the journal fails to mention. Walter Kelly's cabin was farther out in this wilderness than any other habitation, at the mouth of Kelly's Creek in Kanawha County, West Va. On the fate of Kelly see *post*, and Wither's *Border Warfare*, pp. 159–161.—ED.

[63] The Burning Spring of the Kanawha, located in the county of that name about fifteen miles above Charleston, W. Va., was first discovered by Arbuckle's party in 1773. It was a pool of water through which natural-gas forced its way and kept burning over the surface of the water. In 1775 the place was located by Washington and Col. Andrew Lewis. The former intended to leave his portion as public property, but for some reason this plan was never carried out, and the

4 inches of the water, and immediately the water will be in a flame, & Continue so until it is put out by the Force of wind. The Springs are small and boil continually like a Pot on the Fire; the water is black & has a Taste of Nitre. The spring never rises above its Bank, nor does any water run from it above ground, tho' it continually boils up. One of the springs was dry, at the time we were there—and the earth in the hole of it was burning.

16th. We proceeded to Elk River,[64] 6 miles & found the canoe on the opposite shore of New River. Mr Floyd and a stranger went out to hunt; whilst we finished the canoe, which was done when he returned, after shooting a Deer & a Pike 43 inches long.

17th. We called our canoe the Good-Hope, imbarked on board of her, sailed 9 miles down the river, there saw two canoes ashore, which caused us to land, We found Majr Fields[65] in company, who gave us some

---

land was sold to private parties, who in 1843 bored a natural-gas well at this place. See Fleming's description in his *Journal, post.* ED.

[64] The mouth of Elk River was a well-known landmark in the Kanawha Valley. In 1773 Colonel Bullitt surveyed the tract for himself, and no settlement was made thereupon until 1788, when George Clendennin purchased the land, and built the first house in what is now Charleston, established as a town in 1794.—ED.

[65] John Field was born in Culpeper County in 1720. He was of a good pioneer family, and early showed the traits of a popular leader. He was in service during the French and Indian War, protecting the frontier in 1756, and serving as captain under Forbes in 1758. Being out with Bouquet as major in 1764, that title became the most popular one, although after serving in the legislature (1765) he was made colonel of militia (1766). Concerning his narrow escape from the Indians in this exploring trip on the Kanawha in July, 1774, see Stuart's "Narrative," as cited above. His son and negro maid were captured, and in revenge Field enlisted a

Bear meat, which was acceptable at that time, as we had no Provisions. The People informed us, that the Indians had placed themselves on both sides of the Ohio, and that they intended war. The Delaware Indians told them that the Shawnese intended to rob the Pensylvainans & kill the Virginians where ever they could meet with them, We parted with them & proceeded to Crab River 3 miles.

18th. We surveyed 2000 acres of Land for Col. Washington, bordered by Coal River & the Canawagh.[66] Mr. Dandridge crossed Coal River, & lost himself, which put Mr. Floyd to a great deal of trouble to find him in the night. Mr. Taylor and his company joined us. The Bottoms or Low Grounds here are but narrow & not very good. We catched a Cat fish that weighed 40 pounds.

19th. We passed on from hence, passing Pokatalico River at 6 miles, to a bottom Mr. Hogg is improving in all 14 miles,[67] Mr. Hogg confirmed the news we had of the Indians, He says there were 13 People who intended to settle on the Ohio, and the Indians came upon them and a battle ensued, The white People killed 3

---

company of forty men in his own county, and joined Lewis's army at Camp Union. There is a tradition that he considered himself entitled to outrank Colonel Lewis. For his fall on the field of battle, see accounts *post*. His son Ephraim was rescued from captivity, emigrated to Kentucky, and was slain at the battle of Blue Licks (1782).—ED.

[66] For Washington's plan to improve this land, see his *Writings* (edition of 1889), ii, pp. 451–455, 459–462.—ED.

[67] Hogg and two or three of his men were killed soon after this at the mouth of the river. See *Amer. Archives*, i, pp. 707, 1015. Some of his clothes were found by the army; see Fleming's *Journal, post*.—ED.

HANSON'S JOURNAL 115

Indians (imagined to be Chiefs) and then fled.[68] This caused the Indians to hold a council & they are determined to kill the Virginians and rob the Pensylvanians. This is a very good bottom, & there is a Pine, & a Cherry Tree, within 19 feet of each other; they are 3 feet in Diameter.

20th. We proceeded to the mouth of the Kanawha, 26 miles. At our arrival we found 26 People there on different designs — Some to cultivate land, others to attend the surveyors, They confirm the same story of the Indians. One of them could speak Indian language, therefore Mr. Floyd & the other Surveyors offered him 3 per month to go with them, which he refused, and told us to take care of our scalps. We passed but one bottom which is within 7 miles of the mouth of the River, & I am informed it runs 20 miles deep & is good Land, is on the South Side about 6 miles broad on the side of the River. On the North point, where we met the People is very fit for a fort, and to my opinion does not overflow which is not the case of the other bottoms.[69] Mr. Floyd and the other Surveyors were received with great joy by the people here.

21st. Mr. Floyd wrote to Coln. Preston letting him know how affairs are at present & what happened on

---

[68] This must be the fight referred to by George Rogers Clark in his letter of 1798, when he says: "Only eighty or ninety men assembled at the place of rendezvous [mouth of Little Kanawha], where we lay some days; a small party of hunters which lay about ten miles below us were fired upon by the Indians, whom the Hunters beat off and returned to our Camp." Mayer, *Logan and Cresap*, p. 150. Note that this was some days before the Pipe Creek and Yellow Creek massacres.—ED.

[69] The site of the battle of Point Pleasant, and later of Fort Randolph.—ED.

the journey. Mr. Floyd and the rest of the People are in high Spirits, and determined to go down the river, to do the business they came on & try the consequences unless a superior Force should attack them,

22nd. The Company consisting of 18 men with 4 Canoes proceeded down the Ohio River, Messrs. Floyd & Taylor going on foot down the other side about 10· miles to a Creek. On the East Side, the Bottoms are narrow, but on the West side of the Ohio they appear broader. We passed 2 small Islands.

23rd. We aired, and dried our small stores and some of the Company went a hunting.

24th. We proceeded down to the little Ḡiandot 14 miles, the Bottoms good that we passed and even but not very large. We found a Battoe loaded with corn, we took about 3 Bushels of it with us.

25th. We waited for the rest of the Company that we left at the mouth of New River The River Ohio fell 2 feet within 24 Hours and we found a spring at the foot of the Bank.

26th. At 3 o'clock this afternoon 3 men came to our Camp, who had been 20 miles below us and were alarmed by Indians, & made their escapes. 2 of them joined Mr Floyd, viz Nash & Mr. Glen, and Lawrence Darnell joined Mr. Taylor.

27th. Mr Douglas & Mr Hite joined us with 13 men, which makes us 37 strong. But the alarm before mentioned occasioned 4 to return back, viz Mr. Dandridge, Taylor, Holloway & Waggoner, which reduced us to 33 but we proceeded down to Great Giandot 20 miles. We saw 4 Deleware Indian men & about 14 squaws besides children, who gave us to understand that there were 50 Indians below us. The Bottoms we passed are good land, But low consiquently overflow very much.

28th. We were stopt by rainy weather.

29th. We proceeded to Big Sandy Creek, passing little Sandy Creek at six miles, thence to Big Sandy 7 miles is one continued Bottom, in all 13 miles, where we stopet and cooked our kettle, and then embarked in our Canoes, and floated all night. In the morning we discovered that we had floated 25 miles.

30th. We proceeded 15 miles to a Creek called 4 Mile creek,[70] where we stopt to hunt, except Mr. Hite and two of his men, who proceeded. After we had killed some meat, Mr. Floyd did not think it proper to let Mr. Hite go on alone. We therefore proceeded 4 miles lower, which brought us opposite to the mouth of the River Sciota. By this time it was dark, but we saw Mr. Hite's Fire and call to him, but he would not answer, therefore we landed below the Fire, and went thro' the woods with caution, until we discovered it to be Mr. Hite and his men. On the upper side of 4 Mile Creek is very good land, I suppose to the Quantity of 2 or 3000 acres.

May 1st. It being Sunday we took our rest, and looked at an old Fort we found about 4 or 500 yards from the Banks of the River. It is a square Figure, each side 300 Paces long. It has 4 Gates and 2 Sally Ports, and it is so antient, that the Indians cannot tell when it was built, or by whome. There has been an

---

[70] The creek now called Tygert's, so named for Michael Tygert, who explored it in 1773.—ED.

Indian Town there formerly & there is some remains of it to this Day.⁷¹

2nd. We made a survey of this Bottom for Paterick Henry. It contains 4 or 500 acres, of very good land, including the Fort & Town. There is a Sycamore tree 37 feet in Circumferance on this bottom. The River here is 494 1/2 yards wide. At 9 o'clock we embarked, and went down 7 miles, then landed and Surveyed a Bottom, which Contains 5 or 600 acres for Wᵐ. Henry. The land is excessive good. From there we proceeded 13 miles lower down the River, passed Shot Pouch Creek,⁷² five miles below the last Bottom we surveyed. The Bottoms here are but small & not very good. We had rain this night which gave us wet skins, as we were ill provided.

3ʳᵈ. We proceeded 4 miles lower to Salt Lick Creek,⁷³ and made a survey of 200 acres, the Bottoms narrow & beachey, We had a hard frost this night, which killed almost every thing that was green.

4ᵗʰ. We proceeded 5 miles lower, and then Mr. Floyd made a survey of 2000 acres on a large Bottom

---

⁷¹ The first Shawnee town at the mouth of the Scioto was built on the west bank. This being abandoned because of a flood (1753), a less substantial village was erected on the site of Portsmouth, which was abandoned during the French and Indian War for Chillicothe, and villages higher up the Scioto. See Croghan's "Journals," in Thwaites, *Early Western Travels,* i, pp. 133, 134. Croghan had a stone trading house on the Kentucky side of the river, probably the "fort" to which Hanson here refers. See Thwaites, *On the Storied Ohio,* p. 152. From this Shawnee village Mrs. Ingles made her escape in 1755.—ED.

⁷² Apparently Kinniconick Creek, in Lewis County.—ED.

⁷³ Salt Lick Creek, at whose mouth is the modern Vanceburg, was surveyed by Bullitt in 1773. For an account of early salt-making in this region see Cumming's "Tour," in Thwaites, *Early Western Travels,* iv, pp. 164, 165.—ED.

which runs 5 miles down the River, and ends opposite to an Island, whereon we lodged. This night the Frost was very severe,[74] the Island is called Oppony Island.

5th. We proceeded 5 miles lower and then landed on a bottom, which Mr. Floyd surveyed for Mr. John May.[75] It contains about 700 acres, very good land. There was frost again this night. We lay on a very large Island opposite our Survey.

6th. We proceeded 3 miles and then landed on a Bottom, which Mr. Floyd surveyed It runs on the River 3 miles, but is narrow, he finished the survey at a small Creek, which he called Nashes creek[76] from his valiant behaviour on the following occurrence. While we were surveying, Nash hunted thro' the Bottom & at the Creek met with two Indians, who called him Brother, but attempted to change Guns with him, which Nash refused. When they found he would not change, They would have killed him for her, but he was much on his guard, and they had but one Gun between them. Therefore by his Quickness & Alertness, he got Clear. Soon after the Indian that had no Gun overtook one Mc Culloch and took his double barriled Rifel from him. This alarmed us, and 12 men went in search of the Indians, 6 of them one Way & 6 another. The first 6 men saw the Indian, that had taken the Gun & one of the men fired at him but missed him, we kept under arms until evening, and

---

[74] Great May Frost.—L. C. D.
[75] For John May, see *ante*, p. 21.—ED.
[76] The creek now called Sycamore, a very small stream two miles below Ohio Brush Creek. On this Indian alarm, see statement of Sodowsky, in Collins, *Kentucky*, ii, p. 466.—ED.

then embarked & floated 4 miles down the River, & then landed,

7th. We rose early this morning and serched the woods for Indians, but found none. We then embarked and went 14 miles down to a small run, passing Lee's Creek,[77] where lies a small Bottom of land, Surveyed 200 acres on Brackin's Creek[78] for Thos. Hanson good land with a high Ridge on the back of it. We had heavy Rain & Thunder.

8th. We proceeded 19 miles down the river then encamped, The Bottoms narrow & broken.

9th. We proceeded to Locust Creek 12 miles, & there began a Survey on the Bottom which extended 7 miles, & Contains 3000 acres. We lay all night at the end of the bottom. The land very good.

10th. We proceeded down the River, passed Little Miamia at 2 miles went from thence to Licking Creek[79] 8 miles. A survey was made on the upper side of this Creek, good land & there is part of the bottom on the lower side not Surveyed very good, we proceeded 11 miles lower & then encampt; It Thundered & rained this night.

11th. We rose early in the morning, & proceeded down 6 miles, which brought us to a Bottom of good

---

[77] In Mason County, still bearing the same name; the creek was named for Hancock Lee, who explored Kentucky in 1773. The party has passed Limestone Creek, later the entrepôt to the state, without mention.—ED.

[78] Bracken Creek, in the county of the same name, took its cognomen from Matthew Bracken, who surveyed with Hancock Taylor in 1773, and was killed at Point Pleasant in 1774.—ED.

[79] The future site of Cincinnati (settled 1788) and its Kentucky suburbs, Covington and Newport.—ED.

land.[80] We made a survey of the same for Doct. Hugh Mercer, containing 1000 acres. 4 miles below this Bottom, is great Miamia coming in on the Western side of it. There is a fine Bottom on the Eastern side of the Ohio, not surveyed. We proceeded 12 miles lower down to an Island & there encamped.

12th. We proceeded down to a Creek 8 miles which lies within 3 miles of the big Bone Lick. There was 1000 acres surveyed for William Christian, about the Lick. The Land is not so good as the other Bottoms, likewise a little broken. There is a number of large Teeth to [be] seen about this Lick, which the People imagined to be Elephants, There is one Seven Feet & three Inches long. It is nine inches in Diameter at one End and five inches at the other.[81]

13th. Mr. Douglass made a Survey of 2000 acres on the upper side of the Creek for Mr. William Christian, good land. At Mr Douglasses return, we embarked & floated down the River to Kentucky, 47 miles & by daybreak landed. In our passage we came to an Indian Camp, landed & found two Delewares, & a Squaw, we gave them Some Corn & Salt.

14th. Our Company divided, eleven men went up to Harrod's Company one hundred miles up the Kentucky on Louisa River. (n. b. Capt Harrod has been there many months[82] building a kind of Town &c.) in

---

[80] Nearly opposite North Bend, Ohio.—ED.

[81] Nine years earlier (1765), Croghan had visited this lick, and found similar tusks of the extinct mammoth. Fossil bones are still found in this locality. See Croghan's "Journals," in Thwaites, *Early Western Travels*, i, p. 135.—ED.

[82] Harrod's party started in March. A note by Draper is to the effect that the Hixson copy says this phrase should be "but a few days." But see Roosevelt, *Winning of the West*, i, p. 161.—ED.

order to make improvements. This day a quarrel arose between Mr. Lee and Mr. Hyte. Lee cut a stick and gave Hite a whipping with it, upon which Mr. Floyd demanded the Kings Peace, which stopt it sooner than it would have ended if he had not been there.

15th. We lay here in hopes of somebody's coming down to let us know where the Line came down the Ohio, (i. e. the line Col. Donaldson run between us & the Cherokees, which line is said to be Kentucky River itself). We saw a Canoe coming down which stopt as soon as they perceived us, & we saw no more of them.

16th. Mr. Floyd and Mr. Taylor surveyed eight miles & a quarter up the side of the Ohio, but the land is not so good as the other Bottoms we passed, for it is Beachy & of a more sour nature.

17th. Mr. Floyd and Mr. Hite & 5 men with them went 20 miles up Kentucky to a Salt Spring, where we saw about 300 Buffaloes collected together. The Bottoms were broken & Beachy all the way we went up. Mr. Floyd landed several times to look at the land, But found none to please him.

18th. We looked over the land & examined the spring of salt water—The land is worth nothing but the springs if collected together would afford a very good salt work. Mr Floyd offered Mr. Hite his men to assist him to make his Survey there; but Mr. Hite neglected it.

19th. Went into the country for 8 or 10 miles & find it something better than at the springs; but seemed rather of a sour nature. Mr. Floyd with three men went by land to see the country Mr. Hite & 2 men returned to the Canoes & floated down the River.

20th. We found Mr. Floyd & his 3 men within 9 miles of the mouth of the Kentucky at a creek which we called Bear Creek. We all embarked & went down to the mouth of the Kentucky.

21st. Mr. Floyd surveyed 600 acres of land on the lower side of the mouth of Kentucky which takes in little Kentucky for Coln. Preston. The land is very good, but I think some of it overflows.

22nd. In the evening we embarked and went down the river three miles & half, leaving a letter at the mouth of Kentucky to direct any Person or Persons that followed the line how to find us.

23d. As we were on a bottom, Mr Taylor surveyed 1000 acres & then Mr Douglas began at his line, & Surveyed another 1000 acres, which took in the Bottom, except a small point at the lower end. It is 7 miles long. We campt at the lower end, Good land.

24th. Mr. Floyd went on the top of the hill from the River & surveyed a tract of land which is good and well Timbered & watered. We encampt 5 miles below on a small bottom, where it rained in the time.

25th. Mr Floyd surveyed the Bottom and some upland to the Quantity of 1000 acres. It was Showery weather.

26th. We embarked & at the same time saw a canoe coming down the river with a Red flag flying. We hailed them but they would not come to us, therefore we went to them and found them to be 2 Indians. One of them was called Dickirson who had a pass from the Commandant at Fort Pitt, to go down the River in order to collect their Hunters, and cause them to go home, as they expected a war between the white people & the Shawnese. They told us that the people on the river near Fort Pitt had left their Habitations and were gone to the fort, But expected they were returning again to their homes. That they thought it would be made up again. They said the white people & the Indians had a skirmish & that the white people had killed 16 Indians viz. 13 Shawnees 2 Mingoes & 1 Deleware. We parted with them but were afraid that they would follow us. Therefore Mr. Floyd Mr. Taylor Mr. Douglas & and an other man got into a canoe by themselves thinking to have a further conference with the Indians, but they being fearful would not come nigh us any more. This put our people into different opinions as to what to do. Some were for going down the river by way of the Mississippi But Mr. Floyd and the rest of the surveyors were determined to do the business they came on, If not repulsed by a greater force than themselves. We proceeded to Otter Creek, 4 miles and Mr. Taylor surveyed the Bottom containing 1000 acres. Good Land.

27th. We went down the River 7 miles where Mr. Taylor made another survey, and then went 4 miles further where we encampt.

28th. Mr. Floyd made a survey of 2000 acres of upland & proceeded 8 miles down the river to an Island. The upland is very good.

29th. We left the Island & went down to the falls 12 miles, & encampt on an Island at the Fall. Mr. Douglas surveyed the Shore from Harrod's Creek to Bear Grass creek.[83]

---

[83] Harrod's Creek, in Jefferson County, was named for that pioneer on his surveying trip of 1773.—Ed.

30th. Mr Douglass made a survey at the falls, for Dr. Connelly, of 4000 acres.[84] Here is a large body of flat land, which is indifferant next to the River but a Piece back it is very good land.

31st. Our Company divided, Mr. Taylor Mr Douglas & their Companies went towards Harrad's Creek, to make their surveys, & Mr. Floyd with Mr. Hite stayed on the land next to the Falls & surveyed. Floyd made a survey.

June 1st 1774 We made a survey of 1000 acres for Col. Preston. Good land & well watered, including part of Bear Grass Creek, & another small Creek running through it. Mr. Floyd & Mr. Hite made a survey each, of 1000 acres, one for Mr. Boyer & the other for Mr. Ware. Roderick Mc Cra got lost today. Mr. Douglass joined us again, & had surveyed 7000 acres.

3rd. Mr. Floyd & Mr. Douglass made a survey of 1000 acres for Mr. Mc Corkle & Mr. Hite surveyed another 1000 acres. Roderick refused to carry the Chain & went into the country by which means he got lost again.

4th. We waited all day for Roderick fearing the Indians had met with him, therefore left our camp & lodged on a rising Hill that night.

---

[84] This survey had been made by Bullitt in 1773—2,000 acres for Connolly, and 2,000 for another officer, whose claim Connolly had purchased. Preston refused to recognize the survey, as not being made by his own deputy. Lord Dunmore, however, issued the patent Dec. 16, 1773, but Preston insisted on re-surveying the tract. In 1780, after Connolly's adherence to the British cause, the land was declared escheated. See Durrett, "Centenary of Louisville," in Filson Club *Papers*, No. 8.—ED.

5th. We returned to our camp & found that Roderick had been there. We called low & he came to us, then went with our package 4 miles up the Creek & surveyed 1000 acres for Mr. Dandridge.

6th. Mr. Floyd surveyed 1000 acres for himself, very good land & full of springs. Mr. Douglass surveyed another 1000 acres.

7th. The company scattered to look for good land, Mr. Floyd with Allen found a large tract.

8th. Mr. Floyd took 2 men & surveyed the land which he found to be 7000 acres. Mr. Douglass surveyed 2000—one for himself the other for Mr. Christian.

9th. Mr. Floyd & the two men returned this evening.

10th. We went to the waters of Salt River, 3 miles, there are several pieces of land not yet surveyed.

11th. We lay in camp & some hunted for meat, as we were quite out of meat,

June 12th. We packd up our alls & marched for Salt Lick near Salt River,[85] 12 miles bearing to the South West. We passed a large body of good land well watered & well timbered.

13th. Mr. Douglass made a survey for Mr. Christian of 1000 acres, round the Lick, then marched off for Salt River. We went five miles & met with a branch & called it Floyd's River. The land is broken and stony.

14th. We proceeded up Salt River 20 miles & found

---

[85] Bullitt's Old Licks, in the county of the same name, surveyed by Colonel Bullitt in 1773. The first salt-works in Kentucky were established here, three miles from Shepherdsville.—Ed.

it very crooked, the land chiefly stony hills, except one small bottom.

15th. It rained & thundered, which caused us to stay in camp. Nox & Allen seemed very sullen, & left the camp which made us imagine they had a mind to leave us. But in the evening they returned again dried their blankets & stayed with us that night. Mr. Floyd did not like the land here.

June 16th. We rose early and began our journey up the River. Nox & Allen walked so fast that they left the rest of the Company, & we never saw them more.[88] Mr. Douglas killed an Elk, therefore we stopped to breakfast. We travelled 25 miles, the land good for nothing.

17th. We traveled but six miles as it was showery. The land begins to be tolerably good. Mr. Floyd says he is not very well.

18th. Mr. Floyd is very bad & cannot sit up, therefore we must stay, & have no nourishment for him.

19th. Mr. Floyd geting worse we gave him an Indian Sweat, which gave him some ease but weakened him very much. It thundered, & rained this afternoon.

20th. Mr. Floyd being something better Mr. Hite & Mr. Nash went in search of Kentucky river, at night they returned they said they thought they had been on the waters of the little Kentucky.

21st. Mr. Floyd finding himself better ventured to march again. But as he was very weak we only went 6 miles, about N. E. Course, & crossed the river, the land is good.

---

[86] Knox got in to the Holston settlements the last of July. See Preston's letter in *Amer. Archives*, i, p. 707.—ED.

22nd. We rose early this morning & traveled very sloly, for the space of 9 miles. & Roderick was taken ill of Fever & ague, which caused us to stop. The land is good & well watered & timbered. We crossed a branch of Salt river bearing N. E. It rained & thundered most of the night.

23rd. We divided into two Parties, went up a branch to a fork, made by another Creek & then began a survey of 10000 acres, which took us to the waters of Kentucky. We run our End line two miles & half N. and our side line 6 miles & quarter E. 8000 acres of it is good land, the other 2000, is broken next to the waters of the Kentucky. Here we waited for Mr. Douglas and Company.

24th. We were short of provision. Mr. Douglas joined us in the afternoon & as Mr. Nash had kiiled two Elks about 4 miles down the Creek, We went to them, about a N. N. W. Course but was obliged to carry Roderick's pack for him as he was very sick.

25th. We traveled about 17 miles different courses, which brought us to the Kentucky on a small creek. We heard the Voice of one man calling to another, which made us imagine there were Indians about therefore as soon as night came on we went about 3 miles up the river & lay without fire. The land was broken that we traveled over this day.

26th. We traveled 7 miles up the river & made a bark Canoe by which we crossed the river. As soon as we had crossed it we heard the report of a gun, we therefore travelled a little way up the river & then took off into the country. We traveled about 12 miles E. S. E. which brought us to Elk-Horn Creek, where we found some good land.

27th. Mr. Floyd & Mr. Douglas surveyed the good land we saw yesterday, Containing near 3000 acres.
28th. We traveled a S. E. Course to a small Creek, & Mr. Floyd went a land hunting & found Mr. Taylor's last years line, of 20,000 acres, surveyed by him on Elk-Horn Creek.
29th. Mr. Douglas made a survey of 2000 acres which joins Mr. Floyds survey. Mr. Floyd went out to examine land.
30th. Mr. Floyd went to the Creek & there found Mr. Taylor's old corner, & began at the same to survey. He surveyed 6000 acres, but in running the back line found a new marked line, by which he knew that Mr. Taylor had been there, & we left off surveying.

July 1st. 1774. Mr. Floyd & Nash went in search of Taylor & Co., whom they found in a short time, & who took us to their Camp about 8 miles up the river at a large spring. All the land that we passed over today is like a Paradise it is so good & beautiful.

July 2nd. 1774. Mr. Taylor went with Mr. Floyd to shew him where he might begin, to be clear of his survey.

July 3rd. Mr. Taylor returned but Mr. Floyd & Nash went farther into the Country that he might judge how to lay his survey

4th. Mr. Floyd having not returned, Mr. Douglas sent out a man to look out land for him.

5th. Mr. Floyd returned & seemed well pleased at what he had found. It thundered & rained this day,

6th. Mr. Floyd, Nash, Mc Cra & Hanson left the rest of the company with an agreement to meet at Mr. Harrod's Cabbin 20 miles off, higher on the Kentucky, on the first of August, as they thought that we would all be done surveying by that time. We went to one of the main branches of Elk Horn Creek, & there began our survey, it thundered & rained.

7th. We continued our survey & had to swim the Creek, with our Gun, & Packs, on our heads. Our surveys begin on the North branch of the Elk Horn Creek, about 7 or 8 miles from the forks.

8th. We continued our Surveys, the lines all running paralel with each other—running in length N 20 E. in breadth, S. 70 E. The land is so good that I cannot give it its due praise. Its under growth is Clover Pea vine Cane & Nettles—intermixed with Rich weed. Its Timber is Honey Locust, Black walnut, Sugar tree, Hickory, iron wood, Hoop wood, Mulberry, Ash, & Elm, & some Oak.

9th. We surveyed part of the day & then Mr. Floyd & Nash went in search of a spring, which they found, & here abouts we continued our Surveying til the 18th. day of the month, One plot joining another, & all of eaqual goodness, Well watered. Then we returned to Floyd's Spring.[87]

* * * * * * * *

19th. We leveled Mr. Floyd's Spring, & found it to have a fall of 13 feet 7 inches.

20th. We began Mr. Floyds survey of 1000 acres about his spring, which is the largest I have ever seen, in the whole country and forms a creek of itself.

---

[87] Royal Spring, near the site of Georgetown, Scott County. The latter name was given it in 1775; and in that year or early the next, McClelland's Station was established at this place.—ED.

21st. We finished Mr. Floyd's Survey, & set off for the Cabbin & traveled 20 miles & Campt. The land all good & level that we passed over today.

22nd. We changed our course to the S. W. & struck the River in 10 miles traveling, a little above Dicks river which is 10 miles above the Cabbin. We kept down the river about 8 miles. The land near the river is high Hills with Cliffs of Rocks facing the river on both sides, which is lime Stone. (Mr. Floyd says that he observed some free stone there also)

23rd. We Crossed the river, some of us on a Raft with our packs & Guns, & others of us Swam over. we then traveled out straight into the Country 6 miles & lay down.

24th. We Steared West Course to find the road that is between Salt River & the Cabin & we found it in 4 miles travel & proceeded to the Cabin 4 miles further. At our arrival we were surprised to find every thing squandered upon the ground & two fires burning. Mr. Floyd & Nash went down to the landing place & found these words wrote on a tree. "Alarmed by finding some people killed we are gone down this way."[88] Mr. Hite's & Mr. Douglas party that arrived here 2 days before us, which we knew by a note found there, We took a Canoe we found here & crossed the river, &

---

[88] The men killed were James Hamilton and James Cowan, the tragedy occurring July 8, 1774. The survivors escaping to Harrodsburg, warned that party, and they all set out for the settlements, arriving July 29. The notice on the tree puzzled Floyd, who was at a loss to understand the phrase "gone down." It did apply, however, to the descent of Douglas and party to New Orleans. See *ante*, p. 111, note 59; also *American Pioneer*, ii, p. 326; *Amer. Archives*, i, p. 707; and Draper MSS., 3B305, 306.—ED.

traveled 8 miles north into the Country. We made search for Mr. Floyd's saddle bags but could not find them.

25th. We Steered our Course E. S. E. which brought us in sight of the river again, therefore we changed our course E. N. E. 6 miles, & then stopt for the night. We were in a very bad plight for traveling home but about 15 rounds of powder, & none of us knew the way, the land here is good.

26th. We traveled 22 miles —16 of them an E. Course. & 6 N. E. the land all good except 4 miles with several Creeks running through it.

27th. We traveled 22 miles E. Course 12 miles of it good land.

28th. We traveled 20 miles as near E. as the mountains would let us, crossing north branch of Kentucky. The mountains here were so steep, that we were obliged to throw all away that we had, except our Knit Leggins & Mockasons.

29th. We changed our course to the S. E. as we thought we were too far North & traveled but 18 miles, the mountains so steep and tiresome.

30th. We traveled but 9 miles a S. E. course & then were obliged to hunt, as our provisions were out. We crossed another branch of Kentucky,

31st. We traveled about 4 miles on another branch of Kentucky, leading E. Mr. Floyd had a very sore foot which caused us to stop here.

Aug. 1st. 1774 We traveled about 25 miles S. E. & came on another branch of Kentucky that we crossed which did not lead on our course.

2nd. We traveled about 25 miles, & came on the 3rd branch of Kentucky that we crossed.

3rd. We traveled up the river 20 miles. Its chief bearing is a S. E. course small bottoms on the River.

4th. We traveled 5 miles up the river & met with a gang of Buffaloes, killed two & provided ourselves with Provisions.

5th. We traveled 30 miles up the river still bearing to the Southward of East small bottoms along the river.

July [Aug.] 6th. We traveled 17 miles up the River Easterly, then it turned Northward, which made us leave it, & go up a branch bearing Eastward 1 mile. We passed a large Vein of Cole, that makes its appearance in the River Bank.

July [Aug.] 7th. We traveled up the branch—to a large mountain which we found to be Cumberland Mountain. We think we came 30 miles this day.

8th. We had a blazed road which took us through the gap of a large mountain, & brought us to the head of Powels river, where we lost the Blazes, and steared our Course over the mountain, S. E. which brought us on Guess's River a water of Clinch River, running nearly east, & we traveled this day 30 miles.[89]

9th. We kept that River in sight til we came to Clinch river in the afternoon to Mr. Blackburns near the Rye Cove where we found them forted in, prepared for war with the Shawnees.

---

[89] Preston (*Amer. Archives*, i, p. 707) speaks of this as "an extreme, painful, and fatiguing journey of sixteen days through mountains almost inaccessible and ways unknown." Dr. Draper thinks they came through Pound Gap, a depression in Cumberland Mountains in Russell County, Va. Guest's River, a western branch of Clinch, mingles its headwaters with those of Pound Fork of the Big Sandy. Christopher Gist took a similar route in 1751, and the name of the river appears to be a variant of Gist's River. See "First Exploration of Kentucky," in Filson Club *Papers*, No. 13.—ED.

SINKING CREEK MASSACRE DELAYS THE EXPEDITION

[Maj. Arthur Campbell to Capt. Daniel Smith. 4X43.]

ROYAL-OAK, Augt. 9 1774

DEAR SIR—I have this moment Received intelligence of several people being killed last Monday by the Indians on Sinking-Creek about 10 miles from Col^o. Prestons.[90] This makes it necessary that we should be strictly on our guard least some straggling party should visit us. Therefore endeavour without loss of time to get the Inhabitants in your Company collected together into 2 or 3 convenient places for forts, and let them keep up strict and regular Duty until more Men can be sent over to assist them which I will endeavour to have done with all possible speed. This alarm will retard the expedition at least a Week, therefore all young men that chooses to do regular Duty may be taken into pay I expect an Express Tomorrow from Col^o. Preston after which you shall have further Instructions. Pray do every thing in your power for the safety of the Inhabitants.

I am Dr Sir, very sincerely Yours

ARTHUR CAMPBELL

On his Majestys Service To Captain Daniel Smith on Clinch

---

[90] This refers to the massacre of the family of Balser Lybrook—see Robertson's letter of August 12, *post*. The father was wounded, but escaped by hiding in a cave. Of the boys, John was still living in the vicinity in 1836. For his account of the massacre and his own escape, see Draper MSS., 31S, book 3, pp. 47, 55, 57–61; see also Preston's account in *Amer. Archives*, i, p. 707.—ED.

[Maj. Arthur Campbell to Col. William Preston. 3QQ79.]

[Aug. 9, 1774][91]

SIR—I have just Received an account by one Bates (who lodged last Sunday Night at Billey Robinsons) that the Indians had done some damage on Sinking Creek I therefore tho't it my Duty least the Enemy might be out also upon this Quarter, to send Expresses to Capt. Russell and Smith to be on their Guard and to collect the Inhabitants immediately into the Forts. I have also Ordered some of the Captains on this side to draught about 40 Men to join them; I would be glad you would order some Men to be draughted out of Capt. Herberts and the late Capt. Doacks Company, to join Capt. Smith at his Station near the Head of Clinch if those two Companys furnish about 30 Men I think I can compleat ye. two Companys afterwards from this River I am extremely anxious that these draughts may not interfere with the expedition. I have even gone so far as to say that such as has already turned out or Young Men that can be spar'd will not be suffered to get pay if they would go to the Forts. However by accounts from the lower settlement today Capt. Shelby is succeeding very well 20 Men being coming from Wattago to join him I shall make use of this late outrage to Spirit up our people to go on the expedition.

Excuse my anticipating your Orders about sending Men out, as I tho't a Days delay might be dangerous.

---

[91] This letter is undated, but internal evidence proves that it must have been written at the same time as that of Captain Smith.—ED.

Please give me instructions how the Forts is to be provided with Provisions especially Flour viz Whether the Capts. is to engage it themselves or a Commission be appointed to provide it. Before Capt. Harrod[92] returned his Men was billeted out at places that pleased them; They have now concluded to stay here until the Holston Troops March with them to the place of Rendezvous.

I am Sir Your most Obedient Servant
ARTHUR CAMPBELL

FINCASTLE OFFICERS FOR THE EXPEDITION

[Maj. Arthur Campbell to Col. William Preston. 3QQ72.]

ROYAL OAK Augt. 10th. 1774

DEAR SIR—The Bearer Capt. Looney will wait on you about some Business concerning the Expedition It appears by what I am informed by him and Capt. Shelby that there is not quite so good an understanding subsisting between them as I could Wish; however if both could be gratifyed as they are good old hands it might turn out well; If Capt. Russell goes on the Expedition I think there will be an absolutely necessity for Capt. Looney[93] to be put in business on that Quarter as I cannot think of any Officer on this River that will suit so well: I had a Letter Yester-

---

[92] For Capt. James Harrod from Kentucky, see *ante*, p. 108, note 55.—ED.

[93] The Looneys were a well-known pioneer family of Southwest Virginia. Captain Looney did not accompany the expedition.—ED.

day from Capt. Russell who mentions his doubts of raising a Company which if he could not he would rather continue, or, rather be employed, on the Frontiers; he also mentions some tracts lately being discovered. I am inform^d by another hand that his Wife is extremely against his going. I think I can be a judge in a few days whether it would best for him or Capt. Looney to goe on the Expedition. I think also that it will be necessary to appoint Capt. Doacks men to go under Capt. Crockett or Capt. W^m. Campbell As not a Man of that Company I am informed will go under Capt. Herbert. I know you would willingly remove every reasonable objection to forward the Expedition. I dont know as they mens objection is very reasonable against Herbert but yet it may be proper to gratify them. I wish Capt. Herbert may give way on this occasion as perhaps five Capt^s. may do as well with 2 or 3 extraordinary subalterns as the first appointment, or you can be a judge at the place of rendezvous who may be properist to appoint for the sixth.[94] Capt. Looney can inform you how we are embarrassed about finding flour for the Forts. I have not yet heard from Reed Creek perhaps some may be got there. Capt. W^m. Campbell desires me to recommend one John Anderson to you for Ensign to Capt. Looney I believe you are acquainted with the Young Gent. and I think he may be a proper person.[95]

---

[94] The five captains were, William Campbell, William Russell, Evan Shelby, Walter Crockett, and William Herbert. John Floyd also raised a company in this region.—ED.
[95] The Anderson family was one of the oldest in Augusta County, settling there in 1738. This was probably a grandson of the first John, and eldest son of Andrew. See Waddell, *Augusta County*, p. 332.—ED.

I am now waiting with impatience to receive the Letter you promised to write me from Colo. Lewis's; that I may know what department I am to act in. The Expedition is the Principal object of my attention; but if you order the care of this Frontier to me; I will submit.

The late stroke in your Neighborhood is alarming. I hope it will rouse our Spirits to make speedy reprisals.

I am Sir with great Esteem Your Obedient Sert.
                                    ARTHUR CAMPBELL
To Colo. William Preston pr. fr. of Capt. Looney

INDIANS HARASS THE FRONTIER

[James Robertson to Col. William Preston. 3QQ73.]

CULBERSONS 11th August 1774

SIR—I was Expecting Orders to Gone Home to Seen Some What About my Affairs. I have a good deal to do before I Can Start to the Expedition Which I would by no means miss if I Can Possibly make out to go. There has been three or four Indians Visiting the Waste plantations Above us on the River they Burnt a House About five miles above the fort Last Sunday, we got word that night of it and I Set out monday morning Early and was Constantly on Search of them untill Last night but there was So few of them they made not the Least Sign that we Could follow I will Send out A party to day and Watch About the Old Plantations as they will Perhaps be Sculking About, the men Seems Resolute for A Sculp or two, and I have Offered £5 for the first Indians hand that will be brought in to the fort by any of the Compy. John Draper set out Sunday Last with 20 men up Blue Stone as far as the Clover Bottoms, on their march they Came Across the Tracks of four or five Indians they folow'd them Some way but they Scatered so they Could not folow them they were making into new River by their Course about the place where they Burnt the House, they Left a War Club at one of the wasted Plantations well made and mark'd with two Letters I G (well made) So that I think there Party to Range with though they are All Distracted Eight or Ten men that Came with me and mastin I with the Rest that Came with me will Continue untill monday when we must Start as there is Severals of them going on the Expedition.

The party that Came with Draper and Patton will be plenty to Keep the fort and Likewise have a Smart Party to Range with though they are All Distracted Already for Home I Keep the Scouts out as far as the Glades they Cannot See any Signs of the Indians that Road I Supose these Indians Came up Sandy River and In by the Head of Blue Stone. I will make the Scouts go up High on Blue Stone and Watch the Roads that way. Sir I dare say you have a Good Deal of Trouble Geting hands to us, and I am Sure I have a Vaste Deal of Trouble in Keeping them in Tune as they are A Distracted Enough party I assure you my Complmts. to your famyly and Sir I Heartyly wish you Luck from your most Obd S.

JAMES ROBERTSON

N. B. I have had a Severe Spell of a Great Cold and the worst tooth Ache that ever was

JAS. ROBERTSON

To Col. William Preston Pr. Mr. Edmond Vance

[James Robertson to Col. William Preston. 3QQ74.]

CULBERSONS 12th August 1774

SIR—This morning Our Scouts met with a Couple of Poor Little Boys betwen this and Blue Stone one A Son of John McGriffs the Other a Son of Widow Snydoes at Burks fort,[96] that made their Escapes from the Indians Last Tuesday night about midnight away up towards the Clover Bottoms on Blue Stone or Between that and the lower war Road on Blue Stone They were taken from Palser Lybrooks Sunday Last there was two Indians and a white man Only that did the mischief. they Emediately set off from there with the greatest Caution the Boys Says Walking on Stoney Hills the worst way Imaginable they have five or six small sculps, which I Imagine is Poor Lybrooks Children, as they were in A Canoe and the Boys Say they See the Indns. Sculping the Chldn. in the Canoe, they were three poor Sons of Bitches Intirely naked without Either Blankets or match Coats and the Boys Say's they were dividing their Powder with Each Other and they are Sure they had not Ten Loads. I was making up a party to Send out that

---

[96] At Burke's Garden, in Tazewell County, where James Burke had settled in 1753. The original proprietor and all his family were either killed or captured by Indians.—ED.

way where the Boys left the Indns. and I had Sent out a Sarjt. with Eight men this morning by Sun Rise up the River to go as far as Rich Creek East River and Wolf Creek[97] if they were to See any Signs Some of the party at Wood's fort was to Joyn them. there Is 15 men kept there—they had not gone more then three miles along the Road from this Place, on the North Side of the River before they Came on the Tracks of Eight or Ten Indians or whitemen that had gone Since a Grait Rain that was Yesterday about the midle of the day I know not any Chance of white men being that way unless About that number I Discharged yesterday had Delay'd their time though the Bearer Can Inform you. I Sent the party [which] was going on Search of the Indians the Boys left After these Signs nighest Home we have about 36 men here besides the party at woods though some of them has been a month out almost and Drapers & Pattons Party is Distracted to get Home already as their famylys in a great measure is the frontiers

Sir Unless you keep your own Side of the mountains well Guarded there them Stragling little partys will do Abundance of Damage where People is Gathered in forts there Ought to be men under Pay Just Ready on any Occasion these Small partys passes Scouts and Companys with out Possibly being Discovered if my Life and Honour and the Lives of all my Relations and the Lives of all my well wishers was at Stake I Can do no more then I have, or is Ever

---

[97] For Rich Creek, see *ante*, p. 112, note 62. East River and Wolf Creek are western affluents of the New, in Giles County.—ED.

Willing to do. You'l Please to make the Oficers Draft Some of their Compy. that has not yet been on Duty and Send them out, as the party that Come with me is all Expecting to Set of[f] monday Next and Against. they get Home they will be a month out I had A thought of Seting home next monday but I wont Atempt it untill I' See if we Can Rub up these Yalow Dogs A Little I supose my helpless famyly is in Great fear, and Indeed not with out Reason. Perhaps I look on you to be in A Dangerouser Station there then we are here and would advise you to keep a party Constantly on their Watch, as there is white men amongst them they Undoubtedly know men of the Best Circumstance and that is What they Generaly Aim at

Dear Sir I am Your most H^{bl}. Servant

JAMES ROBERTSON

N. B. Sir I have been in the Greatest misery Ever any felow was in, Since Last monday with A pain in my Jaw one of my Eyes Has been Shut up Ever Since and has hardly Either Eat or Slept I Declare

J R

we never heard of the Damage being done untill the Boys Came in, the party Came up Sandy and Cross by the Clover Bottoms and I Imagine is going that way Again

---

ARRANGEMENTS FOR ENLISTING

[Maj. Arthur Campbell to Col. William Preston. 3QQ75.]

ROYAL-OAK Augt. 12th 1774

SIR—Yesterday I had a meeting of the Inhabitants of the three upper Companys on this River at the

Town-House And am Sorry to find too many of the Officers making partys; in going on the Expedition, One Vance Capt. W^m. Campbells Ensign his effectually put a stop to the Men in Capt. Smiths Company from going under Capt. Russell and Joseph Drake has made a party in Capt. W^m. Campbells Company; I did all I could to divert them from such irregular proceedings; But Mr. Drake persisted and became very noisy, and nine Men which I observed was Crabtrees late adherents together with Richardson turned out and refused to go without Mr. Drake went their Officer. The Men in the other two Companys insists that they may have an Officer out of their own Company over them and that they will have no connection with Crabtrees Friends: I had tho'ts of first Ordering Mr. Drake to the Fort, but upon further consideration I will encourage the whole to go to the Camp at Mr. Thompsons; and I have left it to Capt. W^m. Campbell to make report to you, of the whole proceeding.

On my way home I met with your Letter of the 8th Ins. which was a little unlucky it came to hand so late; as I could sent the Orders From y^e. Town-House with speed to Cap^{ts}. Shelby and Russell however no time shall now be lost as I will hire Expresses, To day for that purpose

By Capt. Floyd and other accounts Capt. Russell seems now inclined to decline going on the Expedition provided he can be employed on the Frontiers. He has generously offered what Men he can raise to Capt. Floyd who is fond of going. I wish this alteration may take place; as you will soon know what Capt.

Floyds Merit on late Occasions intitles him to. And I know your willingness to serve him. Perhaps between Russell and Harrod some thing can be done and perhaps [it] may be seen proper that Herbert stays at home.

But of these matters I only aim at now giving you a hint When the whole meets at y^e. Camp at M^r. Thompsons matters can then be more precisely regulated. I shall use my utmost influence to get as many as possible started down there; and I believe several supernumery Officers which I expect when they have started that far, will choose to go as single Volunteers rather than turn back.

Want of Powder for the Forts is a general cry, indeed I dont know what they Men, that goes out will do for want of it. and I also find great difficulty of providing Flour I believe I shall have to purchase it at a certain Price at my own risque:—However I hope to receive a Letter from you in a few Days; with a further account of the Expedition and more particular extensive Orders to me if I stay at home or if you dont Order it to the contrary before that time I intend to wait on you the 20th Ins. at the Camp at M^r. Thompsons especially as several of the Officers going on the Expedition has requested it of me I shall only order a subaltern to Head of Clinch in y^e. Room of the late Capt. Doack until I see or hear from you: I believe Capt. Thompson will be deceived in geting Men without drafting however I shall wait until he makes trial. Excuse my prolixty, I heartily Wish your Family safety from so near dangerous visitants

And am Sir Your most Obedient Servant

ARTHUR CAMPBELL

ENLISTMENTS

[Col. William Preston to Maj. Arthur Campbell. 3QQ76.]

SMITHFIELD Augt. 13th. 1774

SIR—I rec^d. yours by Capt Loony, & have given him Instructions to raise a Company so as not to interfere with any of the Captains already appointed. This need not preclude Capt. Russell as his Company will also be necessary if it is Consistant with his private affairs to go out; as I am apprehensive there will be Occasion for as many as can be raised. I would be glad to know his full determination on this Head as Soon as Possible.

I wrote to you last Monday agreeable to my Promise at the meeting of the Officers. The Letter I expected the Governor would send to Colo. Lewis had not come to his hand yesterday Evening when I left that Place.

The News of Capt. Doacks Death came to me after I wrote you, So that some Lieuts, must be sent to the Head of Sandy with a proper Party to range there. I have demanded 100 Men with proper Officers from the County Lieuts. of Pittsilvania to cover the Frontiers in the absence of the Troops. Those will be employed from the Head of Clinch to Culbersons. I hope men enough can be raised in the County to guard the Western Frontier.

I can't think of applying to Capt. Herbert to drop the Expedition a Second Time, when he gave it up so genteely at first, & now he has gone so far in the Business. When the men Assemble at M^r. Thomsons I hope it will be so contrived as to give Sattisfaction to all.

I expect Major Ingles here to Day or to morrow & shall endeavour to engage him to lay in Some Flour at your House

The Governor has ordered me to Stay on the Frontiers, Colo. Byrd is gone down the Country & Colo. Christian will, I believe go on the Expedition, Therefore I cannot see how you can be Spared from Holston where it is absolutely Necessary there should be a Field Officer.

I beg of you to Press the Officers to put their men in motion, as it will encourage the People not only in this, but the Neighbouring Counties to prepare for the Journey; & indeed there is no time to be lost.

I am Sir your most Obedt Servt.

Wm. Preston

[Col. William Preston to Capt. John L. Joanes. 3QQ147.]

Smithfield Augst 13th 1774

Sir—I returned from Botetourt Court about two hours ago, I was at Colo. Lewis's yesterday Where I met with Colo. Fleeming & Colo. Christian when amongst other things which we consulted concerning the expedition it was concluded that I should write to you agreeable to my promises; and let you know that your kind offer of raising 50 men fit for the Expedition is thankfully accepted of & that you will meet with all due encouragement according to the Number of men you can engage for that necessary service. It is therefore hoped & expected that you will not Loose a moment in raising the Men & having them prepared for the journey & to march them immediately to Mr. W^m. Thompsons within Ten Miles of New River where the necessary Provisions will be prepared for them. this I hope you will be able to effect by the 24th or 25th Inst. at furthest but I would rather you Could do it sooner as the Men will Rendezvous at the Levels of greenbrier before the 30th You may assure your Men that they will be Paid & Regulated in the same manner as the militia from Fincastle and all the other Counties are & that their duty will be as easy as the nature of the service will admit at any Rate it will be no harder than our neighbours & friends who are engaged in the same service.

I would have no objections to your engageing ten or fifteen more than ye Company to stay on the Frontiers dureing the absence of the Forces these men would be under my direction & you may be assured they shall be well used Perhaps a few might engage in this part of the service that might not incline to go on the expedition but I would not have you loose a moment in Complying with this last requist as the season is so far advanced every Minute is Precious

I wish you success in Raising the men & am Sir your verry Hble Set

[WILLIAM PRESTON]

Capt. John Litton Joanes

[Col. William Preston to Capt. David Long. 3QQ140.]

S^IR—As I make no doubt but Capt. Shelby & Capt. W^m. Campbell have before this Time compleated their

Companys for the expedition & as it would be for the Honour & Interest of the County to send out a large Body of Men on the Occasion & the rather as we are not Limited to any Particular number I would therefore be glad you could raise a company capable for Service. You tell me you can get 25 or 20 Men off Watawgo provided they can have Robt. Lucas for a Lieutenant. I have no Objection to him on these Terms. Mr. John Anderson or Mr. Abraham Bledsoe[98] will be your Ensign, & I make no doubt of his endeavouring to get some Men for the service; but you must by no means attempt to engage any one man in any Company that has promised to go with either Capt. Shelby or Capt. Campbell or their Officers this would breed endless confusion and perhaps retard if not ruin the expedition

The time of Rendesvouz is near at hand therefore you have not a moment to Loose in raising prepairing & marching your men to Join the other Companies at Mr. William Thompsons should you be a Day or two behind you might overtake them before they asemble at Greenbrier. I would be glad to hear from you soon that I may act accordingly.

I wish you health & success & am Sir. yr. Hble Sert
[WILLIAM PRESTON]

August 13th 1774
To Capt David Long

---

[98] Abraham was a younger brother of Isaac and Anthony Bledsoe.—ED.

ENLISTMENTS

[Col. Andrew Lewis to Col. William Preston. 3QQ77.]

RICHFIELD[99] August y^e. 14th 1774

SIR—By John Crinar I have received 1 & 2 half barrels gun Powder. 1 ½ of which Sent by Robt. Donald. he has for you 1 ½ barrels as he tells me. I have likewise received by him 16 galls Spirits & Sundry other Articles which exclusive of the Spirits will weg^t. about 150 lbs. This I mention that on your giving him a certificat this may be included any thing else he has for ye Expedition You will Order out by Your Troops & I hop[e] you will send by them all ye powder that you can posably spare. Pray let me know as soon as Posable what Success your officers have had in Recruteing. Capt. Love will have very few Crocket Less & I am told Rentfrow will have none. it is sayed ye Little River people are all fled.[1] I am afread Draughting must [MS. torn] and this I have no opinion of I am [MS. torn.]
The Bearer had 2 Bushals Corn from me

DUNMORE PREPARES FOR WAR

[Lord Dunmore to Lord Dartmouth. 15J149.]

FREDERICK COUNTY, Aug. 14. 1774.

I wrote your Lordship that I expected a War with the Indians, since that the Shawnees, Mingoes, and

---

[99] The home of General Lewis, whither he removed from the neighborhood of Staunton in 1770. It was near Salem, on the Roanoke, then in Botetourt, now in Roanoke County.—ED.

[1] Little River is an eastern affluent of New, entering it in Montgomery County, above Ingles's Ferry.—ED.

some of the Delawares, have fallen on our frontiers, killed, scalped, and most cruelly murdered, a great many men, women and children. I have ordered out a good many parties of our Militia, one of which fell upon one of their towns called Wahatomakie on the Muskingham waters, where they took a few scalps, killed some and made one prisoner, destroyed their Town and totally erased their plantations, but I find that has not yet called those home that were out on this side of the mountain, for whilst I was at dinner yesterday, I was informed by a person who made his escape, that they were murdering a family about fourteen miles from me, but I hope in eight or ten days to march with a body of men over the Alleghany Mountains, and then down the Ohio to the mouth of the Scioto, and if I can possibly fall upon these lower towns undiscovered I think I shall be able to put an end to this most cruel war in which there is neither honor, pleasure, nor profit. Enclosed I send your Lordship the Resolutions and Instructions of the Delegates of the different counties of this Colony; and I think it is but justice to His Majesty's Attorney General here, to send your Lordship his Considerations on the present state of Virginia, published by him on this occasion.

[DUNMORE]

RAVAGES ON THE FRONTIER; RETURN OF SURVEYORS

[Extract from a letter of Col. William Preston to George Washington. 15S80.[2] Consult also letter of Preston, Aug. 13, 1774, in *Amer. Archives*, i, pp. 707, 708.]

SMITHFIELD Aug. 15th, 1774:

Mr. Thomas Hog who brought the plats of your land on Cole River from Capt. Floyd in April last with two other men has never since been heard of, so that there is no doubt of their being killed or taken, but I fear the former is the case. Capt. Floyd with three others came in last Saturday; the other surveyors with a party of men are still out, but there is some reason to hope they are safe.

* * * * * * * *

We are greatly harrassed by the enemy in this country: Abt. ten days ago, a small party killed five persons, mostly children, & took three prisoners about 15 miles from this place, which is greatly exposed. I began yesterday to build a fort about my house for the defence of my family.

McDONALD'S EXPEDITION

[Extracts from a letter from Maj. Angus McDonald to Maj. John Connolly. Reprinted from English Historical Manuscripts Commission, 11th *Report*, v, p. 359.][3]

On the 2d instant I and my party attacked the

---

[2] This extract was copied by Dr. Draper from the Washington MSS. in the State Department, Washington.—ED.

[3] The following extracts were enclosed in a letter from Thomas Walpole to the Earl of Dartmouth, dated Oct. 27.—ED.

Upper Shawnesse towns; I destroyed their corn fields, burnt their cabins, took three scalps and made one prisoner; I had two men killed and six wounded. Simon Girty[4] being returned from Wheeling to Pittsburgh gives the following information the 11th August, 1774. That he met David Owens and twelve men upon Captina, on their return from attacking the upper Shawnesse Towns, where they had been with Major McDonald,[5] who told him that the day before

---

[4] Simon Girty, frequently known as the renegade, or "White Indian," was born in Pennsylvania in 1741. At the age of fifteen he was captured by the Indians, and lived among the Seneca for three years. After his return he served as interpreter, and learning the Delaware language was made a chief of their tribe. He accompanied Dunmore as interpreter, and early in the Revolution enlisted men in the neighborhood of Fort Pitt for the Continental service. In 1778 he left Fort Pitt with McKee and Elliott, to join the British forces at Detroit. For five years he lived among the Indians, leading their raids against the border settlements—work which brought much obliquy upon him. He is said to have consented to the torture of Crawford, and is known to have been at St. Clair's defeat (1791) and Wayne's victory (1794). Soon after this he settled on the Canada side of Detroit River, where he died in 1818. See Butterfield, *History of the Girtys* (Cincinnati, 1890).—ED.

[5] Angus McDonald was a Scotch Highlander of clan Glengarry, born about 1727, and reared and educated in Glasgow. Having participated in the rebellion of 1745, he fled to America and about 1754 removed to the then far-western town of Winchester (Va.). He served in defense of the frontier during the earlier Indian wars, and retired (1763) with the rank of captain, entitling him to 2,000 acres of Virginia land, which was to be surveyed by Hancock Taylor. In 1769 he was appointed major of militia for Frederick County, and at the close of this expedition (December, 1774), lieutenant-colonel. Although a staunch Whig, he refused to enter the Continental army, being unwilling to serve second in command to a colonel without military experience. He died early in 1779. Major McDonald was a man of commanding figure and strong personality, and a rigid disciplinarian with his troops. After this Wakatomica expedition, McDonald served under

the pilots (Owens being one) had reached Wackitomika;[6] they came across an Indian coming towards them at whom Owens fired but missed him, then the guides found a horse with some baggage on him. And upon their arrival at Wackitomika, they were informed by a prisoner (afterwards taken) that this Indian was going for bears' oil at some adjacent encampment. That they encamped that night, and the next morning proceeded on their march when three men (pilots or spies) being forward they heard a kind of noise, like a cough on the path before them which alarming them, they saw an Indian coming up towards them on the road, at whom they fired but missed him, advancing a little further they perceived where the Indians had made blinds on the path side to waylay the party who they expected to be coming against them, after proceeding a little further they were fired upon by a party of Indians by which five white men were wounded and two killed; and one Indian supposed to be a Delaware also killed, but how many

---

Dunmore until the close of the war. In an autograph letter of Jan. 1775, he says "all the Country is well pleased with the Governours Expeditions." (Draper MSS., 4NN22).—ED.

[6] Wakatomica (Wapatomica) was a group of Shawnee towns on the Muskingum, in the county of that name, not far from the site of the present Dresden. These were the easternmost of the Shawnee villages, and the home of the most hostile of that tribe. Zeisberger, the Moravian missionary, preached here in 1773 and hoped for their conversion; but the wrongs of Logan and other Ohio Indians were discussed at this place with much rancor, and from here war-parties had gone out against the frontier in spite of the intercession of the friendly Delawares. Early in the summer of 1774, the Shawnee had deserted the Muskingum towns in anticipation of an attack—see *Penna. Archives,* iv, pp. 552, 554, 559; this being so long delayed, they had returned, and defended their homes against the Virginia invasion.—ED.

Indians were wounded is unknown, but they suspected there were some more either killed or wounded. Leaving 25 men to guard the wounded, they pursued the Indians into the Snakes' Town, and the advanced party observing an Indian making from the water up the bank, whom they suspecting to be in the preceding battle, fired at and wounded him, the main body then coming to the opposite side of the river to the said town, Joseph Nicholson called over to the Indians and told them that he was one of the six nations; the Indians reply and asked if he was Simon Girty, Nicholson answered that he was not Simon Girty, for that he was at Fort Pitt, upon which four of the Indians came over. Major McDonald then gave it out in orders that no white man should attempt to come near them or molest them. A council then commencing between Major McDonald and these Indians, one of his men fired across the river and killed an Indian. The Indians after receiving orders from Major McDonald to bring over two white women they had prisoners, which they promised to obey, were dismissed, however none of them returned except one Indian an Onondaga but without the prisoners, and him they detained as a prisoner. They then crossed the river and attacked the Snakes' Town, where they found some Indians on whom they fired, killed one, and one of their own men was wounded, last of all they proceeded on through the several upper towns, destroying them all and all the corn they found standing as likewise between three and four hundred bushels of old corn.[7]

---

[7] The best single account of McDonald's expedition is the unpublished one by Dr. Draper in Draper MSS., 3D5-11.

[Contemporary newspaper extract—*Maryland Journal* for Wednesday, Sept. 7, 1774. 2JJ66.]

WILLIAMSBURG, Aug. 15:

By an Express from the frontiers we learn, that Col. Mc Donald had just arrived from Wahatomakie, a Shawanese town on the Muskingum, which he has destroyed with all the plantations round it, taken three scalps, killed several of the Indians, and made one prisoner, with the loss of only two of his people & six wounded: and that an expedition is planned against some of their other towns, which, if

---

Consult also *Amer. Archives*, i, pp. 682, 684, 722–724; *Washington–Crawford Letters*, p. 95; *Penna. Archives*, iv, pp. 558, 574; Roosevelt, *Winning of the West*, i, p. 216; Withers (Thwaites ed.), *Border Warfare*, pp. 153–155; Crumrine, *Washington County, Pa.*, p. 55; Howe, *Ohio* (Cincinnati, 1852), pp. 382–384; and Jacob, *Life of Cresap*, pp. 67–70.

Early in June Dunmore planned an expedition against the Indian towns, but it was not until July that McDonald succeeded in securing a force sufficient to move out. About 400 were then recruited, chiefly on the Monongahela and Youghiogheny, under the following captains: Michael Cresap, Michael Cresap, Jr. (nephew of the preceding), Hancock Lee, Daniel Morgan, James Wood, Henry Hoagland, and probably two others. Marching across country and joining Crawford at Wheeling, where he was left in command of Fort Fincastle, McDonald ordered every man to take seven days' provisions in his pack, and crossed the river (July 26) at the mouth of Fish Creek, some twenty-four miles below Wheeling, whither they had floated down in canoes. George Rogers Clark, who had a land-claim in this vicinity, was a subaltern in Cresap's command. From the point of crossing, the towns were about ninety miles distant. No enemy was seen until within six miles of Wakatomica, where about thirty Indians awaited the columns, in ambush at the head of a swampy crossing. A slight skirmish of thirty minutes resulted in the killing of four Indians and wounding others, when the enemy broke and fled. The whites lost two killed and five wounded, among the former a frontiersman named Martin; among the latter Nathaniel Fox, William Linn, and John Hardin. Leaving a small party to care for the wounded, the army pushed on to

successful, will probably put an end to the war. Several parties of Indians are daily seen on this side of the Allegheny Mountains, but they have done little mischief of late, except scalping one family on the head of Cedar Creek.

FINCASTLE MEN MARCH OUT

[Capt. William Russell to Col. William Preston. 3QQ78.]

D^R. Col.^{o}.—I have long expected to have been releived, by Men at our Forts, that the Volunteers might

---

the Muskingum, where they arrived about nightfall of the second of August. The Indians were posted on the opposite bank, prepared to dispute the passage, and protect the first town. After some sharp-shooting, darkness put an end to the combat, and the whites withdrew to hold a council of war on the expediency of forcing passage across the stream. Cresap's and Hoagland's companies were detached to deploy some miles below, and at the break of day cross and make a flank movement on the towns. Meanwhile an interpreter brought in a Delaware and Mingo, who requested peace. The former was told that strict orders had been issued to molest no friendly Indians, the latter was sent to bring hostages from the Shawnee. He returned later unsuccessful, and was the prisoner brought back by the expedition. Cresap spent the night in preparation, and moved out two hours before dawn, crossed the river, and had a slight skirmish in which the leader himself killed one Indian, and others were wounded. The towns were found abandoned. After burning five villages, and cutting down seventy acres of standing corn, the army, then almost entirely destitute of provisions, crossed country to Wheeling. A small party of Pennsylvanians, led by Devereux Smith, and of Delaware Indians under White Eyes, had come to Wheeling two days after the army had started on their out-going march. Crawford discouraged their attempting to overtake the expedition, whereupon they returned to Pittsburg. The results of the expedition were slight, ravages upon the frontiers thereafter increasing rather than diminishing. But the body of men who had been enlisted, awaited at Redstone the wing of the army taken out by Lord Dunmore.—ED.

COMMISSION OF CAPT. GEORGE ROGERS CLARK, IN THE DUNMORE WAR

Reduced facsimile from original in the Draper MSS.—48J1

March, to the appointed place of Rendezvous: such relief was promised the Men when they Engaged and such they must have; other ways are ready, only some brown Linen which Mr. Brander told me, should be up before the Army Marched from Rendezvous. I have been apply'd to by Majr. Campbell to resign my Interest to Capt. Floyd, of the Volunteers: this [I] wood gladly do, to serve my good Friend; which I proposed to himselfe, and am still Anxious, if I can get the Command of a Company on Clinch, till his return, or at least as long as it shall be thought necessary, to keep Men under pay, in this Quarter.

I have heard Capt. Thompson is appointed to Command a Company at Blackmores, should I be granted a Command, and it shall be agreeable to you, and Capt. Thompson, should be proud it could be your pleasure, to appoint him towards the head of the River, as that will give him a more Immediate opportunity, of Securing the Inhabitants about his Fathers, and even his own, and I think Sir You will think it absolutely necessary to have two Captains to Command on Clinch, at this Critical season, that ought to be Ranging, besides those in the Forts, as Constant Guards, to the Inhabitants.

Could I meet with this Indulgence, will use all my endeavours to get the Men to go with Capt. Floyd, as it is my sinceer desire [to] serve him: but otherways must still hope for your promisd favours, of Joining some of the Ensigns Recruits in the County, to my Company to Complete it; there are about thirty that will certainly go with me; and Capt. Smith says Wm.

Bowen[8] has about four with him that will gladly go with me; I hope to have Orders (if my next is to march for the Expedition) to take Horses proportionable, with what has been granted to Capt. Shelby, as the Men look for the same Indulgence. I hope to here from You as soon as possible, in the Interim, relying on your Charatable, and beneign Endeavoures to serve me, subscribe my selfe Dr. Colo.

your Most Obedt Humb. Servt.

W Russell

F^T. Preston August the 16th. 1774

N. B. The Scout give Accts of Scattering Tracts, about Powels Mt^n. supposed to be Indians

On his Majestys Service To Col^o. William Preston on New River P^r. fav. of Mj^r. Campbell

---

[Maj. Arthur Campbell to Col. William Preston. 3QQ80.]

Sir—About ten Minutes ago I Received yours of the 17th and as I have now an Oppertunity by Mr. Logan will write to Capt. Looney. I wrote Capt. Russell Yesterday much to the same purport you now desire me and shall now press him more earnestly, not to loose a moment. I expect he will be at New

---

[8] William Bowen was born in Maryland in 1744. When very young he emigrated to Augusta County, and as a lad of fifteen joined Christian in pursuit of an Indian party (1759). At the battle of Point Pleasant, he had a terrific hand-to-hand struggle with an Indian antagonist, whom he finally overpowered. Ten years later (1784), he removed to what is now Sumner County, Tenn., where he passed the remainder of his life. (Information furnished Dr. Draper by his daughter in 1844. Draper MSS., 6C17).—Ed.

River by the 26th. This day the Capts. Shelby, Wm. Campbell & Harwood [Herbert] March in high Spirits from this place with upwards of 80 Men Looney and Drake has done hurt to Shelby, & Billey Campbell and one Vance has done the like in Capt. Smiths company to the prejudice of Russell, however I will endeavour to humour all parties until the[y] come to rendezvous, and perhaps you can fall on some method then for the best, as I now find most of the Men would make it a matter of indifference, to join their first proposed Officers, and go on the Expedition cheerfully If some matters is once explained by you: in regard to their pay. I propose meeting you at Mr. Thompsons against ye. 22d. That I may receive Orders fully in regard how I am to act on the Frontier; and I wish you to be there to Review the Holston Voluntiers.

I am Sir [MS. torn] most Humble Servt.

[MS. torn] CAMPBELL

ROYAL-OAK Augt. 19th. 1774

On his Majestys Service To Colo. William Preston

AUGUSTA COUNTY CONTINGENT

[Rev. John Brown to Col. William Preston. 3QQ81.]

VERY DR. SIR—The frequent alarms that reach my Ears from your quarter of the Indians appearing & killing your Neighbours gives me a melancholy damp, when I think on your dangerous situation, & your confinement to it, by both your Business & honour, that forbidd your moving from it. I hope your prudence will direct you to every apparent method that will tend to secure your dr. Family from the barbarious intention of the heathen, as it is in your power to order men for the deffence of the Fronteers; let not your Courage or modesty prevent keeping a sufficient gaurd about your own House as a means of preservation. I trust in God that he will preserve (my dr. Friend) from all Enemies.

I was in Town last week Capt. Mathies[9] & Mc Clanachan[10] Marched with noble Companies all cheerfully

---

[9] Capt. George Matthews was of Irish descent, born in Augusta County in 1739. At the age of twenty-two he pursued a raiding party of Indians, and defeated and killed nine of their number. After the battle of Point Pleasant, he joined the Revolutionary army as colonel of the 9th Virginia, was captured at the battle of Germantown, and confined upon a prison ship in New York harbor until his exchange (1781), in time to join Greene's army at the head of the 3d Virginia regiment. A few years later he removed to Georgia, and was twice governor of the state (1787-89; 1793-96). In his first term he befriended Sevier and the Franklin government; in his second, he signed the notorious Yazoo acts, and although not charged with personal corruption was discredited therefor. He was a member of the Georgia constitutional convention, and first representative in congress from the state. In 1811 he was appointed commissioner to settle the East Florida troubles, and in 1812 incited a rebellion therein against Spanish authority, which the government at Washington suppressed and repudiated. Matthew's anger thereat was great, and he started for Washington to remonstrate with the authorities, but was taken ill of a fever and died at Augusta, Ga. (1812). He was a unique and pronounced character. For personal anecdotes see Gilmer, *First Settlers of Upper Georgia* (New York, 1855). The officers of his company in Lord Dunmore's War, according to Draper MSS., 2ZZ52, were: William Robertson, 1st lieutenant; George Gibson, 2nd lieutenant; William Kennerly, sergeant, the latter being left with sixteen men in command of a Greenbrier fort.—Ed.

[10] The McClanahans were a prominent family of Augusta County. Robert, the father, settled near Staunton about 1735; he was in command of the militia, and high sheriff until 1709. Two sons commanded companies in Lord Dunmore's War.

DEFENSE OF FRONTIER 161

willing to go to the Shanee towns. Capt. McDowel[11] marched thursday last; but had not the number of men allotted to him by the Colo. viz. 75. I understand that 25 that were drafted refuse to go with him & design to run the hazzard of the fine I am sorry that both parents & those that have refused speak & act so unreasonablly relative to the present expedition, but men act like themselves.

I am dr. sr. your Brother in the Strictest friendship
JOHN BROWN
August 22d. 1774
To Col. William Preston in Smith-Fields N. River

DEFENSE OF FRONTIER

[Col. William Preston to Maj. Arthur Campbell. 3QQ82.]

SIR—Agreeable to the Conclusion come to by a Council of the Militia Officers of this County, the second of this Month, for the Defence of the Frontiers, in the absence of the Troops,[12] I ordered Capt. Thompson with sixty men to guard the lower settlements on Clinch, which Duty I suppose he is upon by or before this time; & as the upper Settlements are still uncovered, I would have you appoint Capt. Daniel Smith to that Service, with such Officers as you think

---

This was the elder, Alexander, named for his maternal grandfather, Alexander Breckinridge. He was colonel of the 7th Virginia in the Revolution, resigning in 1778; later, he was county clerk of Augusta for many years. His wife was a sister of Patrick Henry's first wife.—ED.

[11] Capt. Samuel McDowell, see *ante*, p. 25, note 41.—ED.

[12] The Indians continued their depredations; see reports in *Amer. Archives*, i, p. 737.—ED.

proper; & there must be thirty men draughted from Capt. Herbert's & the late Capt. Doacks Companies. The men are to be disposed of along that Frontier as was agreed on at the meeting of the Officers above mentioned. In appointing the Subalterns, I would recommend it to you to send them from the Companies which produces most men; And you are to be particularly careful that each person concerned, performs the Duty incumbent on him.

I would also request that you would examine carefully into the number of Scouts on that Quarter, & if you see it necessary, to abridge them. You will likewise make enquiry, how they, & each of them, have performed the trust reposed in them, and make report to me accordingly.

W^M. PRESTON,

[To Major Campbell]
Augt. 25th. 1774

[Maj. Arthur Campbell to Col. William Preston. 3QQ83.]

ROYAL OAK Augt. 26. 1774

SIR—By a Petition I seen to day and the information of Capt. Russell and Smith, it appears that the Inhabitants on Clinch, desire to be employed in the Service; the[y] further intimated that the[y] hoped you would enlarge the Number on Duty; this I could by no means en[cou]rage until I had Orders from you: This far I let th[e] Gentlemen know, that the Inhabitants that strictly did regular Duty might be continued on the Lists unti[l] a sufficient Number of Draughts might arrive to compleat the Companys, and

RECRUITING 163

then I would recommend it to the Officers to keep the best Woodsmen of ye Inhabitants in pay for the purpose of ranging in preference to any that might offer themselves from Holston or New-River; This much don't seem to give satisfaction I would therefore be glad to receive your particular Orders on this subject; I am afraid if the Inhabit[ants] is not indulged in some measure at least: that the[y] may lea[ve] the settlement. Capt. Smith informs me that he thin[ks] there was an Indian in his Cornfield a few Days ago It is likely some scattering fellows is about, for what intent I cannot certainly judge

I am Sir Your most Humble Servt

ARTHUR CAMPBELL

To Colo. William Preston

RECRUITING FOR THE EXPEDITION

[Capt. John Floyd to Col. William Preston. 33S35-49.]

ROYAL OAK, 26th Aug. 1774.

Dr. SIR—I have engaged only 3 men on my way to this place; there are several others about the Mines & Cripple creek;[18] I have sent Ephm. Drake that way with a few lines, who says he makes no doubt of getting eight more: There are four on the south fork which I am told will go with me. I can't inform you how many Jos. Drake has got since; but I understood there are near forty at the Town House waiting till I

---

[18] For the lead mines near Fort Chiswell, see *ante,* p. 52, note 90. Cripple Creek is a tributary of the upper New River, whose waters interlace with those of the upper Holston.—ED.

go down; he writes me that the men wouldn't go on as you directed before he started himself, & now declare they will not go under any Captain except he is also along. I am told he disclosed his orders before he endeavored to send down the men; but by his letter to me it is not so. Major Campbell & his brother are much incensed against him, & I understand the Major has sent word to Capt. Shelby that Drake is stopping his men as they come by, but I am told he has only engaged two that came from Watauga. I hope you will not take too much notice of news you hear before I go down, & I'll write you exactly how it is. I shall use my endeavors to send down every man to their captain if I find they had promised them to go; but if they will not go under any of the officers already marched, I shall bring all I can, & the matter may be settled when they all meet. Upon the whole I make no doubt of getting my number of men & overtake the army in due time.

You will hear by Capt. Russell of the death of Mr. H. Taylor & one of his company, my poor brother sufferers, whose death I hope to revenge yet.[14]

I am Dr. Sir, yours affectionately, while

Jn. Floyd.

To Col⁰. Wᵐ. Preston   Fincastle   Pʳ. Capt. Russell

Col. Wᴍ. Preston, Dear Sir—The chief of the men Mr. Drake has engaged, as well as those he before

---

[14] Hancock Taylor, the surveyor who was killed by Indians in Kentucky, together with one James Strother. See *ante*, p. 23, note 38.—Ed.

promised, are now ready to march. There were five men of the number he before promised that have already gone and joined their captains: He will let you know who they are, & also tell you how many of those with him were listed since he last returned. There are ten on the way from Watago, & we expect some from Clinch. I should be glad M^r. Drake could return & assist me; you may depend on my sending down all the men as fast as they are ready. Perhaps if M^r. Drake should not return, those from Watago may not be so well satisfied, as I am not acquainted with them.

If M^r. Bledsoe resigns his interest to us, I think we can soon be ready to follow the army, which I shall know immediately on his brother's return from Carolina which he hourly expects. M^r. Drake can inform you how things are here better than I can write, as he is in haste. Pray let have the news, if any, by all opportunities. I am D^r. Sir your most obt. servant,

J^N. FLOYD.

29[27]th Aug. 1774.[15]

P. S. The six men that joined their captains are— W^m. Rodgers, W^m. Fowler, Thos. Baker,—Horn, James Barnet, &—Champe.

TOWN HOUSE, August 28th. 1774

MY DEAR SIR—I this moment rec^d. yours, & have prevailed with the men to march down with Vance.

---

[15] In the copy, the letter is dated 29th Aug.; but as it is placed before the letters of the 28th, and the context seems to show precedence, the assumption is it should be the 27th.—ED.

I have promised them nothing in particular, but told them when they came to you they would be dealt fairly & candidly with, & that you would do everything in your power to make them easy. The chief of the men, I think, wants to go with us; I have told them if they were not satisfied, we should endeavor to exchange one for another.

I read part of your letter to them which seems to make them fully satisfied. I wrote you yesterday that I made no doubt of raising my company, but when I came to enquire particularly of Drake, I find he has engaged but few, I imagine about 15 with what I engaged going out: Had I not recd. your letter, I was in a fair way to get the men sent down with Vance. There are several of the men engaged with Drake who did not live in Mr. Campbell's bounds, & others that did not live in the colony, but I have sent them all along. My dearest friend, I know you are often confused & put out of humor with settling differences. I shall endeavor to carry on things here in such a manner as to give you as little concern as possible; but I now wish I had done as I think you would have advised me if you had not seen I was anxious to go— but I always intended, & for the future always will be directed by you in all my future undertakings. You are sensible of the expense I have been at, and as I have undertaken it I would willingly go. Capt. Bledsoe has wrote you about going out, but does not know whether it will be agreeable to you, but he is now here & says if has not fortune in getting men from Carolina by his brother, he will resign his interest and assist me all he can. If he has done anything that may displease you, pray write kindly to him as I think it may be an advantage to me as I know with his help I can get a company. Vance thinks you'll be angry with him, & says that he has done nothing that he thought contrary to your orders, please to speak calmly to him & the men, & endeavor to satisfy them, as they rely much on what you wrote me. They are not all ready, but shall try to start them this evening or soon of the morning. I have heard every man's sentiments with regard to Joseph Drake's conduct & upon the whole when you are made more sensible of it, I hope you will not be quite of the same opinion. Mr. Lewis's certificate I think you may rely on. I think the men yet expect to go with us, as they say Capt. Campbell has his full company, & suppose it will make no difference with him; but I know they will do as you order them. I am unwell and confused by people pressing on me to hear news; but I will write you again by every opportunity

August 28th. 1774.

Dr. Sir—I thought a few hours ago I had everything in order, & the soldiers to march down immediately with Vance; since which Vance has refused to go, the men revolted & say (the greatest part of them) they will go with nobody but Capt. Drake, who was not here when the men agreed to go with Vance. Billy Bowen can tell you by word better how it is, or how he thinks it is managed. I cannot judge what is the reason why Vance declines, or why the men refuse to go without Drake. Since the men are last determined, they blame me and say I wanted them to go with Vance to get some of my own ends answered. In short, my dear sir, I don't know upon what terms I am here myself; I again wish I never had undertaken any such thing as raising a company, but as I have, I would not be disappointed for a £100, as I never yet undertook with more ardency.

You will hear of Mr. Boone's return, & desire of going out.[16] If Mr. Drake gets a birth down there & does not immediately return to me, & assist according to your instructions, I may let Boone join me and try. Capt. Bledsoe says Boone has more interest [influence] than any man now disengaged; & you know what Boone has done for me by your kind directions, for which reason I love the man. But yet do as you think proper in every thing respecting me. Drake wants to see you, he says, to clear up his character. Pray let me hear from you by Mr. Ramsey,[17] or if he has come away by the first opportunity possible, & excuse my letter, for I am angry, confused & sick.

Jn. Floyd.

---

[16] Boone reached the settlements Aug. 27th. See *ante*, for his setting out.—Ed.

[17] Josiah Ramsey, son of Thomas, of western Virginia, was captured by Indians when a child, being returned to the settlements after Bouquet's treaty (1764). He was at the battle of Point Pleasant, and suffered from lack of provisions on the homeward route. He was a scout in the Cherokee campaign of 1776; and in 1780 removed to Kentucky, the next year going to the Cumberland settlement, where he was major of militia, and frequently served against the Indians. He died at an advanced age, at his son's home in Missouri. See Draper MSS., 5S57–63.—Ed.

RECRUITING

[Anthony Bledsoe to Col. William Preston. 3QQ86.]

Town house Augt. 28th. 1774

Sir—The call of the Contrey on me for my Cattle hath detained me from making so great a Progress in Rasing a Company as I otherways should have done, after what pas'd at Court at the Council of Officers I concluded if you ware Desirous that I should have recruited a Company, in North Carolinia, you would have given me orders for that Purpose, on my receiving Col^o. Christians Instructions I declair'd my Intentions to go on the Expedition and engaged some men, not thinking it might give umbraige to any Gen^t. and am heartyly sorry to be inform's it Disaffected you at my Proceedings, I should not have Attempted it had it not been the Officers from those Parts had marched

I sent to Carolinia as I look'd on [considered that] the delay of the Cattle might be more disagreeable then the delay of fifty Men, I have not yet had any return from Carolinia until Which return I shall Continue to engage all the men in these Parts, except forbid by your Orders. I hope you will Condescend to give me all Indulgence the nature of the case will allow. I am desirous of Gowing on the Expedition and have at all Times shewed a Willingness to Serve my Contrey in any Station Whereunto I was call'd, your perticular Instructions by M^r. Ramsey will greatly oblige

Dear Sir your most hum^l Servt

Anthony Bledsoe

N. B. Please to excuse hast

On his Majestys Service To Col^o. William Preston Pr Fav^r. of M^r. Ramsey

[Maj. Arthur Campbell to Col. William Preston. 3QQ85.]

S ir—This morning I went to the Town-House with Mr. Bowen; As Capt. W^m. Campbell requested me in Order to notify some of his Men that former faults or breaches of their Words would now be overlook'd, provided the[y] march^d. to the Camp according to your directions: All the Men I conversed with seem'd very well agreed to what I told them and professed an anxiety to go on the Expedition without loss of time. Capt. Floyd communicated your Instructions to Vance which he agreed to: soon after Mr. Drake came, and your letter was delivered him, he seemed confused for some time at length I observ'd him to have several private consultations with Vance and some of the Men, after which it was signified to me that Vance would not March to the Camp; although he had agreed to do so not an Hour before. I then asked and required him in a public Manner to go which he also refused; Mr. Bowen was then proposed to march the men down: when Mr. Drake interposed in a Clamourous manner, and said, he would March them down himself. He was expostulated with on the impropriety of such a proceedure since your Orders could not then be obey'd in assisting Capt. Floyd to raise his Company: however he obstinately persisted, and I was not willing to bring matters here to any further hight, and then agreed to furnish him with provisions for the Journey and Vance immediately went off home. I don't know by what term to express the idea I have of Mr. Drakes Character and behaviour it seems to be a complication of such Qualities as deserves a

RECRUITING

very coarse name; I should have tho't according to my idea of Military regulations; that if the first Officers in the county under you, had, so prevaricated, and trampled on Orders the[y] would deserve to be severely cashiered; But these matters you know best how to manage at this critical juncture.

Capt. Floyd seems uneasy at the way Drake has used him as he now plainly discovers, that he was expecting to be appointed to a separate command. For this reason and to relieve Mr. Floyds anxiety I wrote pressingly to Mr. Boon to raise men with all expedition to join Capt. Floyd; and I did not doubt but you would do everything in your power to encourage him. And what induced me particularly to apply to Mr. Boon was seeing his Journal last Night, and a Letter to Capt. Russell wherein he professes a great desire to go on the Expedition, & I am well informed he is a very popular Officer where he is known So I hope Capt. Floyd will still succeed as I have good reason to believe Mr. Boon will get all in Capt. Looneys Company that intended to go with Bledsoe, and perhaps you can asist a Little out of Waggoners recruits as I have heard to day he is likely to get some Men. I have been informed that Mr. Boon tract a small party of Indians from Cumberland Gap, to near the Settlement, upon this intelligence I wrote pressingly to Capt. Thompson to have a constant look out and to urge the Spys strictly to do their duty

I am embarrassed about geting Flour, Billy Sayers[18] half says he can get some, but I believe he is

---

[18] The Sayers were one of the earliest families to remove to Fincastle County, of which William Sayers was deputy sheriff in 1776.—ED.

not to be depended on, I have purchased some Corn, which the men must do with until a supply can be got of Flour. I was apply'd to Yesterday to know if Crabtree could be taken into the service at the Forts; I discouraged such a step but agreed I would inform you, and be guided accordingly. It may be best not to drive the Wretch to despair at this time. Donelson can easily be taken if there is a Warrant sent.

I am Sir with much Esteem Your most Humble Servant

ARTHUR CAMPBELL

Aug^s. 28th. 1774

[Capt. William Russell to Col. William Preston. 3QQ84.]

DR. COLO.—I have got as fare as Mr. Branders with a handful of Men out of my own Company. I think our Number of private Men is thirty one; in what Manner our Company is to be compleated; you, I hope can best Determin. the Men I' have, are fit for the business, but are badly fix'd, for want of Hunting shirts, and Blankets; but as I hear Mr. Branders Waggon, is on this side New River; I hope we shall get supply'd. Mr. Jno. Green and three others of Mr. Taylors Company have Arrived on Clinch,[19] but did not see them, as they only came to Blackmores the Night before we Started: and this Day an Express, from Mr. Boone overtook me, to informe me of his return; and desire, to go on the Expedition. Mr. Taylor with two others of his Company was fired on

---

[19] John Bell, Abraham Hempinstall, and one whose name has not been preserved.—ED.

by the Indians, in the Kentuck, on their way down the River, to bring up some Provisions &c, they had left. Mr. Taylor Received two balls in his Boddy, one of which proved Mortal: he traveled two or three days, and his Company carried him, two more; before his Death: the Company Buried him the first of this Instant: one more of the Compy. was shot ded in the Canoe but the Works are brought in, except one Survey.

I hope to be near the Camp, at Mr. Thompsons tomorrow night, if not quite there; when I hope to see You, and Colo. Christian, with the other Gentlemen for the Expedition. I shall be glad Sir., if it can be done, to have a Gun provided against we come down, as I have a very good Hand without: when I was in the service before, there was near twenty press'd Guns: which the Country freely pay'd for, and I doubt not, but the same necessity will be allowed now. Till I have the pleasure to see you; am Dr. Colo.

your most Obedt. Humb. servt.

W. RUSSELL

Sunday August the 28th. 1774
[Enclosure in above.]

To Col. William Preston at Camp at Capt. Thompsons pr. David Gass[20]

---

[20] David Gass was a native of Pennsylvania, born about 1729. In early life he removed to Albemarle County, Va., and about 1769 came out to Castle Woods, on Clinch. He prepared to remove with his family to Kentucky, in Boone's company (1773); but the party were deterred by the killing of Boone's and Russell's sons, and returned to the Clinch, where the Boones passed the next few years, neighbors to the Gass family. In 1774, Gass was employed as a scout, and the next year went with Boone to Kentucky, where he died in Madison County (1806). These facts were obtained from correspondence with his son. See Draper MSS., 24C74, 84, 92.—ED.

Recd from Robt Preston[21] for the Use of the Expedition the Articles following Viz one Cask of Powder & 250lb of Lead Nine sacks of Salt & twenty nine Axes also two baggs Witness my hand this 27th Day of August 1774

W: BUCHANAN[22]

[James Robertson to Col. William Preston. 3QQ88.]

SIR—I thought to been at your House friday or saturday but Cannot be there untill Sunday night or monday. I have been through the whole Company and meets with poor Success though picked up Some. I Gather them all Together Saturday and Pretends to make A Draft by your Orders I tell them, and dont want to Concern with any that has famylys, but Only these Hulking younge dogs that Can be well Spar'd. if you please give me a Line or two to Back me I would be Glad you would desire the Oficers in Capt. Cloyd's and Capt. Taylers Compy. to Stir up Some Backward Scoundr[els] in their Companys to turn Out or Else force them for no Honour nor Intreateys

---

[21] Robert Preston was a distant relative of Col. William, and became first surveyor of Washington County, which office he held for over fifty years. He left a large patrimony to his son John, who married Margaret, daughter of Col. William Preston.—ED.

[22] William Buchanan was afterwards (1776) captain of a militia company from Montgomery County, employed in rangranging in Kentucky. A tree in Warren County, of the latter state, bore his name with the inscription "1775." In 1778, he was at Boonesborough, being one of the nine selected to treat with the Indians, from whom they had a narrow escape. He was killed in Holder's Defeat (1782), and left no descendants.—ED.

will move them. I Could Stay untill the midle of next week and Overtake the Army before they go to the falls. Perhaps you have Seen Some what of Capt. Woods, or heard what number he has to Joyn us
I am Sir Your Obedt. Servant

JAMES ROBERTSON

1st. of Sep br. 1774
To Colo. William Preston   Pr Mr. Thos. Lewis

N. B. I have had more uneaseyness this Eight days Amongst these Deels Buckeys then I have had this three years there is some procarious Gent. amongst us who makes some mutiny amongst the men as they want Compns.

[Michael Woods to Col. William Preston. 3QQ88.]

I thought to have Come over to you my Selfe to Recd., Such order as you Should think fit: but I am Disappointed in geting a horse: therefore I thought it was proper to acquaint you that I have got about 14 men that appears to be willing to go to the Shawanese towns; also to Let you know that there is some that has Engaged with me some time agone that Refuses: besides there is several in those parts that has little or nothing to Keep them Excepting hunting and Killing of the Dear: therefore Sir I hope you will send me orders how to proceed with such persons: also to Let you know that I Expect Mr. Stephen Inglish up out of pitsylvenia County with about 20 or 25 Men with him for me and whether I am disappointed of them or not I am will[ing] to Join Companies with

Mjor. Robertson as I do not Expect to make up a full Company my self
All from yr. Servt. at Command

MICHAEL WOODS[23]

3 Sept. 1774
To Coln. William Preston in fincastle County

MARCHING TO THE RENDEZVOUS

[Col. William Christian to Col. William Preston. 3QQ89.]

HEAD OF RICH CREEK, Septr. 3: 1774

SIR—Yesterday I reached this place, which is about 32 miles from Mr. Thompsons & about 42 from the levels. I am greatly detained by the Cattle as they are long gathering every morning, there are now about 200.

I have lodged at Woods Fort between 7 and eight hundred pounds of Flour, as it would have been more than a days journey out of our way to have gone near there. I have ordered four of the men in pay at Woods fort to take over to your house some horses with bad Saddles & some with none, as I heard you proposed that they should be better fixed, and sent with the other Men.

I have desired Capt Wood to go over to your house this day to see what he is to do: I told him he had

---

[23] Michael Woods was one of the first emigrants to the Valley of Virginia, coming through Wood's Gap and settling west of the Blue Ridge about 1734. The Captain Woods who indites this letter was probably a grandson of the pioneer settler.—ED.

better join Maj^r. Robertson; which he inclines to do as he comes along.

I think it will be next tuesday before we can get to the rendezvous this day is rainey & I doubt we can go but a little way; several of our horses are not found, altho it is at least 10 OClock in the day. The Cattle cannot travel in the heat of the day. we are also much plagued with the pack horses.

I will inclose you a return of the Men, which is the same or nearly as at Mr Thompsons, none have deserted since. Jacob Starn & Thomas Robinson from Capt. Herberts, and Joseph McCall from Capt Crockets, I did not know of the last until the day after we marched. I wish you would Advertize them as Deserters

Capt. Thompsons men say that you did promise them that John Read should neither draw pay nor act as Ensign in Capt. Campbells Comp^y, some of them say you told them so in the house after what passed out of doors, which they can make oath to. I mention this, that you may know every circumstance, M^r. Read still says he thinks he can make himself agreeable.

I am informed that Men & provisions were moving from Stanton Wednesday and thursday was a week and that several Comp^{ys} were at the Warm Springs. It is also said Mathews dont propose taking out all the flour at once, but to send back the pack horses from the mouth of Elk. That L^d. Dunmore wrote to Ch. Lewis that some of his men had taken some little Towns & killed three or [four] people & that his Lordship was at fort Pitt. The above news came by one of the Woods's. He says also that there is Jents plenty and all goods necessary for the men such as Shirts Blankets Leggons.

Stevens is just come and says that Drake came down with the Men & that you had prevailed on those of D. Smiths Compy to Join Capt. Russell but says he did not understand anything was done about Capt. Campbells men as he thinks the men insisted Mr Campbell had no right to them. Capt Campbell says that several of them were of his own Compy at Holston & even some of them turned out as volunteers, at Clinch to go with him, which he is sure they would have done, had they been dealt with in the same manner he did with other Companys, & he still thinks he ought to have them

Capt. Shelby bids me also mention that he expects you will order his men to Join him.

Capt. Shelby and Capt. Campbell both desires me to write to you that as they have both been at great trouble &c that they hope you will at least direct that all those men they claim & have a right to may be Joined in their pay rolls, several men are Sick, Two of the Packmen have the fever & ague and must be left at Woods: they catched it I suppose at the big lick

Majr. Robertson, if he has no Cattle may get here easy in two days & to the levels in two more: I hope to see him there next week. I could wish we had 300 men before we march from there. tis reported here that the first party Marches next tuesday, but no certainty

I shall write you at large from the levels by Allsup, I take him there on purpose.

THE COMMISSARIAT 179

Capt Herbert wants Jamey Newell to Act as Ensign & to take his Chance of pay. I told him I thought you had no objections
I would be glad of a Letter from you by Majr. Robertson about every particular step you would have me take.
I am sir with respect yr. Servant
W^M. CHRISTIAN

Capt. Crocket & Draper sets up a claim to the two Manifields & Grayson because they were in Madisons Compy. where Draper lived Since I wrote the Captains, desire me to write that they dont propose, or desire that you should take any step that would make the men run away, but begs that you will give me directions what to do in it

Colo. Wm. Preston Smithfield

PROVISIONING THE EXPEDITION

[James Robertson to Col. William Preston. 3QQ91.]

SIR—I am this minet Return'd from Greasey Creek after a parcel of Fellows that Engagd with Tomey Ingles[24] Some time Agoe they are Every one of them

---

[24] Thomas Ingles, son of William and Mary, was captured with his mother (1755) when about four years old. His parents did not succeed in recovering him from the Indians until 1768, when he was found to be practically a young Indian in his habits and manner of living. Sent to Dr. Thomas Walker of Albemarle County, he acquired something of an education during the next three or four years; but he never became entirely accustomed to civilized life. During his

gone to ye mountains for fear. The Orders you Sent me I will put in Execution with the Help of my good Freind Davey Hughs. I apointed a muster Yesterday and Left Some of the Clevir fellows that goes with me to do what they Could, but not one of the younge fellows Apeared that Could go I would [have] Sent you 3 or 4 Beaves Yesterday but Could not find them untill to day I will send them to morow there is no word yet from Madison or Kent about the flower. Jacob Lorton told me that Joe Gray had 200 Bushels of Corn he would fondly spare to ye Expedition as the mill is handy to it you might perhaps be supplyd. there is Two Cursed Scoundrels Old Pate and his son Jacob has Corn Beef and Old Bacon Plenty to Spare and will by no means Let it go with out the Ready Cash I would fondly furnish them, from what I Imagine they do all they Can to Hurt the Expedition

    I am Dr. Sir your H{bl}. Servant

                      JAMES ROBERTSON

4th Septr. 1774

N, B. the Bearer is in want of A gun and has no Chance of Geting One I wish we Could fall on Some Method to furnish him Perhaps you Could Spare him one   J R

    To Col. William Preston pr. Favour of Mr. David Hughs

---

winter at Point Pleasant, where he remained in garrison after the battle, he visited his Indian friends on the Scioto. The following year he married and settled at various places in southwestern Virginia, where in 1782 his wife was captured and his home burned by Indian marauders. Later he removed to Tennessee, thence to Mississippi, where he finally died. See Hale, *Trans-Allegheny Pioneers*, pp. 115-143.—ED.

THE CAMP AT GREENBRIER

[Col. William Fleming to his wife. 2ZZ1.]

Union Camp on the Levels G[reen] B[rier][25] Sept[r]. 4. 1774

My D[r]. Nancy.—I have by Accident met with an Opportunity to the Court house, and am in hopes it will reach you. I reached this place on Monday last having delayed a day or two on purpose to fall in with some provision eschorts tho without effect. I found Col Charles Lewis here from Augusta there will be Six hundred or near it from that County. Col[o] Lewis came here the first Sept[r]. and Companies have been coming in every day, since. a party Marches to morrow or next day, to fall somewhere on New River near Kellys place I imagine it will be the Augusta Voluntiers. when I shall march will be uncertain. there are some Indian Spies attending us, and now and then firing on a stragling person they can have an advantage over, that is not too near the camp. as our motions will fully imploy them I think the Inhabitants will be altogether safe whilst we are out, and would not have you give way to Apprehensions of dainger. Col Lewis informs me he has ordered three Men to Belmont,[26] if they behave well, with Allen & the other, they will

---

[25] The place was designated as Camp Union because the forces from the different counties were here united. The rendezvous chosen was known as "The Savannah" or "Big Levels of the Greenbrier," where an early settlement had been raided by Comstock in 1763. The fort at this place was again attacked in 1778, in revenge for Cornstalk's murder. The town of Lewisburg was established here by law in 1782.—Ed.

[26] In 1768 Colonel Fleming removed to an estate in Montgomery (then Botetourt) County, which he named Belmont, where he resided the remainder of his life.—Ed.

be sufficient if they are troublesome Capt Trigg who I understand commands the Compy. will Chainge them, should you be Apprehensive of dainger, or dismiss them alltogether at your discretion. there has bein no damage done here since we came out, but one man Slightly wounded, and one Shot through the Jaw these were country People near little Forts about 3 miles from this. there are not above two parties of Indians of three or four in each party on these fronteers so that you must give no Attention to any Reports you hear that may Allarm You. I am thus perticular to remove any uneasiness you might be under. I have been in good health since I left home, and have met with nothing that gives me uneasiness, but the Absence of my horses. I imagine they have made homewards from this place, and mention'd it that should they get home you need not be surprized. or if they are taken up, you may chance to hear of them, and get them. I have inclos'd a description of them as I advertized them in a Camp advertizement. I have nothing more perticular to write but Sentiments not proper to commit to paper, you know my warmest wishes are for your and my Lenny[27] happiness. I shall take Opportunities as they offer to Acquaint you with our Motions. Remember me to all My Friends. And believe me faithfully Yours whilst

Wm. Fleming

P. S. I expect your brother here this week.[28]

To Mrs. Fleming, Belmont. Recommended to the care of Mr Pat^k Lockheart Merch^t. Botetourt

---

[27] Leonard Israel Fleming, eldest son of the writer, was born in June, 1764. In later life he became a pioneer of Kentucky.—Ed

[28] Col. William Christian.—Ed.

AT CAMP UNION

[Col. William Fleming to his wife. 2ZZ2.]

Union Camp Septr. 7. 1774

My Dearest Nancy—I have an Opportunity which I gladly embrace to let you hear that I am well, I wrote to you once since we reach'd this Place, which I imagine you have receiv'd we have had nothing happen'd new since. Your Brother & the Companies from Fincastle reach'd this place Yesterday Mr. Jones informd me, he cal'd, and that you were all well & that you were in good Spirits. this gave me great satisfaction. Trust in God and you need have no fear. I wrote you that my horses were Missing and that I imagined they were gone homewards. I have got them again so that I am as easy as a person can be that has left so near & dear conections behind him. but consider my D^r. Girl the Cause engaged in is a good one, and Our Seperation only for a small time. but I must stop writing on this subject. You surely know my reasons for it. I have heard of Sympathizing thoughts posessing the breasts of two Distant Lovers if there is anything in this fond Oppinion You must know what passes in my heart at present and not accuse this letter of coldness. more I need not say, nor would it be prudent to commit more to paper. Col^o. Charles Lewis march'd Yesterday with Six hundred Men. Col^o. A. Lewis and myself Marches on Monday Next, with four or five hundred, & your Brother in a few days after with two or three hundred more. My Lord Dunmore is near Pitsburg by this. he will have upwards of Seven hundred with him, that is 400 that march'd with Maj. McDonnald

& three hundred with himself. you have heard that McDonnald with a part of his men destroyed an Indian town Wakatomakee. &c: Remember me to Lenny tell him I would have sent him his horse, but I think he will stand the Journy bettar than any I can get here, however if I can get two I will send both him and Eurus in. and tell my boy to learn his book & write every day, that I may see what a fine boy he is when I return I have got the horses Appraised that if he should be lost tell him he will get Six pounds for him. Remember me affectionatly to Your Mammy who I hope is still with you and to Rosy, Prissy & Polly[29] If I have an Opportunity I will write before we march, if not I recommend You & the Family to the Protection & Guidance of Divine Providence. And I hope that All Sufficient power will grant us a happy meeting again in a little time. till which my Dr. Nancy I remain Your Affectt & Faithfull.

Wᴹ. Fleming

P. S. I have met with an Opportunity and have sent in our horses by Martin McFerrin,[30] and a Son of Samˡ. McRoberts, who will deliver them to Mr Lockheart.

Wm. F.

---

[29] Mrs. Fleming's nieces, daughters of Col. William Christian. Rose later married Judge Caleb Wallace; Mary (Polly), Col. Stephen Trigg; and Priscilla died young.—Ed.

[30] Martin McFerran was later (1788) colleague of Col. William Fleming at the Virginia convention to ratify the constitution of the United States, and voted against the adoption of that instrument.—Ed.

AT CAMP UNION

[Col. William Christian to Col. William Preston. 3QQ92.][31]

CAMP UNION at the GREAT LEVELS. Septr. 7. 1774

DEAR SIR—I reached this place yesterday; a little after Colo Chas. Lewis marched with about 600 Augusta men. His business is to proceed as far as the mouth of Elk & there to make Canoes to take down the Flour. He took with him 500 P[ack] Horses carrying 54,000 pounds of Flour & 108 Beeves. Colo. Andrew Lewis talks that himself & Colo. Fleming will march next monday with a large body of men & 200 P Horses, there are about 450 men from Botetourt. He signifies that I must stay and bring up the Rear some days after him. What to do I dont know when our men hears they are to stay behind, I doubt they will be much dissatisfied. I intend to try to get our men all to be together which I find they earnestly wish for. Colo. Field marched this evening with about 35 & he expects 100 more will be here to morrow, He proposes joining C. Lewis He brought orders from Lord Dunmore to Colo. Lewis requiring him to be received with his men.

On the 30th. of August His Lordship was on his way at Cresops,[32] about 80 miles from Winchester. He will have about 700 men with him, & Colo Fields thinks will be at Mouth of great Kanhawa some days after the 20th. I wish we may get [there] soon

---

[31] Roosevelt in *Winning of the West*, i, p. 223, epitomizes this letter, which, however, he had only from a copy. The original is in tl Draper MSS., and the date is September 7, not 9.—ED.

[32] The home of Col. Thomas Cresap, at the site of Oldtown, Maryland.—ED.

enough. Colo. Lewis seems to think the number of men greatly exceeds his expectations, and that you may as well or had better let but about 100 more men follow me, that our County may have Compleat or some little more than 300 Rank [&] file, And that you could employ Any others that are raised to protect your Fronteers I think it was last Friday, one John McGuire was badly wounded by a party of Indians, a day or two after another man was wounded. A party of Indians was discovered in the Woods on Horseback, about Sunday but had their blankets over their heads & deceived our men or the foremost man who first discovered them cried "here they are boys." which alarmed them & gave them time to slip off the Horses and run away without being fired at. They were mounted on some of the Pack Horses & others that grazed near the Camp but tis supposed by the Signs that they had not discovered the Camp when they shott at McGuire, but tis believed they did since.

Colo. Fields says Majr McDonald with 400 men, being Ld. Dunmores advanced party below Fort Dunmore were boldly attacked by about 30 Indians. His men were marched in 3 Columns, himself at the head of the middle one, which was attacked, and about 4 men killed & 6 wounded. He ordered they right & left Columns to File of[f] & try to Surround the Enemy which could not be effected but they killed 3 or four Indians & took one, McDonald afterwards marched into a little Town and found his mens scalps hung up like Colours but the Town evacuated. Fields says the Shawnese with their near friends can meet us with about 1200 good men on short warning.

This Camp is about 140 miles from the Mouth of Kanhawa & from that into the Town[s] 70, in all 210 miles.

I cannot think of any particular occurrence respecting your Men, since I left you to inform you of. Every body has done as well as could be expected. And tis said here that no Troops have yet appeared, equal in goodness to them. And if I may add none disciplined, or equal to them, as to the order of their march &c. Henry Paullen[33] "says, he bore the Crack till we come but now he gives up" So much for that part.

May I request you to hurry on Maj^r. Robertson & the men you choose to send after, if I am to be left behind, pray let us go on together, & try to overtake the rest at mouth of Elk or at the Mouth of the river. I would not for all I am worth be behind crossing the Ohio, and that we should miss lending our Assistance. I believe from my heart that our men would all turn home if they thought they could not be with the foremost. As the men you send will have a good many Pack Horses & but little Flour I hope they will come quick. It may be 70 miles to your house, & from the road I think they may easily march in here the fourth day. Capt Russell marched 25 miles one day, there

---

[33] Capt. Henry Pauling led a company of Botetourt troops, for the muster-roll of which, see *post*. In 1777 he went out with Col. Bowman at the head of a militia company, to succor the hard-pressed settlers of Kentucky, especially those at St. Asaph's. Later he settled in Kentucky, was a member from Lincoln County to the convention ratifying the United States Constitution. Like most others from his section, he was against that instrument. The next year, he represented the the same county in the Virginia assembly.—ED.

is no bad road but Rich creek & Toms Creek mountains.

Jn⁰ Taylor Went off with Cʰ. Lewis with a Brigade of horses he was well. There was no [Beeves] left here when I came I fear beef will be Scarce tho Mc [MS. torn] he expects agrea [MS. torn] soon. Matthews is to have brought out 160000 weight 54 is gone 26 is here & the rest on the way. The 400 horses that are started, will return as fast as they can. Tis said that about 800 horses are employed. I observed a letter from Matthews directed to Messrs Ingles, Simm[s], Hamilton, & Hill Companys giving orders what to do. Ingles goes on & Barnes is to assist him.

I hope to see Mr. Floyd with Majʳ. Robertson if Johney has no Tent there is room in mine. He need not provide one.

I will inclose you a return & am Dear Sir Your Most Humble Servt.

Wᴹ Cʜʀɪsᴛɪᴀɴ

A Return of the Militia from Fincastle Septemr. 7. 1774. Camp Union

Field Officers	Companies	Captains	Lieuts.	Ensigns	Serjts	Drums	Fifes	Rank and File					Chaplain	Armourer	Butcher	Occurrences
								fit for duty	Sick	Bawmen	P. H. men & drivers	Total				
	Capt. Crockett	1	1	1	3			40	2	1	5	48				1 sick near Mr Thompsons 1 at Stewarts fort.
	Capt. Herbert	1	1		3			38	2			40				the sick at Rich creek
	Capt. Russell	1	1	1	2	1		42				42				
	Capt. Shelbey	1	1	1	3	1		37	2			39				1 sick at Mr Thompsons 1 in Camp
	Capt. Campbell	1	1		3			40	1			41				the sick man at Mr Thompsons
1	Capt. Harrod	1		1	2			22				22	1	1	2	
1		6	5	4	16	2		219	7	1	5	232	1	1	2	

WILLIAM CHRISTIAN

To Col. William Preston, Fincastle By Allsup

THE EXPEDITION MARCHES

[Col. Andrew Lewis to Col. William Preston. 3QQ93.]

CAMP UNION on the GREAT LEVELS Sept. 8th 1774[34]
DEAR SIR—On the 1t. day [of] this month I reached this place where was the most of ye Augusta Troops and part of those of Botetourt. Colo. Christian Joined us tuesday last. from Augusta we have 600. of this County about 450 Majr. Field is joined with 40 & has about 100 more on ye way, by Order of his Lordship, & should yours be Augmented to 300 we shall on ye whole have 1490. some of which that are least fit for service I purpose leaveing to Gareson ye small Forts: but still we shall have a much Larger Number than was Expected, & consequently must have an Equal addition of Provitions, which is ordered, & can be Brough[t] out, & carryed from this Camp by ye Last Marching Party to ye Mouth of Elk where it must be stored, & taken down by water as we shall have ocation for it. My Brother with ye Augusta Troops & Capt Arbuckles Compy Marched for ye Mouth of Elk on Teusday. & I propose Marching with Botetourt & one Compy of the Fincastle Troops Next monday. It is with pleasure I can inform you that I have had but little trouble with ye Troops to what I expected, and I hop[e] they will continue to do their duty with the same cheerfulness. I received a letter from his Lordship last sunday Morning, which

---

[34] Roosevelt, *Winning of the West*, i, p. 222, note 2, prints part of this letter from a copy. We follow the text of the original.—ED.

was dated ye 30th August, at old Town, which I take to be chrisops   He then, I am told, had Colo. Stephens[35] & Major Connoly at his elbow as might be easily discovered by ye contents of his Letter, which expressed his Lordships warmest wishes, that I would with all the troops from this quarter Join him at ye Mouth of the Little Kanaway   I wrote his Lordship that it was not in my Power to alter our rout, and men-

---

[35] Gen. Adam Stephen was a Scotchman educated as a physician; he early removed to Virginia and settled in the lower valley. In 1754 he was the senior captain in Col. Joshua Fry's regiment, and when Washington took command Stephen was made major. He was with Washington at Great Meadows, and the next year was severely wounded at Braddock's defeat; recovering, he served throughout the French and Indian War, and commanded the Virginia regiment raised in Pontiac's War (1763). The following year he was magistrate of Frederick County, and when Berkeley was laid off (1772) was made high sheriff thereof. In Lord Dunmore's War, he served second in command to the governor, and at Fort Gower made a speech in favor of the colonial cause. Stephen was an ardent Whig, and in communication with the Virginia leaders of the Revolution. A member of the convention of 1775, the next year he was made brigadier-general of troops, serving at Princeton, Trenton, and elsewhere in New Jersey. Early in 1777 he was promoted to a major-generalship, serving with honor at the Brandywine. But after the battle of Germantown, he was cashiered for having been intoxicated upon that important occasion. He retired to his home at Martinsburg, Va., whence he was several times sent to the Virginia assembly (1780-85). In 1788, he was a member of the Virginia ratifying convention, and made several vigorous speeches in favor of the constitution, attacking the opposition, especially that shown by Patrick Henry. See "History of Virginia Federal Convention" in *Virginia Historical Collections,* new series, ix, x. Three years later (1791), General Stephen died at an advanced age at his home in Martinsburg. He was a man of great stature and powerful strength, much feared by the Indians, although beloved by his friends—see letter of Fleming to Stephen, *post.* One of his daughters was the wife of Alexander Spottswood Dandridge. This note is abbreviated from a sketch by Dr. Draper in his MSS., 3D, chap. xvi.—ED.

tioned to him such circumstances as I thought Necessary for him to know. I wish he had done so in his letter to me. If more troops should offer their service to you for this Expedition then [than] would make the Number you have sent me 300 please to make some other use of them, if need be. the Next day after I came to this place ye Indians wounded a man within 2 miles of us & ye Next day they wounded another. from this we may expect they will be picking about us all ye March. Had I time to sit I might think of many other little circumstances to inform you of at present I can only tell you, what you I hope, will at all times believe, that I am

Your Most affectionat friend & very Humble Servt.

[ANDREW LEWIS.]

P. S. Should you send any addition to your Fincastle troops Now with me furnish them with Powder we shall not have more than ¼ lb p^r. Man. I am &c

LEWIS

On His Majestys Service To Col^o. William Preston Fincastle

GUARDING THE FRONTIER

[Maj. Arthur Campbell to Col. William Preston. 3QQ94.]

ROYAL-OAK Sept. 9th. 1774

Sir—Yesterday Morning early, One John Henry was dangerously wounded; upon Clinch about four Miles from Capt. Smiths Station, and it is supposed his Wife, and three small Children, is taken Prisoners. Henry was standing in his door, when two Indians fired at him, his Wife and Children was in

Bed; He immediately ran to the Woods; and shortly after, accidently met with Old Jno. Hamilton who concealed him in a Thicket until he should go and alarm the Fort, and bring him assistance[36] Hamilton had the courage, to go by Henrys House; but seen nothing, either of the Indians, or the Woman and Children, afterwards, he took one Bradshaws on his way; who just before he came was alarmed by some Indian Signs in his Cornfield Bradshaw immediately set out for the Settlement, thro the Woods after he came about 3 Miles past the place, where the Mischief had been done, in the morning, he came upon a place where about 12 or 15 Indians had Breakfasted they leaving behind them, some of their Provisions. Afterwards he followed the Tracts a small distance, and found they seemed to steer their Course toward this River. He then made the best of his way towards the settlement in the Rich Valley which he alarmed last Night and this morning. The principal part of which is just now arrived here in a distressed situation. I have sent out Orders, to this and the two next Companys on Holston, for all the Men that has Arms, or any ammunition to assemble Tomorrow, in Order to patroll a few Days, in the Rich Valley, and some of the best hands to go over, to see what is become of Capt. Smith; as he is very weak at his own Station, having only 8 Men the last Acct.; and notwithstanding repeated Orders and requests, there has not yet gone a Man out of Doacks or Herberts Companys,

---

[36] John Henry had settled on this piece of land in the present Tazewell County, the preceding May. He afterwards died of his wounds. See *Amer. Archives*, 4th series, i, p. 808.—ED.

to join him. The Forts at Glade-Hollow, Elk-Garden and Maiden Spring, has their compliments compleat, and it was Capt. Smiths Choice to have his own Station at Maxwells-Mill,[37] the last to be compleated as there was no Familys, in the Fort, and the recruits from New River, and Reed-Creek, was alloted for that Station Please write pressingly to Lieut. Peirce to send out the 15 Men you formerly Ordered, as I am well informed it might easily be done, out of that Company that is covered by so thick a settlement as Reed-Creek, and besides there is few if any Men gone on the Expedition from the upper settlements on New River and those of Elk Creek.

I shall be glad if you should think it proper, to allow me a few Men at this place, as I am Obliged frequently to be abroad, to provide Provision for the Men on Duty and to stir up others for the Service. besides my House is now a Frontier except what Forts is on Clinch.

I hope you will now think it expedient, to enlarge the number of Men on Duty, at least for a few Weeks; as the Head of Clinch and the lower settlement on Holston is but weakly-Guarded. I hope the Levies from Bedford and Pittsylvania is arrived at New-River. If you should think it proper for a Subaltern Command to join Capt Smith as I am afraid the men

---

[37] For the location of these forts (in Russell County, Va.), see Smith's MS. map. His own fort was called Fort Christian; that at Glade Hollow, twelve miles east of Russell's, was garrisoned by fifteen men, under John Duncan; the Elk Garden fort, six miles east of the present Lebanon, had fifteen men commanded by Serj. John Kinkead; the Maiden Spring fort had five men under Serj. John Crow. See Summers, *Southwest Virginia*, p. 157.—ED.

out of Herberts and Doacks Companys may not be got. The want of Ammunition is still a general cry, indeed we have very little, as the Inhabitants was so incautious to shot away their late supply to save their Crops.

Flour will soon be wanted, I hope Mr. Buchanan is on his way out by this time.

Should the Enemy be so strong as to be able to follow up their blow, it is likely they will be met with Tomorrow as I expect they will follow up the peoples footing that is fled. And I have directed the patrollers to march by three different routs to the Rich Valley and Clinch.

Please favour me with an Answer by the Bearer I am Sir Your most Obedient Servt.

[To Colonel Preston]   ARTHUR CAMPBELL

AT CAMP UNION

[Capt. Philip Love to Col. William Preston. 3QQ95.]

DEAR COLL—If I had time I would Write you a long Epistle of our present situation, our Intended Movements &c. but the Botetourt Troops Marches in a few [h]ours for the Mouth of Elk, our next Post from this therefor can only tell you that I am satisfied with the Survey made for me on the Cantuck by Hencock Taylor & would be glad to have my Plot Accordingly I conclud with the sinceare wishes for your healt[h] & Safty & that of your Family's & am D[ear] Coll. your Affc Servt.

Big Levels 12th of Sept 1774   PHIL. LOVE

[Col. William Christian to Col. William Preston. 3QQ146.]

CAMP UNION Septr. 12, 1774

DEAR SIR—Colo. Lewis has just marched with Colo. Fleming & the Botetourt Troops, with an addition of Capt. Shelbey & Capt. Russell's Companies from Fincastle and has left under my care the remaining part of the Fincastle men, a few Culpepper, Dunmore & Augusta men, and ordered me to stay for the return of the pack horses that went with Ch: Lewis which I shall look for [a]long this day week. I have dispatched Mr. Posey[38] towards Stanton to hurry out all the flour possible by that time, and Several persons are employed in gathering Beeves. There is gone on about 72,000^{wt} of flour. There is now here about 8 thousand   130 horse loads to be here to Morrow night. 96 loads at the warm Springs Which I have to Send back for, & I suppose there is between 30 and 40,000 weight beyond the Springs. I purpose to march, this day week with all that can be had or day or two after

---

[38] Thomas Posey, who acted as commissary in this campaign, was born (1750) near Potomac River, but at the age of nineteen removed to Augusta County. He had a long and adventurous career, serving on the Augusta County committee of safety (1775), as captain under Matthews, and later under Morgan in the Revolutionary War. At the storming of Stony Point, he was major in command, and aided against Cornwallis (1781). A few years later, he removed to Spotsylvania County, where he served as county lieutenant (1786-93). He held high rank in Wayne's army (1794), and after the Indian wars removed to Kentucky where he was in the state senate, acting lieutenant-governor, and major general of militia (1809). About 1812, he removed to Louisiana, and was appointed to the United States army for a brief term (1812-13). The same year he was chosen governor of Indiana Territory; and in 1816 was appointed Indian agent, whereupon he removed to Shawneetown, Ill., where he died Mar. 19, 1818.—ED.

if possible. As the Colo. proposes building Canoes, and a Fort at the mouth of Elk, and a Fort at the mouth of Kanhawa, He Says I need not be under any Apprehensions but that I will get down in time to Cross the Ohio with him. Sometimes he talked of Setting off from there the middle of October, or not much Sooner. He seems extremely anxious that I Should make haste with the provisions. I wish Major Robertson could be here with all the Fincastle men yet to Come on Sunday or monday Next, and that he would do his endeavour to get Some beeves, on the way perhaps he could raise 30. Colo. Lewis when he counted up the Escort I am to Command counted 100 Men to come and mentioned Maj^r. Robertson as a proper person for me to have with a Company to take on what Provisions I could not get readay. He seemed unwilling to trust any of the low landers. But I doubt my neighbour will hate to be Left. Colo Field marched with about 40 men a few days ago, about 80 men of his are now come Colo. Slaughter from Dunmore[39] with about 40 is here: he Sent 80 with the

---

[39] Col. Francis Slaughter married the daughter of Robert Coleman, and removed to Kentucky about 1785 and settled in Hardin County. Lawrence and George Slaughter were both in this campaign, in the company of their father-in-law, Col. John Field. Col. George Slaughter raised a company in 1776, and joined the 8th Virginia regiment participating in the battles of Brandywine and Germantown. Returning to western Virginia, he joined Shelby in his Chickamauga campaign in 1779, and late in the same year started with re-inforcements for George Rogers Clark in the Illinois. His company was obliged to winter in the mountains, arriving at Louisville in June, 1780. After aiding Clark in the Piqua campaign, Slaughter returned to Virginia and in 1784 was a member of the house of delegates. Later he settled in Jefferson County, Ky., removing thence to Charlestown, Ind., where he died June 17, 1818.—ED.

Govr. The kettles and Tents were chiefly distributed before I came I could get but 16 or 17 tin battered kettles for all Fincastle & but few Tents But I am told oxen brigs 🝝 enough for Tents will be brought with the Pack horses to morrow If the major is not marched when you get this Intelligence I really think we ough[t] to send over that whole Country and try to buy beg or borrow kettles for to do withougt is very hard almost [im]possible It will presently make men sick to live on Roasted meat without broath. Some Scouts returned from Gawley about fifty odd miles from here Saturday evening & reported that they saw 5 Indians on tuesday morning with horses going away & on friday morning they saw three comming in I have been afraid all this day that Somebody would be killed in the naighbourhood as poeple travels about very Car[l]essly Tho it may be they ere [are] come to watch the motions of the army only.

I really think theare is great need of your keeping out a considerable body of men on the Frontiers of Fincastle least Several partys of Indians should be set out before they heard of our Troops nor do I think that the number should be reducd on the Frontiers untill you hear of the Armys being at or near the Mouth of the N[ew] River Lestwichs Company is diseried [distributed] thro this part of the Country as well as [a] number of men who appeared unfit for the Journey. at Jamey Buchanans desir I have let him go in He talks of returning soon if he is well But his helth semes bad & his [constitution] week so that I hardly think him equ[a]l to the Task if so he had beter stay at home Billey is hardey nothing will hurt him but Billy Johney is gone out but I doubt is a bad boy. He is with Capt. Love who is extremely kind to him & treat[s] him friendly Jamey behaves well & will be advised. Colo. Lewis wont suffer any changes with Companies Several application have been made to get into our Companies. There is but Little alteration in our returns Since I sent you one only my Leaving out the Sick Left on the way whom I suppose you will station at the forts There is such a Number of our men driving horses and Cattle & gone to work at Canoes that I have but about a few more than 100 for duty here. I wish you may think fit to send about 100 rank & file men if they Can be got with convenience. It was Said in Camp that there would be no danger of the frontiers when we Started but the officers & I believe men all confides in you that you will not Leave the people unguarded. If I think of any thing more to write you before Jamey starts I will. on my marching from here I will le[t] you [k]now all the nuse.

In the mean time I am Sir Your Obliged Sarvant
WILLIAM CHRISTIAN[40]

LATE RECRUITS

[Maj. James Robertson to Col. William Preston. 3QQ96.]

RICH CREEK 15th Septbr. 1774

SIR—we are Stop'd a day to Get what Beeves and Cattles We Can Pick up. Capt. woods and his Party

---

[40] This letter is not an original, having been copied for Colonel Preston by an unknown hand.—ED.

is Joynd me Which makes our number of the Whole 55 the Soldiers I had at M^r. Woods Desird Discharges from me which I have given them, though they are willing to Inlist again, if you See Cause.

I have sent you an Acct. of their time Likewise finding their Provisions for the time.

Mitchel Clay   51 days on Duty   found his own Provisions
Zekil Clay   51 Days   found his Provisions
David Clay   51 Days   found   D^o
Rich^d. Blankenship 44 Days   D^o

N. B. The above I give a Certifycate for their Provisions and Entered in the Accts. I left with you untill the 17th August, not Including that day

James Will[ia]ms   51 Days   Diets & D^o [Provisions]
Samuel Campbell   51 Days   Diets   D^o
Joshua Inglis   51 Days   Diets   D^o
Andrew Woods   51 Days   Diets   D^o Express 6 Days
Francis Farlen   25 Days   Diets   D^o
Henry Atkins as Express four Days

JAMES ROBERTSON

P. S. I must be for Ever Obliged to all my good freinds for assisting me in Geting my Compy made up as I thought it was meerely Impossible to do it in the time and I am sure there is not Such an Other Compy for the Quaintyty of men belonging to the Whole Dr. Sir I wish you Every thing that Would make you Happy.

I am your Obdt. Servant

JAMES ROBERTSON

To Col. William Preston

[Michael Woods and James Robertson to Col. William Preston. 3QQ97.]

Sir—I Draughted Philip Cavanough John farley Richard Blankingship John [H]umphres francis farley & george pack who all Refused; and I understand there is some of them going over to you to try and get off But Major Robertson & I has Consulted and we desire that you may not Countenance any of them; and we Expect to get them and some more and if they go I shall have 2 [MS. torn] besides myself which is all from yr. Servt. & wellwisher

MICHAEL WOODS

RICH CREEK 16th Sept. 1774

To Cornl. William Preston in fincastle County on his Majesties Service

N B Prhaps Cavender & John Farlen will aply to you for Certyfycates for the time they were Scouts but I have told them that [their] money is stop'd to pay their fine should they not go with us.

I am yr. Serv.

JAS. ROBERTSON

We are Just starting for the Levels. J. R.

PROVISIONING DUNMORE'S ARMY

[Dorsey Pentecost to Capt. William Harrod. 4NN13.]

16th. September 1774

Dr. Bill—The bearer Mr. McCarmick will commune with you, who is to come up to assist you in Gathering up the Cattle, he [is] appointed by the Governour under me to go Down the River, and therefore hath full authority to do anything that may be wanting as well as if I was there my self, you must (whether you will or no) Excuse my not Coming myself as I am under such orders from my Lord that I cannot come, do for the best & be Exped'ious. Capt. Kincaid is to Rec[eiv]e them.

I am y^r. O'b^d.

DORSEY PENTCOST

Mr. Mc Carmick will inform you of my Situation & the News. Pray D^r. Bill do Everything in your Power & if any acc^s. that require my Settling before you go Down send them to me and I will do Everything for you in my Power. I am ordered not to Leave this Post or I would have come my Self and therefore you know it is out of my Power

I, as before

D. PENTCOST

On his Majestys Service To Capt. William Harrod Ten Mile Creek [41]

RENEWED ATTACKS ON THE FRONTIER

[Maj. Arthur Campbell to Col. William Preston. 3QQ98.]

ROYAL-OAK Sep^t. 17th. 1774

SIR—The same day J^{no}. Henry was wounded on Clinch There was one Samuel Lemmey taken Prisoner on the North fork of Holstein, about a Mile from the

---

[41] Pentecost, being detained at Fort Pitt, assigns the task of collecting provisions to Harrod, who is at his home in western Pennsylvania. Ten Mile Creek is an affluent of the Monongahela.—ED.

upper End of Campbells Choice (now called the Clay-Lick) and John & Archibald Buchanans Familys narrowly escaped.

Tuesday 13th three Indians attacked one of Capt. Smiths Soldiers about half-Mile from the Maiden-Spring Station he is tho't to have killed one of them; and escaped himself without being hurt: a party of our people happened to be within 300 Yards when the Guns fired; they soon were at the place of action, and give the remaining two Indians a good Chase the wounded fellow, found means to get into a large Cave or Pit within 70 or 80 Yds. of the place he was shot; in which it is supposed he is Dead, as he fell when he was shot, and Bled a good deal; I have one [of] the plugs now in my House that burst out of his wound a few steps from the Tree he stood behind when he received the Shot. The Pit is to be search'd by means of leting a Man down in it by ropes with lights as our Men is anxious to get his Scalp.

The same Evening of ye. 13th. Capt. Smiths Scouts discovered the tracts of a party of the Enemy going off with Horses and it is supposed the prisoners. he immediately set out with a party of 21 Men, in pursuit of them, which I am perswaded he will follow a considerable way, or else overtake them.[42] I have made strict enquiry into the Conduct of the Spys and find, it was not their fault, the leting the Enemy in undiscovered. The different passes they were ordered to watch, lay at such a distance, that it took several days

---

[42] Colonel Preston reports these occurrences in a letter published in *Amer. Archives*, i, p. 808, in which he states that Captain Smith's party was unable to overtake the Indians, who had stolen horses upon which to ride away.—ED.

before the[y] could go, to each, when they came to Sandy River the[y] found the Enemys footing; and immediately ran to the station, but as they were 30 Miles off and the Enemy had 2 or 3 Days start the damage was done before they got in to give the Alarm. I am much obliged to the most of the Militia that was called upon, on this occasion, as they shewed great willingness both to go out, and do what service [lay] in their power

The Principal part of the party now in pursuit of the Enemy under Capt. Smith is of those that I sent out as I mentioned in my last Letter. There is a few obstinate Wretches, that selfishly refuses Duty, when in their power, to perform it; Please give Orders what course is to be taken with such, for if they go unpunished it will set a bad example to others. Also one of the party, that went out on this occasion; behaved but indifferently; They proceeded to the place the Man was wounded at, made some small search there, from when[ce] the[y] went to Capt. Smith Station and drew three days provision, on pretence, they intended to search the Country round for the Enemys footing; but instead of doing so; the[y] precipitately returned home; altho, on their way back, they were informed of fresh Signs of the Indians and was requested to go in search of them; which they refused. I should think less of this Piece of ill-Conduct, had it not been for the deception about the Provision; as it was some Bacon that was kept in reserve, for to carry out in case of a pursuit and for the use of the Spys, and besides Meat is but scarce on Clinch. Your late instructions will enable me to satisfy every reasonable request of the Inhabitants; and if we had Powder; I hope in the Almighty we shall be able to give a good account of the Enemy, if the[y] trouble us with any more Visits.

I shall take it as a favour if you will let me know the News from the Army as often as you receive Intelligence.

Herberts Men is not yet come: 12 is gone out of Doacks Company and I believe two more will be along in a few Days the fifteenth Man, I am informed, is an obstinate Gent, that despises Authority. I have not yet seen Capt. Wilson, But I expect he will dispose his Men in the best Manner he can on Reed-Creek and in the Rich-Valley in Order to protect the Inhabitants and encourage them to stay at home, to save their Crops.

Capt. Floyd was to have some Plots made out before he went away, for Col. Byrd, Capt. Harrison and myself I hope he has not forgot to inform you about them.

I am Sir With great Respect your Obedient Servant
ARTHUR CAMPBELL

COLONEL CHRISTIAN'S DIVISION

[Col. William Christian to Mrs. William Fleming. 2ZZ10.]

CAMP UNION Sept. 18. 1774

DEAR SISTER—I am just sending over to Bot[etourt] Ct. house for some powder. and take the oppy to tell you that I am well & intends marching from here the 25 Instant or 26. Mr Fleming went from here Monday the 12th. he was well. I dont expect to be at Ohio before 10 or 12 October, as I have a large convoy of Provisions & about 400 men. Tho I expect to be there in time to cross over with the advanced partys.

Yesterday week about 30 miles from here, an Indian killed a white man of the advanced party and another white man killed the Indian, they were spys I suppose, I dont look for any more partys coming in.

I dont know whether my Father & mother are with you yet or at New river, & so cant write. But if they are with you, say all I could say. I shall write my dear parents, before I leave this, when I am ready to set of. I do expect to settle in Botetourt somewhere that will suit them & me, & not over New river again. I doubt not of being back in time to have all fixed before winter.

The messenger is waiting & I will conclude, Dear sister, Yours affectionately

W^M CHRISTIAN

Write Mrs Christian[43] if possible.

[Capt. John Floyd to Col. William Preston. 33S42, 43.]

D^R SIR— Sept. 18th 1774

* * * * * * * *

I am in hopes we shall make out pretty well

---

[43] Mrs. William Christian was Anne, sister of Patrick Henry. After her husband's death in Kentucky at the hands of Indians (1786), she fell into a decline, returned to Virginia with her children, spent a winter in the West Indies for the sake of her health, and died the day after she landed at Norfolk (1787). The foregoing is from information given to Dr. Draper in 1843 by Mrs. Eliza Ramsey, daughter of William Fleming. See Draper MSS., 8ZZ4.—ED.

about kettles we are also allowed 60 yards of tent cloth for a company. You may depend upon my using my endeavors to have your stiller fetched home this winter. I shall take your advice about returning home this fall, if the season is too far advanced for me to return by the way of Kentucky, & finish my business this winter, which I shall be a better judge of when the expedition is over. I think it seems to go on slowly. There are three of the Mc Afees[44] & Saml. Adams joined my company since I came here; there were some Bottetourt men not allowed by Col. Lewis to join the Fincastle captains, but Col. Christian says I shall not lose these. The affair with Capt. Campbell is not yet settled about the men; it is to lie over until we return, & be settled then the men go in

---

[44] There were five McAfee brothers, who lived with their families on Sinking Creek, Botetourt County—James, Robert, George, William, and Samuel. The first three of these, with James McConn, Jr., and Samuel Adams (then a youth of eighteen years of age), explored Kentucky in 1773, together with Colonel Bullitt and Hancock Taylor. After exploring the interior of the country and making several locations, they returned home by way of Powell's Valley and Clinch River, having endured many hardships, and at one time nearly perishing of starvation. The same party, re-inforced by the other brothers and several neighbors, sought Kentucky again in 1775. Two of them joined Henderson's Transylvania party; but after the failure of that company returned to Virginia, whence the final emigration, with all the families, was made in 1779. McAfee's Station was on Salt River, in Mercer County, about six miles below Harrodsburg; in 1781 it vigorously sustained an Indian attack, the assailants being driven off. William McAfee was killed on Clark's Piqua campaign of 1780; George died on his farm on Salt River, 1803; Samuel in 1801; James in 1814. Robert went to New Orleans with a cargo of produce in 1795, and was there killed by a Spaniard, who attempted to rob him. The McAfee MSS. are in the possession of Col. Reuben Durrett of Louisville, Ky.; copies thereof are found in the Draper MSS., 14CC.—E<small>D</small>.

my company; it has been fairly stated before Col. Christian; he seems to think I ought to lose three if not four.

* * * * * * * *

If I come that way, Col. Christian thinks I had as well take with me the captain's commission you gave me last spring. it is in my field book which I had on Kentuck. if the messenger returns, pray send it.

[JOHN FLOYD]

To Col. Wm Preston

FORAYS AGAINST THE BORDER

[Circular letter of William Cocke. 3QQ103.]

GENT.—As a friend to my Country and being informd the melencholy news of John Robertses Family Being taken[45] think it my Indespensable duty to do Every thing in my Power to promote the Honour & Safety of this Fronteer I would therefore advise & Request you to Erect a fort at Some Suitable place as near the line as Possable not to Give the Indians one foot of Ground for by Flying we not only make them Sensable of Our incapasity to Receave them but Give up our property for their Surport. I have Rote to my

---

[45] The family of John Roberts, living on Reedy Creek, an affluent of the North Fork of Holston, in the present Sullivan County, Tenn. Quite remote from the scene of any former outrages, they had not sought the shelter of the forts, deeming themselves safe. Roberts, his wife, and several children were killed; the eldest child James, a lad of ten years of age, being carried into captivity. One of the children lived some days after being tomahawked and scalped. See *post;* also *Amer. Archives*, i, p. 808; *Amer. Pioneer*, i, pp. 14, 208.—ED.

Sergent to take what men is in my Company Out for your Amedeate protection and shall Go amedeately my Self to Carrolinia and Raise what men I can there to Join his forces with out any further Delay which Conduct I hope will be aprovd of By the Gent that is at the Helm of affairs or wheather they Should or not I Can assure you that my Life and little all is always Ready to Be Risked in your Defence. Therefore shall pursue Every meathod that I think may be for your Safety and that God of his Infinate mercy may Keep you all from the hands of those Barberous Savages is the Sincear wish of Gent your Friend & m. obt

Wᴍ Cocke

25th September 1774.
To Inhabitants on the Fronteer of Holson

[Maj. Arthur Campbell to Col. William Preston. 3QQ104. MS. torn along the edge.]

Monday Morning 5 OClock [Sept. 26]

Dear Sir—Last Night about Midnight I Received Letters from Clinch and the lower settlement on Holston giving me an account of the distressed situation of those places, on Account of the expected approach of a large [body] of this Enemy.

Friday the 23d. Two Negros was Captured from [Moore's][46] and a considerable number of Cattle and

---

[46] This was the fort of which Daniel Boone was in charge. The Indians made the captured negroes run the gauntlet in front of the fort. whose garrison was too weak to sally to their assistance.—Ed.

Horses [stolen] The 24th. in the Evening a Family was killed and [scalped on] Reedy-Creek near Kings-Mill[47]

Yesterday morning about Sunrise there was [shouting] and firing heard at several Houses.. The d[amage] done was not known when the Express cam[e away.]

From several concurring circumstances; th[is attack] is made by the Cherokee parties mentioned in [Shoats] and Taylers depositions[48] so that there is now but little probability of avoiding an open rupture with them Which if the case, you know what measures will be necessary for the preservation of this Country The want of Ammunition is truly disheartning at this crisis. The people was gathering together at [Kings Fort?] in Order to make a stand; I have Ordered Co[cke] to go down with what Men he can raise. I intend also to send for part of Capt. Wilsons [men to go with] him. I hope you will judge it proper to send [an express to] the Army to hurry the return of the Men [from this] County especially the Capts. Russell, Shelby and [MS. torn] whos Familys is in distress.

It was very unfortunate that Capt Thompson had [left] Blackmores only two Days before the damage

---

[47] This was the Roberts family, see *ante.*—ED.

[48] Archibald Taylor, and a settler named Shoat, who had been trading with the Cherokee returned to Holston a few days before this, and notified Capt. William Cocke that two war-parties of this tribe had left their villages, whether to go to the aid of the Shawnee or to attack the settlements was not known. Cocke had sent their depositions to Major Campbell (Draper MSS., 3QQ99, 102), who had forwarded them to Colonel Preston. The marauders on Reedy Creek did not prove to be Cherokee, but a Shawnee and Mingo party under the leadership of Logan.—ED.

was done as he had his full compliment of men: When the [enemy] came there was only 12, and some of them indifferent Flour is wanted badly at Blackmores and the hea[d of Clinch?]
I am respectfully Yours

ARTHUR CAMPBELL

On his Majestys Service To Colo. William Preston

[Maj. Arthur Campbell to Col. William Preston. 3QQ105. MS. torn along edge.]

DEAR SIR—I have just thot since I closed my Letter, that Lead is like to be a scarce article also.

I imagine if you were to write Charles Divereaux and Evan Williams; they would set to Work; and make a sufficient supply for this Country. consider if they [were] to get some asistance from the Country if it would not be cheaper than sending to Warwic. I have authority to give them liberty from Colonel Byrd on reasonable terms.

I am Sir Your Humble [servant]

ARTHUR CAMPBELL,

Sept. 26 1774
To Colo. William Preston

SIR—I am just informed that Archibald Taylor is a Man that his Word be depended on. Shoat I would not depend so much upon were it not that his deposition corresponds with Taylors.

I am informed of further particulars that Oconostota left the Council, when he found the Shawanese faction was strong, saying he had used his unwearied endeavours, to keep Peace with the English. But if they would go to War he would have no hand in it. I will forward your Letter to him with all Speed, perhaps it may help him to reasume his authority: and we may at least carry our point so far that the time may be lengthened out by negotiations until we are better prepared. I have wrote a long Letter to my acquaintance Mr. Cameron by way of Carolina.

I hope the Almighty will bless our endeavours for the Safety of the helpless

I am yours as before

A CAMPBELL

On his Majestys Service To Colº. William Preston To be forwarded by Mr. Brander

EXPEDITION AT ELK RIVER

[Col. William Fleming to his wife 2ZZ5.]

MY DR. NANCY—Agreeable to my Promise I take every Opportunity of letting you hear from me, convinced it will afford you the same satisfaction in reading that it gives me in writing to you, even though I have nothing to add to my former but that I continue in health & that nothing extraordinary has hapned as yet. we are within Five days march of the Ohio, and have dispatched five Scouts to the Mouth of the N[ew] River in search of his Lordship from whom we have heard nothing since we left Camp Union on Green

ELK RIVER EXPEDITION

Briar. We will March from this on Friday Next. the Men have been employed in Making Canoes since we came here and will have 18 large ones loaded on thursday Evening. This comes by Jos. Scot, and as conveyance will be uncertain after we leave this You will perhaps not hear from me till we reach the End of our March, or are about to Return I scarce expect your Brother who is yet on Green Briar will join us before we Cross the Ohio if then. My Dr. Nancy, that You & Lenny are daily in my thoughts, you need not doubt, but as much as I love & Regard you both, I can not Allow myself to wish me with you, till the expedition is finishd knowing that it would Sink me in your esteem, & that you would dispise a wretch that could desert an honourable Cause, a Cause undertaken for the good of his Country in general, and more immediately for the Protection of his Family, as included amongst the Frontier settlers let thoughts like these Animate you and support your Spirits, and remember my Dr Girl that the Divine Being is Omnipresent as well as Omnipotent, that He who rides on the Wings of the Tempest, and derects the Artillery of Heaven, beholds with serenity, the Rage of a Battle & derects each deadly Shaft where to strike—for a Sparrow falls not to the Ground without his knowledge. His Mercy is more conspicuously displayed, in instances of Preservation & Protection in the fiersest Battles and greatest daingers, than in a calm undisturbed Rotation of time in a quiet peaceble life. thefor My Dr. think me as safe on this Expedition, tho we should have a Skirmish or two with the Indians, as if at home. And should it be the Will of God, that I should fall, I must & can not otherwise think, but that he who dies in the Service of & in the defence of his Country, dies in an Act of Religion. and circumstances considered, dies the death of the Rightious. but my D^r. I hope in a few Months to have the Pleasure of personally telling You & my Little Son more perticularly of our proceedings, and till then I Recommend You, him & the Family, to the Protection of that Being who is equally present at this Moment, and at all times, both with You and me, Who knows our most secret thoughts both Now and Always, and is equally Able to preserve you & protect me.

I am My D^r. Nancy Yours whilst

W^M. FLEMING

Tuesday Sep^t. 27. 1774, The Mouth of Elk River

COLONEL CHRISTIAN'S DIVISION

[John Floyd to Col. William Preston 33S43, 44.]

Sept. 28th. 1774.

DEAR SIR—

* * * * * * * *

I have heard by Saml. Newell[49] your lady was again mending from her relapse &c.

---

[49] Samuel Newell was born (1754) on the ocean, while his parents were emigrating from Ireland to America. They settled first in Frederick County, but early removed to the Holston, where young Newell was active in the Indian wars, and the border battles of the Revolution. He was a lieutenant at King's Mountain (1780), where he was severely wounded. The next year, being chosen captain of militia,

We are now marched three miles from the camp, & in a fair way of going on without any more loss of time. It is Col. Christian's opinion there will be a peace made with the Indians by the time we get down or soon after. You will receive this by Mr. Vance, who returned home with my consent. He is a poor man & has a large crop of corn &c. left by his family; he also promises to take care of the affairs of those in my company who live in that quarter, which makes them all agree to stay contentedly; he wants to be employed on the frontiers if there is any body wanted; I think he can be of as much service in that part as most people.

I have no news worth mentioning & am really afraid to say much lest you should be in more trouble (if possible) than I left you. I cannot rest till I hear from you again.

My company seem all anxious to come by Kentucky, but if I can't do it time enough to be at your house by Christmas I shall return & go down early in the spring. I will say no more now, but most earnestly pray to Heaven that you may be restored to your former peace of mind, & will be always your most affectionate

JN. FLOYD

Col. Wm. Preston

---

and having removed to French Broad River, he was active in the founding of the abortive State of Franklin. In 1797 he removed to Somerset, Ky., where for many years he was a judge. In the latter years of his life he retired to Montgomery County, Ind., where he died in 1841, leaving many descendants in Kentucky and Indiana.—ED.

FEAR OF CHEROKEE WAR; OFFER OF AID FROM CAROLINA

[Maj. Arthur Campbell to Col. William Preston. 3QQ106, 107.]

Royal-Oak Sep^t. 29, 1774.

Dear Sir—We have frequent alarms since the late damage; Indian Signs has been seen in the very Heart of the settlement; and a Man upon the South Fork narrowly escaped being taken Prisoner, about Twilight in the Evening. I believe they are only Spys. I have had the good fortune notwithstanding the general consternation the late alarms occasioned to keep the people from flying the Country; endeavouring to divert them from believing that it is the Cherokees which seems to be their greatest terror. And giving them assurances that every thing will be done in your power, to have Ammunition speedily brought into the Country: I have prevailed with the most of the Inhabitants on this River to erect Forts, which I expect will be chiefly compleated this Week, and I make no doubt now but we will dispute the Country valiantly if once provided with ammunition: even if it should be a Cherokee War.

I am still in a doubt whether it was Cherokees did the late mischief, altho' there was one of their War Clubs and some other Cherokee Signs left. But the general Clamour, here is against that nation and indeed several circumstances seems suspicious It may be well for us to be prepared.

I had a Message from a Gentleman in Carolina, that fifty Catawba Indians was desirous of being employed against the Shawanese and he could send fifty prime White-men along with them their Neighbours and acquaintance: I returned him Answer it might be well for to get them in readiness; as they might have occasion for them in their own Government: and if they choose to march as volunteers to the great Island I would endeavour that they should meet with all possible encouragement. Pray consider if there is no need for them against the Cherokees whether it might not be doing a Service, if they come, to March them thro' Cumberland Gap, to the Ohio, where it is likely they could be employed in the Scouting way to good purpose, the ensuing Winter. Please let me know your Sentiments about this Scheme as I must let the Gentleman know if it is disapproved of. Capt. Cocke set out to Carolina before I Received yours of the 25th. but as he is a stranger it is likely he wont succeed. It is certain We want Men badly as it is now impossible to get a Man to leave this River to go to Clinch as they look upon themselves in equal danger. Blackmores & the Head of Clinch is extremely thin, so that it is out of Capt. Looneys or Capt. Smiths power to pursue the Enemy if there was but a dozen of them.

Capt. Wilson if Provision was plenty (or rather flour) would be agreed to go further back than Mr. Doacks, as many of his Men is not pleased with their lodgings and say they would rather you would Order them to be stationed in the Woods. Consider whether it would not be better for them to be towards the Head of Blue Stone and Clinch; as they would then as effectually cover the Frontier part of Reed Creek as where they are, and it is bad to give ground, and have they War among us. The middle Stations on Clinch is pretty strong of the Inhabitants and of late they are so close Garrisoned that they are afraid to mind there Crops; And now employ themselves in small ranging parties. Mr. Boon is very diligent at Castle-Woods and keeps up good Orders. I have reason to believe they have lately been remiss at Blackmores, and the Spys there did not do their duty.

I have tho't it would be well to have a whole Company stationed at or near the Great-Island, to secure that important pass, in case of a Cherokee War. of this matter Please favour me with your Sentiments.

You will lay me under the greatest Obligation to favour me frequently with your Instructions; as they business this way is likely to become Weighty.

I am Dear Sir With usual Respect Your Obedient Servant

ARTHUR CAMPBELL

P. S. There is but one Family as I yet hear of murdered. they spared none one Child Scalped and Tomhaked could speak Sensibly.[50] the other Family had fled to the Woods. A. C.

---

[50] In a later letter, of which only the final part has been preserved, Major Campbell gives the Roberts child's history as follows: "upon whose first appearance, my little hero ran off, his Uncle called, he knew his voice and turned and ran to him rejoiced; his Uncle questioned him, and he returned sensible Answers, Shewed his murdered Parents and sisters his Brother is not found, and I suppose captivated. He received but one Blow with a Tomhake on the back of the Head, which cut thro his scull, but it is generally believed his Brains is safe, as he continues to talk sensibly, and being an active wise Boy, what he relates is Credited. For my part I don't know as I ever had tenderer feelings of compasion, for any of the human Species. I have sent for him, and employed an Old Man that has some Skill to attend him. I

P. S. I luckily procured one pound & half of Powder before the Militia went out, which I divided to such as had none, 3 loads apiece, which they went very cheerfully out on. If you could possibly spare me, one or two pounds I would divide it in the same, sparing manner, in case of another alarm.

I intend to send to you, as soon as Capt. Smith returns to let you know the event of his journey by which Opportunity the Powder if you can Spare it can come If a good opportunity dont offer before.

I am Yours &c

A CAMPBELL

Please hurry ye. Flour out as there is great need of it There is Beef enough bought and bespoke.

On his Majestys Service To Col⁰. William Preston To be forwarded by Mr. Brander

---

[Maj. Arthur Campbell to Col. William Preston. 3QQ109.]

Saturday Octb. 1 1774

Dear Sir—Last Thursday [Sept. 29] between sunset and dark, three Men was fired at within 300 Yds [of] Moors Fort on Clinch one John Duncom was shot dead on the Spot; and Scalped, altho a party of Men ran out of the Fort to the place as soon as the Guns fired; The Indians ran off and Night prevented them

---

wish I could get Doctr. Lloyd to him. If he cannot come, please try if the Doctor could not send me up some Medicines with directions. I have been too tedious, and circumstantial, in relating the little hero's story, but as it seems to be a singular instance I am perswaded you won't be displeased with it." (Draper MSS., 3QQ111.)—ED.

then being followed. The Express came of[f] next morning early. Mr. Boone was preparing to go in search of the Enemy. Mr. Boone also informs me that the Indians has been frequently about Blackmores, since the Negroes was taken; And Capt. Looney has so few Men that he cannot venture to go in pursuit of them, having only eleven Men I have had no Word yet from Doack, Thompson, Montgomery or Cox, and indeed I am afraid there will few if any come, If I may now judge of their conduct from that in time of the former alarms. If the[y] don't come I hope you will judge it expedient to endeavour to raise Men elsewhere. I Wrote Capt. Thomas Bryan[51] lately who has a large stock on Mockison, that I would be glad he could come over and bring a parcel of good Woodsmen with him, but as I give himself no encouragement to be employed asistance from there is uncertain.

Mr. Boone has sent me the War Club that was left it is diffirent from that left at Blackmores; Mr. Boone thinks it is the Cherokees that is now annoying us, I rather believe it is some of Major M·Donalds desper-

---

[51] The Bryans were a large family who came from Ireland, and first settled on Opequon Creek in the lower part of the Valley of Virginia. Later they removed to North Carolina, and formed a large settlement known by their name, on the upper Yadkin. The Bryans intermarried with the Boones, and a party of forty from their settlement joined Daniel Boone in his proposed migration to Kentucky, which was checked owing to the slaying by Indians in Powell's Valley of sons of Boone and Russell. Probably Capt. Thomas Bryan was one of this party, as they were all good woodsmen. He was the youngest son of the first emigrant, Morgan Bryan, grandfather of Boone's wife. The Bryans later (1779) settled a station of that name in Kentucky, but Thomas does not appear to have been of their number. One of his name was a Loyalist leader in North Carolina, and perished at the Battle of Shallow Ford (Oct. 15, 1780).—Ed.

ate fugitives that has taken refuge some where on the Ohio [to] the back of us; and would willingly deceive us into a belief that it is the Cherokees, that they may succeed that way to create a misunderstanding between us and the old Chiefs. Your Letter to Ocanassoto I expect will have a speedy conveyance as there is at Wattaga two Cherokees friends of ours who I expect will carry it for a small reward; and I have wrote to Mr. Carter[52] that the Messenger must bring an Answer, before he gets his pay For which I will wait with impatience, as it may clear up the Present doubts.

I have inclosed a letter of Abraham Bledsoe to me. The Man is a good Woodsman, as to the other parts of his Character I am but a stranger to. I don't know as Col. Wright or Armstrong[53] is to be trusted as I am well informed they behaved with extreme duplicity to Capt. Jones on a late occasion; besides I understand Armstrong wants to get possession of that part of Colo. Donelsons purchase between Holston and the

---

[52] John Carter was one of the prominent pioneers of east Tennessee. Of superior education and good family, his advantages gave him leadership in the new community. As early as 1772, he opened an Indian trading establishment west of the Holston, in what was known as Carter's Valley. In the Treaty of Sycamore Shoals (1775) he received indemnity for being robbed by the Indians. About this time he removed his residence to Watauga, where he was chairman of the court, and of the committee of safety, as well as colonel of the militia. Colonel Carter embarked in the State of Franklin enterprise, and was one of its leading magistrates. He acquired a large landed estate, and Carter County, Tenn., was named in his honor.—ED.

[53] Col. Gideon Wright and Col. Martin Armstrong were prominent citizens of upper North Carolina. The former was a Loyalist in the Revolution; the latter, a Whig, took command of the American troops after the battle of King's Mountain.—ED.

West Line As Armstrong looks upon it he has a right to the emoluments of that bent [bend] as a Surveyor in North-Carolina. Capt. Tom. Bryan is a good honest fellow if he raises Men I wish you would encourage him. If you have an oppertunity Please let Capt. Bledsoe know I have ordered Men to be stationed at his House; besides there is upwards of 20 Men ranging between him and the North-fork. It may be well to let him know this piece of News, as the present alarms may go to the levels worse than it is, and he may do a disservice if he should turn home. I shall have a particular attention to all the Gents. Ladies that is on the Expedition, and shall afford them all reasonable assistance in my power.

I am Dear Sir Your most Obedient Servant

ARTHUR CAMPBELL

To Colo. Preston.

BRINGING UP THE REAR

[Anthony Bledsoe to Col. William Preston. 3QQ108.]

CAMP UNION 1st October 1774

DEAR SIR—The unexpected delays Attending the Expedition Occasioned me to be no farther on my March then this place, some Company being obliged to wait till the return of the Horses from the Advanced Partys Six brigades of which return'd last night, Though so much Worsted that they will not possiably be able to go [to] the Springs for their loads till about Monday. Colo. Lewis by his Writing to

Colo. Christian expected in all probarbility the whole of the fluor Order'd by him for the Expedition was are [ere] now at this place, though upwards of two hundred & fifty Loads not yet Arived. One hundred & fifty of them not left Santown [Staunton], the Other hundred now at the Warm Springs, which I have to wait for and shall be oblig'd to send Horses to Stantown [for] the hundred & fifty Loads Still there, as Mr. Mathews[54] Writes it is quite [out] of his power to send them, though am not oblig'd to wait any longer then the Hundred loads can be brought from the Warm Springs, which I doubt will be too late to See any thing more [than] the trouble of the Pack horses & the badness of the Road, though Colo. Lewis it is likely told Severall of the Pack Masters that they would be [in] time Enough to go to the Towns, if so, I shall, though I much dout it. Colo. Charles by report would start this Week to the Mouth of the Kanawoway from Elk. I Judge every person finds the Expedition more teadious then it was generally expected.

I have sent inclosd a Copy of Colo. Andw Lewis Letter to Colo. Christian.

Colo. Christian Started from this place last Tuesday Evening, nothing remarkable since my arivall here. I have much use for a hospital and Doctor, as all the sick from the [w]hole regiment is left here, which ren-

---

[54] Sampson Matthews, brother of George, was the keeper of the ordinary at Staunton, and a man of prominence in Augusta County. He had served as commissary in the French and Indian War, also as deputy sheriff and justice of the peace. In 1781 he was colonel of a regiment raised to repel Arnold's invasion of Virginia. He was officially styled "Master driver of cattle," in Charles Lewis's Augusta regiment on the Point Pleasant compaign.—ED.

ders may stay very disagreeable. if anything worther of notice happens before my depart[ure] I shall Acquaint you, if any thing has appeard to you since I came away from your House please to let me knowe. I do not expect to leave this place till about the 15th Instant.

 I am, Dear Sir Your most Hble Servt

ANTHONY BLEDSOE.

 To Col. William Preston in Smith Field Fincastle County p^r fav^r. of M^r. James Gilmore

---

TROOPS FOR BORDER DEFENSE

[John Montgomery to Col. William Preston. 3QQ110.]

DEAR SIR—I Received your Leter wherin you desired I should use My influence with Regard to raising 15 men to Go to the assistance of the Distressed People of Holston. Agreeable to which I appointed Michael Dougherty Ensign to Command that party, if they Could be raised in Capt. Crocketts Company, but as his bounds is not large & the Most part of them went out with himself to the Campaign, that Number I realy believe Cannot be rais^d in Capt. Crocketts Company, unless Men were to Leave their wives and Children exposed to the Mercy of the Enemy, which we in reason Cannot Expect. M^r. Dougherty is Still willing to serve if you Can but Contrive how he may Make up that Number of men. he has used all Deligence ever since I acquanted him of the Matter & hath no Certanty of More than 5 or 6 men, as the Cheif of the

but if you will Give him authority to make up the Number out of any other Company where you think they can be best Spared Mr. Dougherty will freely Serve and begs that you may Send further instructions as Soon as you Conveniantly Can, And Conclude with Subscribing myself Dear Sir your most Obdiant & Hble. Servt.

JOHN MONTGOMERY[55]

2ᵈ. Octbʳ. 1774
To Colᵒ. William Preston, Fincastle, These.

---

[55] Col. John Montgomery was a native of western Virginia, of Irish parents, being born within the limits of Botetourt County, about 1748. His natural gifts were great, and he was readily recognized as a leader in the young community, being made magistrate of Botetourt (1770), later of Fincastle County (1772), and a member of the committee of safety in 1775. He is usually supposed to have gone on the Point Pleasant expedition with Christian; but this letter proves he was elsewhere occupied upon the frontier. In the Cherokee campaign of 1776 he commanded a company under Christian, and was stationed at Long Island at its close In 1778 he was ordered out with George Rogers Clark, to Kentucky, thus becoming one of Clark's four captains on the Illinois campaign. After the taking of Kaskaskia, Montgomery was sent to Virginia with dispatches, and there ordered to enroll a regiment for Clark's re-inforcement, of which he was to be lieutenant-colonel. The alarm from the back settlements led him, however, to join Shelby's Chickamauga expedition (1779), thus delaying his return to Illinois until May of that year. He continued in the Illinois until the close of the war, when he settled in southwest Kentucky, later removing to the Cumberland, and founding Clarksville (Tenn.), named in honor of his former commander. He was actively engaged in the Genet expedition (1793-94), of which Clark was to take command. After its collapse, he went out on the Nickajack campaign, distinguishing himself for his daring. The same year (1794), however, he fell victim to Indian hostility, being killed while on a hunting excursion, not far from the mouth of the Cumberland. Most of these details are found in Draper MSS., 36J22.—ED.

DISTRESS OF THE FRONTIER

[Maj. Arthur Campbell to Col. William Preston. 3QQ112.]

ROYAL-OAK, Octr. 4th. 1774

DEAR SIR—Since I closed my Letter Yesterday[56] Capt. Thompson came here; and give me a particular account of the situation of the People in the lower Settlement; he was much put to it to get Men to go out of the Inhabitants, however with 9 Men he venture thro' Mockison Gap, and somewhere between the North-fork and Clinch mountain he came upon fresh tracks but could not make them out any distance.

Upon the late alarm I ordered out Sergt. Commands to range along the back side the Settlement on Holston so that there is now a second Chain of rangers from the Great Island up   I also Ordered 4 Men to Mr. Bledsoe 4 to Mr. Shelby and 4 to Mr. Cummins for their particular protection;

Upon consulting with Capt. Thompson it was agreed that I should make application to you for his having the Command of these upon Duty in this Side Clinch mountain, and that he would endeavour to have a party of 20 always with himself to range. besides It was necessary that some Officer on Duty should be among the lower Inhabitants at this time to encourage them and regulate matters.

Since I wrote the above I received yours by Mr. Montgomery and am glad to receive Orders anticipat-

---

[56] This was the letter referring to the Roberts child. See *ante*, p. 208, note 45.—ED.

ing my application for a third Capt. on Duty, and I make no doubt but you will approve my appointment of Capt. Thompson, especially as I find it is the best way he can do any thing at his other business which it is rendered very difficult for him to perform on account of the confusion among the Inhabitants. I make no doubt but your last supply of Ammunition will encourage the Inhabitants much, as I think every Man have 1/2 doz shoots a piece having direct[ed] the Powder to be divided by their Gun-Measures.

I am Sir your Obedient Servt.

ARTHUR CAMPBELL

P. S. I have sent you a Paper delivered me by Capt. Thompson by which you may see Cockes resolution.

To Colo. William Preston pr fr. of Mr. Trimble

[George Adams to Col. William Preston. 3QQ113.]

HOLSTON RIVER October ye 4th 1774

SIR—I need not Relate ye Distresed Circumstances of those Parts to you I imagain you have Such acounts too Frequent ye Mockinson people is Left home Some time ago and some of them is Now at my hous where there is a few of us Gathered and hopes to tary here untill we heare how Circmstances promis With our Army at ye Same time if it is in your Power and you Will Be so Kind as to alow them a few men the time they are Gathering theire Crops they then can Suport there familys and if not they canot suport theire famileys here they mus unavoidably Remove theire Famileys from Those Parts they have Large Crops it is a pity y^t so much Grain Should be Lost I Would beg ye favour of you to Write if you Can aford them aney asistance as ye vermin is now Distroying theire Grain very fast I Could Equally Beg for maney other places But I dout y^t Every Place Canot be Suplyed With men.

Amunition is very scarce With us Which is ye ocasion of abundanc of Feare from Sir your Humble Servt With Esteeme

Gore. Adams

To Colo^n. W^m. Preston, this.

[Capt. Daniel Smith to Col. William Preston. 3QQ114.]

D^r. Sir—The late Invasions of Indians hath so much alarm'd the Inhabitants of this River that without more men come to their Assistance from other parts, some of the most timorous among us will remove to a place of Safety, and when once the example is set I fear it will be followed by many. By what I can learn the terror is as great on Holston, so that we've no room to hope for 'Assistance from that quarter. M^r. Kingkeid is an intelligent man and can give you an account of the Situation of the Clinch inhabitants; To him I refer you for the same. I am just going to the Assistance of the Castles Woods men with what force could be

THE DISTRESSED FRONTIER 229

spared from this upper district. I am Dr Sir Yours most respectfully

DAN SMITH

Elk Garden 4th. Octr. 1774.

Vincent Hobbs
Thos. Shannon
Robert Brown
Saul Cecil
John Smith
Wm Baylstone
Holton Money
Sam^{ll} Money

W^m. M^caDoo
John Mares
Joseph Mares
David Pattom
Israel Harmon
Thos. Maxwell
Joseph Turner
W^m. Magee[57]

to Col. William Preston at Smithfield P^r. M^r. Jno. Kingkead.

[Maj. Arthur Campbell to Col. William Preston. 3QQ114.]

DEAR SIR—John Cox is just arrived here with 24 Men I shall send him down the River, to range about Reedy-Creek and Mockison Gap until the Flour you mentioned arrives and then he may serve as an Escort to the provisions over to Blackmores; Mr. Cummins will wait upon you, and he can inform you his Sentiments of the situation, I wish you could do something for him I have done all I can.

I am Dear Sir your most Obedient Servt.

ARTHUR CAMPBELL

Oct. 5, 1774.

pr fa^v. of Rev. Chas. Cummins.

---

[57] Evidently a list of the garrison at Elk Garden.—ED.

[Maj. Arthur Campbell to Col. William Preston. 3QQ115.]

ROYAL-OAK Oct°. 6. 1774

SIR—The Evening after M^r. Cummins left this, I Received your Letter of ye 1st. Inst. sent out by Paddy Brown; who tho't proper, to carry the Letter past, and it was returned me this day open. I wish it was in my power to humour every Inhabitant, consistant with Justice to the Service; but there is many of them so unreasonably selfish I dispair of succeeding in every case.

Paddy Brown is an Old Weaver Body, that lives with one of the Doughertys, he came here one day and applied for to get in for a Spy, I very flatly refused him; he then went off in dudgeon.

Upon the alarm of Lammey being taken, Vances & Fowlers Wives with several other Families convened at M^r. Harrisons[58] which lyes upon the Main path to Clinch, in the Rich Valley, opposit to the Town-House, upon the request of several Inhabitants in both sides, I ordered Six Men to be Stationed there for ten Days; two of which was always to be out ranging. Hen^y. & Jos°. Dougherty moved their Families to this side the mountain, disagreeing with y^e. Majority of y^e. Inhabitants, as to the place to build a Fort. M^r. John Campbells Wife has been in this side the mountain this two months past, and himself has acted as Ensign to

---

[58] The Harrisons were a prominent family of western Virginia but whether connected with the Frederick County Harrisons, from whom the presidents descended, is uncertain although it is probable, for a Benjamin Harrison was killed on Holston in 1754. See Preston register, in Draper MSS., 1QQ83.—ED.

Capt. Smith, on Clynch ever since that Gent. was Ordered on Duty. Archibald & John Buchanans Familys,[59] and Andw. Lammeys came here; who has continued in this side yet; Capt. Wilson went Immediately with 15 Men, and ranged near a Week in the Neighbourhood where Lammey was taken, and he left four of his best Woodsmen with the Neighbours, for several days longer. I also ordered two of the most trusty persons I could get, for to act as Spys along Clynch Mountain for 10 days which they performed I am satisfyed faithfully; besides they Six Men, at Harrisons, I ordered Mrs. Vance & Fowlers Wife 3 Men a Week particularly, to asist about saving their fodder, which they got removed with safety.

All the Men stationed in this side Clynch, I give particular directions that they should if possible, be Young Men; and be ready to march to other places if called upon; Indeed when I first Ordered these men I had a Scheme in it, to send such good hands as could be best Spared out of them over to fill up Capt. Looneys and Smiths Companys on Clynch when the fears of the people in this side was a little abated. It has fell out extremely unlucky, that both them Gentlemens ranging Stations, was very thin when ye. Indians came. Capt. Smith having to wait until he was reinforced

---

[59] In the early days of Augusta County, Col. John Buchanan was deputy surveyor for Col. James Patton, and located many valuable tracts of land upon Holston River, where his descendents lived. Archibald lived on the North Fork, and the August court of this year (1774) had ordered a road surveyed thither from Arthur Campbell's. John Buchanan served as lieutenant of the 7th Virginia continental regiment, and was killed in battle in 1777.—ED.

from this side before he could pursue. And at Blackmores the other Day the Indians coursd one of the Negroes they took, near a quarter of an Hour, several times in view of the Fort.

In short the most of the people in this Country, seem to have a private plan of their own, for their own particular defence.

The people in the Wolf–Hill Settlement,[60] will have the Indians, to come up the Valley & North fork, opposite to them, and then make a Right-Angle to their habitations, they people on ye. South fork will have the Enemy, to steal Slyly, up the Iron Mountain, and make one Grand attack, on the Head of Holston, and Sweep the River down before them; The Head of New River will have it, that the Cherokees will fetch a Compass, round Wattago Settlement, and come down New River, on a particular Search for their Scalps. The Rich–Valley and North fork people will have Sandy the dangerous pass. for proof of which the[y] quot[e] former and recent Instances; to wit Stalnaker & Henrys Family being carried out the same road.[61] You may thus see what a task one would have to remove every ones wears; I wish I could be instrumental in defending from real ones, imaginary dangers would give me less anxiety.

* * * * * * * *

I am Sir Your most Obedient

ARTHUR CAMPBELL

---

[60] The present Abingdon, Washington County.—ED.
[61] Stalnaker's family was attacked June 18, 1755. The reference to Henry's family is to the incident mentioned *ante*, pp. 192, 193.—ED.

THE DISTRESSED FRONTIER

[Maj. Arthur Campbell to Col. William Preston. 3QQ116.]

Thursday Evening Octr. 6. 1774

S$_{IR}$—Samuel Shannon came here to day with 21 head of Cattle several of them very indifferent. I have detained him until the Beginning of next Week as he says he wont go further without a guard; by which time I expect the flour Waggons will be up, and I can send both together to Mockison Gap, you will see by Capt. Smiths Letter that there is near cattle enough engaged for his Fort. One of the Snodgrasses says he seen an Indian a little below Capt. Thompsons the day before Yesterday, I rather think if he seen anything it was some of Donelsons and Masons party in disguise as I hear they have threatened the Sheriff. The Boy that was scalped is dead, he was an extraordinary example of patience and resolution to his last, frequently lamenting "he was not able to fight enough for to save his mammy." I divided the last of the 8^{lb}. Powder that came by Vance to Lieut. Cox Men yesterday The[y] had 4 Shoots apiece and with perswasions I got them to go down the River, they said the[y] would turn home if they did not get more next Week. I hope Branders powder will be up by that time.

I am Sir Your most H^{bl}. Servt.

A$_{RTHUR}$ C$_{AMPBELL}$

	Men	Miles	
Blackmores	16		Serg^t Moor
Moores	20	20	Boone
Russells	20	4	W. Poage Serg^t.
Glado Hollow	15	12	John Dunken Serg^t.
Elk Garden	18	14	John Kinkead Serg^t.
Maiden Springs	5	23	Joseph Craven D^o.
Whittons, big Crab Orcha	3	12	Ensign Campbell [62]

To Col^o. William Preston. p^r. fv^r. of M^r. Hen. Thompson

[Capt. Abraham Penn to Capt. Joseph Martin. 1XX3.]

SMITHFIELD.

DEAR SIR—I have proceeded on my Journey Home as for our Discharge it will not be till November at Least. the Col^o. wont agree that any of my men Shall go Home, but I am to git three or four Whilst gone to Relieve those few that Necessity Requires at Home. Philip Cavenaugh must be Imployed as a Spye, and pray keep them all at there Constant Duty, for the Indians have made Four Brakes on Holston and the People are all forting with all Dexterity so that We may Expect the Next Stroke in our parts. be Constant on your Gard and Keep a Strict Search in them parts. let the People know that it is thought they are in Danger, as they May be on there Defence. I think

---

[62] This list of the forts and their garrisons is on the backing of the letter. Crab Orchard was in the present Tazewell County, the first settlement made within its borders by Carr and Butler in 1766–67. In 1771, Butler sold out to Thomas Witten (Whitton). The fort was about three miles west of Jeffersonville. See Bickley, *Tazewell County*, pp. 55, 56.—ED.

Gatliff and Clay had better Move there families back again, as they are in a Back place, for I should be very Sorry any Mischief Should be Done in them parts. pray Dont let one Charge of powder be shot In Vain for I Expect we Shall be in great Want before any Supply can be got. Colo. preston Says he will stop Alsups Wages for you If it comes to his hands. I expect Colo. will Send a Supply of provisions to you Soon No more but am your Sincere Friend and Humble Sert

ABRAHAM PENN[63]

Oct. 7th 1774
To Capt. Joseph Martin[64] at Culbersons Bottom

---

[63] Capt. Abraham Penn was evidently at Smithfield, Colonel Preston's residence, when he wrote this letter to Capt. Joseph Martin; the latter, although holding a commission of equal rank with Penn, served as his subordinate at the Culbertson Bottom fort. Penn was an old resident of this region, and Martin, a new-comer, chose to serve under him rather than be omitted from the service. Penn lived on New River the remainder of his life and rose to be colonel of militia. (Information given to Dr. Draper by Martin's son, in Draper MSS., 3XX18.)—ED.

[64] Gen. Joseph Martin was one of the influential borderers of his time. Born in Albemarle County (1740) he was a schoolmate of Gen. Thomas Sumter, and Col. Benjamin Cleveland. A boy of great energy, he was rebellious toward discipline and ran away to join the army (1756) at Fort Pitt. He afterwards became a trapper and hunter, and in the course of his explorations visited Powell's Valley, and determined to make it the site of his station. In 1769, under the leadership of Dr. Thomas Walker, he took up a large tract therein and planted corn. After the war of 1774, in which Martin was occupied in defense of a frontier fort, and as a leader of scouts, he became the Powell's Valley agent of the Transylvania land company, and established a colony fifty miles westward of the settlements. He was always active in Indian warfare, commanded a company against the Cherokee in 1776, and the following year was appointed by the new government as Indian agent, a position of responsibility and power. In discharge of his du-

POINT PLEASANT CAMP BEFORE THE BATTLE

[Col. William Fleming to Col. Adam Stephen. 2ZZ71.]

To Colo Stephens at the Mouth of Hockhocking [Oct. 8]⁶⁵

Dᴿ Sɪʀ—I was very agreeably surprized this morning when Colo Lewis favoured me with a sight of yours from Hockhocking. to know you was so near, and that we were to make an excursion again together after so long an Interval of ease, rousd in my breast, sentiments I know not what to call them, but surely they are warmer than common lifeless Friendships contracted in indolence or over a bottle A Soldiers connections in this light may be compared to Gun Powder which keapt dry, will with a spark kindle into a blaze this [will] I hope be a sufficient excuse for my giving you a true state of our Situation at present. Agreeable to My Lords. instructions From Augusta Botetourt & Fincastle, Colo Andw Lewis march[ed] to

---

ties he resided many years at Long Island on the Holston, and was frequently a commissioner to draw up treaties such as that at Hopewell (1785), which made possible the King's Mountain Campaign (1780); and his influence was potent in counteracting British intrigues. In 1789 he resigned his office. Retiring to Virginia he served in the legislature, where he aided Madison with the resolutions of 1798; he also ran the boundary line between Virginia and Tennessee (1800), and died at his home in Henry County, Dec. 18, 1808. He was a man of much physical and mental vigor a born leader, brave to a fault, and devotedly served by his friends. See letters of his sons in Draper MSS., 3XX13, 18, 29; 8ZZ2.—Ed.

⁶⁵ This letter is undated; but a comparison with Fleming's Journal shows that the message was received from Dunmore and Stephen the morning of the eighth. Fleming and Stephen had campaigned together in the French and Indian War.—Ed.

this place 800 effective R[ank] & File the most of them Woodsmen well Armed & such as may be depended on. Our rear of 200 & odd men are within 60 miles of us. Officers & Attendants are not included in the Above. With such a force Colo Stephens would the Shawnese & Mingoes be more than a Breakfast. We have had a verry fatiguing march. Our horses are wore out. Our Canoes are sent back to Elk for flower so that it is impossible to leave this, before the rear joins us with Flower & Bullocks. I am heartily sorry it is inconvenient for the troops with you to meet us here, as it may be Attended with disagreeable Consequences both from the reasons above, And likewise the Officers & mens being sensible that they are as near the Shawnese towns or perhaps nearer than at Hockhocking. They look on the Enemy as within their grasp and though marching 70 or 80 miles out of their course as giving the Enemy an Opportunity to Escape They likewise know the mouth of the Kanhaway to be a considerable pass into the frontiers of Augusta Botetourt & Fincastle and deserting such a pass or neglecting it by marching up the river is leaving their Friends & Families exposed, but still they are willing should these reasons be Over ballanced [by] others of more weight to march where ever they are ordered. But Dr Sir I am Affraid it would blunt the keen edge they have at present which might be keept sharp for the Shawnese &c: I am convinced it would be Attended by considerable desertions. And perhaps raise a Spirit of Discontent not easily Queld amongst the best regulated Troops, but much more so amongst men unused to the Yoak of

Military Discipline. which way so ever we march be Assured it gives me the greatest Pleasure to have the Honour of serving under His Lordship especially as Col⁰ Stephens will be with us. I am &c.

W. F.

THE FRONTIER STILL EXPOSED

[Maj. Arthur Campbell to Col. William Preston. 3QQ117.]

ROYAL-OAK Oct⁰. 9. 1774

DEAR SIR—Last Thursday Evening the Indians took a Negroe Wench Prisoner, belonging to Capt. Shelby within 300 Y^{ds}. of the House.[66] After they took her some distance they examined her, how many Guns was in the Fort, and other questions relative to the strength of the place. They also asked if the store was kept there now.

After they had carried her off about a Mile, they seen or heard, a Boy coming from Mill, they immediately tyed the Wench, and went off to catch they Boy, while they were gone, the Wench luckily got loose, and made her escape; She says they knocked her down twice, when she refused to tell in what situation the Fort was, and she says One was a large Man much Whiter than the rest and talked good English. It was they same kind of a person Mr. Blackmore saw in pursuit of the Negroe he believed; some think

---

[66] Shelby's house was on the site of Bristol, Tenn., or Sapling Grove, as it was called in frontier times.—ED.

Capt. John Logan[67] is about yet—others that it is Will Emery, a half Breed Cherokee as he was one mentioned by Shoat that was out, and he is known to be for some time past, in the Shawanese Interest he was the Interpreter when Col. Donelson run the line. and it was he robed Knox & Skeggs.[68]

---

[67] The party employed in this marauding expedition was the one organized by Logan; see his message, *post*.—ED.

[68] This refers to the plundering of the Station Camp of the Long Hunters (1771), in Green County, Ky., when they carved on the bark of a tree, "Fifteen hundred skins gone to ruination." Dr. Draper describes this event in Draper MSS., 3B 230-238; he also gives the following sketch of the leaders. "Henry Skaggs and brothers were a noted family of hunters, and nothing but hunters; and keeping pace with the advancing settlements, they pushed forward to Clinch River, and were in 1777 at Shadrack White's Station in the neighborhood of Maiden Spring Fork of Clinch. In 1779, Henry Skaggs, accompanied by upwards of twenty men, started for Kentucky, were attacked by Indians in Powell's Valley, lost part of their horses, when all returned, save Skaggs, his son John a mere youth, and a man named Sinclair. With eleven horses they went to the Green River country to hunt, and during the succeeding hard winter Sinclair got lost, probably drowned in Green River, and young Skaggs sickened and died, and amidst the severities of the season a hollow log was his burial place. His father was left alone to finish the hunt, and return home with the horses, pelts and furs. He settled on Pitman's Creek in the Green River country, within the present Taylor County, Ky., in 1789, with his children and connections around him, sharing freely in the Indian difficulties of the times; and there he died in 1808 or '09, aged upwards of eighty years. Possessing a large and bony frame, he was bold, enterprising and fearless. His brothers Charles and Richard also settled in that region, lived to a good old age."

James Knox, a native of Ireland, served as a scout with Christian in 1774, headed one of Morgan's companies of riflemen at Saratoga and Stillwater, and retired with the rank of major. After the Revolution he settled in Kentucky, married the widow of Benjamin Logan, and died in 1822, respected and wealthy.—ED.

Jno. Young came here last night, with two load of flour I could not possibly prevail upon him, to carry it any farther, I am afraid I shant get a Waggon for two or three days to carry it to Reedy-Creek; at Blackmores they are in great Want. Mr. Lewis has not sent the Skins you mentioned, he told me Crabtree had disappointed Capt. Lewis We shall try to have some by next Waggons.

I am informed Capt. Cocke has sent Word over that he is likely to get a large Company. Pray Write me what I shall say to him: his Public Spirit is much talked of by many of the Inhabitants; indeed the want of men is a general cry.

I am Dr. Sir Yours Respectfully

ARTHUR CAMPBELL

P. S. By the letters Mr. Biddle brought me last night from the Mouth of Elk, It appears that it is Capt. Russell & Shelbys intentions to come home by the way of Kentucke, and they have appointed to meet Mr. Boone the 15th. of November at the mouth of Dicks River with Horses. Please let me know whether I shall let Boone go or not. What would you think of employing Capt. Cocke that way as he is so hot for the fatigues of Marching.

I forgot to mention Capt. Thompson was on his march with about 30 Men near Capt. Cockes when he got the news about Shelbys Wench. perhaps our sculking Enemies may be found out this Week.

Yours

A. C.

To Colo. William Preston. On his Majestys Service

[Col. William Preston to Capt. Daniel Smith. 4XX44.]

Octr. 9th. 1774

DEAR SIR—I rec^d. yours by Mr. Kinkead and am really concerned for the distrest situation of the Inhabitants on Clinch and Holston. I would to God it was in my Power to give them such Assistance as their Dangerous Circumstances Demand. The scarcity of Men as well as Ammunition is very Alarming. I have sent 24 men out of Capt Herberts & 22 out of Capt Doacks Companies to Major Campbell; I have also ordered out Capt. Wilson with about 30 Pittsylvanians. I am also in hopes that Mr William Doack and one Dougherty will take out upwards of 20 men in a very little time.

I have also by Mr. Kinkead given express Orders to Capt. Cloyd to draught as many single men as are in his Company, and get as many married men as are willing to go, which will in all I hope be above twenty, & either to send an Officer or march them out himself to Clinch by the Way of Walkers Creek, & to be disposed of on that River by Major Campbell to the best Advantage for the Defence of the Inhabitants. I shall try before they go out to procure two Pounds of Powder to send with them.

On hearing of the late Murders on your Quarter I sent an Express to the President Imploring some Relief for this County particularly in the Article of Ammunition.[69] I also wrote to the merchants at Rocky

---

[69] Probably this is the letter of Preston published in *Amer. Archives*, i. p. 808. The president of the council at this time was Thomas Nelson, who had long been secretary of

Ridge on the same subject; and to several Gentlemen, particularly Doct^r Walker and Col^o Pendleton,[70] but as the President don't Act as Commander in Chief while the Governor is in the Colony I expect the Express will be detained untill to morrow that the Coun-

---

that body. He was younger brother of William, former president of the council, and uncle of Thomas, signer of the Declaration ot Independence. Secretary Nelson was born in Yorktown in 1716, and died at the same place in 1782. He was leader of the moderate party among the Virginia patriots, and received forty-five votes in the convention that elected the first governor of Virginia, being defeated by Patrick Henry. Too old for military service, he sent three sons into the Revol•‌tionary army.—ED.

[70] Dr. Thomas Walker was born in King and Queen County in 1715, and educated for a physician. In 1748 he became interested in Western lands, and accompanied Patton and Buchanan into southwest Virginia, an expedition resulting two years later in further exploration beyond the Alleghanies; at which time Cumberland Mountains, Gap and River, and Kentucky River were named. In the French and Indian War, Dr. Walker acted as commissary with the rank of major; in 1768 he was Virginia commissioner at the Treaty of Fort Stannix, and several times served in similar capacities. An ardent Whig, he was a member of the Revolutionary committee and that of safety, and later (1777), of the council of state, and the general assembly (1782). He was much interested in science, and is said to have stimulated Jefferson's interest in scientific pursuits and Western discovery. Dr. Walker died (1794) at his estate of Castle Hill, in Albemarle County, where his descendants still reside. See "First Exploration of Kentucky," in Filson Club *Papers*, No. 13, for further details of Dr. Walker's career.

Col. Edmund Pendleton was born in Caroline County, Va., in 1721 and, although having but few early advantages, by sheer force of ability rose to the front rank of Virginia statesmen. He was a member of the assembly as early as 1752, and in almost continuous public service until after the ratifying convention of 1788, whose presidency he held. Preston wrote to him as a county-lieutenant for Caroline, to which office he had been appointed in 1774. It would appear that Preston was ignorant of his absence in Philadelphia as one of the Virginia delegation to the first continental congress.—ED.

cil meets, when I have the greatest hopes something will be done for our Defence; and that without loss of Time. I shall endeavour all I can to get a few men to Garrison the Important Pass at Culbersons Bottom & if I succeed therein, I will order the Party there to your Assistance. This is all I can do if my own Family was at any one Fort on your River, and each of my sisters Families at the others.

If any Method could be fallen on to enable the Inhabitants to secure their Crops it would be carrying a great Point; as the loss of them must undoubtedly Ruin the People. If Mr. Cloyd sends the men, I hope it will be a good step toward it.

I can by no means be of Opinion that the Cherokee Nation are engaged some straggling fellows of them may have Joined a Party of Shawnese who were lately at their Town, in committing the late Murders & Roberries. Nor can I think the Ohio Indians, if they intend to defend their Country at all, can spare any Number to annoy us this season, at least till the matter is tryed with the Army, the greatest part of which is at the mouth of New River, before this time.

I make no Doubt of your doing all in your Power for the Ease & Defence of the People, in which laudable Business may Heaven succeed your Endeavours.

I am Dr Sir your affectionate & very h'ble servt
WM. PRESTON

On His Majesty's Service To Capt. Daniel Smith

[Maj. Arthur Campbell to Col. William Preston. 3QQ118.]

ROYAL-OAK Octr. 12th. 1774.

Yesterday your letter by M^r. Cummins and instructions by John Kinkead came to hand; which Instructions I will strictly adhere to, as far as I think your general intentions for the protection of the whole Frontier will anywise admit.

Yesterday also I had an Express from Clynch, with the following intelligence. Thursday y^e. 6th. In^s. at Blackmores one Deal Carter was killed and Scalped within 55 Steps of the Fort. M^r. Anderson who had a man with him, fired at the Indian as he was Scalping the Man killed, while the other Man shot at another Indian. The Indians fired several shots at Anderson & the other, when they fired off the Bastion at them. The Indians had like to done Andersons Job, having struck into the stockade a few Inches from his Head.

Evidently the indians intentions was to have made a bold push to enter the Fort as the People was ch[i]efly all some distance away from the Gate upon Logs, the Enemy it seems had silently crept along under Bank of the River completely out of view, until poor Carter discovered them, he immediately commenced hallooing Murder; one Gun fired and missed—another shot him thro the Thigh, but not mortal, he could not Escape, as he was too lame: One fellow more bold than the rest, soon ran up and tomahaked and scalped him, the remainder of the enemy escaped at the distance of about 100 Y^{ds}. and fired as mentioned before.

The next day Capt. Smith came to Blackmores with a party of 30 men in connection with Boon; The Night afterwards they had Six horses out of Seven taken out (by the Indians) of a small inclosure, which the Fort Walls made part, the next Morning early Captⁿ. Smith & Boon set out with 26 choice Hands greatly anxious to proceed: they found some footing and Horse tracts not far distant from the Fort, which I hope they will be able to trace & enable them to overtake the Enemy; M^r. Anderson also informs me, that an Indian was seen behind a Smith Shop at Blackmores Sunday 9th. at break of Day. This unlucky affair happened when there were but few men in the Fort and Capt. Looney happened to be in this settlement, & Lieut. Cox had not got out. It is remarkable that Capt. Shelbys Wench was taken the Same day, and about the same time of the Day, that this affair happened on Clinch:[71] so many attacks in so short a time, give the inhabitants very alarming apprehensions; Christian's Fine Stock of Cattle, and Horses is missing; a considerable number of the Cattle and Horses about the Fort, is either killed or carryed off; Want of Ammunition and scarcity of provisions again become a general Cry; Since I began this Letter I am mortified with the Sight of a Family flying by. If Ammunition don't come soon, I will have no Argument that will have any force to detain them.

If our Army is not able to keep a Garrison at Point Pleasant & the Falls the ensuing Winter, I expect we shall be troubled with similar visits the greatest part

---

[71] The two attacks were at places more than forty miles apart.—ED.

of the ensuing Season. It is more than probable that all these late attacks were made by the Indians, that fled from the upper Shawanese town observed. I expect in a day or two to receive Some intelligence from the Cherokees, as the messenger was expected back Yesterday at from that quarter.

I am Dear Sir

ARTHUR CAMPBELL.

P. S. I have sent you inclosed Logins Original Letter which came to hand this Day.

A. C.

The Words of the Original Letter.[72]

TO CAPTAIN CRESSAP—What did you kill my people on Yellow Creek for. The white People killed my kin at Coneestoga a great while ago,[73] & I though[t nothing of that.] But you killed my kin again on Yellow Creek, and took m[y cousin prisoner] then I

---

[72] This is a contemporary copy, somewhat torn, apparently made by Colonel Preston from the original letter sent to him by Major Campbell; it is upon the lower half of the latter's letter. This is, probably, the most authentic transcript of this well-known document. The letter was written by a prisoner named William Robinson, who was captured on the Monongahela July 12, carried to the Indian towns, saved from the stake by Logan, and adopted into an Indian family. For his deposition in regard to these circumstances, see *American Pioneer*, i. pp. 14-16, 208; or Jefferson, *Notes on Virginia* (later editions), appendix. The letter was left at the house of Roberts, where the massacre occurred Sept. 24th. See letters of Harry Innes and Benjamin Sharp, *op. cit.* Judge Innes has evidently confused the date of the receipt with that of the writing of the letter.—ED.

[73] Logan here refers to what was known as the Paxton riot in 1763, when twenty inoffensive Conestoga Indians were killed by a border mob. See Parkman, *Half Century of Conflict*, ii, pp. 115-128.—ED.

thought I must kill too; and I have been three time[s to war since but] the Indians is not Angry only myself.

CAPTAIN JOH[N LOGAN]

July 21st. Day.

[Col. William Preston to Capt. Joseph Martin. 1XX4.]

SIR—Yours of the 10th. Instant came to Hand Just now. I have for several Days past expected a Waggon Load of Flour, of which I should have endeavoured to contrive you a Part; & shall do it as soon as it comes. In the Mean Time I have directed the Bearer to endeavour to forward two or three Load from Mr. Thompsons to keep you doing. I have heard that there are several Beeves belonging to the Country at Wolf Creek on the West side the River and at Rich Creek. I heartily wish you could have some of them drove to the Fort for the Use of the Company. It would save the Country a great deal of Expence, which ought to be strictly taken Notice of. These Beeves if they cant be secured now will I doubt be lost. But if they cant be found, I shall, as soon as Mr. Shannon returns from Holston, which I expect will be in a very few Days, send out some Beeves for your use. I beg of you be very careful in giving out the Provisions that there be no waste, nor no Person fed thereon but such as belong to the Company or are employed as Expresses, Drivers or the like. The orderly Sergeant should make Dayly Returns & the Provisions drawn accordingly.

I make no Doubt of your Care and Industry to Discover the Enemy. I know you have made Several long fatiguing Scouts with your Men, for which I am much obliged to you. The Pass is Important & I am fully Satisfied you will do all you can to Guard it.

I have ordered the Scouts to be under the Direction of Capt Penn & in his Absence to be under your Command; should any of them Disobey Orders, or be Refractory, let me know it; & the first step shall be to Appoint another; & the next will be to give him a Sweat for his Pay. I am almost Confident William Mc. Mullen

The satisfaction you Express on the Recovery of my Family from their late Distress, is most thankfully received. It was what I little Expected when I saw you last & for weeks after.

I am Dear Sir your most Obedt. Servt.

WM. PRESTON

12th. Octr. 1774

On His Majesty's Service to Capt Joseph Martin at Culbersons Bottom.

[Capt. Daniel Smith to Col. William Preston. 3QQ119.]

CASTLE'S WOODS 13th. Octr. 1774

DEAR SIR—I am this far on my return from the lower Settlement to the head of the river; Mr. Boon can inform you of the bad success we've had after the inhuman savages,—the murders they've committed, and the mortification we've suffer'd of putting horses into a Pen adjoining to the fort, for the Indians to take away, and whose trace we could by no means discover. I shall be as expeditious as possible in getting to the head of the River lest they should invade those parts that are particularly under my care.

Whilst I was in the lower settlement I was shown a paper signed by many of the inhabitants representing their situation to be dangerous because they've been so irregularly supply'd with the number of men allotted to the district; and also requesting you [to] appoint Mr. Boon to be a Captain, and to take charge of these lower forts, that so he may be at liberty to act without orders from Holston captains who by their frequent absence leave the inhabitants sometimes in disorder. Instead of signing this paper I chose to speak my sentiments to you concerning Mr. Boon and the paper which I suppose he will shew you. As to the paper I believe it contains the sense of the majority of the inhabitants in this settlement. Mr. Boon is an excellent woodsman. If that only would qualify him for the Office no man would be more proper. I do not know of any Objection that could be made to his character which would make you think him an improper person for that office. There may be possibly be some impropriety in it Because of Capt. Russell when he returns, but of this you are much the best judge.

I am in great haste but am Dr Sir with much esteem Your very humble Serv.

DAN SMITH

To Col. William Preston. at Smithfield

[Maj. Arthur Campbell to Col. William Preston. 3QQ123.]

[Oct. 13, 1774][74]

DEAR SIR—As Mr. Boon is to be the Bearer hereof he can inform you particularly of the News this Way.

You will see by the inclosed your Old acquaintance W^m. Poage wants a Commission. he now acts as Serjeant at Fort Preston I believe he is a fit Man enough on many accounts for to be an officer; which I would be glad you could gratify him with if it don't interfere with others already appointed, which I am afraid it will, as either Vance or Capt. Looneys Ensign is int nded for that Station, I wish M^r. Boons application or rather y^e. people for him may not have a similar tendency. I think it is men, and not particular Officers, they stand in most need of. This much I am informed that it was not proposed by M^r. Boon for to Petition you as they do; But it arose from a notion that a distant Officer would not be so particularly interested for their safety as he who lives among them. And some disgust at Capt. Looney for being away at home the time of the late alarm, which he pleads in excuse that he wanted to see to the safety of his own Family, when Roberts was Killed in his Neighbourhood.

Mic. Dougherty was here Yesterday and complains about some Men that is stationed at Herberts who when he drafted them went there for an Excuse. It seems Mic. is in the right certainly there is no need

---

[74] This letter is undated, but was doubtless sent at the same time as Capt. Daniel Smith's. Boone being the bearer of both.—ED.

THE FRONTIER EXPOSED   251

yet for Men at that place, his party is only Seven and himself which I have sent to Reedy Creek to asist as Guards in carrying out Flour to Clinch.

Please Send me a News Paper or two. I have sent by Mr. Boon one perhaps you have not seen.

I am Sir Your very Humble Servt.
ARTHUR CAMPBELL.
To Colo. William Preston. pr. fr. of Mr. Boon

[Maj. Arthur Campbell to Col. William Preston. 3QQ120.]

Octr. 13th. 1774

DEAR SIR—I have just Received an Express from Capt. Cocke, That an Indian was seen Tuesday about Sun-Set near Benjamine Logans. And that he went out with a party Yesterday Morning to make discoveries, and near the place the Indian was seen the Evening before, he observed a Man run into a thicket, which He followed, but could not come up with, But found several Mockison tracts.

This Day Ensign Armstrong of Capt. Wilsons Compy. with 22 Men left this place one half of which is to stop at Mr. Cummins and the other to proceed about 10 Miles lower to one Fulkisons where there is a Number of People Assembled. also Seven Men from Capt. Crockets Company, which I have directed as low as Kings Mill where Lieut. Christian is stationed;[75] which place I am obliged to make use of as

---

[75] Belonging to a collateral branch of the family of Col. William Christian. Gilbert, son of Robert, was born about 1734. Settling in the Holston country, he commanded a company on the Cherokee campaign (1776), on the Chickamauga

a Store-House, from whence the flour is Packed to Blackmores, by the way of Mockison Gap.

Capt. Cocke also mentions that no Men came with him from Carolina. But that he expects one Colo. Walker, will send 20 or 30 in to him this Week. And he Demands of me positive Instructions what he shall do with them, when they come. Please write the Gentleman yourself. I imagine if any Men should come they wont have any objection to serve under Virginia Officers.

If the Enemy keeps alarming the Inhabitants, as they have done for some time past; we shall be hard put to it, to save the Crops of Corn. I wish that Capt. Pens Company was on the Head of Clinch. Then Capt. Smith could be removed to Elk-Garden where he would be convenient to assist either way; which might be very serviceable as he is a diligent, Active Officer.

I am Sir Your most Obedient Servant

ARTHUR CAMPBELL

P. S. I had to send some of the Men down without a Single Shoot of Powder. Please inform M^r. Buchanan that our Salt is near out.

Yours A. C.

On his Majestys Service. To Col. William Preston. p^r. M^r. Anthony Head

---

expedition (1779), and at King's Mountain (1780). He was prominent in the State of Franklin, and acted as colonel in the Cherokee War (1788). He died at Knoxville in November, 1793. King's Mill station was at the mouth of Reedy Creek, on the site of the present Kingsport, Sullivan County, Tenn.—ED.

FLEMING'S ACCOUNT OF THE BATTLE OF POINT PLEASANT

[Col. Fleming to his wife. 2ZZ6.][76]

My DR Nancy—I take this Opportunity to write you that you may be convinced I am yet amongst the living on Munday last, we were Alarmed by some from Camp that had been pursued by Indians. on the News being confirmed 150 from Augusta line & as many from the Botetourt, were ordered out. we marched in two Colums Colo. Ch: Lewis led the Augusta, I was at the head of the Botetourt line we had not march[ed] above three quarters of a mile before the Right line or Augusta line was Attack'd & in a second of time the Botetourt line likewise. the fire became general & very heavy. Colo. C. Lewis Receivd a mortal wound. I receivd three balls two through my left Arm, & one in my left breast, but I praise the Almighty, I did not fall and had strength with Assistance to reach my tent where I heard C[ol.] C. Lewis was just come in after I was dresd I went to see him. Colo. Lewis who as we did not expect a general engagement was in Camp behaved with the greatest Conduct & prudence and by timely & Opportunely supporting the lines secured under God both the Victory & prevented the Enemys Attempts to

---

[76] This is the first letter published by us, written by a participant in the battle. It is interesting to note that it was penned by one of the badly wounded officers. Although his left arm was shot in two places and he was wounded in the breast, the handwriting is clear and firm.—Ed.

break into Camp[77] it was a hard fought Battle, lasted from 7 in the Morning to an hour by sun the Indians were computed at 1000. but for a perticular Acct I must referr you to another time. I Bless God my wounds are in a good way. if it please God to spare me I propose coming in to the Inhabitants the first Opportunity. I am my Dr Nancy Yours &.

Wm Fleming

Octob^r. 13. 1774

Richd Wilson & Smith are both well Attend me Closely & will Return with me God willing

---

[Col. William Fleming to William Bowyer. 2ZZ7.][78]

Dr Will—Agreeable to my Last from Belmont, I set out on Monday Aug. 21st. and without any thing Remarkable Reached this place. ye 6th Inst. where we continued without Interruption till Monday the 10th. when about Sunrise we had intelligence of a Man being kild' & several closly pursued, by a large party or parties of Indians. Col^o A: Lewis ordered 300 Men from the two Lines of Augusta & Botetourt Forces to go in Quest of the Enemy, little Imagining

---

[77] This is valuable testimony to Col. Andrew Lewis's military conduct in the battle. By some of the ignorant backwoodsmen, he was accused of cowardice because he did not in person lead the line of battle against the enemy.—Ed.

[78] This letter is undated, but we have included it with Fleming's letter to his wife. The Bowyers were a family of Augusta pioneers supposed to be of French origin. William was a brother-in-law of Fleming, and served his term as militia officer; both in 1776 and 1781 he was a lieutenant-colonel. He died at Staunton about 1808.—Ed.

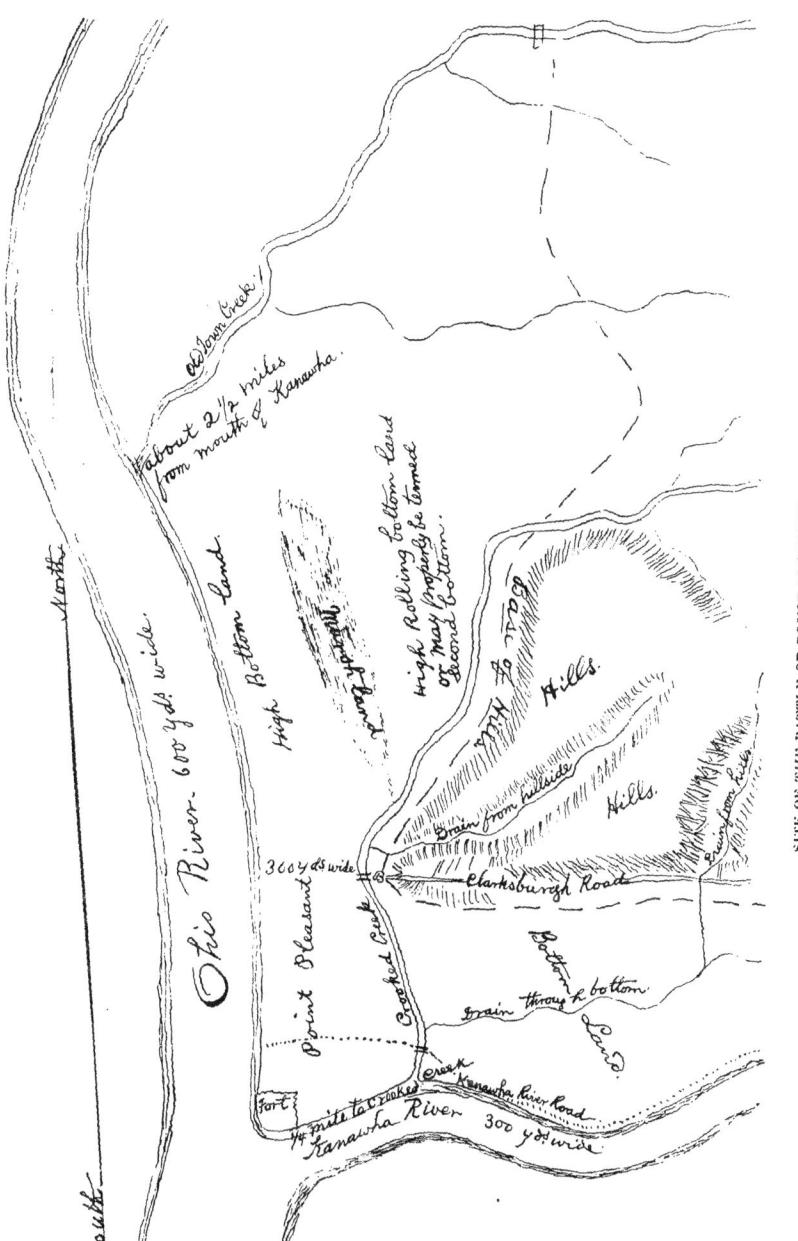

SITE OF THE BATTLE OF POINT PLEASANT
Reduced facsimile from original in the Draper MSS.—2ZZ58.

as we afterwards found it to be the Case that we were to engage the whole United Force of the Enemy Ohio Indians. we Marched from Camp in two lines Colo. Charles Lewis led the Right line. I led the left. about 3/4 of a mile from Camp, the Indians began the Attack on the right & in a Second of time the Left line was Attacked. I must refer you to perticular Accounts of which no doubt you will see several, and only Observe generals, as I am ill at ease to write. soon after or in the first Fire Colo. C. Lewis received a Mortal wound, and was brought to his tent with some Assistance. he died a few hours after, very much Regretted by the whole Army much about or soone after this hapned on the Right, I receivd three balls in the left Line two struck my left arm below the Elbow broke both the bones, & I find one of them is lodged in my arm. a third entered my breast about three Inches below my left Nipple and is lodged some where in the Chest. on finding my self effectually disabled I quitted the Field. when I came to be drest, I found my Lungs forced through the wound in my breast, as long as one of my fingars. Watkins Attempted to reduce them ineffectually. he got some part returned but not the whole. being in considerable pain, some time afterwards, I got the whole Returned by the Assistance of one of my Own Attendants. since which I thank the Almighty I have been in a surprizing state of ease. Nor did I ever know such daingerous wounds, Attended with so little inconvenience, and yet the wounds in my arm are in a bad condition. they do not digest and run but verry little. what will be the consequence as yet I know not, but I write you circumstantially that you may if it is not too much trouble, write perticularly to my wife. We had 7 or 800 Warriors to deal with. Never did Indians stick closer to it, nor behave bolder. the Engagement lasted from half an hour after [sunrise], to the same time before Sunset. And let me add I believe the Indians never had such a Scourging from the English before. they Scalpd many of their own dead to prevent their falling into Our hands, burried numbers, threw many into the Ohio and no doubt carried off many wounded. We found 70 Rafts. we tooke 18 or 20 Scalps, the most of them principle Warriors amongst the Shawnese &c, as we were informed by One McCulloch[79] who came to us from his Lordship two days after the Ingagement, who viewed the Scalps & bodies & personally Knew them he says there is not a Noted Warriour left amongst the Shawnese. After the Ingagement Colo Lewis sent off some Scouts to his Lordship two of them are since Returned. His Lordship had Marchd from Hockhocking where he had been in Camp for some days. he was joined by White Eyes the Delaware who told his Lordship 700 Warriors were gon to the South, to speak with the Army there, & that they had been followed by another Nation, that they would begin with them, in the morning and their business would be over by Breakfast time. and then they would speak with his Lordship. that they came fully convinced they would beat us I think is certain.

---

[79] William McCulloch, a prominent Indian trader, probably the same who later became one of the first settlers of Zanesville, Ohio.—ED.

they cros'd the River & encamped the same side with us the Evening before, brought over with them their goods Deer Skins &c: took no pains to conceal themselves, And were boldly Marching to Attack Our Camp when we met them Our Camp is situate on the Junction of the Kanhaway & Ohio in the Upper fork the Enemy in expectation of forcing us into the Ohio had lind the Opposite bank with some & the lower forks likewise was not neglected. the Enemy had brought their boys and squaas to knock us in the head I suppose, but God disappointed their Savage presumption. And tho Many brave Men lost their lives, Yet I hope in its consequences, it will be a general Good to the Country, and this engagement will be long Remembered to the Memory & Honour of those who purchas'd the Victory by their deaths. I am &c:

WM. FLEMING

Be sure to write my wife the Substance of this, or enclose it to her.

To Mr. William Bowyer Mercht Stanton pr Mr Klendenning

BATTLE OF POINT PLEASANT DESCRIBED BY PARTICIPANTS

[Capt. William Ingles to Col. William Preston. 3QQ121.]

POINT PLESENT at the MOUTH OF GREATE KANAWAY, October 14th 1774

SIR—I have taken this first Oppertunity of Informing you of the Particulars of Our March from the Levels to this Post we Marched from the levels the 12th of Septemr. & arrived at the mouth of Elk the 24 of sd Month where we Built several Canoes which we Loded with flower and swam our horses and Bullocks over the River on the 2d of Octobr & Continued our march to this Post without aney Molistation from the Enemy where we arrived on the 6th. and Encamped in the forks of the river where we looked on ourselves in Safe Possision of a fine Encampment and thought our Selves a terror to all the Indian Tribes on the Ohio & thus Luld in saftey till Sunday the 9th & after hearring a Good Sarman Preached by the Revd. Mr. Terrey went to Repose [wit]h Our Gards Properly Posted at a Distance from the camp as usual little Expecting to be Attackd. by any Party of Enemy as we looked upon them to be so much inferiour to us in Number, but they takeing the Advantage of the Night the[y] Crossed the Ohio on Rafts & Poisted themselves Within one mile of our Camp where the[y] lay till morning with an intent as we Suppose to force our Camp had not Providence in a Partickular manner Interposed in our behalf the[y] ware discovered by Some of our hunting Partys that hapned to turn out that Morning Verry Early and one of Our men was fird upon by them & Kild and one of them Was Kild in his Place that fireing Alarmd. the Whole Camp and two Detachments was Sent out of a hundred & fifty each the one Commanded by Colo. Charles Lewis of Agustia the Other by Colo. William Fleming the[y] soon fell in with the Enemy & a hot Engagement Ensued which Lasted three hours Very doubtfull the Enemy being much Suppirour in Number to the first Detachments Disputed the Ground with the Greatest Obstinacey often Runing up to the Very Muzels of our Gunes where the[y] as often fell Victims to thire Rage Several more Detachments being Sent from the Camp they were obligd tc Give Ground which the[y] Disputed inch by inch t'll at Lenth the[y] Posted themselves on an Advantagus peese of Ground Where the[y] Continued at Shooting now & then untill night putt an End to that Tragical Seen & left many a brave fellow Waltirring in his Gore we had the Sattisfaction of Carr[y]ing of[f] all our wounded & Kild with Very litle Lose of Sculps we Sculped 20 of them on the Field several the[y] have sculped thimselves thire wounded the[y] Carryed of[f] in the Night after the Battle and several of them the[y] Dragd into the River [Our] Loss of Men is very Considerable & it is the General oppionon of All the Officeours and men that thire Loss is Equle if not Suppirour to Ours I have been Partickular in Collecting A Catallogue of the Kild & Wounded Which I have sent you a List of

I am Dr Sir Your Humble Servt

W: INGLES.

To Col. William Preston. Fincastle These

Write to Jo McMurtory to Send in Green & not to Insist on the Jobb My Sister wants him to put in wheat.[80]

---

[80] This postscript is in a different handwriting from the letter.—ED.

NEWS OF THE REAR GUARD

[Anthony Bledsoe to Col. William Preston. 3QQ122.]

CAMP UNION. 15th. Octr. 1774.

SIR—I received yours of the 8 Instant & am ever oblig'd to you for your Inteleligence & more so for your Perticular ceare of the frunteers in generall. I communicated your Promise to Severall men at this place who had families, who Greatfully Acknowledg'd the favour & seem'd Satisfy'd. I understand by Mr. Jones that he see a Letter at your House that was left at Roberts Subscribed by one Loggens Directed to Crissop [Cresap]. There is two young men now in my Company that says they know one Loggens a mixt breed in the Shawonee Nation, one of whom I can Depend on the Other a Stranger. they both agree in Sentament as to Loggens being a notoreous Villion. I received a letter from Colo. Christian of the 6th. Ult dated at the Mouth of Elk though Nothing Perticular happend sence his departure. he had Arived at Elk in 8 days from this place, next day cross Elk with the fincastle troops for the mouth of the new river with all Possible Despatch, Colo. Lewis being started 9 days before him by some Accounts I have received) Christian informs he fou[nd] no letter at the Mouth of Elk nor no person. I last night got Inteligence from Colo. Lewis by some Desertters who say the Cannoose that carried down the floure for Colo. Lewis returnd to Elk last Monday night & that there was no Accounts from the Governer at the Mouth of the New river. I expect an express every Moment if anything Perticular shall let you know Colo. Christian informs me he had sent Express to Colo. Lewis which he expected would be back at the Mouth of Elk in four days from the 6th which was to come to me As soon as possiable. Colo. Slaughter is left at Elk With Several Compenies till further Orders I purpose starting from this place Tomorrow with about 200 Horses & 80 Cattle & hope to reach the Mouth of new River in 12 days if the Weather be good. it Measures 103 Miles from this Camp to Elk. Pray should you have any Oppertunity Write me if any thing happens worthy of your notice. Pray write to my Wife to Acquaint her that I & my Company are in health & purpose marching tomorrow as the Bearer cannot Wait till I can Write,

I am your most Obedient & Sir your most Hble Servt

ANTHONY BLEDSOE.

On his Majestys Service To Col. William Preston.

REPORT FROM BATTLEFIELD

[Col. William Christian to Col. William Preston.] [81]

CAMP at POINT PLEASANT, at MOUTH of ye GREAT KANAWHA. 15th Oct. 1774.

DEAR SIR—I have been enquiring for some days for an opp'y to send some letters to Greenbryer, as I

---

[81] This letter is printed from a careful draft of the original, in the possession of M. L. Preston, of Marion, Va. We are indebted to J. T. McAllister, of Hot Springs, Va., for being placed in communication with the Preston family, and thus obtaining this draft of a paper, which is an essential link in the chain of documentary evidence.—ED.

wanted to write to you and some other friends. I can find no certain one, but I have some thought that some person will be going off tomorrow or next day as several talk of it. About one hour ago Col. Lewis asked me if I had written to you, I told him I had not, but would this evening. He desired me to tell you that he was hurryed and that my letter you would please to accept of from both; as I was to include you a state of the battle fought here on Monday the 10th instant, which I will do, I have a copy ready as drawn up by Col Lewis himself, from which you can have an idea of it.[82] I will also inclose you a state of the killed and wounded. I made it today from what scattering accounts I could gather. I have been through all the camps and believe that many more men will die. There are many shot in two places, one in particular I observed with two bullit, some in three. They are really in a deplorable ..uation, bad doctors, few medicines, nothing to eat or dress with proper for them makes it still worse. I intended being here on Tuesday, but on Monday evening about 12 or 15 miles off I heard they were fighting and reached it about midnight. The cries of the wounded prevented our resting any that night. We are building a breastwork. The Fincastle men have just finished their proportion and I hope all will be done tomorrow. We should have crossed the Ohio for the Towns ere now, but we must secure our wounded. His Lordship was to march with 1200 men last Thursday morning for the Towns, and wrote to Col. Lewis to meet him about 20 miles on this

---

[82] This is the report accompanying Shelby's letter; see *post.*—ED.

POINT PLEASANT BATTLE

side of Chillicossee at a large ridge. Chillicossee lyes about 20 miles farther than the Towns we intended for and is of course 90 from here, our pilot says 100. His orders were to meet next Tuesday at noon, that we cant do, as we dont propose crossing Ohio before Monday, perhaps some may Sunday in the night James Fowler, James McAnore and Sam Huff started on Wednesday morning from here with an acco[unt] of the battle, begging him to fall down in his vessels. On Thursday morning by day a little Billey Mann and some others who had been sent up by land, came down in a canoe, with the Govr's orders. I mentioned we were then embarrased not knowing what his Lordship would do on hearing how we were situated. I have hopes we will hear from him Monday night, Col Lewis thinks S nday night. If no accident happened him, he wou' d be gone 2 days before our scouts got to his Camp, which was at Heekhocking, 15 miles on this side of Little Kanawha. His Lordship has about 170 beeves, 250,000 of flour for 1300 men, about 100 of which would remain at Camp. Tis said that he had about 30 pack horses to take and that he would drive with him 100 beeves. Perhaps humanity will induce him to return and come to us if he is found but a little way off as Col. Lewis earnestly begged he would do so by Fowler. But should he not our wounded must be done with the best we can—And if we dont hear more from him before, we shall march on Tuesday morning with about 12 days provisions. Tis said the Enemy's whole forces and families are assembled at Chillicossee where they have homes and plenty of provisions—amunition in the greatest plenty They have cleared the weeds and bushes to a great distance around Town. Some here think the Govr's Army will be for pushing on before us, some that they will join us here and send in haste to tell us so. Some that they will stand fast until we are as far forward as them. We shall cross with some more than 1000 men, to-wit:—abt. 400 Augusta, 320 Bot[etourt], Abt. 320 Fincastle and leave between two and three hundred here. All of us that does return home I think will do it in Novr. Mann says that he had persuaded the Govr. to come here, but Major Connelly prevented it.

From what I can gather here I cannot describe the bravery of the enemy in the battle. It exceeded every mans expectations. They had men planted on each river to kill our men as they would swim over, making no doubt I think of gaining a complete victory. Those over the Ohio in the time of battle called to the men to "drive the white dogs in." Their Chiefs ran continually along the line exhorting the men to "lye close" and "shoot well", "fight and be strong". At first our men retreated a good ways and until new forces were sent out on which the enemy beat back slowly and killed and wounded our men at every advance Our people at last formed a line, so did the enemy, they made may attempts to break our lines, at length our men made a stand, on which the enemy challenged them to come up and began to shoot. I conclude a few of their braves did that as in their *rear* [blank in MS.] It was supposed several hundred Tomhake [tomahawks] were employed in cutting saplins to take off their wounded. Our men could have forced them away precipitately but not without great loss, and so concluded to maintain their ground all along the line. Which they did until Sundown, when the enemy were supposed to be all gone. Our people then moved backward, scalping the enemy and bringing in the dead and wounded.

The enemy came over on rafts about six miles up Ohio & set at the same place. They encamped within two miles of this place the night before the battle and killed some of our beeves, their loss I think is great. Late in the evening they called to our men that tomorrow they wd have 2000 men for them, to fight on for they had 1100 men as well as them. They damnd our men often for Sons-of-Bitches, said "Don't you whistle now" (deriding the fife) and made very merry about a treaty.

Ch. Lewis was shot in clear ground as he had not taken a tree while speaking to his men to come on He turned and handed his gun to a man and walked to Camp telling the men as he passed along "I am wounded, but go you on and be brave"

Col. Field was killed behind a great tree, looking for an Indian who was tal[k]ing to amuse him whilst some others were above him on his right hand among some loggs, who shot him dead.

Col. Flemming was shot with three balls, two in the left arm and one in the left breast, while speaking to his division in a peace of clear ground, with great coolness and deliberation he stept slowly back and told them not to mind him but to go up and fight.

Poor Col. Lewis soon after he reached the camp died & I fear poor Flemming will. I hope and fear for him may times in ye day. His loss here is irreprable, If Col. Thomas don't come down with medicines,

Col. Lewis wrote his Lordship who had informed him he would have "all requisites" he was begged for medicines and a surgeon. We have Watkins here. I wish you would write P. Henry if you can have an Opp'y something about ye battle, as I want my dear wife to know that I am well.

God Bless you & yours, I am your very well wisher.
WM. CHRISTIAN.

P. C. 16. Poor Flemming seems like living today, has some hopes that the ball was far spent and has not gone far through his body. He got up just now and seems hearty. Yesterday we gave him over for lost If he mends fast he can see to nursing ye wounded soon, It is getting dark

---

FLOYD'S ACCOUNT

[Capt. John Floyd to Col. William Preston. 33S44-49.]

MOUTH OF THE GREAT KANHAWA, Oct. 16, 1774.

MY DEAR SIR—I have heard for some days past that there was some person going into the inhabitants; I have gone through the camp to find an opportunity of sending you a few lines, but I don't yet know of any sure of going.

I think I wrote you by Vance the time we marched from the Levels; we went on without loss of time & arrived at the mouth of Elk in eight days, where we understood Col. Lewis with all the troops had set out for this place five days before. Col. Christian thought it necessary for Col. Slaughter with all the Lowlanders to wait at Elk for the return of the canoes which took down flour for the advanced party, & to guard the flour left there by us. as all the pack-horses were disloaded at Elk.

As Col Christian had no instructions left at Elk how to act, and as he had before marched from the Levels sooner than his orders allowed him, he thought proper to send down the scouts, Knox, Smith & two others, to see how things stood, and at the same time wrote Col. Lewis he should follow on the day after they left him, which we did being the 6th. instant, with about 350 beeves and left 24000lbs of flour with Col. Slaughter The 9th about 12 o'clock we met the scouts on their return, with a letter from Col. Lewis, directing Col. Christian to leave 50 beeves at Elk for those who would be there from time to time; & that our junction at that time would only serve to eat one another up. These instructions he could not comply with, without sending some of us back; he therefore called the officers together, & with their advice thought proper to march on as we were. The tenth in the afternoon about twelve or fifteen miles from the Ohio, the news met us that the army was attacked that morning early by a large body of Indians. We pushed on and got in about midnight, where we were very kindly received; and I imagine if our number had been double what we were, we should not have been complained of for that. I understand we were much prayed for that day in time of the engagement. Col. Christian has wrote you so full about the battle, and enclosed you a list of the killed &c, that he says I may refer you to him about that. I will just mention what my opinion is about some things, as there are many conjectures with regard to the number of Indians &c; some think eight hundred, some one thousand. Col. Christian and the party which marched out with him went up the Ohio next day, as it was said they intended to fight that day also; and in searching about & seeing the track the Indians made and the rafts they crossed the river on, it is my opinion there were not more than five hundred at most, but they fought desperately, I believe, & retreated in such a manner as to carry off all their wounded & only retired to a thick place where there had been a town & damned the white men for sons of bitches, to come on; which they did not chose to do, & retreated also. It really appears to me to have been partly a drawn battle: Some gentlemen tell me it appeared doubtful for some time, and sure it is that our men drew back once about the first of the engagement far enough for the Indians to scalp three of our men. I am also told there were never more than three or four hundred of our men in action at once, but the trees & logs the whole way from the camp to where the line of battle was formed, served as shelters for those who could not be prevailed on to advance to where the fire was.

There was no one officer who had his own men; there were first 300 sent out, some from each company, and when they found there was fighting enough for the whole, it was impossible for the officers to collect their own men so that when they saw any doing no good, and ordered them to advance, they refused and said they would be commanded by their own officers. Certain it is, that about the number I mentioned & many of the officers fought with a great deal of courage and behaved like heroes, while others lurked behind and could by no means be induced to advance to the front.

Col. Christian has told you all that is to be done, and also about the Governor, so that I can say nothing that will give you more knowledge of what is in hand. It is the opinion of many who pretend to be judges, that we shall have fighting enough before long.

The season is so far advanced, I imagine I shan't return by Kentucky this time; if I don't, I shall lose no time after this affair is over in returning to finish my business in the settlement, if I live to return at all; and will ever be, my dear sir, your most affectionate, and obedient servt., while

Jn. Floyd.

Hope to have a line from you before long.

SHELBY'S DESCRIPTION OF THE BATTLE

[Isaac Shelby to John Shelby. 7ZZ2.][83]

Camp Opposite to the mouth of Great Canaway October 16th 1774

Dr. Uncle—I Gladly imbrace this oppertunity to

---

[83] The portion of this letter beginning "For the satisfaction of the people in your parts," and ending with the list of killed and wounded, may be considered as practically the official report of the battle. It was probably drawn up by Andrew

Acquaint You that we are all three[84] yet alive th[r]o Gods Mercies & I Sinceerly wish that this may find you & your Family in the Station of Health that we left you. I never had any thing Worth Notice to quaint you with since I left you till now, the Express seems to be Hurrying that I Cant write you with the same Coolness & Deliberation as I would; we arrived at the mouth [of] Canaway Thursday 6th. Octr. and incampd on a fine piece of Ground with an intent to wait for the Governor & his party but hearing that he was going another way we Contented our selves to stay there a few days to rest the troops &c when we looked upon our selves to be in safety till Monday morning the 10th Instant when two of our Compys.

Lewis (see Prestons letter f Oct. 31, *post*) and copied as desired by those sending word to the inhabitants. It was printed in several contemporary newspapers, even so far away as Belfast, Ireland See Hale, *Trans-Allegheny Pioneers*, pp. 187-190. In 1817 Charles S. Todd sent a copy to *Niles's Register*, which appeared in volume xii, p. 145. He reports that this was in the handwriting of Capt. William Russell, who was "the best scholar in camp." This was reprinted in *Virginia Historical Register*, v, pp. 191-193. It is also printed in *Amer. Archives*, i, p. 1016. Roosevelt (*Winning of the West*, i, pp. 225, 341-344) gives the entire letter from a copy in the Campbell MSS. We print directly from the original.—ED.

[84] Capt. Evan Shelby, and his two sons, Isaac and James— the former being lieutenant of the company. Born in Maryland in 1750. Isaac removed to Holston in 1771, and this campaign was the first of his public services. The following year (1775) he surveyed in Kentucky and took out a pre-emption right to a farm in Lincoln County, where he finally settled in 1782, after distinguished services against the British in North Carolina. He was first governor of Kentucky (1792-96), and served again in that capacity during the second war with England (1812-15). He refused the portfolio of war under Monroe, and died at his home in Kentucky (1826). His brother James was born in 1752, and killed by Indians near Crab Orchard, Ky., in 1781.—ED.

POINT PLEASANT BATTLE 271.

went out before day to hunt, To wit Val. Sevier & Jas Robison & Discovered a party of indians;[85] as I expect you will hear something of our Battle before you get this I have here stated this affair nearly to you. For the Satisfaction of the people in your parts in this they have a true state of the Memorable Battle faught at the mouth of the great Canaway on the 10th. Instant; Monday morning about half an Hour before sunrise two of Capt Russels Compy. Discovered a large party of indians about a mile from Camp one of which men was killed the Other made his Escape & brought in his intilligence;[86] in two or three minutes

---

[85] According to the reminiscences which Thomas, son of Isaac Shelby, related to Dr. Draper (18S215), James Shelby was ill of a fever, and his father requested these two friends to "perch a turkey" for him, early on the morning of Oct. 10. In so doing they discovered the Indian camp.

Valentine was the younger brother of the noted Gen. John Sevier. Born in Rockingham County in 1747, he removed to the neighborhood of the Shelbys in 1773, and was sergeant in Evan Shelby's company. He served in the Cherokee campaign of 1776; was captain in that of Chickamauga (1779), and led a company to the campaign against the British in North Carolina (1780), which culminated in the battle of King's Mountain. After other military services, in which he rose to the rank of militia colonel, he removed to Clarksville, Tenn., where he died in 1800.

Sevier's companion-in-arms, James Robertson, was later the "father of Middle Tennessee." He was born in Virginia in 1742, and at an early age removed to North Carolina, where he married in 1768, and two years later settled on the Watauga. In 1778-79 he explored the Cumberland region, and in the autumn of the latter year led out a party that founded Nashville. For many years thereafter, Robertson was employed in defense of the new settlement and in treating with the Indians. In 1812 he was appointed agent for the Chickasaw, and died at the agency two years later. In 1825, his remains were removed to Nashville, and re-interred with much honor.—ED.

[86] These were Joseph Hughey, of Shelby's company, and James Mooney, of Russell's. The former was killed by a

affter two of Capt Shelbys. Compy. Came in and Confirmed the Account. Colo. Andrew Lewis being Informed thereof Immediately ordered Colo. Charles Lewis to take the Command of 150 men from Augusta and with him went Capt. Dickison. Capt. Harrison. Capt Willson. Capt. Jno. Lewis from Augusta and Capt. Lockridge which made the first division [87] Colo.

---

white renegade, Tavenor Ross, while the latter brought the news to camp. Mooney was a former neighbor of Daniel Boone, upon the Yadkin in North Carolina, and had accompanied him upon the disastrous Kentucky hunting expedition of 1769. He was killed at Point Pleasant.—ED.

[87] Col. John Dickinson was a son of Adam, a pioneer settler of what is now Bath County, Va. He served actively on the frontier during the French and Indian War, and from his fort Arthur Campbell was captured (1751). During Pontiac's War, Dickinson aided in a retaliatory pursuit of Cornstalk's party, after the massacre of Carr's Creek. In 1777 a raid upon the Shawnee towns was planned, for which Dickinson acted as colonel from Augusta County. This was brought to naught by the slaying of Cornstalk in the fort at Point Pleasant. Colonel Dickinson remained one of the distinguished citizens of Bath County, until his death in 1799. See *West Virginia Historical Magazine*, ii, p. 54.

Capt. Benjamin Harrison, son of Daniel, belonged to the Rockingham family of that name, founders of Harrisonburg. He was born in 1741, and after his service at Point Pleasant acted as colonel in McIntosh's campaign (1777). He was lieutenant colonel of his county, and led troops to aid Lafayette (1781) against Cornwallis. He died in 1819. This information was furnished to Dr. Draper by his son, Peachy R. Harrison, who died in 1848. See Draper MSS., 8ZZ68.

Of Capt. Samuel Wilson little is known, save that he was a son of John Wilson, an early settler of Augusta, who for many years represented the county in the Virginia assembly.

Capt. John Lewis, of Augusta, was the eldest son of Thomas, brother of Andrew and Charles. John was born in 1749, and although wounded in the battle of Point Pleasant, served in the Revolution, being with Washington at Valley Forge and in the Jerseys, and at the surrender of Cornwallis. He died in 1788, leaving four children.

Capt. Andrew Lockridge lived on Bullpasture River, in Augusta (now Highland) County. He was married in 1762.

Fleming was also ordered to take the Command of one hundred & fifty more Consisting of Botetourt Fincastle and Bedford Troops Viz. Capt. Buford of Bedford[88] Capt. Love of Botetourt[89] Capt. Shelby & Capt. Russell of Fincastle which made the second Division. Colo. Lewis marched with his Division to the Right some Distance up from the Ohio. Colo. Fleming with his Division up the banck of the Ohio to the left: Colo. Lewiss Division had not marchd. little more than a quarter of a mile from Camp; when about sunrise, an Attact was made on the front of his Division in a most Vigorous manner by the United tribes of Indians—Shawnees; Delewares, Mingoes, Taways,[90] and of several Other Nations in Number not less than

---

During the Revolution he was in active service, defending the frontiers against Indian invasion, commanding at a fort near Warm Springs (Bath County) and at Clover Lick (1777-79).—ED.

[88] Capt. Thomas Buford came of a well-known family of Bedford County. His cousin Abraham was colonel of the Virginia regiment that was cut to pieces by Tarleton at Waxhaw Creek (May 1780), on its way to the relief of Charleston. Col. Abraham Buford afterwards removed to Kentucky, and took a prominent part in the early political affairs of that state. See Speed, "Political Club," in Filson Club *Papers*, No. 9. He was long thought to have been lieutenant in his cousin's company at Point Pleasant, but the muster roll which we publish does not contain his name.—ED.

[89] Capt. Philip Love was in 1770 a magistrate of Botetourt, and in 1776 served as colonel in Christian's Cherokee campaign, having in the previous year removed from Augusta County to what is now Wythe. A collateral branch is represented by the Love family of Tennessee.—ED.

[90] The Ottawa, a Northwestern tribe long under the domination of the French. Pontiac was an Ottawa chief, and the tribesmen still harbored a grudge against their English conquerors. For the speech of one of the Ottawa, reputed to be a son of Pontiac, see *American Archives*, 4th series, iii, p. 1542.—ED.

Eight Hundred and by many thaught to be a thousand; in this Heavy Attact Colonel Charles Lewis received a wound which soon after Caused his Death and several of his men fell in the spott in fact the Augusta Division was forced to give way to the heavy fire of the Enemy In about a second of a minute after the Attact on Colo. Lewiss Division the Enemy Engaged the Front of Colo. Flemings Division on the Ohio; and in a short time Colo. Fleming rec^d. two balls thro his left Arm and one thro his breast; and after annimating the Captains and soldiers in a Calm manner to the pursuit of Victory returned to Camp, the loss of the Brave Colonels was Sensibly felt by the Officers in perticular, But the Augusta troops being shortly Reinforced from Camp by Colonel Field with his Company together with Capt. M'Dowel, Capt. Mathews & Capt. Stuart from Augusta, Capt. John Lewis,[91] Capt. Paulin Capt. Arbuckle & Capt. M'Clanahan from Botetourt, the Enemy no longer able to Maintain their Ground was forced to give way till they were in a Line with the troops left in action on Bancks of Ohio, by Colo Fleming in this precipitate retreat Colo. Field was killed, after which Capt. Shelby was ordered to take the Comm^d. During this time which was till after twelve of the Clock, the Action continued Extreemly Hott, the Close underwood many steep

---

[91] Capt. John Lewis, of Botetourt, born about 1750, was the eldest son of Col. Andrew Lewis, and a noted Indian fighter. There is a family tradition that he secured a commission in the British army, but resigned and came home to marry Patsy Love, the belle of Alexandria, Va. He settled on some of the Western lands inherited from his father, and was killed by his own negroes. See Gilmer, *First Settlers of Upper Georgia*, pp. 56, 57.—Ed.

bancks & Loggs greatly favoured their retreat, and the Bravest of their men made the use of themselves, whilst others were throwing their dead into the Ohio, and Carrying of[f] their wounded, after twelve the Action in a small degree abated but Continued sharp Enough till after one oClock Their Long retreat gave them a most advantages spot of ground; from whence it Appeared to the Officers so difficult to dislodge them; that it was thought most adviseable to stand as the line then was formed which was about a mile and a quarter in length, and had till then sustained a Constant and Equal weight of fire from wing to wing. it was till half an Hour of Sun sett they Continued firing on us which we returned to their Disadvantage at length Night Coming on they found a safe retreat They had not the satisfaction of scalping any of our men save One or two straglers whom they Killed before the ingagement many of their dead they scalped rather than we should have them but our troops scalped upwards of Twenty of those who were first killed; Its Beyond a Doubt their Loss in Number farr Exceeds ours, which is Considirable.

Field Officers killed Colo. Charles Lewis, and Colo. Jno. Fields, Field Officers wounded Colo. Willm Fleming; Capts. killed John Murray[92] Capt. Saml. Willson Capt. Robt. McClanahan, Capt. Jas. Ward, Captains wounded Thos Buford, John Dickison &

---

[92] Capt. John Murray was a brother-in-law of Charles Lewis. Charles Cameron, later a militia officer of prominence in Bath County, in the battle lost his brother, George Cameron, his half-brother, Capt. John Murray, and his brother-in-law Charles Lewis.—ED.

John Scidmore,[93] Subbalterns Killed Lieutenant Hugh Allen,[94] Ensign Mathew Brakin Ensign Cundiff,[95] Subbalterns wounded, Lieut. Lard; Lieut. Vance Lieut. Goldman[96] Lieut. Jas. Robison about 46 killed & about 80 wounded from this Sir you may Judge that we had a Very hard day its realy Impossible for me to Express or you to Concieve Acclamations that we were under, sometimes, the Hidious Cries of the Enemy and the groans of our wound[ed] men lying around was Enough to shuder the stoutest hart its the general Opinion of the Officers that we shall

---

[93] James Ward was born in Ireland about 1727, emigrated to America in infancy, and settled in Augusta County, where (about 1749) he married the daughter of Patrick Lockhart. He was a lieutenant in the French and Indian War, being with Forbes and Bouquet. In 1769 he removed with his brother-in-law, Matthew Arbuckle, to the Greenbrier country. At his death he left seven children. Two of his sons, James and Charles, were pioneer Kentuckians. See Draper MSS., 2DD54–59.

Of Capt. John Scidmore nothing is known.—ED.

[94] Lieut. Hugh Allen had served in the Shawnee expedition of 1756, and in the autumn of the same year was sent with a message from Governor Dinwiddie to the Cherokee chiefs. In 1773 Dunmore issued to him a patent for 2,000 acres of land, in reward, for his services (Draper MSS., 2QQ152). He left three sons—John, William, and Hugh. It is a family tradition that the sapling behind which Allen was sheltered, bore the marks of sixty to seventy bullets, and that he was finally killed from behind. His widow afterward married William Craig. Allen was a lieutenant in Capt. George Matthews's Augusta company.—ED.

[95] Jonathan Cundiff was ensign in Captain Buford's company, from Bedford County. He was survived by two sons, who emigrated to Montgomery County, Missouri, and left numerous descendants. See Bryan and Rose, *Pioneer Families of Missouri* (St Louis, 1876), p. 251.—ED.

[96] Samuel Vance was a lieutenant in the company of John Lewis of Augusta; Edward Goldman, in that of Pauling. See muster-rolls, *post*.—ED.

soon have another Ingagement as we have now got Over into the Enemys Country; we Expect to meet the Governor about forty or fifty miles from here nothing will save us from another Battle Unless they Attact the Governors Party, five men that Came in Dadys [daddy's] Company were killed, I dont know that you were Acquainted with any of them Except Marck Williams who lived with Roger Top. Acquaint Mr Carmack that his son was slightly wounded thro the shoulder and arm & that he is in a likely way of Recovery we leave him at mouth of Canaway & one Very Carefull hand to take Care of him; there is a garrison & three Hundred men left at that place with a surgeon to Heal the wounded we Expect to Return to the Garrison in about 16 days from the Shawny Towns.

I have nothing more Perticular to Acquaint you with Concerning the Battle. as to the Country I cant now say much in praise of any that I have yet seen. Dady intended writing to you but did not know of the Express till the time was too short I have wrote to Ma[m]my tho not so fully as to you as I then Expected the Express was Just going. we seem to be all in a Moving Posture Just going from this place so that I must Conclude wishing you health and prosperity till I see you & Your Family in the meantime I am y^r. truly Effectionate Friend & Humble Servt

Isaac Shelby

To M^r. John Shelby Holstons River Fincastle County fav^r. by M^r. Benj^a. Gray

THE SOUTHWESTERN FRONTIER

[Maj. Arthur Campbell to Col. William Preston. 3QQ124.]

ROYAL OAK Oct⁰. 16. 1774

Sir—Last Night I received a Letter from Capt. Thompson who had just returned from a trip of Ranging as far as Capt. Shelbys. He informs me that one Murphy an half Breed Cherokee had come into Wattago, as a Messenger from some of the Chiefs, to inform the Inhabitants that a Number of their Young Men had gone out to War contrary to their consent; and that they had put to Death one of the Indians that was concerned in the Murder of Capt. Russells Son and had the other in confinement. The Capt. then observes that perhaps all this is only Indian policy; which I am well satisfyed will be the case should the Shawanese and their Allies be Successful in repulsing our Army. He also informs me that he could not get a Man to go as Spy towards the Cherokee nation. As I proposed they should go to the Fork of the Paths that goes to Nola-Chuckee and that to the Island, about w[h]ere they say Indians is almost always hunting.

One of Capt. Thompsons Men had his Arm Shattered in a dangerous manner by one of his companions foolishly struggling about a Gun. Quere don't we want a Doctor in these parts. Capt. Smith was not returned the last accounts. I expect to hear every Day of his having an Action.

There was an account came here last Night that a Woman & two Children was killed or taken near

Blackmores since the Murder of Carter. But as it has come thro several hands by way of report I hope it is not true; as the people in that Quarter suffer of late a kind of Seige, and I think Women and children would not be straggling out.

I am Obliged to continue Shannon out here sometime as he is a forward careful hand, And I am of late much put to it to get Provisions carried out to Blackmores.

I am Sir Your most Humble Servt
ARTHUR CAMPBELL,

To Colo. William Preston. at Smithfield p. Boydstone

NEWS FROM THE BATTLEFIELD

[John Madison to Mrs. William Fleming. 2ZZ9.][97]

MADAM—You have heard of the Battle on the Ohio [the] 10th. of October I dare Say, I shall not dwell on Particula[rs at] Present but hasten to Acquaint you with what most Concerns you. Colo. Flemings behaviour on that day [was an] Honour to him and all his Connexions it is true he re[ceived] three wounds two in his left Arm and a Slight [one] in his Brest, but I have the Inexpressible Pleasure of Assuring you they are not Mortal. Every Letter Confirms this Acct. to Impose on you would be a ps. of Dishonesty I am not Capable [of] believe me Dr. Mrs. Fleming & be happy.

---

[97] This letter is undated, but could not have been written much before Oct. 31, when Preston received word of the battle.—ED.

You are no doubt anxious to hear who [was killed] on that fatal day, I will Insert their names be[low] tho' I know it will Cost you a tear. Excuse this [hasty] Epistle & believe [me] to be with much Esteem Madam

yr. Obt. hble Se[rvant]
JOHN MAD[ISON][98]

[*Killed*]	*Wounded*
Colo. Chas Lewis	Colo Wm Fleming
Colo. John Fields	Capt Tho Blueford [Buford]
Capts. Saml Wilson	Jno Dickenson
Robt. M Clenachan	Skidmore
James Ward,	Lieut. Vance
John Murry	Goldman
Lieutenants	Lard
Hugh Allen	
Jno Cunduff	
Mathew Braken	
John Frogg of Staunton [99]	

---

[98] John Madison was cousin of the father of President Madison, and himself father of James (first bishop of Virginia), Thomas, Rowland, and George, of Kentucky. He was the first clerk of Augusta County, and delegate to the Virginia assembly 1751-52. His wife was a Miss Strother, whose sisters married Thomas Lewis and Gabriel Jones, all of them living in the neighborhood of Port Republic, in the present Rockingham County.—ED.

[99] John Frogg was the nephew of Mrs. Thomas Lewis (née Strother), and had married her daughter Agatha. Their home was in Staunton, and he accompanied the army as sutler. A young, handsome man, he was generous and gallant, and fond of display, and the day of the battle was attired in a brilliant red jacket which made him a prominent mark for the savages. William White, of Augusta, related that when Frogg fell an Indian bounded forward to scalp him, but he and four others bent on a similar errand, were shot. After the battle, Frogg was found with the five dead savages in a heap above his body (Draper MSS., 8ZZ71). A tradition was also current in the family, that on Oct. 10 his little daughter awakened three times, clinging to her

The private mens names not Mentioned the Whole number of the Killed & wounded amount to 147.

Colo Preston would have written to you but he is so hurry'd with express's at present it was out of his Power

To Mrs. Ann Fleming

COL. WILLIAM FLEMING'S JOURNAL

[Fleming's description of the expedition. 2ZZ71, pp. 47-56.]

An Extract from a Journal keept by An Officer in the Army under Colo Andw. Lewis on the expidition against Our Enemy Ohio Indians.[1]

In consequence of a Plan laid down by my Lord Dunmore, in which the Forces under Colo. Andw. Lewis were to Join His Lordship at the Mouth of New River, Camp Union at the big levels of Green Brier was appointed the place of Rendevouse for the Augusta Botetourt & Fincastle County troops, at which place they were Assembling from August ye. 27th. Septr. ye. 2d. we were Alarmed by a report that Stewarts

---

mother, crying out that the Indians were killing her father— a fact of which the household did not receive notice until a number of days later; see Gilmer, *Settlers of Upper Georgia*, pp. 49-51. Frogg's widow married Capt. John Stuart, of this same expedition; and his daughter was the wife of one of the Estill family.—ED.

[1] This journal of Fleming's, in his own handwriting, is found at the end of his Orderly Book, and evidently is an abbreviated account written from the data in the book, so as to present a connected description of the expedition.—ED.

Fort, four miles from Camp was Attack'd by Indians. A party being sent out found that only one man had been fired at and escaped with a verry slight wound but next day Septr. ye. 3d. McGuire a Countryman was brought in from another Quarter into Camp much wounded & had a bullet cut out of his Cheek. Septr. ye 4th. Parties as the day before were sent out in quest of the Enemy, and discovered three or four who had horses, but had no Opportunity of firing on them, tho they recovered the horses, and several Buffalo hide halters a tomhawk &c. were found. These Indians being a Party who had, as was customary come in to do what mischeif was in their power, and then push home with as many horses as they could pick up. The 5th. Parties on horseback had orders to scour the woods for two or three miles round camp. And a Capt. &c: & fifty private went in pursuit of the Enemy discovered yesterday.

Col: Andw. Lewis Joind the troops Septr. 1st. as Commander in Chief.

6th. Colo. Charles Lewis with the greatest part of the Augusta troops and Arbuckles Compy. from Botetourt march'd from Camp union with all the Cattle collected there at that time and [four] hundred pack horses loaded with Flower, Salt, & Tools, for [the] mouth of Elk River and had orders to build a small store house, for the provisions, And get Canoes made, sufficient to transport the Flower &c: from that Place down the New River to the Ohio. The 10th. One of Our Spies came in from Gauly and reported that on the 6th. Inst he discovered a party of Indians with horses on their return from the Inhabitants, And on

The Form of the March

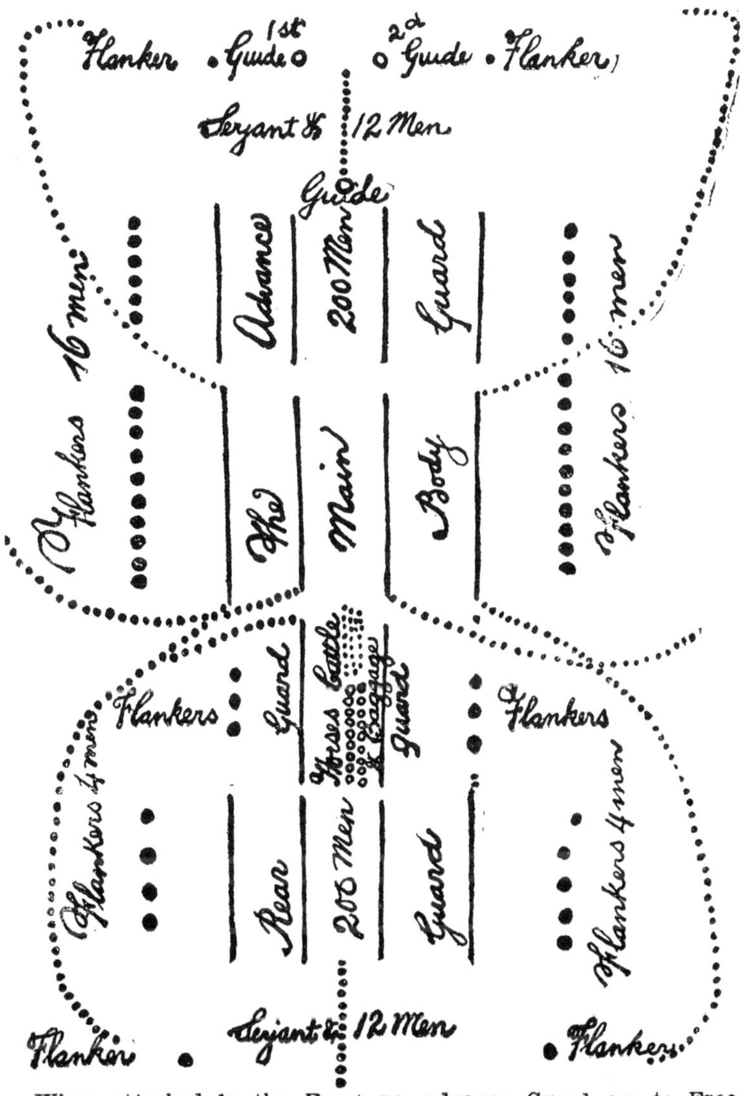
Flanker
1st Guide
2d Guide
Flanker
Serjant & 12 Men
Guide
16 men
Advance
200 Men
Guard
16 men
Flankers
The
Main
Body
Flankers
Flankers
Guard
Horses Cattle & Baggage
Guard
Flankers
Flankers 4 men
Rear
200 Men
Guard
Flankers 4 men
Flanker
Serjant & 12 Men
Flanker

When attached in the Front ye. advance Guard are to Free themselves & Stand the Charge while the Right & Left hand Columns Are to move towards Right & Left as Pr dotted Circular Lines &c. Endiavouring to outflank the Enemy & then Close in &c. If the Right or Left Columns Should be Attacted they are to be Supported by the Advance or Rear Guard who are to out Flank the Enemy &c while the Party attacted in whatever Quarter, Column or Van Or Rear Guard are to Stand the Charge while the Distant Columns Flank them.

the mòrning of the ninth another party coming in, from this time we have reason to believe that Our motions were narrowly watched by the Enemy.

Septr. the 12th Colo. Andw. Lewis with the Botetourt troops & Capt^s. Shelby Russels & Bufords Comp^{ies} left Camp Union & took with them all the Beeves & Pack horses that were then Collected. In the Evening a man from Col^o. C. Lewis party came into Camp & reported that Col^o. Fields from Culpepper County who Joind us with about 30 men & had marchd after Colo. C. Lewis on the 10 Inst. his men being out hunting had one of them [been] shot down by an Indian but that the Indian was kild before he scalpd him. This Indian proved to be a Tawa.

19th Crossed Gauly Mountain, which I take to be a Continuation of that Chain of mountains caled the Alegany Mountain, to the Northward and we Met with sudden & frequent Showers of Rain as is usual near these Mountains. It is pritty difficult to Cross being about a mile & half in Ascent & as much in descent

The 21st we fell in with New River or the Big Kanhaway a little below Kellys Place. and marching down the River Eight or Nine miles passed two curious Springs, the Vapour of which kindles quick as Gunpowder & burns with a surprizing force.

The 23. we Joind Col: C. Lewis who was encamped on the Banks of Elk river about a mile above its influx into New River by Computation 108 Miles from Camp Union.

Imployed to the 30th. in building a storehouse & making Canoes for transporting the stores. The 24th

the Scouts were sent different ways for the discovery of the Enimy. The 25th One of the Scouts that had Crosed the Kanhaway returnd & reported that about four miles from Camp, a Small party of Indians had passed them in the Night with horses on their way down the Kanhaway. Colo. Lewis sent some Scouts this Evening to the Ohio to wait on his Lordship, As we expected about this time His Excellency with the Troops from the Northward would be arrived. And the 29th One of them returnd when about 15 miles from the Ohio, on their discovering Indian fires on the banks of the Kanhaway, and this Scout likewise on his way up discovered another party of Indians.

The 30th. Cros'd the Elk & marchd down to its mouth where we encamped. Octr. 1st.

The Troops were ordered to form two Colums in their march from this, each Colum made two grand divisions The Botetourt Troops formd the Right, the Augusta the left Colum. Capt. Jno Lewis of Botctourt with his Company Marchd advanced a little way in the front of the Colums Bullocks & Pack horses fell in betwixt the Front & Rear divisions, and had each Flank covered with One hundred Men.[2] 6th. reach'd the Junction of the Great Kanhaway with the Ohio. we have met with a lettar from My Lord Dunmore[3] The spies sent from Elk came in this Even-

---

[2] See accompanying plan of march, drawn by Fleming.—ED.

[3] This message was left in a hollow tree by Dunmore's scouts, who arrived before the advent of Lewis's army. The messengers are claimed to have been Simon Kenton, Simon Girty, and Peter Parchment. See Dr. Draper's MS. notes; Butterfield, *History of the Girtys*, p. 27; Hildreth, *Pioneer History*, p. 88. Another list, given by Samuel Murphy, comprises Simon Girty, John Turner, and Joseph and Thomas Nicholson. See Draper MSS., 3S11.—ED.

ing, and told us they had quitted their Canoe, after sending back the messenger formerly mentiond, and came by land to the point, where not finding His Lordship, they had continued amongst the hills, without being discovered by several parties of Indians that were hunting Buffaloes. Colo Lewis sent up by some of our Spies a lettar in return to His Lordships to Hockhocking. The 8th. Some messengers from My Lord with lettars came down by water & returnd in a few houres.[4]

The 10th. some men who had left Camp at about three miles distance, fell in with a large Party of Indians a little after day break. One of Capt Russels men was shot down one escaped, & brought us the first intelligence which in a few minutes was confirmed by several Others being chased into Camp. Imagining this to be some scouting party, Colo. Lewis ordered a detatchment from every Company. so as to make up One hundred & fifty men from each line, to go in quest of them   Colo. Charles Lewis led the Augusta Detachment   And had with him Capts Dickinson, Harrison & Skidmore, & Colo. Fleming the Botetourt. and had with him Capts Shelby, Russel, Buford & Love. & the Augusta line marchd on the Right near the foot of the hills. The Botetourt along the Banks of the Ohio, at about 200 Yards distance: We Marched Briskly 3/4 of a mile or better from Camp, the Sun then, near an hour high, when a few guns were fired on the

---

[4] One of these messengers mysteriously intimated to Captain Stuart that the Indians were preparing for an attack. See Stuart's "Narrative," in *Virginia Historical Collections,* 1st series, i, pp. 36-56; *Magazine of American History,* i, pp. 668-679, 740-750.—ED.

Right, & succeeded by a heavy fire, which in an Instant extended to the left and the two lines were hotly engaged. Early in the ingagement Colo. Charles Lewis on the Right received a mortal wound, and was led out of the Field. He died in a few houres, much beloved, universally esteemed, & greatly lamented by the whole troops. Soon afterward Colo. Fleming on the left, was daingerously wounded in the breast & Arm & Obleedged to quit the Field. The Fire continuing very warm & the Indians pushing our men, forced them to retreat 150 or 200 Yards, but being timely supported by reinforcements sent from Camp, they recovered the ground they had lost, & in turn drove the Eninyy. Colo. Fields who came out with reinforcement was unhappily kild. the Action continued verry warm till near twelve o'Clock, when the Fire tho pritty constant was not so heavy. As the Enimy whenever they met with an advantagious piece of ground in their retreat, made a resolute stand, during which some of them were employed to remove their dead, dying & wounded. in the Afternoon they had gained such an advantagious post that it was thought imprudent to Attempt to dislodge them, & firing ceased on both sides about half an hour before Sunset, from this place the Enemy made a final retreat and crossed the Ohio with their wounded. Some of their dead were slightly covered in the Field of Battle, some were drag'd down, & thrown into the Ohio And others they had scalped themselves to prevent our people. whilst this passed in the Field, Colo. Lewis was fully imployed in Camp, in sending necessary reinforcements where wanted on the different quarters. The Troops were encamped on the Banks of the N[ew] River & Ohio, extending up both Rivers near half a Mile the Point betwixt the Rivers was full of large trees & very brushy, from the furthest extent of the tents on both Rivers he cleard a line across & with the brush & trees Made a breastwork and lined it with the men that were left in Camp. The following is a list of the kild & Wounded Those markd with Asterisks died after the engagement Kild of the Augusta line, Colo. Charles Lewis * Colo. Jno. Field, Capt. Saml. Wilson, Lieutt. Hugh Allen. Eighteen private[s] Wounded of the Augusta line Capts. Dickenson. Skidmore Lieutts. Leard & Vance with 51 private. Kild of the Botetourt line Capts. Murray, Robt. McClennachan * Ward * Thos. Buford *. Lieutts. Bracken & Goldman, with Ensign Cundiff & 17 Private. Wounded Colo. Fleming Lieut. Robison & 35 private. We had the morning of the engagement upwards of Eleven hundred effective men.

About 12 o'Clock at Night Colo Christian with the Fincastle troops came into Camp. the 11th. Large parties were sent out in search of the Enimy when they found all the Indians had crosd the Ohio.

The 12th Imployed in gathering in the dispers'd Bullocks & horses & in clearing the Camp of Underwood. this day the Guns Blankets &c taken from the Indians, sold by Vendue amounted to near £100. The 13th. the Express that first went to his Lordship returnd with Instructions for Colo Lewis to march towards the Shawnese Towns and Join His Lordship at a certain place by the way

The 14th. 15th. & 16th. imployed in finishing a store

house & running up a breastwork, which was Raised two logs high, with part of a Bastion. we cros'd the Ohio the 17, After leaving all our Indisposed, lame, & those Judged unfit for Duty at the point, and their wounds some time after the engagement

Botetourt line	Augusta line
Botetourt line	Col^o. C. Lewis
Capt Murray	Col^o J. Fields
" Robt McClennachan	Capt. Saml. Wilson
" Ja^s. Ward	Lieut^t Hugh Allen
" Buford	Eighteen Private
Lieut. Bracken	
" Goldman	Wounded
Ensg^n Condiff	Capt. Jno Dickinson
Seventeen Private	" Skidmore
	Lieut^t. Leard
Wounded	" Vance
Col^o. Fleming	fifty one private
Lieut Robinson	
thirty five private	

29.

Col^o Lewis came into Camp last evening. when he had got to some distance from the Towns the Governor sent an Express to inform him that He had very near concluded a peace and that he was to halt his troops there. the place being inconvenient to encamp and Col^o Lewis men being fired on that morning he marchd on Next Morning He received another Express informing him the Peace was in a manner concluded that the Shawnese had agreed to his terms and therefor Col^o Lewis was to encamp where he was. & that he & any Officers he tho't proper might come over to his Camp. Col^o Lewis did not imagine it would be prudent to go to his lordships Cam[p] with only two or three Officers, and therefore marchd thither with a design to Join his Lordship but the Guide mistook the path & took a path that led betwixt the towns & his Lordships Camp. this put the Indians into a fright they expected Colo Lewis was going to Attack their towns they left his Lordship, and run off. His Lordship rode down to Colo Lewis's Camp in the 18th begun Our March for the Shawnese Towns. When about 15 miles from them. we had an Express from His Lordship, Accquainting us a Peace with the Indians was Almost concluded, inviting Colo Lewis & such of his Officers as he choose, to come over to his Camp. we continued to march forward & in some houres afterwards another express arrived with the News that a Peace was concluded & brought orders for the Army to halt, as the place was inconvenient for the Troops to encamp, we marched on to water which the Indians observing struck them with a dread that we were going to Attack their towns, as we by a mistake of the Guide had gct rather betwixt his Lordships Camp & the Towns & much nearer than we imagined.[5] All the Indians with his Lordship, immediately quitted His Camp, except White Fish, who with Gibson a trader, Attended His Lordship to Our Army. My Lord informd us the Shawnise had agreed to all his Terms, and that as Our Presence could be of

---

[5] The Indian towns here referred to were on the Pickaway Plains, in the county and township of the same name, a few miles below the present Circleville, Ohio. According to the traditions of the pioneers of that region, Lewis halted below Kinnickinnik Creek, in Green Township, Ross County; but finding the place inconvenient for a camp, pressed on across the creek, and took a trail to the northwest, leading directly to Grenadier Squaw's Town. He halted between Congo and Scippo Creeks, in Pickaway Township, and there received the visit from Dunmore.—Ed.

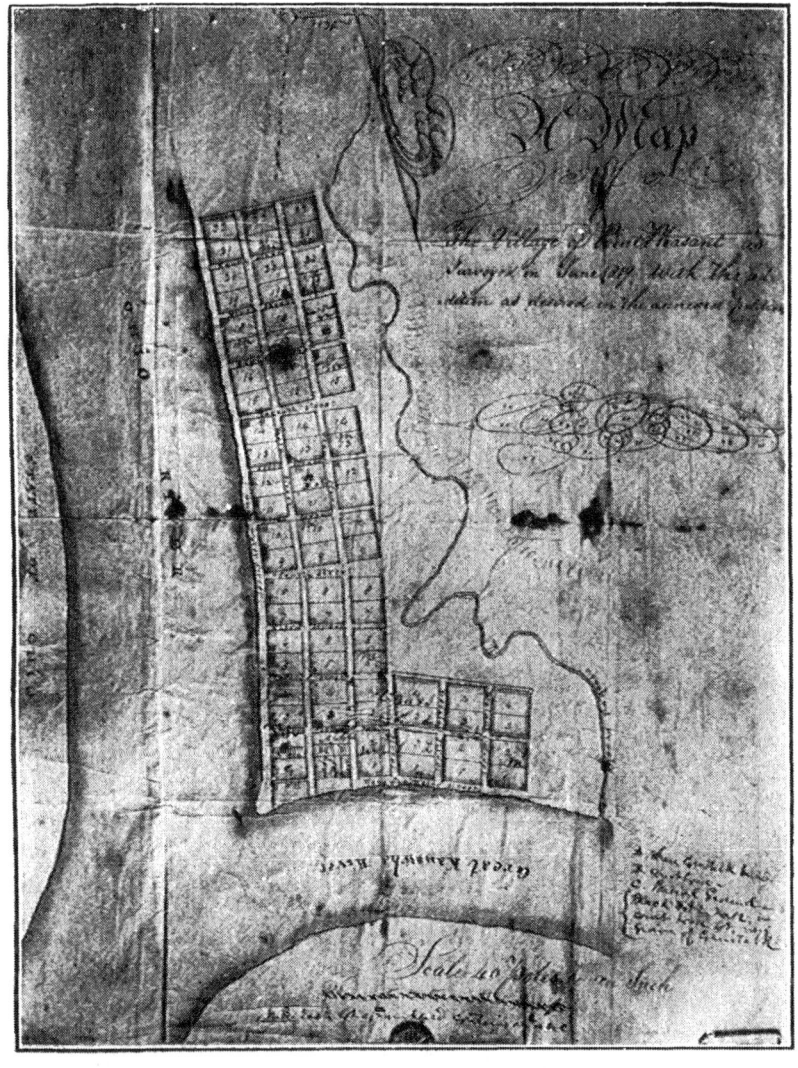

MAP OF THE VILLAGE OF POINT PLEASANT AS SURVEYED IN JUNE, 181'
Reduced facsimile from original in Draper MSS.—2ZZ56

Legend: A, where Cornstalk was buried; B, courthouse; C, burial ground. Black dot in No. 12, in court house lot, near grave of Cornstalk

no service, but rather a hindrance to the peace being concluded he ordered the whole to return, which we did the next day. We reachd the Point the 28th where we found the Breast work very near compleated from which Place we filed off homeward by [MS. torn].

PRESTON'S REPORT OF THE BATTLE

[Col. William Preston to Patrick Henry. 3QQ128.][6]

October ye 31st. 1774

DEAR SIR—Being on my way from home to Fincastle Court was overtaken this Evening by Letters from Colo. Christian and other Gentlemen on the Expedition, giving an Account of a Battle which was fought between our Troops & the Enemy Indians on the 10th Instant in the Fork of the Ohio & the great Kanhawa

The Particulars of the Action drawn up by Colo. Andw. Lewis I have Sent you inclosed, also a Return of the killed and wounded; by which you will see that we have lost many Brave and valluable Officers & soldiers whose loss to their Families, as well as to the Community is very great.

---

[6] Roosevelt (*Winning of the West*, i, pp. 227, 344-347) gives this letter from a copy in the Campbell MSS. We print direct from the original, upon which Dr. Draper wrote: "The following letter by Colonel Preston, dated Oct. 31st, 1774, was found among Patrick Henry's papers and preserved by his grandson Col. Patrick H. Fontaine, of Pontotoc, Mississippi, whose son Charles D. Fontaine gave it to me in 1840 or 1841, when I resided there. The reference to Mrs. Christian, near the close of the letter is very natural, as she was a sister of Patrick Henry."—ED.

Col⁰. Christian with the Fincastle Troops, (except the Companies Commanded by Capts. Russell & Shelby who were in the Action) were on their march, and on the Evening of that Day about 15 Miles from the Field of Battle heard that the Action began in the Morning. They Marched hard & got to the Camp about midnight. The Cries of the Wounded without any Persons of Skill or any thing to Nourish People in their unhappy Situation was Striking. The Indians had crossed the River on Rafts 6 or Eight Miles above the Forks in the night and it is believed intended to Attack the Camp had they not been prevented by our men meeting them at the Distance of half a Mile. It is said the Enemy behaved with Bravery & great Caution, that they frequently Damn'd our men for white Sons of Bitches why did not the[y] Whistle now (alluding to the Fifes) & that they would learn them to Shoot.

The Governor was then at Hockhocking about 12 or 15 Miles below the Mouth of little Kanhawa from whence he intended to march his Party to a Place called Chillicossee about 20 Miles further than the Towns where it was Said the Shawanesse had Assembled with their Families and Alies to make a Stand, as they had good Houses & plenty of Ammunition & Provisions & had cleared the Woods to a great distance from the Place.[7] His Party who were to march from

---

[7] Chillicothe is said to mean "chief town," also "town on leaning bank." The name was applied to various localities at different times—to a village three miles north of Xenia, Ohio; to one on the site of Frankfort, Ross County; and the one on the site of the present Chillicothe. That referred to here, was on the west bank of the Scioto, about fifteen miles above Chillicothe, and five or six below Circleville. At one time there

the Camp was about 1200 & to Join Colo. Lewis's Party about 28 Miles from Chillicossee. But whether the Action above mentioned would disconcert this Plan or not I think appears a little uncertain, as there is a probabillity that his Excellency on hearing the news might, with his Party fall down the River & Join Colo. Lewis's Party & March together against the Enemy.

They were about Building a Breast Work at the Forks & after leaving a proper party to take Care of the Wounded & the Provisions there that Colo. Lewis could March upwards of a Thousand Men to Join his Lordship. So that the whole when they meet will be about 2200 Choice Men. What may be their Success God only knows; that it is highly probable the matter is decided before this Time.

Colo. Christian says from the Accounts he had, the Enemy behaved with inconceivable Bravery. The Head men walked about in the Time of Action Exhorting their Men "To lie close, shoot well, be strong & fight." They had Parties planted on the opposite side of both Rivers to shoot our men as they swam over, not doubting, as is supposed, but they would gain a complete Victory. In the Evening late they called to our Men "That they had 2000 Men for them to morrow and that they had 1100 Men now as well as they." They also made very merry about a Treaty.

Poor Colo. Charles Lewis was shot on a Clear piece of Ground, as he had not taken a tree, encouraging

---

was a village there known as Westfall, but the site is now farm land. The bank at this place was high; there was but one fording place, just below the site, and the whole was easily defensible by a large body of Indians.—ED.

his Men to Advance. On being wounded he handed his Gun to a person nigh him and retired to the Camp telling his Men as he passed, "I am Wounded, but go on & be Brave." If the loss of a good man, a sincere Friend & a Brave Officer claims a Tear, He certainly is entitled to it.

Colo. Fields was shot at a great tree by two Indians on his Right while one on his Left was amusing him with talk & the Colo. endeavouring to get a shot at him.

Beside the loss the troops met with in Action by Colo. Fleming who was obliged to retire from the Field, which was very great; The Wounded met with the most Irreparable Loss in an able & skillful Surgeon. Colo. Christian says that his Lungs or part of them came out of the Wound in his Breast but were pushed back, & by the last part of his Letter which was dated the 16th Instant he has some hopes of his recovery.

Thus Sir I have given you an Account of the Action from the Several Letters I recd. & have only to add that Colo. Christian desires me to Inform Mrs. Christian of his Wellfare, which with great Pleasure I do thro' this Channel; and should any further News come which I much Expect soon I shall take the earliest oppy. of communicating the same to you. It is believed the Troops will surely return in Novr.

I write in a hurry & amidst a Crowd of Inquisitive People therefore hopes you'll excuse the Inaccuracy of Dr. Sir

Your Sincere Wellwisher & most Obedt Servt
                                                    Wm. Preston.

P. S. if you Please you may give Mr. Purdie a Copy of the inclosed Papers & any thing else you think worth the notice of the Public[8]

FURTHER DETAILS OF THE BATTLE

[Extract from a letter from Staunton, Virginia, dated November 4, 1774, published in Pennsylvania *Gazette* Nov. 16, 1774. 14J57.]

On the 10th of October, our Army being encamped in the Fork of the Great Kanhawa, two men went out early to hunt, but were fired upon by a number of Indians, when one of them was killed, the other made his escape, and brought the intelligence to the camp. Colonel Lewis immediately ordered out 300 men, who, after marching about three quarters of a mile, before sun-rise, were attacked by a number (supposed to be from 800 to 1000) of desperate savages; they soon made our men retreat about one quarter of a mile, when a reinforcement coming up, they continued fighting in this place till noon, and were never above twenty yards apart, often within six, and sometimes close together, tomahawking one another. The Indians then began to fall back, but continued fighting at a distance till night came on and parted them. Such a battle with the Indians, it is imagined, was never heard of before. We had upwards of 50

---

[8] Alexander Purdie was a Scotchman who had emigrated to America and entered the printing business at Williamsburg, Va., where he published the *Virginia Gazette*. He died in 1779.—ED.

men killed, and 90 wounded. Amongst the slain were many brave men, both officers and privates; and a Magistrate of this place, Mr. Frog, a very worthy Gentleman, was also killed so eager were the Indians for his scalp, that one man shot three of them over him, endeavoring by turns to scalp him. The number of Indians killed cannot be ascertained, as they were continually carrying them off, and throwing them into the river, but from the tracks of blood, the number must have been great. Our men got upwards of 20 scalps, 80 blankets, about 40 guns, and a great many tomahawks; and intended in a few days to go over the river, to meet the Governor, 20 or 25 miles from their towns. The Indians the Governor lately concluded a peace with, it is assured, were in this battle. We suppose they have had the other struggle before this time, and are very impatient to know the issue.

A Gentleman from Virginia has favoured us with the following list of officers killed and wounded in the above engagement, viz. Killed. Col. Charles Lewis, Col. John Field; Captains John Murray, Robert M'Clenagan, Samuel Wilson, and James Ward; Lieutenant Hugh Allen; and Ensigns Baker[9] and Candiff.

Wounded, Captains William Fleming (since dead) John Dickinson, Thomas Blueford [Buford] and

---

[9] Samuel Baker was ensign in Henry Pauling's company of Botetourt troops. Apparently, the report of his death was a mistake. He lay behind a log that was raised an inch or two from the ground, and had fired several shots around the end, when a bullet took off the tip of his mocassin. Upon finding himself discovered, he left the place. See Draper MSS., 12CC2.—ED.

John Skidman [Skidmore]; Lieutenants **Goldman**, Robinson, Lard and Vance.

44 privates killed, and 79 wounded.

HOMEWARD ROUTE

[Maj. Arthur Campbell to Col. William Preston. 3QQ129.]

ROYAL OAK Nov. 4. 1774

DEAR SIR—After I parted with you at Sayers, I was informed by Ben. Gray, that the Men from Holstein and Clinch, on the Expedition fully intended to return by the Kentucke, or up Sandy Creek; he mentions so many of their reasons for returning that way That I am perswaded they will attempt it, except they get a severe Stroke at they Towns.

In order to facilitate their March up Sandy, Capt. Smith intends to set out next Monday, with a small party to go down that River, about 10 or 15 Miles below w[h]ere Col. Lewis returned from,[10] and should he not meet any of them, he is to mark they way back, and give directions by Writing where they best hunting is; and if he can kill some meat, when out, he intends Barbicuing it, and Scaffolding it up, leaving directions at particular passes where they may find it.

---

[10] This refers to the Sandy Creek expedition of 1756, led by Colonel (then Major) Andrew Lewis. When within a few miles of the Ohio, they were obliged to return because of the scarcity of provisions. Colonel Preston's MS. journal of the expedition, in which he commanded a company, is in Draper MSS., 1QQ96.—ED.

I have also Wrote to M^r. Boone to be in readiness to march by the 15th, Int., should there be a Necessity for him to go the other way, to meet Capt. Russell I have also directed him to send out two or three trusty Hands, immediately, down Louisa to make discovery and to return by the way of Cumberland Gap. As soon as you hear from the Army again, you can be a judge, whether it will be expedient for M^r. Boone to take the above mentioned trip, Capt. Smith expects to return, time enough to go with him; They want only to take a small party of 40 or 50 on pay and I Believe twice that Number will go on their own cost to meet their Friends.

My Mother, and Mother in Law, is extremely uneasy since they heard of the late Battle. Please favour me by some Speedy method with the first accounts you may hear from the Towns, as several Persons is waiting to know which way to go to meet their Friends.

I am Sir very Respectfully Yours,
ARTHUR CAMPBELL

To Col^o. William Preston p^r. fv^r. of M. Lorton

FRONTIER GUARDS DISBANDED

[Col. William Preston to Capt. Joseph Martin. 1XX5.]

SIR—I rec^d. yours by the Bearer in which your Request some more ammunition but as I wrote last night to Capt. Penn to discharge the Company, I suppose there will not be Occasion for any more. Hearing from the Army, and the reasonableness to believe that the Enemy will find employment enough beyond the Ohio induced me to take this step; and the rather as the season was far advanced & the soldiers beyond their Expectation when they came out.

I Beg you will tell the Scouts [to] return home as I forgot to mention it last night to Captain Penn.

The Schooll Master has been engaged two days in drawing Copies of the Papers sent to me to send to Gentlemen below. I have however made him send you the Return of the killed and Wounded. & the State of the Battle shall be ready for you as you return.

I am Dr Sir your most hble servt

W^M. PRESTON

4th Novr. 1774.

To Capt Joseph Martin

NEWS OF THE WOUNDED

[William Bowyer to Mrs. William Fleming. 7ZZ43.][11]

STAUNTON, Nov. the 6^t. 1774

My Dearest Sister—I am Sincearly Sorry to write or inclose you Tidings That I know will give you much Trouble. I would not have done so but for fear bad as they are that they might be exagerated. I think from what my Dear friend writes he will stil Return to continue you happy. I hope he will, therefore pray do not Anticipate your Trouble before it Realy comes. I know your Tender Heart will Suggest every misfortune that possibly might attend the

---

[11] Evidently accompanying and enclosing Col. William Flemings letter of October 13, to his wife, see *ante,* pp. 253, 254.—ED.

accident, but pray do not so. he is stil In the hands & under the protection of the same kind preserver of us all youl. Observe many worthy men were Imediately Call^d. off the Stage of action at or near the same time he Receiv^d. [h]is wounds. he is stil alive therefore instead of being Sorrowfull I think you ought to Rejoice that he was not amoungst the dead. give your thoughts a Turn this way & I think it will give you some Relief. The man is waiting I cant say more. I wish time would admit I would come & see you my Children are well they Both Last night after in bed hop^d. there Dady Fleming was well & not Dead. I assure you that they Both are much affected. Polly[12] says she will go & see her Dady Fleming for she is sure her mammy will Cry all Day. Pruey says her Dady Fleming is not so bad or he would not write so long a letter & that she is sure mammy fleming will not Cry when she sees how long & well he writes this Little pratling of theres I cannot Curb or stop it gives me joy to see so early a Senceability of affection in my Little ones. Pruey says she wishes Dady fleming were here that she might Help to dress his wounds I will nor have I time to ad[d] more but this fur I would beg of you once more not to Suggest the worst but hope for the Best. Other acc^{ts}. that I have Receiv^d intimate that the wounds are not very Dangerous, & that they may not [be] I sincearly Join you to hope.

 I am with Sincear affection your Brother
W^M. BOWYER

---

[12] Mary (Polly) Bowyer afterwards married her cousin Leonard, son of Col. William Fleming.—E<small>D</small>.

CLOSE OF CAMPAIGN 301

Note The Dead of your acquaintance of any Distinction are Collo Charles Lewis Majr. John Fields Capt Bob M'Clenehan Capt John Murry Capt Samuel Wilson Capt James Ward poor John Frogg George Cameron
No doubt but you [will] see before this comes to hand a perticular acct. of all Killd & wounded.

CLOSE OF THE CAMPAIGN

[Col. William Christian to Col. William Preston. 3QQ130.]

SMITHFIELD Tuesday the 8 Novr '74[13]

MY DEAR SIR—About 7OClock this morning Capt Floyd & myself got there [here] on our return from the Indian Country. I hear you are not expected home before Sunday, if You stay in the neighbourhood of the Town a few days or come up Roanoak I hope to see you But in the mean time I will say a little about our Journey.

This day 3 weeks [Oct. 18] our Army about 1150 in number marched from the Ohio, and on the Monday evening following we encamped within about 3 miles from A Shawnese Town where their greatest force were Assembled.[14] His Lordships Camp was

---

[13] Christian and Floyd arrived at Preston's home only to find that the latter had gone East on business. They had made the return journey from the mouth of the Kanawha in eight days.—ED.

[14] Grenadier Squaw's Town; but in the event of the failure of the treaty the Indians intended to make their final stand at Chillicothe (Westfall)—see *ante*, p. 292, note 7. There were several small towns in the Pickaway Plains: Grenadier Squaw's was on Scippo Creek, about half a mile above its junction with Congo Creek; Cornstalk's, about a half mile farther north, beyond Scippo Creek.—ED.

then about 7 miles from us & about 6 miles from the Town. we intended for his Camp but passed the path that took off to our right hand expecting he had encamped nearer the Towns.[15] That day we were met

---

[15] Dunmore had arrived at Fort Pitt about the end of August, and for several weeks was occupied in fruitless negotiations with the Delaware, Mingo, and Shawnee chiefs, the latter of whom were requested to meet him and make a treaty somewhere lower down the Ohio (*Amer. Archives*, 4th series, i, pp. 873-875). Accordingly the governor, with seven hundred men, set out in canoes, while five hundred more, under the command of Maj. William Crawford, marched by land and conveyed the beeves to the fort at the site of Wheeling, where they arrived Sept. 30 (*Washington-Crawford Letters*, pp. 54, 97). From this point Crawford marched to the mouth of Hockhocking, and crossing his forces began a small stockade named Fort Gower, in honor of the English earl of that name. This fort was on the upper or east side of the Hockhocking, quite near the junction of the two rivers. See Hildreth, *Pioneer History of Ohio Valley* (Cincinnati, 1848), p. 93. A few days later, the remainder of the army arrived, under Dunmore's immediate command; but no Indians appeared, save White-Eyes, the friendly Delaware, and John Montour, the former of whom was sent with a message to the Shawnee. They soon returned, bringing word of the absence of their warriors, who "had gone to the Southward to speak with the army there." Oct. 10, the sound of musketry was heard at Fort Gower; and the following day Dunmore took up his march for the Indian towns, hoping to get between them and the warrior's band. The army camped the first night at Federal, and the second at Sunday Creek, both in Athens County. At the third camp, near the village of Nelsonville, news was brought from Lewis of his victory which occasioned great joy among the troops. See Draper MSS., 3S5-17. Two days later, a messenger from Cornstalk appeared, suing for peace; but next day the army advanced to the bank of Scippo Creek, on what was later the Winship farm, in the southwest quarter of section twelve, township twelve, range twenty-one, where a rude camp was formed, named by the governor for the English queen, Camp Charlotte. The name was written with red chalk on a peeled sapling and placed in the centre of the enclosure. At Camp Charlotte, the negotiations with the Shawnee chiefs had made considerable progress, when the approach of Lewis's army alarmed the Indians.—ED.

by several expresses from his Lordship, the last one informing us that he had concluded a peace. As we went on further than was expected The Indians who watched every motion of our army, informed the Govr. that we had not stopt but were pushing strait for their Towns & would be in that day (which we could have done). His Lordship with the Interpreter Mr. Gibson & an Indian Chief & 50 men came to our Camp at Dusk.[16] The next day he called the Captains together, told what he had [done] & desired us to return home. We began our March that day, all but about 50 Fincastle men who went to the other Camp. on Friday night we reached Point Pleasant. on Sunday evening the greatest part of the Fincastle & Augusta Troops set out for home, every body being anxious.

Capt. Russell is to remain with 50 men at point Pleasant untill the Assembly can be applyd to.

The Mingoes refused to comply with the terms of the Treaty, when his Lordship was at our Camp he had about 8 of their men under confinement. Tuesday night after he returned to his own Camp he detached 250 men who reached a mingo Town the following night, killed 5 & took 14 prisoners chiefly Women & Children the rest escaping under Cover of the Night.[17] The Plunder to a considerable Amount

---

[16] In later years, Col. Andrew Lewis's son wrote to Dr. Campbell that his father was obliged to double or treble the guard around his tent, while the governor was present, in order to preserve him from the wrath of the backwoods soldiers, who were incensed at being turned back when in sight of their prey. See *Va. Hist. Register*, i, p. 32.—ED.

[17] This was the expedition led by Maj. William Crawford, which conducted the only offensive action of Dunmore's division of the army. George Rogers Clark and Joseph Bow-

was brought away, & the Town burned down.[18] This Intelligence came by Jno. Howe who was with the Party & overtook me at Elk. There is another Mingo Town nearer Pt. Pleasant.[19] I doubt the Govr. cannot take that for want of Provisions

The Shawnese proposed laying themselves at the Govrs. mercy & told him to make the Terms & they should be complied with. He proposed their delivering up all the Prisoners & paying for what Stores &c they had taken since last war. And never more to make war or disturb us. for the Two first he takes two of their Chiefs with him to Wm.burg & for the last four Chiefs or the Sons of such. I dont know abt. the other articles but Knox & howe tells me that there is something about their never coming over to our settlements but to Trade.[20]

---

man, later concerned with the capture of the Illinois, were members of this party. The town visited by them was known as Seekonk, or Salt Lick Town (sometimes Hill Town), and was situated on the west bank of the Scioto, near Columbus, about opposite the Ohio state penitentiary. Two other small Mingo villages were in the vicinity. For account of this raid written, by the leader, see *Washington-Crawford Letters*, pp. 55, 56. The numbers of men and enemy killed differ slightly from Christian's account. For traditions of this event, see Lee, *City of Columbus* (N. Y. and Chicago, 1892), pp. 97–99.—Ed.

[18] The booty taken was sold for £305, 15 shillings, and was to be divided among Crawford's men. The booty from McDonald's Wakatomica expedition, reported at the same time, was only £35, 11 shillings, 3 pence. See *Journal* of Virginia House of Delegates, Dec. 9, 1776.—Ed.

[19] Probably Horse-head Bottom town, situated on Pine Creek, an affluent of the Little Scioto in the county of that name. This was the Mingo town that the party from the neighborhood of Wheeling started to attack in April, 1774, from which enterprise they were dissuaded by Capt. Michael Cresap. See Mayer, *Logan and Cresap*, pp. 88, 150.—Ed.

[20] Compare with these terms those reported by Crawford (*Washington-Crawford Letters*, p. 54), and Dunmore's ac-

Last Friday was two weeks [Oct. 21] Logan a famous Chief[21] went home with a little boy a son of Roberts on Holston & two of Blackmores Negroes. He said He had taken them on the Fronteers next the Cherokee Country & had killed I think either 5 or 7 people. The boy and negroes will be soon in.

count in his letter of Dec. 24, *post*. For a history of the subsequent negotiations see Preface to the present volume. Three of the hostages were Chenusaw, also called "the Judge," Cuttenwa, and Newa.—ED.

[21] The following brief biography of Logan is abridged from a manuscript life in the Draper MSS., 2D, chap. 12. The father of Logan was a French child who, captured when quite young, had been adopted into the Oneida tribe, and became a chief of much influence among the Indians of the Susquehanna. Logan's mother was a Cayuga, hence this was his tribe. For many years he lived at Shamokin (now Sunbury), in the Susquehanna valley, and was usually known as John Shikellimo, his appellation Logan being in honor of James Logan, secretary of the province; his Indian name was Tachnechdorus (branching oak of the forest). During the French and Indian War he maintained a strict neutrality, even seeking refuge in Philadelphia from the wiles of the savage allies of the French. Obliged to abandon his ancestral home, he lived in various places in Pennsylvania—for several years in the Kishacoquillas valley, whose pioneers later told tales of his kindness, generosity, and general goodwill except when under the influence of liquor. About 1772, he removed to the Ohio, and it was at his town on Yellow Creek that the affray occurred on April 30, 1774, that has been cited as the occasion for Dunmore's War. Having glutted his vengeance by four prolonged raids, during the summer and autumn of this year, Logan returned to the native towns, after the negotiations with Lord Dunmore for peace had begun. The date of his arrival, as here given by Christian, is proof that he was not in the battle at Point Pleasant. Noticing his absence, Lord Dunmore sent his interpreter, John Gibson, to bring him to the conference. Logan refused to go, and upon that occasion delivered the now famous speech, so generally quoted as an example of Indian eloquence, to which Jefferson paid high tribute in his *Notes on Virginia*. There grew up an animated controversy concerning the genuineness of this speech, and its attribution of the murder to Cresap.

It is a general opinion in the Gov^rs. army that the peace with the Shawnese will be lasting.²²

Many of our wounded men died since the Accounts of the battle came in, I think there are near 70 Dead. Capt. Buford & Lieut. Goldman & 7 or 8 more died whilst we were over Ohio & more will yet die.

Col^o. Fleming is in a fair way to recover and I think out of danger if he dont catch cold. Him & Capt. Dickeson sett of[f] Monday was a week from the Point in a Canoe & will come from Elk or Kellys on horseback.²³ all the wounded are coming in who Can ride, some must Stay untill they get better.

I dare say the Army is now scattered from Elk to the levels, perhaps from Point pleasant to the Warm Springs, all in little Companys. Many of the Fin-

---

It is now admitted that the substance of the speech, as it has come down to us, was actually delivered by Logan, but that he was mistaken in attributing the murder of his family to Cresap. See Jacob, *Life of Cresap;* Mayer, *Logan and Cresap* (especially documents in appendix to edition of 1867); Roosevelt, *Winning of the West,* i, pp. 236-239, 347-352. The rest of Logan's life is sunk in obscurity. He removed to Pluggy's Town, on the Scioto, then to the waters of Mad River, in Logan County, and later to the neighborhood of Detroit. He saved Kenton from the stake in 1778, and the next year was recognized in a savage raiding party in southwest Virginia. See Draper MSS., 5QQ11. He was killed by one of his own relatives on his way home from Detroit in 1780. His epitaph may be given in his own statement, that "he knew he had two souls, the one good and the other bad; when the good soul had the ascendant, he was kind and humane, and when the bad soul ruled, he was perfectly savage, and delighted in nothing but blood and carnage." See *Amer. Pioneer,* i, p. 350.—Ed.

²² See letter of Arthur St. Clair, Dec. 4, 1774, in *Penna. Archives,* iv, pp. 386, 387.—Ed.

²³ Kelly's Creek is a small affluent of the Kanawha, about twelve miles below the Falls, where Walter Kelly was killed by Indians in the spring of 1774.—Ed.

castle men crossed at P^t. Pleasant & intended to steer for Clinch. others at Kellys. I beg of you if you can get any Opp^y. to inform M^{rs}. Fleming of her husbands being on his way, He walks about constantly all day. He had plenty of people to take care of him. Col^o. Lewis I think will be in the first of next week, perhaps some longer. When I saw the Govr. he said he would hasten to W^m.burg to meet the Assembly whom he expected would adjourn from day to day, untill he could get there. He will go very quick.[24]

Pray show this to M^r. Madison. I will see him the last of this week I hope on my way to Hanover. If I knew certainly of y^r. coming up Catawba I would go that way to meet you. I wish the other road may please you as well.

I am Sir as usual Yours Ever

W^M CHRISTIAN

To Col^o. William Preston. at Bottetourt

---

[24] Dunmore arrived in Williamsburg, December 4. The city, the College of William and Mary, and the governor's council presented him with congratulatory addresses (*Amer. Archives*, i, pp. 1014, 1019, 1043). The following March, the convention of the colony resolved "that the most cordial thanks of the people of this colony are a tribute justly due to our worthy Governour, Lord Dunmore, for his truly noble, wise, and spirited conduct, on the late expedition against our Indian enemy; a conduct which at once evinces his Excellency's attention to the true interests of this colony, and a zeal in the executive department which no dangers can divert, or difficulties hinder, from achieving the most important services to the people who have the happiness to live under his administration" (*Journal* of the Convention 1775, p. 7). This was passed by the political enemies of Dunmore, and those assembled in opposition to the royal party. See also address of Fincastle County inhabitants, in *Amer. Archives,* 4th series, ii, 301.—ED.

THE GARRISON AT POINT PLEASANT

[Capt. William Russell to Col. William Preston. 3QQ132.]

My Dear Colo.—I have at length obtained liberty to return from Hochocing, and did Arrive here yesterday. I took leave of his Lordship at Fort Gower, who, at that Time Embark'd for Fort Pit;[25] Colo. Stephen was ordered to wait there, a Day longer to see, if the Mingoes brought in the Hostages as was expected, during which time Colo. Stephen detain'd me to see, if the Mingoes wood come in, as was expected, and after waiting his Lordships appointed time, that pefidious Tribe fail'd in coming according [to] Appointment; when It appear'd quite uncertain whether, their Determination was for War, or Peace, so that Colo. Stephen ordered the number of fifty, allowed at this Garrison, to be Augmented to seventy five, and a few more to be continued as Artificers, till the Fort is compleated.

At my coming down to this place, I found nothing done to the Fort, sutable for a defensive Garrisson, nor was there more Flower left in the Magazine than will serve us at half allowance, Eight Days. One hundred and sixty Beves Colo. Lewis writes me, the Commissarys return'd left in the Woods, of them I wish we may get 80 or 100 so that at present we are in

---

[25] Dunmore's army broke up into small squads, which found their way back to Fort Pitt as best they might. The men suffered for lack of provisions, and were chiefly dependent upon what game could be killed. One party shot eighteen turkeys on an island in the Ohio. Cornstalk and his sister, the Grenadier Squaw, accompanied Lord Dunmore to Hockhocking. Grim's *Recollections,* Draper MSS., 14J201.—Ed.

(should the Indians prove mischievous) a[s] Defenceless situation as poor wretches ever were. We expect flower down from the Levels of Green Briar but I much fear the men on their return Home, will plunder chief of that, in Short our chieff dependence must be on poor Colo. Fields Corn, or Docter Biscoes up the Ohio. I wood esteem it a favour, that you wood try to procure some Flower for us, if any can be had in your Quarter, or if the season wood Admit, to Write to Mr. Mathews to send us some to Colo. Field's Plantation, from whence, we could Battoe it down to this place.[26] When I took water at Hochocing to come down, two white Men and a Captive Negroe of Blackmores, with a Horse for each Man, sot out to come down by Land. They might have been here two Days past; but at present there is not the least Acct. of them, I much fear the Indians have kill'd them, or as the Governor has a parcel of Prisoners taken at Hill Town, of the Mingoes; I fear they will try to get as many of our People, to redeem theirs, reather then give Hostages, especially if they intend to be troublesome hereafter. When I came to this Place I had not the least thought of remaining here but apply'd to My Ld. by Letter, before I saw him to Indulge me with a Post, if any should be Establish'd at the Falls, or Kentuckey. His Excellency thinking it Inconvenient to have that done, uppon the Receipt of your Letter, and Colo. Christian, thought fit to con-

---

[26] Field's plantation was near Kelly's, at the mouth of the creek of that name. See Stuart's "Narrative" in *Mag. of Amer. History*, i, p. 674. "Battoe it down" means to convey it down the river in a batteau, or flat-bottomed boat.—ED.

tinue me here, but told me he intended to have an Established Post at the Falls, as quick as Possible; when I should be removed their. This favour done me, lays me under the most lasting obligation to you, and am sorry, that my sinceer thanks is all I can return, at this time for so lasting a favour done me wh[ich] I trust in god may be of service to my helpless family who do look upon it as such intended by you. I only hope, should anything Occur hereafter, in which I could serve you, you will pleas to call upon me; when I will exert myselfe, with a most harty willingness

I have much to say to you respecting this Expedition; but my confus'd Business here, at this Time wont permit me, and as I hope to wait on you in the Hollydays, It may not be disagreeable then. I wanted much to write to Capt. Floyd, but as Mr. Jones is in haste, I must beg his excuses. I hope this will find you, and Lady well, and that God may long continue you both so, is the real wish of, my Dr. Col. your most Obedt Humble Servt.

W RUSSELL

Fort Blair, at Point Pleasant Novr. the 12th. 1774[27]

---

[27] Fort Blair was a small palisaded rectangle, about eighty yards long, with blockhouses at two of its corners. The last official act of Lord Dunmore in June, 1775, is said to have been the disbanding of its garrison. See *Amer. Archives*, 4th serie, ii, p. 1189. But the Virginia assembly hastened to reestablish the garrison (*Ibid*, iii, 370), and a short distance up the Ohio, a new stockade was built, called Fort Randolph. Captain Arbuckle commanded here for several years, and here Cornstalk was killed (Nov. 1777). Two different attempts were made by the Shawnee to avenge their chieftain's murder, but the garrison withstood the siege, and the walls of Fort Randolph stood until near the close of the Revolution. Col. Andrew Lewis, Jr., found but slight remains of a fort at this place, in 1784. See *Va. Hist. Register*, i, p. 33.—ED.

N. B. I have Inclosed for your satisfaction; an Address of the Officers with my L^d. considering the greivances of British America, which I shall be glad you wood send to Col^o. Christian.[28]

To Col. William Preston in Fincastle.

CHARLES LEWIS MOURNED

[Thomas Lewis to Col. William Preston. 3QQ131.]

STAUNTON Thursday No^br Court[29] 1774

DEAR WILL—You will readily agree I am not well Situated at this time & place to return your favors, of Nob^r. 4th what Can I Say to you, your have Conjured up a Set of reflections in my breast that had begun to Subside, but you were good in this. I cant Enter on ye Subject. but at ye Same time Cannot forget ye Sentiments you have Expressed with so much Energy; the Dictates of a warm & affectionat Friend-

---

[28] This address was drafted at Fort Gower, Nov. 5, 1774, and states that having lived in the woods three months without intelligence from Boston or the delegates at Philadelphia, the signers fear that their countrymen may be jealous of the use of arms by so large a body of men at such a critical juncture; but they will use them for no other purpose than the honor of America and Virginia. The resolutions assert loyalty to the king while "he delights to reign over a brave and free people," but love of liberty outweighs all other considerations; they also express the respect entertained for Lord Dunmore, and believe that the campaign was undertaken from no other motive than the true interest of this country. See *Amer. Archives*, i, pp. 962, 963.—ED.

[29] About Nov. 15.—L. C. D.

ship.—but no more of this at present.—I am Obliged to you for ye attention you paid to my Information on an Intresting affair. if you Could add any thing to your Kindness to ye memory of your Friend it would be by Saying Something to ye Printer, it Cann't, Come with propriety from me; I have no Talents for a thing of the kind, nor would I have any thing Said of him but the truth. Ye Cherokee paper gives me pleassure, as it promises peace in that Quarter. I perceive you are mistaken in Cressops affair but Cannot now Set you Right, I was on the Ohio at ye time of action & am well Informed of the truth, on the part of Cressop it was murder, may god preserve you in famely & property, may you never feel what I do at present, more Distressing than You Can Conceive adue Dr. Friend

THOS. LEWIS[30]

---

[30] Thomas Lewis, elder brother of Andrew and Charles, was born in Ireland in 1718. Emigrating with his father to Augusta County, he became prominent in public affairs, although by defective eyesight debarred from military service. A man of culture and refinement, he had one of the largest libraries in the West, and was a mathematician of some note. For many years he held the office of surveyor of Augusta County, and frequently served in the house of burgesses. In 1775 he was delegate to the Virginia convention, and later voted for the United States constitution in the ratifying convention (1788). He was also employed as Indian commissioner, and for many years was a local magistrate. He died at his home, named "Lewiston," in Rockingham County, Jan. 31. 1790.—ED.

COLONEL FLEMING'S ORDERLY BOOK

[Journal of the Expedition. 2ZZ72.][31]

[Se]pt^r. 4 CAMP UN[ION]

The Guard to mount this day as Yester[day] Capt. 1 Lieutt. 1 Ensign. 3 Sergeants & fifty [MS. torn] [in]quest of the Enemy & Divide in such small parties [MS. torn] thought most likely to discover & Annoy the Enemy. [MS. torn] but little or no probability of coming up with them to d[MS. torn] they may return to Camp. I beg the Officers to exert themselves in preventing the men of their respective Compies. from the infamous practice of shooting away their Ammunition; let the weather be ever so wett they are not to fire without the leave of their Officers. if this order be not complied with no more ammunition can be distributed at his Camp and I hope the Capts. will read or cause to be read to their men every order by which their conduct is to be regulated. A Sergeant & 12 men to march to the ford of the River Green Briar in order to eschort any Baggage or Brigades that may be coming in to day. if none arrives at the foard to day the party is to [MS. torn] morrow.

---

[31] The manuscript book of Col. William Fleming, used for orderly purposes, and containing also a journal of the expedition, was obtained by Dr. Draper from the descendants of Colonel Fleming. The book is 7½×6 inches in size, and composed of 28 sheets, some of which are considerably mutilated on the corners and edges. As will be seen later, the entries after Fleming was wounded at Point Pleasant, are in the handwriting of John Todd.—ED.

Sept'. 5th. [Parole] Scotland

The Guard as Usual. 20 Men to be paraded immediately & to be Mounted on horses, which the pack horse Masters are to furnish to scour the Woods all round the Camp at about two miles distance in order to dislodge any Scouting Indians & make it safe for the Pack horse men to gather up their horses. A Capt. & 50 Men properly assigned to go in quest of the Indians that were discovered Yesterday to be divided into parties & to Return in the Evening unless they have a probability of overtaking them. If Mr Posey has not sent off the full Number of Horses to the Warm Springs Yesterday that were ordered [he is] to send off this day the Remainder [MS. torn]

CAMP UNION Sept' 6, 1774

[MS. torn] illiam [MS. torn] 1 Capt. 1 Lieut. 1 Ensign. 2 Sergts. 1 Corp. [blank in MS.] R[ank] & File of Botetourt Line to Mount Guard. Colo. Lewis with the [Au]gusta Troops. & Capt. Arbuckles Compy. from Botetourt to march as soon as they possibly can get in Readiness to take with him 400 horses loaded with Flower, Salt & Tools & what beef Cattle are at this place. the Kettles that are expected this Morning are to be distributed amongst the whole in equal proportion to the Number of each line. the Compys. that are to March to be compleated to 1/4 lb powder & 1/2 lb ball each man. One of the Acting Comisarys to attend the Marching division

FLEMING'S ORDERLY BOOK

Return [of] Troops from Botetourt on the Expedi-[t]ion against the Ohio Indians 1774 Septr. 7

Companies. Colo. W^m. Fleming	Commiss^d Officers		Non Commissiond O^s			Rank & File
	Lieut^s	Ensgⁿ	Serg^t	Fifer	Drumm^r	
Capt. Phil Love		1	3	.. ....	......	38
Capt Thos. Buford	1	1	4	.. ....	......	44
Capt. Arbuckle	1	1	4	......	1	59
Capt. Jno. Lewis	1	1	4	1	1	64
Capt. Jno. Murray	2	1	5	......	......	67
Capt. Jno. Stewart	1	......	3	......	......	34
Capt. Robt. McClennachan	1	1	4	......	1	41
Capt. Henry Paulin	1	1	4	1	1	53
	9	7	31	2	4	400
						53
						453
Shelby 52						
Fields 38						
Russel 50						32 140
						595

CAMP UNION ON THE LEVELS OF GREEN[BRIER Sept. 7.]

The Guard the same as Yesterday. Mr Posey is order'd to have the Packhorses that are Missing ga[thered] in with all possible speed and to Charge the Packhorse Masters to hold their Respective Brigades as they come in in Readiness at a call. And the Com-

---

[32] These were the companies at Camp Union, included in the Botetourt regiment under Colonel Fleming, but enlisted in Fincastle and Culpeper counties.—ED.

missarys are to have all the Cattle that have been lost on the way or at this Camp to be gathered in and to look out a proper place as convenient, as can be found to the Camp for a bullock Pasture that a guard may be ordered to such place. The Sutlers are forbid distributing Liquors in such Quantities as will make any of the Troops drunk—otherwise a totall stop will be put to the Retailing of Liquors. The Butchers to have a Slaughtering pen made, that they may kill the Cattle otherwise than by Shooting them

CAMP UNION Septr. 8th. 1774   Parole Boston

A Capt^s Guard to mount as usual. A Sergiant & 12 men for a Grass Guard. four faling & one broad Ax to be delivered to each Company the Capt^s. to cause them to be ground & helved And the greatest care taken that they be not lost either in Camp or on the March. Mr Posey to report the Number of Pack horses he has at this place and the Commissary to cause the bullocks that were lost to be gathered together, & Report the Number of Cattle every Evening. The Grass Guard to be kept at the Field in which the Cattle were last Night in which Field the[y are to be] kept every night.[33]

---

[33] In the Draper MSS. (11ZZ1–13) there is the copy of an orderly book kept by James Newell, who acted as ensign in Captain Herbert's company—see Christian's letter of Sept. 3, *ante*. This was given to Dr. Draper by Ben Rush Floyd, who procured the original from a daughter of Newell, Mrs. Adams Sanders, of Wythe County, Va. As this has recently been published in the *Virginia Historical Magazine*, xi, pp. 242–253, from a transcript made from the Draper MSS., and as the orders but duplicate those in Colonel Fleming's book, we have decided to give, in the form of notes, only such portions of Newell's journal as present additional material; and where Fleming's journal is torn, we supply the lacunæ from Newell's.—ED.

FLEMING'S ORDERLY BOOK

[Return of] Troops from Fincastle on the Expedition against the Ohio Indians Sept 9th. 1774

Companies.	Commis^d Offrs.			Non Com^d D^o			Rank & File						
	Capt	Lieut	Ensign	Sergt	Fifer	Drummrs	Rank & File	Chaplain to the Army	Armourer	Butchers	Commissarys	Pack Horsemen	Drovers
Col^o. Wm Christian	.	.	.	.	.	.							
Capt Walt^r Crocket	1	1	1	3	.	.	48						
Capt. Wm Herbert	1	1	.	3	.	.	40						
Capt. Wm Russel	1	1	1	2	.	1	42						
Capt. Evan Shelby	1	.	1	3	.	1	41						
Capt. W^m. Campbel	1	1	.	3	.	1	40						
Capt. Ja^s. Harrod	1	1	1	2	.	.	22	1	1	2	1		
	6	5	4	16	.	3	233	1	1	2	1		

CAMP UNION Septr. 9th Parole York

A Capt^s. Guard to mount as usual. [Sergeant and 12 men] for the Grass Guard. each Capt to inspect his Comp[any, and report the] Number of such, as also of such as they may think [not fully fit] to undergo the fatigue of the Expedition. Maj. Ingliss [to report] the Number of Pack Horses at this Camp exclusive of [those] from Fincastle. Mr Simms[34] to

---

[34] Charles Simms afterwards entered the continental army, being first major of the 12th Virginia, then lieutenant-colonel of the 6th, and later transferred to the 2nd. He resigned from the army, Dec. 7, 1777, and began the practice of law at Alexandria, where he spent the remainder of his life. The family tradition was, that Col. Charles Lewis died in his arms. See Draper MSS., 8ZZ21.—ED.

Report the Quantity of Salt and the Quarter Master to have all the Tools that are not ordered out for the use of the Companies made up in loads.

Septr. 10. Parole [England]

A Capt's & the Grass Guard as Yesterday. The Troops from Botetourt with Capt Bufords Compy. from Bedford, And Capts Shelby & Russels Companies from Fincastle to prepare for a march & hold themselves in Readiness to move on the Shortest Notice. Each Capt. to draw up his Compy. & examine into the state of the Amunition they have distributed among the Men, And make a Report Accordingly. Maj^r. Ingless, Mr Posey & the Q^r. M. to have the beeves & Packhorses under their respective Charge in readiness at a Call, & to have a breastplate fixd to each packsadle if possible.

This day one of the Spies from Gauly came in & reported he had discovered five Indians with 3 horses going out on teusday & on Friday Morning last three coming in [MS. torn].

[CAMP UNION] ON THE G^T. LEVELS OF GREEN BRIAR

Sep. 11 Parole George.

[1 ensign] 1 Serg^t & 1 Corp^l with 18 private for Guard & 6 R. & F. for the Grass Guard. The Guard to be taken from the Comp[anies] that are not under Marching orders of Yesterday, & those who were to hold themselves in readiness are to march to morrow morning Maj^r. Ingless & Mr Posey to cause all the pack horses to be loaded as early as possible & the Quarter Master to have the Brigade under his care to

FLEMING'S ORDERLY BOOK 319

be loaded with all the tools & Ammunition. Divine Service to begin at 12 o'Clock.[35]

Marched from Camp Union Sept. 12th. 7 miles to Camp Plesant crossing Muddy Creek Mountain.

☽ Camp 2nd. Sepr. 12th. 1774 Parole Frederick

A Capt. 1 Lieutenant 1 Ensign 3 Sergeants 1 Corporal & 50 Rank & file for Guard. The packhorse Masters & those who have Charge of the Cattle to have their respective Charges in readiness as it is necessary to march as early tomorrow as possible. A Man from the Advanced detachd party under Colo. C. Lewis came in to Camp [MS. torn] Fields party of 30 [MS. torn] that on Saturday one of his Men named Clay had [MS. torn] Indian and the Indian was shot down [MS. torn] party,[36] he further reported that Colo. C. Lewis [MS. torn] near Fields on Sunday night last that he had [MS. torn] hunting horses & that the Appearance of two Indians had forced him to come towards the Inhabitants when he fell in on our Camp, from 2d Camp we pas'd Hamiltons plantation, Francis Jacksons, and encamped on a Branch of Muddy Creek— distance from 2 Camp 11 Miles, a bad place both for food & good water.[37]

---

[35] From the close of this entry, nothing appears in Newell's *Journal* until Sept. 23, when he was ordered, with Captain Herbert's company, to march from Camp Union, which Fleming's detachment left Sept. 12.—Ed.

[36] For a fuller account of this episode, by which the Shawnee were informed of the approach of the army, see Withers, *Border Warfare*, pp. 163-165.—Ed.

[37] Muddy Creek is a northern affluent of Greenbrier, in the county of the latter name. The first settlers in this region were cut off (1763) by an Indian party led by Cornstalk, who first professed friendship, and then at a given signal began the work of death. See Withers, *Border Warfare*, pp. 92-93, 172, 173.—Ed.

CAMP 3ᵈ Septʳ. 13. ♂ Parole George

1 Captᵗ. 1 Lieutt. 1 Engn. 2 Sergᵗˢ. 1 Corporal & 50 R & F for guard to prevent a Repitition of Orders, let it be observd for the future that in case of an Alarm each Compy. is to form on the Ground, [where] they [are] encamp'd and face outwards, & stand fast untill they receive orders. those who have charges of the Bullocks drivers are to report the Number of Cattle every Evening & to have them gathered in every Morning as Early as possible & in case of any Missing Majʳ. Ingless to report the same before a March. a drisling wet days March & hard rain all night.

Sept. 14ᵗʰ. ☿

Marched from Camp 3 up a branch [MS. torn] about 1½ Miles then [MS. torn] Meadow Creek, or Walkers Cr³⁸ [MS. torn]

[CAMP] 4ᵀᴴ. ON WALKERS CREEK
Septʳ. 14ᵗʰ. 1774   Parole Quebec

A Captains Guard to mount immediately. The General to beat tomorrow at day break. The Packhorses & Bullocks to be gathered in as early as possible The Scouts to take a Range with the Guide that he may be more certain of the way.

Marchd from Camp 4ᵗʰ up the Buffaloe Spring Lick over some easy risings & some meadow ground fell

---

³⁸ Meadow River, a southern affluent of Gauley, rises in southwest Greenbrier County. The route pursued, appears to have been a well-known Indian trace; it was followed by the marauding party of 1778. The scouts Hammond and Prior, sent to warn the settlements, passed the Indians on Meadow River. This should be distinguished from the Walker's Creek which flows into New River.—ED.

in with Col: C. Lewis path about a mile & half from Camp and marchd about a mile & half further to Camp 5th

♃ CAMP 5TH. ON BUFFALOE LICK BRANCH[39]
Sept\\r. 15. 1774 Parole Washington

A Capt\\s. Guard to Mount from which a Sergeants guard to be detatched to the Bullock drivers Camp. As we are now [on] ground much frequented by the Enemy, the firing of Guns which has been so frequently forbid are again repeated. And how ever disagreeable it may be to fall on any method that would look like Stigmatising a man who has come out on the Honourable footing of a Volunteer any Person that is found firing his Gun without first Ob[tain]ing leave may depend on being deem'd a refractory [MS. torn] shall be treated accordingly it is like [MS. torn] the troops that in case of any firing behind, that a party will be [MS. torn] of the Enemy, as we must take it for gr [MS. torn] person will take that Liberty. And such party [MS. torn] to fire on any persons who will endeavour either [MS. torn] make their Escape. And it is hoped every Officer will ex[ert them]selves in preventing this, as well as any other irregularity the Pack horses & Bullocks to be gathered in as early to-Morrow as possible. here we were Joind by Capt R M\\cClennahan & Capt Paulings Comp\\ys. who were left behind to bring up some Bullocks that had been lost.

---

[39] Buffalo Fork is a western affluent of Meadow River; the camp for this night was in the southeastern corner of Fayette County.—ED.

♀ CAMP THE 6TH Septr. 16. 1774 Parole Byrd
A Captains Guard to Mount immediately from which a Sergeants Guard to be detatched to the Camp of the Bullock drivers. the General to beat at daybreak to morrow morning & the whole to be in rediness to march as early as possible. No Compy. to march from their ground before the beating of the Assembly. Marched about ten Miles over two smart hills to a Savannah, or Meaddow ground, to where C^o. C. Lewis had encamped, near the place where Maj^r. Fields party had kild the Indian Mentiond above.

Septr. 17th. 1774 Parole Nelson
[A Captain's] guard to mount from which a Sergeant & 12 to be [deta]ched as a guard to the Bullock drivers Camp. the whole to be in readdiness to march as early to morrow morning as possible. the Adjutant to inform the Packhorse masters that they must Attend this Evening for Instructions. they received orders to go out wth. their horse leaders, on different Quarters of the Camp & drive in all the horses & Bullocks they met with. we marchd this day about ten Miles over Chestnut ridges, and some steep little ridges, pasd Great & Little Laurel Runs, the first of which empties into N[ew] R^r: by the Warrior's foarding.[40] passd W. Mans hunting Camp.[41]

☉ CAMP 8th Septr. 18th. 74 Parole Corbin
A Cap^{ts} Guard to Mount imediately from which a

---

[40] Near the present town of Quinnimont, in Fayette County, West Virginia.—ED.
[41] A small eastern branch of the Kanawha (New River) still retains the name of Mann's Creek.—ED.

Serg^t & 12 to be detatched as usual to the Bullock drivers Camp, whole to be in readiness to march to morrow morning as early as possible. we marched this day about Eleven or twelve miles, broken ridges, chiefly Chestnut and encamped about two miles from [MS. torn] on a Laural run that empties [MS. torn]

☽ Camp ye 9th. Septr. 19th 1774   Parole Page

The Guards as usual & the whole to be [in] readiness to march tomorrow morning as early as possible. this day all cros'd Gauly Mountain we came from Camp to a holl[ow] Bottom, & the Flowring Poplar very frequent the Scouts tooke us up a different ridge from that the Advanced party had taken it was easy in Assent. we had only on[e] steep declivity to come down which continued for about ½ a mile & fell on the head of Rich Creek when we Approached the Mountain. we had as is usual near the main Allegany mountains, frequent sudden Showers of Rain intermix'd with Sun Shine. this Mountain being a Continuation of the Alleghany ridge from the N^{o}ward we March'd by Computation 6 miles, three & a half was in Asending & descending the mountain and encamped on the head of Rich Creek.

♂ Camp the 10th Septr. 20. 74   Parole Johnston

The Guards as before. The Capt. of each Comp^y to inspect his Mens Arms & Amunition to morrow morning and in case of wet Charges to have them drawn if possible the whole to be in readiness to march as early tomorrow as possible. this day we March'd five Miles down Rich Creek wrongly so called.⁴² it is a little Cree.. running confinedly betwixt the hills we Cros'd it a great number of times before we came to Gauly which collects the waters from the Mountains betwixt Green Briar River & Elk River, and empties into the N[ew] River about three Miles above the falls, it was about 100 Y^{ds}. wide a stony ugly foarding.⁴³ the Banks that have been washd by the floods discover not above half a foot [of] soil, & then a white or redish sand & Clay or grity earth. we cros'd this river at two foardings below this in the distance of 1½ miles, both good foardings and came upon Lick Creek.⁴⁴ there is a small bottom in the forks, pretty good land up the river & cross the Creek. we encampd on this Creek about 11 Miles from our last encampment, had frequent Showers all day..

☿ CAMP THE 11th. Septr. 21st. 1774 Parole Kanhaway

The Guard as Usual, the whole to march to morrow morning very early. We marchd up Lick Creek about five miles, cros'd a ridge pritty steep perticularly in the desent came on the head of Pallys Creek, or Kellys Creek thick with Laurel for about 2 miles the mountains begun then to fall away, and the bottom to Open.

---

⁴² The expedition marched about parallel with the Kanawha River, on the east side, and about ten or twelve miles back from the river bank. Rich Creek is a southeastern branch of Gauley River. Fleming means that the land which it drains is not deserving of the name "Rich."—ED.

⁴³ The expedition crossed Gauley River at the mouth of Rich Creek, passing from the present county of Fayette to that of Nicholas.—ED.

⁴⁴ Now called Bell Creek (one of whose branches is still Lick Branch), the boundary line between Fayette and Nicholas counties. Its head waters mingle with those of Hurricane Fork of Kelly's Creek.—ED.

these Creeks in the bottoms [are] stock[ed] with Sugar, Papa [pawpaw] trees, & beech, flowring Poplar, & leather wood. some peavine & buffaloe grass. we marchd about five mile down this run & encampd by Computation 2 Miles from Kellys place. On our March down this Creek we met freq [MS. torn] of good coal that had been washd down with the flood [from the] mountains in the Channel, that burnt very well. the timber trees intermixd with sweet Gum, the land as we Approached the River improved and turnd very rich. We came upon the River half a mile below Kellys place.[45] it was about 200 Yards wide, seemd deep, with high hills on each side, the Bottoms or loe grounds on this side narrow, for some distance then began to Open to two hundred Yards wide in some places. we crosd two running and one dry Creek which was ye second from Kellys place.[46] in several places were swampy places with falen timber something like mosses we march'd by Computation 13 Miles, a Creek came in on the other side cald Cabin Creek & formd an Iland at its mouth.[47] we

---

[45] The expedition passed across country, by the route herein described with such accuracy, in order to avoid the great gorge worn by New River and Kanawha Falls. They came upon the Kanawha at the mouth of Kelly's Creek, some twelve miles above Charleston, having passed over one of the richest coal fields in West Virginia. In 1901 there were six mines upon Kelly's Creek, and many others in the immediate vicinity.—ED.

[46] There are several very small runs below Kelly's Creek, known as Mile Branch, Watson Branch, Dickerson Branch, and Witcher Creek—the latter has an affluent now known as Dry Branch. It being autumn when the expedition passed, the waters were low.—ED.

[47] The first settlers on Cabin Creek were a family named Flinn, who were attacked by Indians (1786). The father was killed, and the mother, two daughters and a son captured, while another daughter escaped. Chloe, one of the captive

pas'd a rapid in which were some rocks above water a mile & half below Kellys. About nine miles below Kellys a little from the road and next the river, are two Springs, in seeminly high ground in little hollows one of them three or four feet over, the other about 100 Y^{ds} from it about 3 feet over that continually buble up to the hight of 3 or 4 Inches above the Surface, without either emitting Air or heat that I could perceive, but had a Sulphurous smell tho not verry Strong. the water was black occasionally throwing up Cinders of burnt wood which [MS. torn] asionally falen into it. it tasted unctious. a [MS. torn] flashd over either of the Springs at the distance of 4 [or] 5 Inches, the flame communicates itself to the surface of the water, and burns with a Surprising force like a Culinary fire made of Ash wood, and consumes any thing that is thrown into it, and is with very great difficulty extinguished it will continue burning for a very long time. the water heats & evaporates after it has been some time burning, and if the expense by evaporation is more than the Spring Supplies, it will burn dry & go out the little basons in which these springs are have no Outlet the water soaking through a fatish earth. from them there is a desent to a miry place with falen trees and a fat black Mud, with grass. I had not time to be more perticular in my observations. we endeavored to extinguish one of the Springs by covering it with green grass without effect as it consumd the Grass at Kelly place, the Advanc'd party discover'd Ind^{ns}. and Our party some Signs or tracts.

---

daughters, was later redeemed by Daniel Boone. See Hale, *Trans-Allegheny Pioneers*, p. 171; also Draper MSS., 14C30-68.—ED.

CAMP Yᴇ 12ᵗʰ ON THE KANHAWAY
Septʳ. yᵉ 22. 1774   Parole Charlestown
The Guards as before the Pack horses & Bullocks to be gathered as early as possible to morrow morning

♀ Septʳ. 23. 1774
We marched along the [River New] to the Mouth of Elk River. the N[ew] River widned [MS. torn] or more, in its general breadth. Joind the troops encamp'd in the Forks, discovered by Our [MS. torn] three Indian tracts up a branch a little way from the last Camp. One of the tracts remarkably long when [me]asured being 14 Inches.

CAMP AT ELK RIVER Sept 23[48]   Parole Dunkirk
1 Capt. 1 Lieutt. 1 Ensgⁿ. 2 Sergts 1 Corpl & 50 R & File for Guard to morrow the Compⁿˢ that Arrivd this day to report to morrow morning the number of Artificers in the Respective Compˢ that are willing to be employed in making Canoes & other work that is necessary   All the tools that are here to be put in working order. The Scouts to Attend very early to morrow morning for Instructions.

---

[48] Newell's *Journal* contains the following entry for this date:

Camp Union Sepʳ 23, 1774

The companies are to prepare to march on Short worning. the Captains are to have all their men in the neighborhood called in by to-morrow evening and see that their men are ready for marching. Each Captain to have 3 horses and no more for himself and company. Gaming is forbid in Camp after this day, and the officers are to take notice, that this order is complied with. the pack-horse masters to have road (as made) completed if possible, and all ready to start off on Sunday evening. the pack-horse masters to have hobbles for every horse & breast plates for their saddles.

♄ 24 Sept.ʳ 74. CAMP ON ELK RIVER Parole Bedford

A Court Martial to Sit at 10 O'clock AM. for tryal of Timothy Fitzpatrick Prisoner. Col: Wᵐ. Fleming Presdt. 5 Capts. Fitzpatrick was a Servt belonging to —Pharo in the Forks had run away & taken with him a Gun belonging to —Paxton. He was committed by Capt. McDowal, as the Crime did not come properly before a Court Martial he was discharged from confinement & joind Capt McDowals Compy who had orders from his master about him. Three Brigades of horses was sent back to Camp Union for flower the men employed in making Canoes. The Flower & Ammunition was lodged in a [Ma]gazine built for that purpose. different Scouts were sent three up Elk toward Pocotilico, three across N[ew] R. to Cole River, and some were down the Kanhaway on this side. The Guard as usual. Divine Service to begin to morrow at 12 o'Clock the Officers to inspect the mens arms and those who have wet Charges to have their guns unbreeched by the Armourer. Rated the Sutlers liquor Sprts. 30 shillings W[orth] Rum 22 shillings W[orth], C. Do. 18 s.

☉ 25 Sept.ʳ 1774.

This Morning Moony one of the Scouts who went of[f] Yesterday for Cole River returnd & reported that about 4 miles below camp on the other side of the Kanhaway, they had turnd out of the path to encamp and coming on the Path early this morning had discoverd the tracts of 3 horses one of them shod & two moccasin tracts that had pasd them in the night going down the River. I suppose them a party of four or five Indians on their return from the Settlement. we Attended Service & had a good discourse. this Afternoon the Scouts for the mouth of the Kanhaway launched their Canoe, after mending a Split Parole Winchester. The Usual Guard to be continued the Armourer to be as [MS. torn] as possible, in repairing the Firelocks, [MS. torn] to repair the locks first, the Scouts that [MS. torn] Camp to Attend early tomorrow morning for [in]structions.

☽ 26. 1774 CAMP ON ELK RIVER Parole Cumberland

The Guard as usual. The Orders Issued the 15th this Month relating to the firing of Guns without first obtaining leave are ordered to be read at the head of each Compy. to morrow morning immediately after the beating of the Reveille. if the troops shall continue to disregard these orders which has so often been repeated they may be Assured an Officer & Party of Men shall be ordered out to Apprehend & Confine them the Capts. are desired to inspect the mens Ammunition of their Respective Compies. & report the names of those who are defficient for such must be the Offenders. the working parties are to be exempted from Guard mounting.

♂ 27 Parole Duke

A Capts. Guard as before. the Pack Horse Masters to have all the Pack horses drove to Camp to morrow & report the number that are fit for Service & hold them in readiness at a Call.

330 DUNMORE'S WAR

[MS. torn] a Return of the Botetourt Troops at the Camp on Elk [MS. torn] near the Mouth Septr. 27th. 1774. Under the Command of Col^o. A: Lewis.

Officers	Companies	Commiss^d Officers			Non Commissioned D^o			R. & File			
		Cap^ts.	Lieuts	Ensg^ns	Sergeants	Fifers	Drumm^r	Fit for duty	Sick	On Comm^d	Total
Botetourt Troops Col^o. A. Lewis Comm^dr in chief Col^o. Wm Fleming											
	Capt. Philip Love	1	1	1	5	.	.	23	1	10	37
	Capt Th^s. Buford	1	1	1	4	.	.	44	.	.	44
	" Arbuckle	1	1	1	4	.	1	53	.	2	55
	" Jno Lewis	1	1	1	4	1	1	57	1	4	62
	" J^no Murray	1	2	1	4	.	.	61	1	.	62
	" Jno Stewart	1	1	.	3	.	.	34	.	.	34
	" R^t McClennachan	1	1	1	3	.	1	27	1	2	30
	" Ja^s Ward	1	.	.	1	.	.	7	.	.	7
	" Hn^y Pauling	1	1	1	4	.	.	45	4	4	50
		9	9	7	32	1	3	351	8	22	381
Fincastle Troops											
	Capt Shelby	4	1	1	3	1	.	45	3	.	48
	Capt Russell	1	1	1	3	.	.	42	1	.	43
	Artificers from Comp^us	.	.	.	.	.	.	12	.	.	12
		11	11	9	38	2	3	450	12	22	484
Culpepper Troops											
	Col. Fields	1	1	.	3	.	.	39	.	.	39
		12	12	9	41	2	3	489	12	22	523
6 Batmen in Capt Loves Comp^y returnd on Command who are prest		.	.	.	.	.	.	.	6	6	.
		12	12	9	41	2	3	489	18	16	523
		Captains	Lieuts	Ensigns	Sergeants	Fifers	Drumm^r	Fit for Duty	Sick	On Comm	Total

FLEMING'S ORDERLY BOOK

A Regimental Return of the Augusta Troops at the Camp on Elk River Under the Command of Col⁰. And'w Lewis Sept'. 27. 1774.

Field Officers Col⁰. C. Lewis	Companies	Capts	Lieuts	Ensgns	Sergts	Fifers	Commissd Offrs. Drummrs	Fit for duty	Sick	On Commd	Total
	Capt Dickinson	1	1	1	2	.	1	19	2	.	21
	" McDowal	1	1	1	4	.	1	44	1	.	45
	" Moffat⁴⁹	1	1	1	4	.	.	51	.	.	51
	" Harrison	1	1	1	4	.	.	40	.	.	40
	" McClennachan	1	2	1	5	.	2	66	2	.	68
	" Mathews	1	2	1	4	1	1	57	3	.	60
	" Lockridge	1	1	.	3	.	.	21	3	4	28
	" Skidmore	1	1	1	3	.	.	32	.	.	32
	" Wilson	1	1	.	2	.	.	25	.	.	25
	" Lewis	1	1	2	3	.	1	56	.	.	56
	" Hains	1	1	1	4	.	.	45	3	3	51
Augusta Troops		11	13	10	38	1	6	456	14	7	477
Botetourt Do		9	9	7	32	1	3	351	14	16	381
Fincastle Do		2	2	2	6	1	.	99	4	.	103
Culpepper Do		1	1	.	3	.	.	39	.	.	39
		23	25	19	79	3	9	945	32	13	1000

⁴⁹ Capt. George Moffatt had had previous experience in Indian warfare. Born in 1735, he was but a young lad when his father disappeared, previous to 1749, on a journey to South Carolina, and was believed to have been killed by the Indians. In 1763 George was captain of a ranging company which was ambushed in pursuing Indians, and lost fifteen men. The next year he pursued a party of savages that had killed his step-father, John Trimble, and made captive his sister and half-brother. In this action he successfully rescued the prisoners. Several of the officers on the campaign of 1774 were his relatives—Col. William Christian was his uncle, and Capt. Samuel McDowell his brother-in-law. During the Revolution in the South, he took an active part, commanding a regiment at Guilford Court House, and acting as county-lieutenant of Augusta, 1781–83. He died at his home in Augusta County, about eight miles northwest of Staunton, in 1811.—ED.

A General Return of the Troops encamped on Elk River near the Mouth under the Command of Colo. Andw Lewis Septr. 28. 1774.

County Troops	Field Offr	Capts.	Lieuts	Ensigns	Adjutt	Quarter M	Surgeon	Chaplain	Sergeants	Fifers	Drummrs	Fit for duty	Sick	Total
Botetourt	1	9	9	7	1	1	.	.	32	1	3	351	14	365
Fincastle	.	2	2	2	.	.	.	1	6	1	.	99	4	103
Culpepper	.	1	1	.	.	.	.	.	3	.	.	39	.	39
Augusta	1	11	13	10	.	.	1	.	38	1	6	456	14	470
Totall	2	23	25	19	1	1	1	1	79	3	9	945	32	977

CAMP ON ELK. Septr. 28. 1774 ☿

The Scouts that were sent out to Cole river returnd & reported they had discovered where 15 Indians had encampd & Shaped their Course towards N[ew] R. Capt. Arbuckle & 50, Officers included, were ordered to go out & endeavour to discover their Course or come up with them. Parole Prince

The usual Guard to be Continued. The Confusion occasioned in Camp by the Sutlers retailing of Liquores in such Quantities & so frequently as to make many of the troops drunk, makes it highly Necessary to forbid the disposing or retailing of any Liquores to the troops otherwise than by orders from the Capts & the Sutlers are likewise to observe that they are not to bring any further Supplies of Liquors as the sale of any more than what is in Camp will not be permitted.

FLEMING'S ORDERLY BOOK 333

♃ 29th Septr. 1774 CAMP ON ELK Parole Westmoreland.
The Guard as Usual. The General to beat to morrow morning at daybreak a Sufficient Number of the Troops most accustomed to conducting Canoes to be collected this Evening & the Canoes to be fitted for receiving their loading with all possible dispatch the pack horses & the Cattle to be gathered as early to morrow as possible & the whole to prepair, for an early march. Elk River is about 100 Y^{ds} over. there is a foarding above the Camp 1 ½ Miles it heads with Green Briar River & of consequence runs much further or beyond Gauly. it is a Still dead running water where we incamp, there is a large flatt of Land on each side

One of the Spies that went down towards the Ohio returned & reported that they were by Computation within 15 miles of the Ohio when they discover'd two fires on the bank of the N. R. that on their making some noise the fires were covered up. on which they pushed over to the other side and on Fowlers return he spied five Indians with 3 horses going down the New R.

♀ Septr 30th. 1774. ELK, Parole King
The Usual Guard to be continued. the Canoe men to have their loading fixd this Evening to the best Advantage the pack horse men & Bullock drivers to have all under their Respective Charges in readiness verry early to morrow morning for a march. the Commissary to issue this evening provisions for the whole for two days. Crosd the Elk and marchd down it for about a mile & encamp^d at the mouth. it Raind hard & continues Rainy.

♄ Octob^r. 1st 1774

The Line of march was form'd the Botetourt troops to march on the Right the Augusta on the left each line divided into two Grand divisions and each grand Division into 4 Subdivisions Capt J. Lewis in the Advance party the Bullocks & horses to fall in the rear of the Front grand division, and the Flanks of the lines to be covered with 100 men on each Colo Fields & Capt. Love to cover the Right Flank Capt^s Shelby Russel Murray & McClennahan to form the Right front Grand Division. Capt^s Buford Stewart Pauling & Arbuckle the Right rear division.[50]

CAMP AT THE MOUTH OF ELK Parole Pitt

The Guard for tomorrow as Usual an Ensign & Eighteen men from the main Guard to be placed over the Canoes & Ammunition And they are not to suffer any person other than the Commissary & Quarter master to enter the Canoes. the Pack Horses & the Cattle to be gathered in as early to morrow morning as possible & the whole to be in readiness to march. we continued in Camp on Acct of Rain

☉ CAMP NEAR THE MOUTH OF COLE RIVER
Octr. 2^d. 74 Parole Burk

From the Capt^s Guard an Ensign & 18 to be placed over the Canoes & Ammunition. The Troops to have as much provisions this Evening as will breakfast them to morrow morning that we may have an Early march the Cattle & Pack horses to be gathered as Early as possible. We Marchd through rich Bottoms & muddy

---

[50] See accompanying sketch of the line of march.—ED.

Swamp Creeks meeting with them every mile or half miles by which the Pack horses were much Jaded. some of the troops went throw [through] an Indian Fort, an Oval 100 Y^ds. Long. the cellar which was full of water 8 feet broad. the Bank about 3 feet above the Surface of the water & 8 broad it is about 2 miles above our Encampment, on the Kanhaway, by Computation 2 miles from the mouth of Cole River. we march'd from Our last incampment about Eight miles in a derect Course tho' we by winding round the Runs made a march of 10. A Sutlers Canoe overset, two guns were lost & some baggage two Canoes were Overset that were fastened together & 27 bags of Flower were floated. they were all recover'd but two or three but much wett: the men had 2 days flower serv'd out. here we had 4 men that deserted. Serg^t Bowes & two men from Capt Paulins Comp^y and One from the Augusta troops. Desertion from the different Troops has been pretty frequent sence we left the Levels, and likewise thefts of Flower & provisions.

☾ Octob^r 3^d. 1774

We marchd through rich bottoms and crossd two or three muddy little Creeks before we reach'd Pocatellico which is a Smart Creek interlocks with the little Kanhaway has very Steep banks was very Muddy & on foarding was about 3 feet or 3½ deep and about 40 Y^ds. over. we encamp'd about a mile below the mouth, this day the Sutlers had a Canoe overset, and one of Our double Canoes Split the flower was mostly saved we marchd this day by Computation ten Miles.

CAMP NEAR THE MOUTH OF POCATELLICO   Parole Dinwiddie.
The Guard as Usual from which an Ensign & 18 for a Guard to the Canoes, the whole to be in readiness for a march verry early to Morrow Morning.

♂ CAMP ON THE GREAT KANHAWAY
Octr. 4th. 1774   Parole Faquire

The Usual Guard to be continued and to be placed as Yesterday the whole to be prepared for an Early march to morrow. For this days march we went through a narrow passage the mountains on both sides running pretty Close to the River on the side we march'd there was several verry large Rocks that had tumbled from the mountain. they were rainged pretty much in a line, the height of most of them exceeded the breadth of the Base. the mountains then extended from the River we marchd by the foot of them, and pass'd by w^t is cald the faling timber or the hurricane, without knowing it, and encamped about two miles below it. the Rocky passage is about 7 Miles from our encampment. we Marchd 14 Miles this day. The falling timber or Hurricane as it is cald is about two miles in breath & extends from the River, about the same distance across the River the mountain is pretty near & Appears swept clear of timber for the same distance, appearing like a Cleard Field, the tops of the trees on this side all lye from the River And on the Other side towards the River some are broke pretty high. the most tore up by the Roots.[51] we pas'd throu[gh] a large tract of good upland, and

---

[51] The present Hurricane Creek, in Putnam County, commemorates the effects of a tornado which had ravaged this area.—ED.

pass'd two or three Creeks the largest of which makes a quantity of good Land.⁵²

☿ CAMP ON THE GREAT KANHAWAY
Octob^r 5th 1774   Parole Charles Town

A Captains guard as before an Ensign & 18 private from the Guard placed over the Ammunition & Canoes. Maj. Ingliss will be pleased to order the Bullock drivers to keep the Cattle together as much as possible, & have them driven in as Early to morrow morning as possible & it is hoped the whole will prepair for an Early march. We marchd this day about twelve miles through several defiles, & over three or four muddy runs with verry high & Steep banks, in many Places the hills came so cloase to the river that the two Colums were obligded to march in One path about two miles from this Camp was the largest of the Runs, when the Rear came into Camp we were informd the Canoe in which the Spies had fell down the River was found floating in the Kanhaway, with some fishing Lines & hooks & some putrefied Fish I suppose the Spies have either been drove from their Canoe the Night Fowler left them, or finding her leaky had run her into the largest Creek we Crosd this day where she had been floated by the Creek rising from Rain, whilst they traveld over the hills to the mouth of the River, as the Fish were in the Canoe when the Spie who Joind us the 29th last left them. some men who stayd behind the troops in our last Camp declared they discovered an Indian, suppos'd a spy to view our Camp after we marched.

---

⁵² Probably Eighteen Mile Creek, in Putnam County.—ED.

♃ 6th Octbr. 1774.

We march'd this day throw many defiles, cros'd many Runs with Steep high & difficult banks, for about 8 miles then enterd a botom which continued to the Junction of the River 3¾ Miles long. in the Mid ground of the Bottom I measur'd nine feet some ten feet high on the trees markd with the Floods. the point is high & Affords a most agreeable prospect. the Ohio is I think 700 Yards over Appears verry level, deep still water the Kanhaway upwards of 400 Yds. and an extensive View up both rivers & down the Ohio. here we met with an Advertizement informing us of a letter lodged in a hollow tree from his Lordship which Accordingly was found see No. [blank in MS.][53] Our Spies that were sent from the mouth of Elk came in and told us they had left their Canoe, on discovering some Indians that night Fowler left them, & that they had come by land to the point, but not finding his Lordship they had continued on the hils, where they had discovered some parties of Indians Buffaloe hunting. when they left their Canoe they pushd her into the River as farr as they could. some of Our Men found a Plowshare & some cleveses about Six Miles above this place. likewise an old fine Shirt which they judged might cost 2/ Stirlg pr. yd. and an Old Cloth Jacket, Sky blew couler, likewise an Under Jaw bone. the plow Share & Cloaths were Judged Toms. Hogs.[54]

---

[53] See *ante*, p. 285, note 3.—ED.
[54] For his death, see Hanson's *Journal*, p. 114, *ante*. This would seem to indicate that he perished by an attack of wild beasts rather than of Indians, who would surely have appropriated the metallic instruments and clothes.—ED.

♃ Camp on point pleasant
Octr. ye 6th 1774   Parole York

An Ensign & Eighteen from the Capt^s. Guard placed in the point to guard the Canoes & Ammunition the Commissary to order the Canoe Men to cover the Flower in the best Manner as it now is placed & the Quarter Master to take Perticular care of the Ammunition. Maj^r. Ingliss to report on Exact state of the Beeves.

♀ Camp on point Pleasant
Octr. 7. 1774   Parole Cork

The Guard to be relieved by an equal Number at 8 o'Clock. The Canoes to be unloaded as soon as possible. The Messrs. Allens[55] to have as many of the Artificers employed as are necessary for making a Shelter for the Stores. Each Compy. to have a Necessary House as soon as possible. otherwise the Camp must become foul & sickly. And it is hoped the Troops will pay so much regard to their own health & Satisfaction as not to ease themselves else where 1 Ensign & 18 [men] with 6 of the Scouts to March to our last encampment & make search for the lost Beeves some of the Cattle drivers to go likewise. Each Capt. to give a list of his Compy. present this Evening.[56]

---

[55] Probably James and Hugh Allen, the latter of whom was killed in the battle. James lived in Augusta County, about eight miles north of Staunton, until his death in 1810. For over sixty years, he was elder of Augusta Stone Church.—ED.

[56] Newell's *Journal* re-commences with entries of the orders on Oct. 7. The orders for this day are with one or two slight verbal changes identical with those of Fleming's *Journal*.—ED.

This day 3 men came from Elk & brought lettars that Colo Christian & 220 Men were there with Bullocks & beeves & Gun Powder. Sergt Trent[57] and a party prepaird for a trip up the River with the Canoes to bring down the Flower.

♄ CAMP ON POINT PLEASANT
Octobr. 8th. 1774 Parole Gooch

This Morning a Canoe came down with some men & lettars from the Governour in which he expresses his surprise that we were not there. My Lord mentions that the Indians had picked up three Officers. And Colo Stephens in his to Colo Lewis says he hears disagreeable news from Boston but can not asert it[58]

The Guard as usual. the Bullock drivers to make a large Penn sufficient to confine their Cattle at Nights & Major Ingless to be perticular in causing them to close up the Beeves every night. The different Lines to Attend divine Service to morrow at 12 o'Clock.[59]

☉ CAMP AT POINT PLEASANT.
Octr. 9th. 1774. Parole Richmond.

The usual Guard to mount tomorrow morning. The masters of the artificers to use all possible dispatch in

---

[57] Sergeant Obadiah H. Trent, of Captain Pauling's company.—ED.

[58] Stephen doubtless referred to the act of General Gage (Sept. 1, 1774), when a detachment of soldiers was sent to Cambridge and carried off two cannon, and to Charlestown, where one hundred kegs of powder were seized. A report was circulated that the troops fired upon the people, but this was later disproved. See *Amer. Archives,* 4th series, i, pp. 762–769.—ED.

[59] At this point in the original MS., the handwriting changes, and the entries from Oct. 9–17 are made by another person, whom Fleming tells us was John Todd. Fleming evidently had failed to enter the orders for Oct. 9, when he was wounded, and required aid in continuing his journal.—ED.

making the House fit for the reception of the provisions &c. The adjutants to give Scouts notice that they are to attend very early for Instructions.

☽ Monday Octob'r the 10th.[60]

This morning before sunrise two men came running into Camp & gave information That a considerable body of Indians were incampt about 2 miles up the Ohio a small distance from it, who made a very formidable appearance. This important intelligence was very quickly confirm'd by two or three more. The drums by order immediately beat to Arms & 150 men were ordered to be paraded out of each line & march against the enemy in two Columns. The right Column headed by Colo. Chas. Lewis with Captains Dickerson, Harrison & Skidmore. The left Column commanded by Colo. Fleming with Captains Shelby, Russell Love & Buford.[61] Thus disposed they marched pretty briskly about 150 or 200 yards apart up the river about half a mile when on a Sudden the Enemy lurking behind Bushes & Trees gave the Augusta Line a heavy fire which was briskly followed by a second & third & returned again by our men with much bravery & Courage. This attack was attended with the death of some of our bravest officers & men also with the deaths of a great number of the Enemy. Nor were the Enemy less tardy in their at-

---

[60] The account of the battle which is inserted in Newell's *Journal* under date of Oct. 14, is the one known as the "official report," already given in Shelby's letter, *ante*, pp. 271-277. The description by Todd is apparently his own, and a new contribution to the reports of the eventful tenth of October.—ED.

[61] The word "Buford" was inserted later, by Fleming.—ED.

tack upon the left Column; for immediately after the fire upon the right line succeeded a heavy one on the left & a return from us with spirit & resolution. As the disposition in which the men were first placed would never promise success against an Indian Enemy the men were forced to quit their ranks & fly to trees in doing this the Enemy made a small advance & forced our men of both lines to retreat the distance of perhaps one or two hundred yards under heavy fires attended with dismal Yells & Screams from the Enemy. About this time we were succoured with a detachm^t from the Camp commanded by Captains Mathews McDowell & others of the Augusta line & some time aftewards by all the Captains of each line except Capt McClenahan of Augusta who was upon guard & Captain Lewis of Botetourt[62] who was ordered to form a line round the Camp for its defence. With the reinforcement from the Camp our men found their strength much increased & making a fierce onset forced the Enemy from their Stations & caused them to retreat by degrees about a mile giving them many brisk fires & hitting many of the leading men as was imagined. We at last with difficulty dislodged them from a fine long ridge leading from a Small slash near the river towards the hills & being discontinued by a small wet bottom again rose & was continued to the

---

[62] This information regarding Captains Alexander McClenahan of Augusta, and John Lewis of Botetourt, is not given in other accounts, and in the case of the latter apparently contradicts the "official report." If Floyd's testimony in regard to the confusion of companies and officers is to be relied upon, these discrepancies are not surprising.—ED.

hills half a mile or more from the river.[63] This advantageous post being gained about 1 o'Clock all the efforts of the enemy to regain it proved fruitless. Tho' they would summon all the force they could raise & make many pushes to break the line; the advantage of the place & the steadiness of the men defined their most furious Essays. About 3 or 4 o'Clock the Enemy growing quite dispirited & all the attempts of their Warriours to rally them proving vain they carried off their dead & wounded, giving us now & then a shot to prevent a pursuit; so that about an hour by sun we were in full possession on the field of Battle. Victory having now declared in our favour We had orders to return in slow pace to our Camp carefully searching for the dead & wounded & to bring them in, as also the Scalps of the Enemy. The day being by this time far advanced with[out] any written orders double Guards were orderd to be mounted Parole Victory.

Killd of the Augusta Line in the Action on the 10th. of Octr. 1774 Colo. Chas. Lewis, Capt. Saml. Willson and Lieut. Hugh Allen, & 18 Privates. 2 Capts, 2 Lieuts. & 51 Private wounded. The above Acct. of the Action was drawn by J. Todd.[64]

---

[63] See maps of the battle ground, included in the present volume. "Slash" was a colloquial Virginia phrase for marsh. The "small wet bottom" is evidently the bed of Crooked Creek, which in time of low water is a very narrow stream with steep, muddy sides. See Draper MSS., 2ZZ57.—ED.

[64] This paragraph, giving the list of killed and wounded from Augusta County, and the information as to the author of the foregoing account of the battle, is in Colonel Fleming's handwriting. John Todd was a native of Pennsylvania (born in 1750); but orphaned at an early age, he was educated at the classical academy of his uncle, John Todd, in Louisa County, Va. Having studied law, he practised for a time in Fincastle, Va.; but on this campaign appears to have officiated as aide or adjutant in John Lewis's company, from Botetourt.

Killed of the Botetourt Line Captains Murray, McClenachan & Ward the two last of which died one on the night & the other a day or two after the battle, Subalterns Ensign Bracken & Cundiff Wounded Colo. Fleming Capt. Buford, Lieut. Goldman, Lieut. Robison 17 Private kild & 35 Wounded. the whole of the kild 46 Sergts & privates & 90 wounded[65]

In 1775 he removed to Kentucky. In the same year he was a member of the Transylvania legislature, and one of the first delegates from Kentucky County to the Virginia assembly. There is some difference of opinion as to his having served in Clark's Kaskaskia campaign; he was certainly not at Vincennes, as frequently stated, but co-operated in raising troops for Clark. In 1778 he was appointed county-lieutenant of the newly-erected Illinois County, and for one year served as its commandant. In 1780, he was again delegate to the Virginia assembly, and married in the same year. Returning to Lexington, Ky., he was chosen county-lieutenant of Fayette, erected the first fort at Lexington, and perished at the battle of Blue Licks, August, 1782.—ED.

[65] There is considerable variation in the lists and numbers of the killed and wounded. Compare with this list of Todd and Fleming, the one given in Fleming's *Journal, ante,* and Bowyer's letter to his wife, where he gives the whole number as 147. Compare also Fleming's list of Oct. 28, *post,* where the number is put at 138. Dr. Draper, who made a very careful estimate from all the original sources, says (Draper MSS., 3D38) that nine commissioned officers and forty-six non-commissioned officers and privates were killed; and ninety-two wounded, of whom fifteen afterwards died. A return from the camp, dated Oct. 23, 1774, reports "seventy-two wounded and four sick" (Draper MSS., 7ZZ4). With the prevalent human tendency to exaggerate the losses in a famous battle, the participants who in later years wrote memoirs, enlarged these figures. Stuart says that seventy-five were killed, and a hundred and forty wounded. Withers and Doddridge follow his authority. Roosevelt (*Winning of the West,* i. 232) accepts Stuart's statement, and thinks that the contemporary reports took no account of any but the badly wounded. We are of the opinion that Stuart is nearly correct, and that a hundred and fifty wounded is approximately the correct number. Counting some nine hundred white troops as engaged in the contest, about one-fourth were incapacitated either by death or wounds.—ED.

♂ CAMP AT POINT PLEASANT
October ye 11th. 1774 Parole Hampton

The Guards to consist of two Capts. & 6 Subaltern officers & one hundred men the Commanding officer of each Company to have their men compleated with ¼ lb. Powder & ½ lb Lead as early as possible & hold them in readiness to take the field that we may as well repulse the Enemy should they Continue about us as gather in the Beeves. Hearty thanks is returned to the brave officers & men who distinguished themselves in the battle of yesterday, by whose gallant behaviour a Victory was under God obtain'd. Let us not be dismayd by the loss of our brave officers & soldiers that fell tho' we cannot help regretting the loss of them; rather let us be inspired with a double degree of Courage and Earnest desire to give our perfidious Enemies on[e] thorough Scourge.

This day were buried the men who were slain yesterday & died last night in different Burying places & the following officers & Gentlemen in the Magazine.[66]

---

[66] In 1875 the legislature of West Virginia appropriated $3,500 towards the work of placing a monument over the graves of those who fell at Point Pleasant; the fund was not used at the time, but being loaned grew to $8,788.33. In 1901, $11,000 had been secured by means of this and private contributions, $9,000 of which was devoted to purchasing and preparing a public park at the angle of the two rivers, as a site for the monument. Oct. 10, 1901, a celebration of the battle occurred, the park being formally opened, and much enthusiasm displayed. The Charles Lewis chapter of the Daughters of the American Revolution, co-operating with a legislative committee appointed by the governor of the state, have the matter in hand, and are preparing to erect a suitable monument as soon as practicable. At the session of 1905, the legislature voted towards this purpose an appropriation of $5,000, payable out of the appropriation of 1906. The members of the chapter are expecting aid from other states interested, also from patriotic hereditary societies in the Old Northwest.—ED.

Towit Colo. Chas. Lewis, Colo. Jno. Field, Capt. Murray with his half brother Geo. Cameron, Capt. McClenachan with Mr. Jno. Frogg, Capt. Wilson Lieutt. Allen.
Omitted before Killed of the Culpepper Troops Colo. Field.
Wounded [blank in MS.] Came to Camp last night Colo. Christien with the Fincastle troops.

☿ CAMP AT POINT PLEASANT
October 12th. 1774 Parole Winsor

The Guard as yesterday. Colo. Christian to send a Capt. & 50 from his line for the Beeves he left on the Kanhaway. Major Ingles to order the Bullock drivers to gather in the Cattle that are dispersed on different quarters. The pack Horses to be brought to the Camp. The master of the artificers to have the storehouse finished as quick as possible Its recommended to each Company to clear off the underwood in the front of their tents so that the whole of the Camp may be made clear. The tools that are most proper for making a breast work to be collected by the quarter master-Sergeant & deliver them to persons by the adjutants orders.

This day The Scalps of Enemy were collected & found to be 17[67] they were dressed & hung upon a pole near the river Bank & the plunder was collected

---

[67] It was the belief of the participants in the battle of Point Pleasant, that the Indians engaged were about equal to their own army in numbers, and that their loss was fully as heavy. A mutilated sheet of manuscript found among the Fleming papers (2ZZ72) makes the following statement:

" * * * told that of 430 Shawnese Warriors or upwards that came out, only 200 had returned, as they were Assisted by the Mingoes, Tawas & Wiandots. and perhaps had several Delawares with them, it confirmed the Judgement we formd

& found to be 23 Guns 80 Blankets 27 Tomahawks with Match coats Skins Shout [shot] pouches pow[d]erhorns Warclubs &c. The Tomhawks Guns & Shout pouches were sold & amounted to near 100 l.

♄ CAMP AT POINT PLEASANT
Oct⁰. 13th. 1774. Parole Alexandria

The Guards to be relieved by an equal number. all the tools to be collected that are not in use by the artificers under Mr. Allen & layd by the store house Mr. Allen will be pleased to have the house in order to receive the flower as soon as possible The Packhorsemen to have all Horses that can possibly find drawn up this day & the Bullock drivers to gather in the Cattle. The Capts. of the different lines to attend at 9 o'Clock.

The following was annexed[68] an address to the

---

of their numbers on the 10th Inst to be somewhere about 800. And that they must have suffered largely, Altho we got only 18 Scalps as they fought bravely & Stood it a long time, making many desperate pushes & resolute stands"

Smith, who had been a prisoner among the Shawnee, stated their loss as twenty-eight. This would not include the Ottawa, Wyandot, and Mingo allies. Only one chieftain is known to have been killed—Puck-e-shin-wa, father of Tecumseh. Dr. Draper gives the following chiefs as participants in the battle: Cornstalk, Blue Jacket, Black Hoof, Red Hawk, Captain Dickson, Elinipisco, and Scoppathus, to which Withers adds Chiyawee, a Wyandot. Charles Clendennin and Thomas Lewis related to Dr. Draper that after the treaty with Dunmore had been signed, the Shawnee chased some white traders away from Chillicothe, saying that they only came to discover how many wounded they had, and to deride them for their losses. Dr. Draper also makes an estimate of two hundred and thirty-three Indians killed and wounded (3D41), but this is doubtless too large a number.—ED.

[68] The writer means that the following address, written by Col. Andrew Lewis, was annexed to the orders for the day.—ED.

Aug^a. Troops as follows: The Augusta line & I have too much reason to condole with one another. You have lost your brave leader & I in him have lost the best of Brothers. A regard to his memory would be inducement enough to me to treat the brave officers & troops of Augusta with all Tenderness & just marks of Esteem even had I never been honoured as I formerly have been with the Command of them. Therefore they may be assured that in everything that regards their rank, interest & satisfaction I shall be anxiously attentive. I shall think myself happy in having it in my power to render them any essential Service either whilst they are under my command on this expedition or hereafter.

This Morning very early returnd the Scouts with Letters from his Lordship to Col^o. Lewis wt. instructions to march soon to the Towns & Join him on ye way.

♀ CAMP AT POINT PLEASANT
Oct^o. 14th. 1774   Parole Portsmouth.

The Guards to mount as usual If the Capts. will be pleased to meet at the Store house & divide the breast work lines so that each Company may have a proportion equal to its number the sooner the work will be accomplished. Capt McKie[69] to succeed Capt.

---

[69] William McKee was a Scotch-Irishman born probably in Ireland (1732). When quite young he removed to the Valley of Virginia, and was active in Indian wars, claiming to have been with Braddock on the day of his famous defeat. He was lieutenant in Captain Murray's company, although having previously ranked as a militia captain. After Dunmore's War, he saw frequent service in the Virginia legislature, and was delegate for Rockbridge in the Virginia constitutional convention, voting, in opposition to his instructions, in favor of the constitution. Shortly afterwards, he removed to Kentucky, where he died in Lincoln County (1816).—ED.

Murray in the command of the Company. Lieutt. Givens to succeed Capt. Sam[l]. Willson & Lieut McCoy[70] to succeed Capt. Ro: McClenachan & Lieutt. Roberts who acted as Lieut. under Colo. Field to take charge of that Company A Return to be given in immediately of the number of Each Company that may be depended on to cross the river to the Towns.

This Night came into Camp Colo. Slaughter with the forces from Dunmore & the Beaves & Flower left by Colo. Christian at Elk.

♄ Camp at point pleasant
Oct[r]. 15th. 1774. Parole Barre

The Guards as usual. 3 men from each Company to be collected & put under the Command of 3 Sergeants one of which is to go up the Ohio 3 or four miles, the Other up the Kanhaway to the first narrows & the 3[d] to take the ridges between the two & make diligent search for horses & drive to camp all they can find. Major Ingles will order all the cattle that can be found to be drive up in the Evening Each Company to draw as much Lead as will complete the men that cross the river to ½ pounds & have it cast into Bullets the men that cross the river to have 5 days beef served out which they are to make ready for Carriage. The Scouts that are fit for Duty to attend for Instructions immediately

☉ Camp at Point Pleasant
October 16th. 1774 Parole Hanover

The Guard as before. all the horses to be gathered

---

[70] An Augusta man of this name, William McCoy, was member of congress from that district (1811-33). He was probably a descendant of Lieutenant McCoy.—Ed.

in after 60 of the strongest Horses are set apart for the carriage of Flower each Company may have a horse to carry their Tents. Major Ingles to have 50 good Beeves in readiness to cross the river & this Evening the troops who cross the river to have two days beef served each man that crosses the river to be compleated to ½ lb Powder 4 of the Scouts to be employd this day in gathering in Horses as they are to have two for the carriage of their bundles that they may the better do their duty It's recommended to the officers who have taken in hand to make the breastwork to have their respective parts finished off this morning as quick as possible.[71]

☽ 17

The Troops Crosd the Ohio & took with them 118 beeves & 10 days Flower. when Colo. Lewis left the Camp he gave me the following Instructions Sir— On my Crossing the River with the Main body of the Troops You are to take Charge of the Officers & troops that remain. Your Principle duty will be to secure this Camp from the Attacks of the Enemy should any Appear & make the Works that are so farr Carried on as compleat as you can. Mr Trent the Canoe master with several Canoe men will be ready to go up to Elk with 4 large Canoes as soon as you can learn by consulting Mr Posey, that the Flower will be at Elk, you are to order up Mr Trent with the 4 large Canoes & what they can not carry down must

---

[71] At this point Colonel Fleming resumes the orderly-book, and it is evident that John Todd crossed the river with the troops and marched for the Indian towns. Newell also crossed the river, and the remainder of his *Journal* is given *post*.—ED.

be brought by the strongest horses that can be found at that place, & perticular derections must be given to the Officer at Elk, to receive & secure all provisions, & have it in readdiness for Issuing as it may be cald for. If you can engage any considerable Number of Men as Artificers and employ them in making a Fort, or rather in preparing timber for it, it would be of service. Hued Logs for Barracks, which might compose the Courtains of a Fort. Vessels should likewise be made for Salting Beef. The Canoes that do not go up Elk to be secured so that they may be had at a Call. If any Lettar should come from the Governor in two or three or even four days send them or it to me.[72] The Capts Dickenson Lockridge Herbert & Slaughter to remain. Lieut Draper & Vance & Ensign Smith Parole Lewis. An officer and 2 sergnts and 30 for gaud [guard].

♂ CAMP AT POINT PLEASANT
Octr. 18th 1774   Parole Finlatton[73]

Capt Lockridge to take the Charge of the augusta Troops that were left Here and Form them Into a Company and have them properly offis[er]ed. Capt. Harbert to take the Charge of the Fincastle Men and Botetourt Exclusive of Capt Bufords and Paulings and have them formed into a Company under his Direction. Capt Slaughter to Form the Culpeper Troops with what arc of Capt Bufords and Capt Paulings into a

---

[72] The original MS. of these orders for Colonel Fleming, in Col. Andrew Lewis's handwriting, is in Draper MSS., 2ZZ73.—ED.

[73] The entries for Oct. 18 and 19 are in a different handwriting, evidently that of one of Colonel Fleming's aids.—ED.

Company properly offs'd. It is Hoped the Capt^{ns}. will have a proper Roole [Roll] of their Companies made out and that they will Engage all the men that Can be spar^d. from guard and tending the Sick, to Compleat the Bastion and Breast Work already almost Finished and to build a stockeade Fort with all Expedition. These ne[ce]ssary works I am in hopes the Men will Cordially join in Compleating as it is not only for the Security of their brave wounded Companions but likewise for their own preservation. and for their Encouragement I can asure them they shall be paid Extraordinary Wages. a subaltern and 30 private men and 2 sergnts for gaurd.

☿ CAM[P] AT POINT PLEASANT.

Octr. 19th 1774 Parole Stephens

The gaurd as before a Centry to be plased over the Canoes Which is to Suffer no Canoes to be taken away but by the Canoe Master or particular orders. Capt Lockridge is Desird to pick out two or 3 of the Most active Men and Best woodsmen in the augusta Line to take a Range as scouts up the Kannaway to morrow morning and from the River Two or 3 miles Round the Camp. Capt Herbert is to Enquire if any men under his Care are fit to range the woods as likewise Capt Slaug[h]ter and make Report of them. the Men are Desird to be as Diligant as possible in they present works they are Employed in and be prepard to attend at the Magazine for Tools to morrow morning when the pioneers March which is to beat which will be an hour after the Revel [Reveille]. Robt McFarling, Wm Blair Scouts

♃ Camp Octr. 20. 1774 Parole Monlin[74]
The Guard as Usual. The Men to be employed on the Breast work &c:

♀ Octr. 21. 1774. Parole Dumfries
The Guard as usual. The Reveille to beat before day break. the line to turn out under Arms & have their Firelocks examined by the Officers of their Companies. the Men for Work to parade as soon as possible & compleat the breast work &c.

♄ Camp at Point Pleasant. Octr. 22. 1774.
The Guard as Usual. What men can be got to work to be imployed. the Guard to be releived to morrow morning at Eight o'Clock.

☉ Camp at Point Pleasant
Octr. 23. 1774 Parole Botetourt
The Reveille to beat tomorrow morning before day The whole Lines are to turn out under Arms, have the Rolls cald and their Firelocks examined & fresh primd if necessary, the different Officers to Attend at the head of their Companies, & see this done. the Men for work are to prepair themselves immediately after, to finish these Necessary works for their own preservation. The Guards to be constantly relieved every Morning at Eight o'Clock, and to consist for the future of one Subaltern, 4 Serg^{ts} & 40 Private men, from which he is to detatch a Serg^t & 8 R & File to the Kanhaway, & a Serg^t & 8 Private up the Ohio, who are to take place on the banks of the River, & keep out two sentinels each the Officer of the Guard

---
[74] Monlin was one of Lord Dunmore's titles.—Ed.

23

is likewise to detatch a Sergt & 8 to the point, who is to have the Canoes in Charge & be Answerable for them. the Men that are on Guard are by no means to leave their Guards and must not expect when on duty to sleep in their tent. the Centinels, on the Approach of any Person to them in the Night or on hearing any unusual noise wch they imagine to proceed from the Enemy, are to chalange briskly, & distinctly. "Who comes there." if they receive no Answer the first & second Challange they are to make readdy, Challange a third time and if they receive no Answer Fire on the Enemy & retire to the Guard, who are to turn out under Arms, on the Centinels Challenging twise without receiving an Answer. The Officer of the Guard is immediately to send a Sergt. & small party to examine into the Cause of the Alarm, & keep himself & Guard in readiness for Action. To keep the men Alert on their Posts it will be necessary for the Officer of the Guard to Visit his Centinels himself, as Rounds, once or twise a night, and have a Sergeant likewise to Visit them especially before daybreak or beating of the reveille it is to be hoped that the men will Chearfully Join in the work to morrow, As it will be a Shame to flinch from the Service of their Country for two or three days work, And will be a constant stain on their honour to their latest posterity, either to be cut off or defeated by the remains of an already beaten Enemy through laiziness of our securing our Post. if this has no effect which I should be both surprized & Sorry to see I must Acquaint those who refuse to Join in so necessary a work that they by their refusall will forfit all claim to the merit of their former good & brave behaviour.

FLEMING'S ORDERLY BOOK 355

☽ Octobr. 24. 1774 Parole Fincastle
The Guards as Yesterday. the Men off duty to be employed on the Breastwork &c.

♂ Octr. 25. 1774 Parole Augusta
The Guards as Usual: the Men off Duty to be imployed on the breastwork, & burning & Clearing Brush

☿ Octr. 26 1774 Parole Culpepper
The Guard as Usual, & the Men to be employed as before a Fish was caught this evening weighing 89 pounds.

♃ 27 Parole Williamsburg.
The Guard & fatigue as usual this day several Men returned from Colo. Lewis & brought Advice of a peace being made with the Indians

♀ 28 Octr. 1774 Parole Peace
The Guards as usual. This day numbers of the Troops crossd the River the Rear is expected tomorrow. A List of the Kild and wounded in the Action of the 10th those markd with a Cross died of their wounds some time after the engagement

Botetourt Line
Capt Murray
*—— Robt McClennachan
*—— Jas. Ward
*—— Buford
Lieut. Bracken
*—— Goldman
Ensgn. Condiff
Seventeen Private

Wounded
Colo. Fleming
Lieut Robinson
thirty five private

Augusta line
Colo. C. Lewis
Colo. T. Fields
Capt. Saml. Wilson
Lieutt Hugh Allen
Eighteen Private

Wounded
Capt. Jno Dickinson
—— —— Skidmore.
Lieutt. Scard
—— Vance
fifty One private

♄ 29.

Colo Lewis came into Camp last evening. and when he had got to some distance from the Towns the Governor sent an Express to inform him that He had very near concluded a peace and that he was to halt his troops there. the place being inconvenient to encamp and Colo Lewis Men being fired on that morning he marchd on. Next Morning He receivd another Express informing him the Peace was in a Manner concluded that the Shawnese had agreed to his terms. and therefor Colo Lewis was to encamp where he was. & that he & any Officers he tho't proper might come over to his Camp, Colo Lewis did not imagine it would be prudent to go to his lordships Camp with only two or three Officers. and therefore marchd thereto with a design to Join his Lordship but the Guide mistook the path & took a path that led betwixt the towns & his Lordships Camp. this put the Indians into a fright they expected Colo Lewis was going to Attack their towns they left his Lordship. and run off. His Lordship rode down to Colo Lewis' Camp in compy with Gibson a trader & Whitefish an Indian. he ask'd Colo Lewis why he did not stop when he was ordered, or if he proposd to push on to the towns. Colo Lewis informd his Lordship the reason of his marching & how he got between his Lordship & the towns, and that his Lordship needed not to be Apprehensive of his Attacking the Towns after receiving his Lordships Orders. the next day his Lordship ordered the Troops with Colo Lewis to return which they did &c:

☉ 30th
sent off some of my baggage with Smith & prepared to go up in a Canoe

☽ 31st
set off from Camp in a Canoe with 4 watermen & Capt dickinson, came up about 5 miles encampd on the S. Side of the Kanhaway.[75]

♂ Novr. 1st.
came up about 17 miles. encampd on the N. side.[76]

☿ 2nd
encamp'd near the Mouth or Opposite Pocatellico on the S. Side.

♃ 3[d]
got up to Elk.

♀ 4th
collected horses to start home and encamped 3 miles from the burning Springs

♄ 5th
encampd 3 miles above Kellys

☉ 6th
encampd ¾ of a mile above the lower foarding of Gauly, which are found very Low, tho it rained on us all day.

☽ 7th
Crosd Gauly twise which we found to our Joy verry low. we Crossd Gauly Mountain had a fine day & the road in excellent order for travelling came down the Augusta Path which we found excessively steep &

---

[75] About opposite the present town of Ambrosia, on the Kanawha & Michigan (part of Toledo & Ohio system) Railway.—ED.

[76] Not far from Midway, opposite the mouth of Hurricane Creek.—ED.

encamp'd at the first water we met south of the Mountain.⁷⁷ Laus Deo.

♂ 8th
encamp'd after crossing several Spurs, & coming down a Steep one in a bottom on a run near the 48 Mile tree. this Night it snowd the earth was covered about 1½ inches. here some of the People found some Bullocks & shot down a Cow that by computation weighd 65 a Quarter.

☿ 9th
Crosd many Chesnut ridges & steep pinches, and encampd on the top of a Mountain near the 33 mile tree a very cold day & night. the encamping ground very bad & Stony

♃ 10th
reachd Wᵐ McClungs on Meadow Creek⁷⁸ all this day I had a fever which increased very much. my wounds enflamed & stopt running, and I had a very bad night but got easier in the morning & marchd about 12 o'Clock on

♀ 11th,
and five miles from thence Met C. C. & W. S: who had set out from town to meet me. had a fever all

---

⁷⁷ Evidently Colonel Fleming returned by the same route over which the troops had marched on their outward journey. By the Augusta path, he refers to the route taken by Col. Charles Lewis's division, which differed slightly, in crossing Gauley Mountain, from that followed by the Botetourt line. See entry for Sept. 19, *ante.*—ED.

⁷⁸ When Hammond and Pryor set out from Fort Randolph, in 1777, to warn the Greenbrier settlements of the large marauding party of Indians on their way thither, they passed the Indian band who were killing and eating hogs at McClung's place on Meadow River, probably in northwestern Greenbrier County.—ED.

night which continued all Saturday I got bled in the Arm my wounds were much enflamed the Arm sweld greatly and the most Violent Shooting flying [pains] in my hand fingers & tho I took some Cocho but without much effect

♄ 12th.

Capt Christian set out on his return[79] My Arm excessivly painfull the feaver very high and verry heartsick. but I thank God I [had] a pritty good night tho the fever continued all the next day & till towards the Evening. this day Daniel McNeill[80] Joind me & staid to come in with me.

☉ 13th.

as mentiond above, but something bettar

☽ 14th.

set out pasd the Levels & got to Spars Foard. lodged there at Mr Andersons.

♂ 15th.

Went to Patrick Daviss. on Howards Creek[81] it snowed in the night

☿ 16th.

Rested there all day. but sent Smith home

---

[79] Not Col. William Christian, but some other member of the family, probably of the collateral branch founded by Gilbert Christian.—ED.

[80] Lieutenant in Captain Philip Love's company.—ED.

[81] About where White Sulphur Springs is now situated, on Howard Creek.—ED.

♃ 17th.

Came over to Greenwoods on Dunlops Creek[82]

♀ 18th.

Got to Fort Young, on Jacksons River[83]

♄ 19th.

Cros'd from Woolys to Crawfords, where we lodged[84]

☉ 20th.

reach'd the Court House.[85]

☽ [21st]

Rested the 21st it raind all day with Sleet Snow & hail & on

♂ the 22d

Reach'd home in safety being Just 3 months gone Praise be to God.

---

[82] On this day's ride Fleming crossed the main ridge of the Alleghany Mountains, passing from the present West Virginia into Virginia, and resting on Dunlap's Creek, a western affluent of Jackson River, a branch of the James in Alleghany County. The present road follows about the same route from White Sulphur Springs to Covington, not far from the line of the Chesapeake & Ohio Railway.—ED.

[83] Fort Young was near the present site of Covington, and had been employed as a frontier defense during the French and Indian War.—ED.

[84] Crossing North Mountain into Botetourt County. Alexander Crawford was a pioneer owning a large estate in western Botetourt County, but he was cut off by the Indians about 1764. See Waddell, *Augusta County,* pp. 191-193. His descendants lived at this place until recently.—ED.

[85] The county of Botetourt was erected from Augusta County in 1769; the first meeting of the magistrates was in February of the following year. Israel Christian, Fleming's father-in-law, donated forty acres to the county for the erection of a court house. This was established as a town by a law of 1772, and named Fincastle, for one of Lord Dunmore's titles. In 1900 the population was 652.—ED.

JOURNAL OF JAMES NEWELL ACROSS THE OHIO

[Portion of Orderly Book and Journal. 11ZZ1-12.][86]

CAMP, ON POINT PLEASANT,
Oct. 17th. 1774. Parole, Murry.

The Horses & Cattle that are to cross the river to be got in readiness as quick as possible three days flour and one of beef to be served out to the whole that crosses the river as the quantity of powder will not afford more than ¼ lb to each man that has been saved since the battle, that is the quantity to be served and the Captains are to receive for their Companies in bulk and have it equally divided

Return of Capt Herberts Comp'ny that crossed the Ohio October 1774 Officers 1, Sergeants 2, privates 26 in all 29.

> Bold Virginians all, each cheer up your heart.
> We will see the Shawnees before that we part,
> We will never desert, nor will we retreat,
> Until that our Victory be quite compleat.
>
> Ye offspring of Britain! Come stain not your name,
> Nor forfeit your right to your forefathers' fame,
> If the Shawnees will fight, we never will fly,
> We'll fight & we'll conquer, or else we will die.
>
> Great Dunmore our General valiant & Bold
> Excels the great Heroes—the Heroes of old;
> When he doth command we will always obey,
> When he bids us fight we will not run away.
>
> Good Lewis our Colo¹. courageous & Brave,
> We wish to command us—our wish let us have.
> In Camp he is pleasant, in War he is bold
> Appears like great Caesar—great Caesar of old.

---

[86] The earlier portion of this journal (as has been explained in preceding notes) has been incorporated with Fleming's Orderly Book. After crossing the Ohio, Newell's record is different, and has a value of its own.—ED.

Our Colonels & Captains commands we'll obey,
If the Shawnees should run we will bid them to stay.
Our Arms, they are Rifles, our men Volunteers
We'll fight & we'll conquer you need have no fears.

Come Gentlemen all, come strive to excel,
Strive not to shoot often, but strive to shoot well.
Each man like a Hero can make the woods ring,
And extend the Dominion of George our Great King.

Then to it, let's go with might & with main,
Tho' some that set forward return not again;
Let us quite lay aside all cowardly fear
In hopes of returning before the new year.

The land it is good, it is just to our mind,
Each will have his part if his Lordship be kind.
The Ohio once ours, we'll live at our ease,
With a Bottle & glass to drink when we please.

Here's a health to King George & Charlotte his mate
Wishing our Victory may soon be complete
And a kind female friend along by our Side
In riches & splendor till Death to abide.

Health to great Dunmore our general also,
Wishing he may conquer wherever he go.
Health to his Lady—may they long happy be
And a health, my good friends, to you & to me.

Parole London.—CAMP ON THE OHIO AGAINST
POINT PLEASANT Octob^r 18, 1774.

1 Capt., 2 Lieuts., 1 Ensg, 75 Private men for the guard. bullock Drivers to gather in and keep all the cattle that crossed the river yesterday. the packhorse masters to have 61 pack horses in readiness for loading as early as possible 60 loads of flour to be brought over from Point pleasant & one sack of Salt. Major Inglis to have 15 more beeves driven over the river as quick as possible.

A general return for the Fincastle troops for 19th Oct. 1774

Captain		Lieut.	Ensigns	Sergnts	Drum	fife	fit for duty	Total
Roberts [87]	1	1	1	2	.	.	37	38
Crockett	1	1	1	3	.	.	28	29
Russell	1	1	1	3	1	.	35	35
Shelby	1	1	1	3	1	.	29	29
Campbell	1	1	.	3	1	.	32	32
Floyd	1	1	1	3	.	.	44	44
Harrod	1	.	1	2	.	.	27	27
Herbert	1	.	1	2	.	.	27	27
1 chaplain, 3 scouts, 1 Butcher				.	.	.	.	261

Wednesday October 19th., 1774.

The guard as before. On this days march the packhorses & cattle to be driven as close as possible and when the ground will admit of it not further back than the rear of the right & left Columns this Camp was on a small creek about 1½ miles from the Ohio where was an Indian Camp, and sundry things found the indians had left on their flight home

Thursday Oct'r 20" [Parole] Essex

The usual guard to mount this morning the packhorse men to drive as close & far forward between the columns as possible & the cattle to be drove between the rear of the other columns in case of an attack. The officers to form in the best manner they can pos-

---

[87] Maj. James Robertson, for whose correspondence with Colonel Preston see *ante*. The majority of the Fincastle troops came in with Colonel Christian, after the battle of Point Pleasant, and were prepared for the advance to the Indian towns.—ED.

sible Judge in order to oppose the enemy according to the ground, place or places, the Enemy may appear In case of an alarm in Camp the officers are to form on their own ground, as they camp to take Care & face outwards. The 19th of this month as we were marching on our way to the Towns, about 15 miles, from the Ohio, there happened an unlucky fellow to shoot off his gun at a deer that run thro' the ranks as we were marching along, and shot my brother through the left knee, and after going 5 or 6 miles further, we was obliged to retreat back to point pleasant on the Ohio.[88] that night we camped with the Army about 20 miles from the Ohio. The next morning there was a large body of Indians seen by the scouts, and there was an alarm in Camp, and all the men turned out and formed a circle and stood about 1½ hours and no enemy appearing they marched off; and we turned the Ohio way, 5 besides my brother, when we expected to be attacked every moment all day till at night we reached point pleasant to our great satisfaction.

Octr 21st. CAMP, ON POINT PLEASANT, Parole—Dumfrise.

The guard as usual. the Revelie to Beat before day break the lines to turn out under arms & have their arms examined by the officers of their Companies, the men for work to parade as soon as possible & compleat the breast work At point pleasant was a stockade fort built to secure the wounded men, who are dieing daily & most shocking sight to see their wounds. Alex McKee caught a cat fish that weighs 57½ lbs.

[88] It would appear that this entry was made by Samuel, brother of James Newell; since, according to the return of wounded men on Oct. 23 (see *post*), James was among the number from Captain Herbert's company.—ED.

CAMP ON POINT PLEASANT Oct 23 1774 Parole Botetourt.

The Revellee to beat to-morrow morning before day the whole lines to turn out under arms, have their Rolls called & their arms examined & fresh primed, if necessary; the different officers to attend at the head of their Companies, & see that this is done. the men for work are to prepare themselves for work immediately after to finish these necessary works for their own preservation. The guard to be relieved continually every morning at 8 oclock & to consist in future of one subaltern, 4 Sergeants & 48 private men from which he is to detach a Sergeant & 8 men up the Kanawha & a Sergeant & 8 men up the Ohio, who are to take place on the bank of the Rivers & keep out 2 Centries each. The officer of the guard is likewise to detach a Sergeant & 8 men to the point who is to have the Canoes in charge & be answerable for them the men that are on guard are by no means to leave their guards, and must not expect when on duty to sleep in their tents. the Centry on the approach of any person to them in the night, or on hearing any unusual noise which they imagine to proceed from the enemy are to challenge briskly and distinctly "who comes there" if they receive no answers the 1st & 2nd challenge they are to make ready at challenging a third time & if they receive no answer to fire on the enemy & return to the guard who are to turn out under arms On the Centinels chalenging twice & receiving no answer the officer of the guard is immediately to send a Sergeant & party to examine into the cause of the alarm & keep himself and guard in readiness for action & to keep the men on their posts it will be necessary for the officer of the guard to visit his Centinels himself as ro[u]nds once or twice a night & have a Sergeant likewise to visit them personally before day break or at beating of the revilie. It is to be hoped the men will cheerfully join in the work tomorrow, as it will be a shame to flinch from the service of this country for two or three days work, & will be a constant stain on the honor of their latest posterity either to be cut off, or defeated by the remains of an already defeated enemy thro the laziness of not securing our posts. If this has no effect which I would be both surprised & sorry to see, I must acquaint those who refuse to join in so necessary a work, that they by their refusal will forfeit all claims to the merit of their former good conduct & brave behaviour

CAMP ON POINT PLEASANT
Octr. 24th. 1774. Parole, Fincastle.

The Guard as yesterday the men that are fit for duty to be employed in the necessary works tomorrow morning as early as possible.

A return of Capt Herbert's Company, Oct. 25th. 1774.

Capt	Lieut	Ensgn	Sergt	Privates	Sick	Wou'd-ed	Waiters on sick	On command	Fit for duty
1	2	2	6	110	10	20	9	6	65

A cat fish caught this day weighed 89 lbs 10 inches between the eyes, 2 ft 4 In. round the head 4^{ft}. 10^{In} long a Blue Cat.

CAMP ON POINT PLEASANT
Octr 25th. 1774. Parole Augusta.

the guard as usual the men for duty except the guard to be employed in the breast works & burning of brush

CAMP AT POINT PLEASANT
Octr. 26, 1774. Parole, Culpepper.

I must insist upon the men on duty to be employed in finishing the breast work & burning the brush the Guard as usual. This day I crossed the Ohio after my horses when I saw Buffalo sign

CAMP Octr. 27, 1774. Parole Williamsburg.

The guard as usual the men for duty to be employed in finishing the works

A General return of the troops Camped at point pleasant commanded by Colonel William Fleming Octr 27 1774

COMSND OFFICERS				NON COMSND OFFICERS.			RANK & FILE					
Compys	Captains	Lieutents	Ensigns	Sergeants	fifes	Drums	fit for duty	sick.	wounded	w[a]liters on wou'd	Boatmen	Cow herds	Pack horses	Total
Cp. Herbert	1	2	2	6	1	.	65	12	20	9	.	.	.	106
Cp. Lockridge	1	1	1	6	.	1	50	8	43	9	5	2	2	119
Cpt. Slaughter	1	1	1	3	.	.	42	3	8	,,	,,	,,	,,	58

CAMP ON POINT PLEASANT Octr [28] 1774

1 Capt 1 Ensn. 3 Sergeants & 50 rank & file to mount guard Immediately all the pack horse men to have all the Horses driven up & confined & report the number every evening to Capt Geo Mathews.

AFFAIRS IN VIRGINIA; THE INDIAN EXPEDITION

[Dunmore to Dartmouth, official report. 15J4-48.][89]

WILLIAMSBURG 24th. December 1774

MY LORD—I have received your Lordships dispatches numbers 9, 10, 11, 12 and 13, but having been, for some months past, in the back parts of the Colony, on Business of a Publick and important nature, of which I shall inform your Lordship, I had not till now an opportunity of acknowledging the receipt of them; but the numbers 12 and 13, particularly the last, so wholly engrosses my thoughts that I am under a Necessity of Answering that letter, before I can proceed to any other consideration.

The perusal of No. 13 has filled me with concern, but not with less astonishment.[90] I have gone over my own letter, No. 16, to which your Lordship alludes, and can only conclude that some other reasons, than any which arise from the complexion of my own rep-

---

[89] The following letter of Lord Dunmore to the Earl of Dartmouth, secretary of state for the colonies, was copied for Dr. Draper in the Public Record Office, London, from the Colonial Papers, "America and West Indies," ccxiii, fol. 13. Portions of it have already been published in *Amer. Archives*, 4th series, i, pp. 1061-1063; and *Magazine of Western History*, i, p. 457.—ED.

[90] From Dunmore's reply it is evident that this letter of Dartmouth contained a rebuke to him for granting lands in the back parts of Virginia, in opposition to the Proclamation of 1763, and thus injuring the prospects of the new company which was to form a colony on the Ohio (see following note). See letter of Dartmouth to Dunmore, dated Oct. 5, 1774, in *Plain Facts* (Phila., 1781), p. 159, reprinted in Bigelow, *Franklin's Works*, x, p. 169.—ED.

resentation of the affair in question, induced your Lordship, and the other of His Majestys Servants, to Set the matter before the King in so Criminal a light, that nothing but His Majestys tenderness and lenity have Saved me from the whole effect of the Royal displeasure, and that, by far, the greatest part of it should actually be inflicted upon me.

However Sensible I am of the kindness of your Lordships intention, in the caution which you are pleased to give me for my future conduct, I must be so free as to declare, that I do not perceive the Misconduct which has made your Lordship think such a caution necessary; neither do I discover the Justice of the heavy rebuke, which your Lordship communicates to me; and that I cannot avail myself of the plea of inadvertancey, which your Lordship has been pleased to put in my way, but that I must depend on the integrity of my actions, and the uprightness of my intentions for my Justification, which if I am not so fortunate as to make His Majesty and your Lordship as fully Sensible of, as I am myself conscious of; the fear of loosing the pecuniary advantages, which I derive from His Majestys favour, will not induce me to use any other means, to ward off the reserved punishment with which I am threatened.

The Policy of Government, respecting the back Country, and the Measures pursued in consequence of it, which your Lordship has been at the pains of explaining to me, I cannot, as you rightly observe, be ignorant of, and I might Suppose your Lordship informed that I was not ignorant of them, for I transmitted, from New York, the 12th: of April 1770 a letter to Lord North, accompanied by a State of all the Arguments, made use of by the People best acquainted with the back Countries of America, against extending any Settlements to the Westward; among which the necessity of adhering to the Policy mentioned by your Lordship is Strongly urged; which Policy Seemed, to every body in this Country, not at all to have been considered, when the Grant to Wallpole and others was intended:[91] and I was then, as I am Still, of opinion that it were best not to extend any Settlements beyond the limits of the Colonies as they Stood then.

When I was removed to this Government I found the boundary line, mentioned by your Lordship to have been Stipulated in the Treaty concluded at Lockaber the 18th of October 1770, putting into execution; the finishing hand was given to that Service after I came here, and I transmitted an Account of it, with a Map of the line, the 20th of March 1772:[92] and My Lord I have invariably taken every Step which depended on me, to prevent any infringment of it by the people of

---

[91] In June, 1769, a petition was presented to the king by a company of Englishmen and Americans, headed by Thomas Walpole, requesting the right to purchase and colonize a large tract of land in America, which had been ceded by the Iroquois at the treaty of Fort Stanwix (1768). The grant was finally ordered by the privy council, Oct. 28, 1773, and only failed of final legal authorization because of the popular disturbances in the American colonies. The new colony was to have been known as Vandalia, with its seat of government at the mouth of the Great Kanawha. See Alden, "New Governments West of the Alleghenies before 1780," in University of Wisconsin *Bulletin*, Histor. series, ii, pp. 20–35; Turner, "Western State Making in the Revolutionary Era," in *Amer. Hist. Rev.*, i, pp. 73, 74; and Bigelow, *Franklin's Works*, x, pp. 346–371.—ED.

[92] See *ante*, p. 5, note 8.—ED.

this Colony; nor, with regard to Grants, has any infringement of it been made, or Settlement either that the power of this Government could prevent.

But My Lord I have learnt from experience that the established Authority of any government in America, and the policy of Government at home, are both insufficient to restrain the Americans; and that they do and will remove as their avidity and restlessness incite them. They acquire no attachment to Place: But wandering about Seems engrafted in their Nature; and it is a weakness incident to it, that they Should for ever immagine the Lands further off, are Still better than those upon which they are already Settled But to be more particular.

I have had, My Lord, frequent opportunities to reflect upon the emigrating Spirit of the Americans, Since my Arrival to this Government. There are considerable bodies of Inhabitants Settled at greater and less distances from the regular frontiers of, I believe, all the Colonies. In this Colony Proclamations have been published from time to time to restrain them: But impressed from their earliest infancy with Sentiments and habits, very different from those acquired by persons of a Similar condition in England, they do not conceive that Government has any right to forbid their taking possession of a Vast tract of Country, either uninhabited, or which Serves only as a Shelter to a few Scattered Tribes of Indians. Nor can they be easily brought to entertain any belief of the permanent obligation of Treaties made with those People, whom they consider, as but little removed from the brute Creation. These notions, My Lord, I beg it may be understood, I by no means pretend to Justify.

I only think it my duty to State matters as they really are: and this being a true Account of them, three Considerations offer themselves for His Majesty's Approbation. The first is, to Suffer these Emigrants to hold their Lands of, and incorporate with the Indians; the dreadfull Consequence of which may be easely foreseen, and which I leave to your Lordships Judgment. The Second, is to permit them to form a Set of Democratical Governments of their own, upon the backs of the old Colonies; a Scheme which, for obvious reasons, I apprehend cannot be allowed to be carried into execution. The last is, that which I proposed to your Lordship, to receive persons in their Circumstances, under the protection of Some of His Majesty's Governments already established, and, in giving this advice, I had no thought of bringing a Dishonour upon the Crown. On the contrary, the measure appeared to me as the wisest, and Safest that could be entered into under the Circumstances above mentioned.

* * * * * * * *

I come now to your Lordships letter N⁰. 12. A circumstantial account of the Transactions, which occasioned such distress and alarm in the Back Settlements, and which, to remove the concern your Lordship may be under on that head, I think proper to anticipate, by acquainting your Lordship that I have been able to put an entire Stop to, will be a full and explicit Answer to all the particulars contained in your Lordships letter:[93] And, I trust, will Satisfy you, that the

---

[93] For this letter of Dartmouth to Dunmore, consult *Penna. Archives*, iv, pp. 577, 579, in which are reported to Dunmore the accusations of the Pennsylvania authorities, that the alarm of the back settlements was occasioned by unprovoked ill-

facts there asserted, are so confounded and Misrepresented, as to manifest only the malicious intentions against me, or the Officeousness and disingenuity of the persons employed in the Channels, through which your Lordship has received the Several intelligences.

The last quarrel with the Indians, as far as the Virginians were concerned in it, took its rise from, or rather never Subsided after, the expedition of Mr. Bouquet.[94] In the Treaty concluded on that occasion, it was Stipulated that all the white prisoners, which the Indians had carried off, should be restored; among which were a great many young Virginia Women and men, and negroes; and the Indians, notwithstanding the treaty, have detained them, till on this late occasion they were compelled to give them up.[95] This has been ever Since a Source of uneasiness in this Country; and

---

treatment of the Indians on the part of the Virginians; that Connolly had re-established the fort at Pittsburg, which the king had ordered demolished; and that he had destroyed the boats used for communication with the Illinois. In answering these charges, Dunmore narrates the course of his expedition.—ED.

[94] Dunmore refers to the expedition of Bouquet to the Muskingum country (1764), when he marched to avenge the massacres of Pontiac's War. See *Bouquet's Expedition against the Ohio Indians* (Cincinnati, 1868). Gen. Henry Bouquet was a Swiss officer who came to America in 1756, served under Forbes (1758), and defeated the Indians at Bushy Run in 1763. The next year he made a peace with the natives, near the Delaware towns on the Muskingum. He died at Pensacola, Fla., in 1766.—ED.

[95] In this statement, Dunmore is somewhat disingenuous. The Indians did restore their captives at Bouquet's treaty (see *Bouquet's Expedition,* pp. 75-81), where a contemporary writer gives a graphic portrayal of the surrender of the white prisoners; nearly three hundred persons being set free. A few preferred to remain with their captors, and a number of fresh captives had been taken in the intervening decade (1764-74).—ED.

it has been aggravated by the continual depredations of the Indians, and some Shocking Murders Committed by them on the people of the Frontiers.[96] The very year after this Treaty a Man was killed on the Frontiers by the Indians;[97] The year after that, eight men were killed upon Cumberland river; Soon after, one Martin, a trader from this Government, was killed with two other men. In the year 1771 a Party of Indians fell upon a Hunting Party of Virginians, and carried off Nineteen horses, as many hundred Deer Skins, their Arms and Cloaths;[98] and the same year the Indians killed one Thomas Man and wounded his brother. The next year they killed one Adam Stroud his wife and Seven Children. The last year they killed one Richards;[99] and the 15th. of October of the same year they killed one Russel, a very promising young man, the Son of a Gentleman of Some distinc-

---

[96] Dr. Draper estimates that the number of both races slain in the interim of supposed peace, was scarcely less than the entire number who perished in the war of 1774. See Draper MSS., 3D, chap. xv.—ED.

[97] Kercheval, *History of the Valley of Virginia* (2nd ed., 1850), pp. 90–96, relates several encounters of the whites and Indians in the Shenandoah Valley during 1765–66.—ED.

[98] The emigrants killed upon Cumberland were a peaceful party removing from Virginia to Mississippi. Governor Fauquier remonstrated with the Cherokee, through Stuart, their Indian agent, who replied that the deed was in retaliation for the unrequited murder of some of their people in the settlements a few years previous. On the murder of Martin, with his companions Guy Meeks and Hartness, see Jacob, *Life of Cresap*, p. 44: and *Amer. Pioneer*, i, p. 312. The robbery was that of the "Long Hunters," in Kentucky. See Arthur Campbell's letter of Oct. 6, *ante*.—ED.

[99] On the massacre of the Stroud family, on Elk River, see Withers's *Border Warfare*, pp. 136, 137. The death of Richards in July, 1773, is reported in *Amer. Archives*, 4th series, i, p. 1015.—ED.

tion in one of the back Counties, together with four men who were in Company with him, and two Negroes attending him. The Father of the Young Man, who was out at the same time, came up to the Ground, and was the first that discovered the dismal Spectacle of the dead body of his Son, Mangled in a horrid manner, and the others in much the same condition.[1]

In hopes of preventing the effects, which were Naturally to be dreaded from these repeated violences of the Indians; and being furnished with depositions, which fixed this last Act upon certain Indians, I wrote to Mr. Stuart the Indian Agent (as appears by the Copy of a letter marked with No. 1 to which I referred your Lordship upon an other occasion) to desire, that he would use his endeavours to perswade the Indians to give up the offenders: But the Indians Shifted the accusation from one tribe to another; that, in Short, the application had no effect.[2]

---

[1] The killing of Henry Russell and James Boone occurred Oct. 10, 1773. See *ante*, p. 2, note 1. This list of Indian depredations is similar to that which Dunmore presented to the Indian envoys in the conference at Fort Pitt. See *Amer. Archives*, 4th series, i, p. 873.—ED.

[2] Capt. John Stuart is thought to have come to America with the Highlanders under Oglethorpe, in 1733, and settled at New Inverness, Ga., whence he marched against the Spaniards on the southern border, in 1740. In 1758 he was second in command at Fort Loudon, being one of the three saved from massacre after the capitulation, by the intervention of the Cherokee chief, Little Carpenter. At the close of the French and Indian War he was appointed superintendent of Indians for the southern department, and in 1764 held a great treaty with them at Mobile, securing most of the Southern tribes to the British interest. In 1769 he was appointed to the king's council for South Carolina, married, and occupied a large house in Charleston. At the outbreak of the Revolution, he was suspected of loyalist sympathies, and as early as 1775 retired to Florida, where he was employed in inciting

At the same time it was known, that messages were interchangeably Sending between all the Tribes along the Ohio, the Western, and Southern Indians; and many indications appeared of some fatal design, which the people in the back Country could not but apprehend was meditated against them: And they were confirmed in their fears by the attacks, Similar to, and much at the same time as those experienced here, which were made by some of the Southern Indians on the white People in their Neighbourhood.

These facts and apprehensions occasioned so great an allarm, that the timorous, and those that had families, began to leave their habitations, by which they exposed themselves to want and misery. I took notice, in my letter of the 2d. of April to your Lordship, of the fears we were then in with regard to this matter.

But these new injuries Stired up the old inveteracy of those who are called the back-woods-men, who are Hunters like the Indians and equally ungovernable; these People took fire all along the Frontiers quite to Maryland, and Pensylvania, and formed Parties, avowedly, against the Indians, which the efforts of Magistrates and Government could not in the least restrain.

It happened that, soon after the Murder of young Russel and his party, a man who had been of that

---

the Indians against the rebellious colonists. His efforts being brought to naught by the Cherokee war of 1776, he retired to England, where he died in 1779. Stuart's application to the Cherokee for the punishment of the murderer of Boone and Russell was effectual; one chief was put to death, and another escaped to the Chickasaw. See *Amer. Archives*, 4th series, i, p. 974.—ED.

party, and the only one who had escaped, was at a horse race at a Place upon the Frontiers, and that two Indian Men and one Woman should come there also. The man immediately fell upon the Indians and murdered one of them, Notwithstanding the interposition of all the other People: all they could do was to Save the other Indian and the woman. The Magistrates endeavoured all they could to have the Murderer apprehended, and offered a reward of £50 as I did also by Proclamation of £100 but both have been fruitless.[3]

This however was the first Indian blood drawn by our People Since the Treaty of Mr. Bouquet.[4] Nor was this followed by any other act of hostility till about the 27th. of last March, that five Indian Cannoes, containing fourteen Indians, going down the Ohio, were followed by one Michael Cressop, a Maryland Trader, with a party of fifteen Men, and a Skirmish ensued in which one Indian and one of Cressops people were killed; but Sixteen keggs of rum, Some Saddles and bridles were taken from the Indians. About the 26th. of April following, two Indians, who were with a white man in a Cannoe on the river, were fired upon from the Shore and killed. This likewise is attributed to Cressop.[5]

---

[3] This was Isaac Crabtree, whose conduct illustrates the darker passions of border life, and the brutality of a certain class of backwoodsmen. See Arthur Campbell's letters, *ante;* and Haywood, *Tennessee,* pp. 43, 44.—ED.

[4] This assertion of Lord Dunmore is contrary to fact. Probably nearly or quite as many Indians were wantonly killed by the whites, as the latter lost of their own race. Compare *N. Y. Colon. Docs.,* vii, pp. 746, 837, 852; see also the massacre of the Bull Town Indians (1772) in Withers, *Border Warfare,* pp. 136-138.—ED.

[5] See *ante,* p. 8, note 13.—ED.

Soon after this, an affair of more importance happned, and which indeed is marked with an extraordinary degree of Cruelty and Inhumanity. A party of Indians, with their women, happening to encamp on the side of the Ohio opposite to the house of one Baker, who, together with a Man of the name of Gratehouse, called to, and invited the Indians to come over and drink with them; two men and as many women came accordingly, and were, at first, well received, but Baker and Gratehouse, who by this time had collected other People, contrived to entoxicate the Indians, and they then Murdered them. Soon after two more came over from the Indian Party in search of their Companions' and these met with the same fate. The remainder of the Indian Party growing uneasy at not Seeing their friends return, five of them got into a Cannoe to go over to the house, but they were soon fired upon by Baker and Gratehouse, and two of the Indians killed and the other three wounded.[6]

If it had been possible, My Lord, to convey intelligence of this atrocious Action to me instantaneously, it would have been impossible for me to take any effectual Step, in the disposition which the People of the Back-Country were then, to bring these Offenders to Justice; But I do assure your Lordship that the pacification, which I have since effected, has not made me relax, in the Smallest degree, my diligence, in finding ways to come at them, and in bringing them to the Punishment due to such enormity: and I have the Satisfaction to acquaint your Lordship that I have

---

[6] See pp. 9–19, *ante*, for other accounts of this affair.—ED.

hopes my endevours for this purpose will not prove unsuccessfull.

The Indians, however, had recently repeated their blows, and given too much cause for these People, not much less Savage then themselves, to Justify their Sanguinary deeds. They had in the beginning of February killed Six men and two Negroes, and, towards the end of the same Month, a Trading Cannoe was attacked, the Men Murdered and the Goods carried to the Shawnese Towns.

While these matters passed, the alarm of the Country Necessarily increased very much; and I received expresses daily, from the principal People of the Counties exposed, entreating my assistance to put them in a State of defence, and to provide means to bring the Indians to terms, which, all our accounts informed us, they were resolved not to listen to; and therefore it was thought the Shortest and most effectual way to accomplish this purpose, was to raise a body of men and Send them directly to the Shawnese Country. When the Assembly met in May, I applied to them by a message (of which I transmit a Copy (N°. 4)) to provide for this Matter. They did not adopt the Plan proposed, but I was referred, as appears by their address on this occasion which I transmit (N°. 5) to an Act, in force, against Invasions and Insurrections, which empowers the Governor to employ the Militia upon those emergencies. Accordingly I ordered the Militia of the Frontier Counties to be imbodied; and the respective Commanding Officers of them to take such Steps as their prudence would direct, and the act of Assembly allow, them in the present exigency:

And I recommended to them to erect Forts in the properest places, as they should Judge, for the neighbouring People to retire to, and defend themselves, in case the Indians penetrated into the Country. I transmit a Copy of the Circular orders which I sent on this occasion (No. 6).[7]

I formerly gave your Lordship an Account, in my letter No. 12, that one of the reasons which occasioned the People Settled about Pittsburg, to apply to the protection of this Government, was that they might have some lawfull Militia establishment, to defend them in case of an attack from the Indians; and that in consequence of this application I had, with the advice of Council, regularly appointed a Militia and Officers to command it, which became part of the Militia of the County of Augusta.

This part of the Country, by its vicinity to Some of, and intercourse with all, the Tribes of the Ohio Indians, was particularly affected by these disturbances. Vast numbers of the Settlers fled. And therefore when the other Militia of the Counties were ordered to assemble, orders were Sent to Captain Conolly, who was the Principal Officer of Militia in this district, to the same effect; and a Fort at this place was Judged particularly requisite, as there is a Settlement of Indians Seperated from it only by the river: And this Fort, which they call Fort Dunmore, had the effect, upon this occasion, of keeping the Neighbouring Indians in awe, for which one had been maintained there so long at the Kings expense; and was the means, together with the great pains taken, and prudence

---

[7] Circular letter of June 10, *ante*.—ED.

observed by Mr. Conolly in Conferring with these Indians, by which they were kept in our interest, and prevailed upon to carry Messages to, and bring intelligence of, the Shawanese and other Tribes by whose incursions the Country had so greatly Suffered. Several accidents happned, indeed, at this place. One of these friendly Indians whom Mr. Conolly had taken with him to reconnoiter the Country, upon a report of a Party of Shawanese approaching, was fired upon, in his return home after he had left Mr. Conolly, by one of the Militia Men; but this man was immediately confined, and a Message was Sent to the Indian Village to assure them he Should be punished. The Traders, who happned to be in the Indian Towns at the time of these transactions, and for Some time Confined there, were released and Sent with an escort to Pittsburg; and this escort, in their return home, were fired upon by a number of white men, and one of them wounded, as it was reported, though it was never known what persons or whose party committed this breach of faith, or, for certain, that it ever was committed.[8] Some time after a Party of the Delawar Neighbouring Indians came to Pittsburg to trade, and were fired upon, by which two of them were killed; but the Perpetrators of this perfideous act were never discovered, Though a reward of £50 was offered by the Commanding Officer at the desire of the Inhabitants, as was also a reward of £100 by me upon my Ar-

---

[8] See *Penna. Archives,* iv, p. 530, for different report of this affair. The Moravian missionaries relate this occurrence, and the fact that the wounded man later recovered. See Heckwelder, *Indian Nations* (Phila., 1819), p. 223; and *Narrative of Mission of United Brethren* (Phila., 1820), p. 132.—ED.

rival there, which happned to be immediately after, and in time to Condole with the Indians and make them Sensible, that no pains Should be neglected to find out, and bring to exemplary punishment the guilty persons, which intirely appeased them: And I can assure your Lordship that, upon the Strictest enquiry which I could make, no one of these facts were attributed either to the design or even negligence of Mr. Conolly (indeed he was above a hundred Miles from the place when the last was Committed) on the contrary, the People of the Country firmly believe, that those two Delawar Indians had been killed treacherously by Some of the Pensylvanians, in order to destroy the good understanding, which Subsisted between the Virginians and those Indians: but which however, this affair, by the care which was observed, did not effect.

In the mean time the ravage of the Indians, where ever they could carry it, was dreadfull:—one Shawanese returned to his Town with the Scalps of forty men Women and Children whom he had killed. On the other hand a Party went out, with my permission, and destroyed one of the Shawanese Towns, and meeting a Small Party of Indians, they killed Six or Seven of them, but this produced no Change in the designs of these People.[9]

The real concern, principally, which the Continuation of these Miseries gave me, and, partly, the Accounts Sent by the Officers of the Militia, of the Mutinous and ungovernable Spirit of their men, whom they could by no means bring to any order or dissi-

---

[9] This refers to McDonald's expedition, for which see pp. 151-156, *ante*.—Ed.

DUNMORE'S ACCOUNT 383

pline or even to Submit to command, determined me to go up into that part of the Country, and to exert my own immediate endeavours on this important occasion. Accordingly, as Soon as the business of the Oyer and Terminer Court in June permitted me, I sett out for Pittsburg where I arrived as has been already related. No time was lost in assembling The Delawar, Six Nations, and all the other Tribes that could be got at, or diligence neglected in Conferring with them on the Subject of the desolating Consequences of Such enterprises as were Carrying on between the Shawense and their abettors, and our people; (I transmitt to your Lordship an Account of the Conferences held on this occasion in a printed Copy (No. 7))[10] I found all those Nations not only disposed to peace, but attached to our Cause, and they promised me, as your Lordship will perceive, that they would go down to the Shawanese (who with one or two less considerable Tribes only were concerned in the depredations that had been Committed) and, if I would appoint a time and place, bring them to Speak with me, and use their influence to incline them to Peace. I determined therefore to go down the Ohio; but I thought it Prudent to take a Force which might effect our purpose if our Negotiation failed: And I collected from the Militia of the Neighbouring Counties about twelve hundred Men, to take with me, Sending orders to a Colonel Lewis to March with as many more, of the Militia of the Southern Counties, across the Country to Join me at the Mouth of the

---

[10] For the report of these negotiations see *Amer. Archives*, 4th series, i, pp. 871–876.—ED.

little Kanhaway, the Place I appointed to meet the Indians at.

I passed down the river with this body of Men, and arrived at the appointed place at the Stated time. The day after Some of our friends the Delawars arrived according to their promise; but they brought us the disagreeable information, that the Shawanese would listen to no terms, and were resolved to prosecute their designs against the People of Virginia.

The Delawars, Notwithstanding, remained Steady in their attachment; and their Chief, named Captain White Eyes, offered me the assistance of himself and whole tribe; but apprehending evil effects from the Jealousy of, and natural dislike in our People to, all Indians, I accepted only of him and two or three: And I received great Service from the faithfullness, the firmness and remarkable good understanding of White Eyes.

Colonel Lewis not Joining me, and being unwilling to encrease the expence of the Country by delay, and, from the accounts we had of the Numbers of the Indians, Judging the Force I had with me Sufficient to defeat them and destroy their Towns, in case they Should refuse the offers of Peace; and after Sending orders to Colonel Lewis, to follow me to a Place I appointed near the Indian Settlements, I crossed the Ohio and proceeded to the Shawanese Towns; in which March, one of our detached Parties encountered an other of Indians laying in Ambush, of whom they killed Six or eight and took Sixteen Prisoners.

When we came up to the Towns we found them deserted, and that the main body of the Indians, to the amount of near five hundred, had Some time before gone off towards the Ohio; and we Soon learnt that they had Crossed that river, near the Mouth of the great Kanhaway, with the design of attacking the Corps under Colonel Lewis. In effect this Body, in their route to Join me, was encamped within a Mile of the Conflux of these two rivers, and near the place where the Indians Crossed, who were discovered by two men, one of which they killed, of Colonel Lewis's Corps at break of Day the 10th. of October. Colonel Lewis, upon receiving intelligence of their being advanced to within half a Mile of his Camp, ordered out three hundred men in two divisions, who upon their approach were immediately attacked by the Indians, and a very warm engagment ensued; Colonel Lewis found it Necessary to reinforce the divisions first Sent out, which (without the main Body of his Corps having engaged) obliged the Indians to retreat, after an Action which lasted till about one O'clock after noon, and little Skermishing till Night, under the favour of which the Indians repassed the river and escaped. Colonel Lewis lost on his side his Brother and two other Colonels of Militia, men of Character and Some Condition in their Counties, and forty Six Men killed, and about eighty wounded. The loss of the Indians by their Accounts amounted to about thirty killed and some wounded.

The event of this Action, proving very different from what the Indians had promised themselves, they at once resolved to make no further efforts against a Power they saw so far Superior to theirs; but determined to throw themselves upon our Mercy: And, with the greatest expedition, they came in Search of the body with which they knew I marched, and found me near their own Towns the Day after I got there.

They presently made known their intentions, and I admitted them immedeately to a Conference, wherein all our differences were Settled. The terms of our reconciliation were, briefly, that the Indians should deliver up all prisoners without reserve; that they should restore all horses and other valuable effects which they had carried off; that they Should not hunt on our Side the Ohio, nor molest any Boats passing thereupon; That they Should promise to agree to such regulations, for their trade with our People, as Should be hereafter dictated by the Kings Instructions, and that they Should deliver into our hands certain Hostages, to be kept by us untill we were convinced of their Sincere intention to adhere to all these Articles. The Indians, finding, contrary to their expectation, no punishment likely to follow, agreed to everything with the greatest alacrity, and gave the most Solemn assurances of their quiet and peacable deportment for the future: and in return I have given them every promise of protection and good treatment on our Side.

Thus this affair, which undoubtedly was attended with circumstances of Shocking inhumanity, may be the means of producing happy effects; for it has impressed an Idea of the power of the White People, upon the minds of the Indians, which they did not before entertain; and, there is reason to believe, it has extinguished the rancour which raged so violently in our People against the Indians: and I think there is a greater probability that these Scenes of distress will never be renewed, than ever was before.

I have given your Lordship a faithfull relation of this Matter from beginning to end, and cannot help conceiving hopes that it will deserve to be Seen in a different view, than that in which M^r. Penns assertion, and other intelligence have endeavoured, I fear with too much Success, to place it. But I must beg leave to remark with respect to the first, that I am possessed of the Message returned from the Assembly to M^r. Penn (a Copy of which I transmitt (N⁰. 8)) whereby it appears that they acknowledged, Notwithstanding the Governors assertion, Some people of that Government had contributed, likewise, to the distress and alarm of the Back Settlements, for the Assembly, in their Message offers a reward for apprehending two Men (Hinkson and Cooper) for Murdering an Indian within the bounds of their Province.[11] And it is manifest, then, from every cir-

---

[11] St. Clair notified the Pennsylvania government of this murder, on May 29 (*Penna. Archives*, iv, pp. 503, 504, 520, 524). The proclamation for the arrest of Hinkson and Cooper was issued July 28 (*Penna. Col. Recs.*, x, p. 199). The governor also sent a message of condolence to the Delaware tribe (*Amer. Archives*, 4th series, i, p. 676). The affair caused much stir in southwestern Pennsylvania, as the perpetrators of the deed were well-known settlers. If tradition is to be believed, Hinkson was in Lord Dunmore's army at the head of a body of rangers (Draper MSS., 3S book 1, 51). The son of Hinkson told Dr. Draper that the killing was in self-defence, that Wipey had a grudge against his father, and threatened to kill him; whereupon Hinkson took the initiative, and waylaid the Indian upon the highway.

Maj. John Hinkson (also Hinkston) was born of Irish parentage, in the province of Pennsylvania. He removed West early in life, and became noted as a scout and woodsman. In 1775 he led into Kentucky a company of settlers,

cumstance, My Lord, that the Proprietary Governor of Pennsylvania hath Sullied the dignity and Solemnity, which belongs to Such an Act as Communicateing the business of the Publick to their representatives, by making it the conveyance of falshood and imposition, which tended only to create dessentions between the people of his Government and their Neighbours of Virginia, and to keep up the aversion in the Indians towards the Inhabitants of this Colony.[12]

In regard to the Fort of Pittsburg, this, your Lordship has Seen in my relation, was done by my order: but if it be seen as it really was, in the light of a temporary work for the defence of a Country, and its terrified Inhabitants in a time of imminent danger, I presume it will appear very different from reestablishing a Fort which had been demolished by the Kings express orders, as if this Act of mine had been contrary to or in disregard of His Majesty's orders: And My Lord, I fear, that it must be owing to the unfavourable opinion which your Lordship conceives of my Administration, that it did not readily occur to

---

who erected a station on Hinkson's Fork of Licking, not far from Paris, in Bourbon County. In July, 1776, they abandoned the settlement through fear of Indian ravages, and returned east by way of Boonesborough. Hinkson brought out his family in the summer of 1780, and had but just arrived at his old station—then called Ruddell's—when it capitulated to Col. Henry Bird, heading a force of Canadians and Indians. Hinkson made his escape on the third day. He became a prominent pioneer of Bourbon County, being chosen major of militia in 1786, and sheriff in 1788. He went out on two Indian campaigns (1786–87), and died at New Madrid in 1789. See Draper MSS., 2S, book 7, pp. 10–13.—ED.

[12] Referring to the message of the governor of Pennsylvania to the house of representatives, July 18, 1774. See *Penna. Archives*, iv, p. 577.—ED.

your Lordship, that the distress and alarm, of which you were apprised at the Same time, however they were occasioned, required that Step, and accounted for it.

As to the information you have received about the boats, I never heard of any destroyed by Mr. Conolly or used by any body, or even that there were any capable of being used or destroyed; but I recollect to have Seen two or three boats which were said to be the Kings lying exposed on the side of the river, every plank entirely rotten and become quite useless: And if any have been destroyed therefore, it must have been thro' the Negligence of the Persons who had the charge of them, and who have thought this a convenient, though a most dishonest, way of accounting for them.

The Assertion of the Proprietary Governor, and the intelligence, which your Lordship informs me, you have received thro' a variety of other Channals; all Spring from the same Source: from the Malevolence which that Gentleman thinks he has cause to manifest towards me. As it may, possibly, be some prejudice to him, he is highly offended at the part I have taken, in putting a Stop to his encroachments upon the Kings Rights.

Instead of manifesting any disposition to reconcile the different opinions, respecting the disputed boundary between this Colony and his Province, his mode of proceeding was, with no little confidence, to exact a full complyance with his demands of this Government, or we were to Suffer the Consequences, declared in a Proclamation; which indeed were terrifying enough; and which I transmit (No. 9) for your Lordships perusal, and mention here, as I conceive it Justifies the Proclamation, which His Majesty's Council of this Colony thought it right to advise me to issue on that occasion, in order to prevent the Magistrates upon the Frontiers of this Colony from being entimidated by that of M^r. Penn, and which Proclamation your Lordship in your letter No. 10 takes notice of.[13] Upon receiving the orders contained in your Lordships letter of 1st. of June I issued the Proclamation herewith inclosed (No. 10)[14] M^r. Penn thought proper, in defyance of His Majesty's orders, to publish the Counter-Proclamation herewith inclosed (No. 11)[15] and every Act of mine, on this occasion, gives fresh offence, which has been the means of occasioning every Species of Calumny to be reported about me; and from both the letters No. 13 and No. 12 which I have received from your Lordship, I cannot but fear that it has gained admittance (where only I could not be indifferent about it) to His Majesty and your Lordship.

It is an easy matter to make people believe that Duty to His Majesty, and Zeal for his Service and interest, could not have been my real motive for interfering in this affair; but that it proceeded from views of emolument to myself. The Philadelphia

---

[13] Governor Penn's first proclamation does not appear to have been preserved. Dunmore's reply, under date of April 25, 1774, is in *Amer. Archives*, 4th series, i, p. 283.—ED.

[14] Found in *Amer. Archives*, 4th series, i, p. 790; issued at Fort Dunmore under date of Sept. 17.—ED.

[15] *Ibid*, p. 856; also in *Penna. Archives*, iv, p. 580; dated Oct. 12.—ED.

Papers, and I dare Say other means, have been used to make it believed, that I acted only in conjunction with a parcel of Land Jobbers, and not by the advice of His Majestys Council or by any good Authority; the Natural inference to be drawn being, that by such means I am procuring Grants of land: The Indian disturbances have been also wonderfully aiding to M^r. Penn's purpose, and he has not neglected them.

The trade carried on with the Ohio Indians has been almost engrossed by the Province of Pennsylvania, which they have draw[n] to themselves, artfully enough, but with what degree of propriety or right I must leave to your Lordships Judgment, by repeated treaties held of their own Authority, and at such times and for such purposes as they think fit. The Traders in General are composed of the most worthless Subjects, such as fail in all other occupations, and become in a manner outcasts of Society. These Men, we have full proof, have made it their constant business to discredit the Virginians (who lye much more convenient for carrying on a Trade with these Indians than the Pennsylvanians) and make the Indians consider them in the most odious light. We know that these Men have bought the Plunder, which the Indians carried off in their incursions.—If the Indians took Skins, they could Sell them cheaper than those they got themselves by hunting, and at the expence of Gun Powder;—if horses, they knew nothing of their value, and anything would purchase them.—It was a lucrative trade to these People, and the means of it, which were the disturbances between the Indians and the Virginians, were encouraged by them.

It is from these Wretches, and People principally concerned in the dispute about the boundary, that Mr. Penn takes the information, upon the ground of which he has not hesitated to Cast, in a declaration to his Assembly, an injurious reflection upon the Justice and Government of Virginia: And that your Lordship may know what Sort of men Mr. Penns friends in the part of the Country about Pittsburg are, I have had affidavits offered to be made, by men well credited and well known, that Several of Mr. Penns Magistrates in that part of the Country had declared they would take my life if they could ever get at me privately. One St. Clair[16] the Clerk of the County in Pennsylvania adjoining Pittsburg whose emoluments, by the great dimenution of the County and Number of Inhabitants, occasioned by the Authority of this Colony's being extended there, are diminished in proportion; and who was the man that committed Mr. Conolly for exercising his functions as a Magistrate under this Government in that district, and the promoter of all the disturbance which has happned between the two Colonies; This Man, I am well informed, is fond of publishing that he has taken care, that a representation of all affairs in that Country Should be carried to His Majesty's Ministers. He was formerly in the Army and an Acquaintance of

---

[16] Gen. Arthur St. Clair, born in Scotland, came to America in 1757, as an officer in the Royal Americans, and resigned in 1762 to settle in Ligonier Valley. In 1776, he embraced the American cause, was made a general, and served throughout the Revolution. Appointed governor of Northwest Territory (1789), he suffered a disastrous defeat therein from the allied Indian tribes, in the autumn of 1791. In 1802, he retired to Pennsylvania where he died in 1818.—Ed.

General Haldemand,[17] with whom I know he has corrisponded on this occasion; and it is not therefore with better information than M^r. Penn's, though I cannot Suppose his motive as bad, that M^r. Haldemand has ventured to transmit to your Lordship intelligence, which with respect to Cressop, he owns he has not had from any proper Authority, and of which, I make no doubt, he will be ashamed, when he finds out that there is no Colonel Cressop except an old Man of Ninety years of age, and who is, and allways was, an Inhabitant of Maryland: And if the General means the Cressop whose name has been mentioned by me, in my relation of the Indian occurencies, he likewise is a Marylander, and never was an Inhabitant of Virginia.[18]

It is true the mistake in this case does not contradict the fact alluded to, or, in the least, lessen the iniquity of it; but the inaccuracy in this, as well as the unfairness in the other piece of intelligence, relative to the building of Forts and destroying of boats, give room to Suspect, that, in the latter, the good of the Service, and, in the former, the interest of hu-

---

[17] Gen. Frederick Haldimand, a Swiss officer, came to America with the British forces, in 1756. He and St. Clair had seen common service in Canada under General Amherst. At this time, Haldimand was commander-in-chief of the American army, with a station at New York. Withdrawn in 1775, he returned to this continent three years later, as governor-general of Canada, an office which he held for six years. He died in Switzerland, in 1791. See McIlwreath, "Sir Frederick Haldimand," in *Makers of Canada* (Toronto, 1904).—ED.

[18] Col. Thomas Cresap, well-known in border history, lived at Oldtown, Maryland; see *ante*. For Capt. Michael Cresap, his son, see *ante,* p. 12, note 22. Dunmore fails to report that he had given the latter a commission in the Virginia militia.—ED.

manity were not the only reasons, which induced the reporter of them, to lay them before your Lordship. For, if he was actuated by nothing but those honourable and Meritorious Motives, he would first have intimated these matters to me, who alone had the immediate power of remedy in my hands, and, not, unless he found I neglected his Monition, taken the round about way of Sending them first to your Lordship: And therefore they must have been Communicated with an intention, that, in passing thro' your Lordships hands, they might leave an unfavourable impression on your mind of my attention to the principal concerns of the Government Committed to my care. I transmit to your Lordship the Copy of a letter (No. 12) which I have thought necessary to write to General Haldiman on this Subject.[19]

The desire of not leaving anything unexplained, and of not omitting anything which is not my duty to represent, in Affairs which must necessarily be interesting to His Majesty, has occasioned me to be very minute; and my anxiety for the removal of the evil opinion, which your Lordships letters No. 13 and No. 12 Carries Such Strong Marks of, has led me, unavoidably, to add so much to the length of my Answer to the Contents of those particular letters, that I can hardly hope your Lordship will bestow a patient Consideration on the Contents of this.

---

[19] See calendar of "Haldimand Papers," in *Canadian Archives*, 1885, p. 226. The letter was dated Williamsburg, Dec. 24, 1774, "remonstrating in sharp terms on General Haldimand having sent to Lord Dartmouth reports of outrages on Indians in Virginia, without having communicated with him (Dunmore)."—ED.

I inclose to your Lordship the Address (Numbers 13, 14 & 15) of the Council of this Colony, the City of Williamsburg and the College, on my return from the expedition against the Indians,[20] which I hope will be admitted as no Small evidence, both to destroy the Assertion of M^r. Penn, and to Convince His Majesty and your Lordship that I have not been careless of the lives of Indians, although I exerted some vigourous Measures to put an end to their disputes with his Majesty's Subjects; or Negligent in any respect of my Duty.[21]

* * * * * * * *

I am, My Lord, Your Lordships Most Obedient humble Servant

DUNMORE

ACCOUNTS TO BE SETTLED

[Maj. Angus McDonald to Capt. William Harrod. 4NN22.]

WINCHESTER 8th. Jany 1775

DEAR CAPTAIN—I am Just Returned from williamsburgh. The news is that all the Country is well pleased with the Governors Expedition and you may Depend we shall be will paid if the Govⁿ. and assembly Dont Differ at meeting: 2^d. Day of Feby is the Day to meet but I am afraid they will not agree if that Should be the Case we shall not be paid this 2 or 3

---

[20] See *ante*, p. 307, note 24.—ED.
[21] The remainder of the letter deals with the pre-Revolutionary movement in Virginia; it may be found in *Amer. Archives*, 4th series, i, pp. 1061–1063.—ED.

years we are all prepairing for war both Virg^a and Maryland is in motion and I believe will fight before they will Suffer themselves to be Imposed on.

* * * * * * * *

I am Dear Sir your most obligd and most obedt Servant

[ANGUS MCDONALD]

To Capt. William Harod on Monongahelia. Pr. favour Moses Pawlings

---

MUSTER ROLLS OF COMPANIES DEFENDING THE FRONTIER

[Undated list. 4XX61.]

A List of Capt. Danie: Smith's Company of Militia in Fincastle County.[22]

Daniel Smith Capt.
W^m. Bowen Lieut.
John Kinckeid Ensign
David Ward Ensign.
Drury Pricket (Pucket)
Robt. Brown
Joseph Horne
James Smith
Ja^s. Scott.
Archelaus Scott
James Price
Joseph Olverson
Saml. Dollarhide
Saml. Vanhook
Christian Bergman
Burton Litton
David Kingkeid Ju^r.
Benjⁿ. Jones
W^m. Neale
Robt. Griffin
Robt. Donalson
Thomas Price
Ja^s. Kendrick
Rich^d. Price
Thos. Mullin
W^m. M^cfarland
Alden Williams
John Courtney
Charles

---

[22] Capt. Daniel Smith was militia officer for Fincastle; see p. 2, note 5, *ante*. The following muster roll is undated, but probably belongs to the spring of 1774.—ED.

MUSTER ROLLS 397

[Michael Woods to Col. William Preston. 3QQ30.]

SIR—I rec^d your Letter Dated the [MS. torn] of this instant and I have conformd my self to it, and I find that there is in that Bounds from Rich Creek Mountain to where the County Line strikes the river thirty men which is

Joseph Inglish	Richard herd
Joshua Inglish	John Nicklas
Wm Cliften	George Scott
And^r Woods	George Sobe
James Williams	[Fr]ancis Rowan
[A]dam Clendinen	[Pe]ter Dingos
Henry Walker	Robert Wiley Senr
[A]dam Woods	Robert Wiley Junr
[R]ich^d. Woods	Thos Wiley
Henry Atkins	Thos. Haket
Charlas Atkins	Samuel Astle
Mich^l. Woods	Ishmall Babit
Samuel Camble	W^m. Lesey
Wm Cavanough Senr	Henry Oharron
Squire Gatleph	Jeremiah Cary
John umphres	

Also there is a few men that lives in a String on the other side of the River that ever will be unconvenient to any other place to Muster at for they would not have above 7 or 8 Miles to a Muster here; and if they must go Elsewhere they Most of them Must Go 15 or 20 Miles to Muster and the names of these is

Charles Cavanough	Charles hays
Philimon Cavanough	Thos. Farlor
James Odear	Francis Farlor
W^m. Cavanough Senr.	John Farlor
Samuel pack	Mitchle Clay
George pack	

and some others that I do not know their names.

Also I must acquaint you that the most of these men

is bad off for arms and ammunition and I believe Cannot get them.

All from yr. Servant at Command

        MICHAEL WOODS [23]

29th May 1774

[Thomas Burk to Col. William Preston. 3QQ31.]

SIR—I have perceedd. According to your Directions as Near as poseble & has oppointd. Eleven out of Thirty four all Able Bodyd. Men. Pleas to Excuse My Short Writting for I Expect to be over With These from your Humb. Sert.

        THOMAS BURK.

May ye 30th 1774

Henry Librough	1	Charles Lucas Jun	7
george Fry Jun.	2	Christy Martin	8
Edward Hale	3	Phillip Martin	9
Thomas Hale	4	Willinton Adkins	10
John Lucus	5	george Martin Jun	11
William Lucus	6		
Joel Cartain		Henley McKinsey	
Umphry Brumfield		Thomas Cashaday	
Richard Chapmon		Charls Lucus Sen	
Andrew Hatfield		John Lucus	
Mordock Mc.Kinsey		William Lucus	20
David gormon		Charls Lucus Jun.	
William Hale		george Martin	
Palser Librough [24]		Christy Martin	
Henry Librough		Phillip Martin	
gorge Fry Senr	10	John Man	
george Fry Junr		Robert Hunter	
John Mc.griff		Philip Williams	
Edward Hale		Parker Adkins	
Thomas Hale		Willinton Adkins	
Patrick Mc.griff		John Cartain	30

[23] For Michael Woods see p. 176, note 23, *ante.*—ED.
[24] For the Indian attack upon the Lybrook (Librough) family see p. 134, note 90, *ante.*—ED.

James Cartain
John Mᶜ.Cartney
Simon Cashaday
george Martin Jun   34
John Young

James Havens
John Havens
Thoˢ. Copley
John Chapman   39 [25]

To Capt. William Preston, Fincastle County, Virginia.

[3QQ34.]

A List of Robert Doack's [26] Company of Militia
June 2ᵈ. 1774

John Stephens Lieut.
William Doack Ensign
Andrew Thompson Enˢ.
William Ward ⎫
James Downy ⎬ Serjeants
William Meek ⎭
David Doack Junʳ.   1
John Downy
John Stephens
Thomas Mead
Adam Walker   5
Arnold Shell
Samuel Doack
Moses Gordon
John Williams
Samuel Moor   10
John Nowell
George Kinder
Jacob Kinder
Hugh Robinson
Andrew Bronstetter   15
Peter Kinder
Thomas Bell
Jacob Dobler
Moses Moor
Samˡ Handly   20
John Gilihan

John Pierce
Martin Staily
Michael Weaver
Christly Weaver   25
John Messersmith
John Bunshell
Barnet Messersmith
Henry Waggoner
Henry Waggoner Junʳ.   30
Michael Grigger
Peter Grigger
Nicholas Cloyne
Campbell Baily
Patrick Johnston   35
Barny Gullion
Charles Fullen
John Gullion   38
Duncan Gullion
Jacob Catron   40
Jacob Kinsor
Walter Kinsor
Michael Kinsor
Wᵐ. King   45
John King
Samuel Campbel
Wᵐ. Campbell
John Maxwell

[25] The last five names were added later, in a different handwriting; thus the original list consisted of thirty-four.—Ed.

[26] Capt. Robert Doack died during the summer of 1774. See pp. 135, 137, *ante;* also his letter to Colonel Preston, dated July 12, p. 78.—Ed.

Bezaleel Maxwell		Robert Stephenson	
David Maxwell	50	William Litz	
John Henderson		George Douglass	
Frederick Rap		James Douglass	
Francis Catron		James Rodgers	85
Jacob Catron		Thomas Rodgers	
Adam Catron	55	Daniel Henderson	
Peter Catron		John Lesly	
Phillip Catron		Samuel Henderson	
Michael Staffy		George Vaut	90
Peter Hedrick		Thomas Mitchell	
Michael Walter	60	James Mitchell	
John Cattes		John Nuland	
Mitchael Wambler		Phillip Dutton	
George Wambler		Alexander Ewing	95
Adam Boh		Samuel Ewing	
Jacob Boh	65	William Ewing	
Frederick Moor		Alexander Ewing Junr	
Isaiah Hamilton		John Reagh	
Jacob Hamilton		Archibald Reagh	100
Francis Hamilton		Paddy Saint Lorrance	
Thomas Hamilton	70	Samuel Paxton	
Michael Catron		Robert Porter	
George Carr		Robert Miller	
James Carr		William Henly	105
William Carr		George Henly	
Ben Butherford	75	Christly Vaut	
Roger Cats		Andrew Vaut	
John Vails		John Carr	
John Crawford		Jacob Blesly	110
John Diver		John Blesly	
John Irvine	80	John Adams	112

[Fragment of Muster-Roll of Capt. Wm. Campbell's Company, July, 1774. 3QQ63.]

These [the left-hand column] were with me upon Clinch, & there engaged to go along with me &c.

Philemon Higgins	W^m. Hopton
Benjamin Richardson	Coonrad Sterns
Joseph Newberry	John Neil
John Johnston	W^m. Richardson
Stephen Hopton	Richard Lyhnam
Richard Woolsey	Wm Champ
John Lewis	John Boles
Auldin Williamson	

The above is a List of the Mens Names belonging to my Company that have engaged to go upon the expedition with Jos. Drake

W<small>M</small>. C<small>AMPBELL</small>,

39 privates upon my Roll.

[5XX2; 6XX106.][27]

A List of the Men in Capt. Daniel Smith's Company. 13th. Augt. 1774

At the Elk Garden Fort.

Robert Brown	Sergeant found bread 15 days M. S. till 23^d. then W.
John Lewis	Listed 13th. Augt. E. G.
Ericus Smith	E. G.
James Laughlin	E. G. These 5 found bread till 29th. Aug^{t}.[28]
William Priest	E. G.
Robert Breeze	E. G.
Benjamin Jones	discharged 29th. Augt. E. G.
Samuel Priest	D^o. E. G. D^o. He found bread.
Thomas Jones	W. he found bread. Listed 14th discharged 29th
Thomas Price	E. G. found bread
Thomas Donelson	E. G. found bread
Robert Donelson	E. G.
Richard Breeze	listed 17th. discharged 29th. W.
Thomas Brumly	M. S.
James Rogers	M. S. Listed 22^d. discharged 29th.
David Priest	E. G. They 2 found bread.
Henry Manadue	E. G.

[27] The following list of garrisons in the border forts (for which see pp. 194, 234, *ante*) is found in two documents, which we have combin_d into one. "E. G." indicates Elk Garden; "M. S.," Maiden-Spring; and "W," Whitton's Crab Orchard fort.—E<small>D</small>.

[28] These five men were discharged Nov. 18, after ninety-eight days' service.—E<small>D</small>.

James Anderson	} E. G.	Listed 23d. discharged 29th.
Richard Price	} E. G.	they found bread.
John Kingkeid	} E. G.	Listed 14th. Augt.
David Kingkeid	} E. G.	found bread.

The 29th. Augt. all the above men except the first five were discharged. Mr. John Kingkeid was then appointed their Sergeant. the 12th. Sept. he took into pay

James Anderson	Robt. Donelson
Ben. Jones	Thomas Price
David Priest	Richard Price
Saml. Priest	David Kingkeid
Henry Manadue	Robert Brown 2nd. Sept.
Thomas Donelson	

At the Glade Hollow fort.

Ensign Hendly Moore
Mr. John Dunkin Sergeant

James Mc Carty
Archibald Scott
James Price   } Listed 29th. Augt.
Drury Pricket
Jeremiah Able

James Scott
Isaac Crisman
Wm. Ferrill   } Listed 19th. Sept.
Richard Thompson
Francis Cooper

Wm. Pharis   29th. Augt. discharged 25th. Octo. W.
Solomon Litton
James Coyl [29]
Wm. Wilmoth   } 29th. Sept.
Joseph Horn
Richard By[rd]
Abm Cooper   Oct. 29–Nov. 18
Archd. Woods   Oct. 31–Nov. 18
Wm Bustar   Nov. 6–Nov. 18 [30]

---

[29] "I do hereby Certify that James Coile Served as a Soldier under my Command Sixteen [days] being then on actual duty & was Regularly discharged the 29 Augt. 1774 Wm. Edmiston"—Draper MS., 5XX4.

[30] The last three names are found only in the second list. Apparently they enlisted after returning from the Point Pleasant expedition.—ED.

MUSTER ROLLS

At the Maiden Springs Station 26th. Augt. 1774

M^r. Robt. Brown Sergeant till 23^d. Sep^t. then Joseph Cravens.
Henry Willis
Joseph Cravens
James M Clehany discharged 19th. Oct. 55 days.
James Cravens
John Jameson listed 29th. Augt. disch. 19th. Oct. 53 days.
James Rogers
Thomas Brumly listed 22^d. Augt. disch. 19th. Oct. 60 days.
And^w. Lammy listed 16th. Augt. 4th. Sept. Saml. Fowler came in his room.
John Flintham listed 14 Augt. disch. 19th. Oct. 68 days.
James Douglas M. S.
John Newland W. ⎫
Samuel Paxton W. ⎬ listed Sep^t. 14th. discharged 22^d. 8 days.
Philip Dutton. W. ⎭
John Cravens. 23^d. Sep^t. M. S.
Rees Bowen Aug. 26—Sep^t 2
David Ward Aug. 26—Sep^t 2
Robt Cravens Nov. 1st—Nov. 18 [31]

At the Upper Station

M^r. John Campbell Ensign

listed 15 Aug^t. ⎧ Isaac Spratt. ⎫ Sergeant
                  ⎪ George Dohorty ⎬ 25th. Sep^t. went away without leave
                  ⎨
                  ⎪ And^w. Steel Oct. 18th disch. 64 days.
                  ⎪ John Hambleton disch. 18th. Oct. 64 days.
                  ⎩ Alex^r. Grant. deserted 8th. Sep^t.

29th. Aug. ⎰ David Bustar
               ⎱ W^m. Thompson

Edward Sharp 7th. Sep^t listed. disch. 21st 14 days.
Michael Glaves. 6th. Sep^t. went away without leave 7th. Oct^r.
James Fullen 5th. Sep^t. disch. 21st 16 days
James Edwards 5th. Sep^t. went away without leave 30th. Sep^t.
John Williams 7th. Sep^t. disch. 16th. 9 days.
Thomas Potter. 5th. Sep^t. went away without leave 7th. Oct. came back
Levi Bishop 8th. Sep^t. D^o D^o 22^d. Sep^t.

---

[31] Of the three preceding men, the first two were apparently discharged to go upon the expedition; the third, upon his return, joined the garrison of Maiden Spring.—ED.

Robert Mauford [Moffet] 8th. Sept.
Alexander Henderson 15th. Sept. went away 12th. Oct.
Francis Hambleton 15th. Sept. went out without leave 25th. Sept. came back
John Crafford 15th. Sept. discharged 24th. 10 days.
Isaiah Hambleton 15th. Sept. 22d. Sept. went away without leave
Benjamin Rediford 15th. Sept. 25th. Sept. Do.
George Vaut 15th. Sept. 26th. went away, came back Octo. 1st.
Andw. Branstead 15th. Sept. 26th. Do } Do
James Mitchell 15th. Sept. 26th. Do }
Rowland Williams. Do.
Mr. Thomas Whitten sen. appointed Sergeant 26th. Sept.
Thomas Whitten jur. Octo. 1st.
John Grinup Do.
Francis Hynes Do.
Samuel Doack. listed Octo. 1st. went away 12th. Oct.
Thos. Rogers. Do. Do.
John Lashly Do. Do.
Wm. King Octo. 1st.
Thos. Meads Do.
Jacob Kindar Do.
Daniel Henderson } Oct. 10th.
Peter Kindar }
Jonathan Edwards. in his brothers room 6th. Oct.
Christian Bergman 5th. Oct.
Michael Razor 24th. Octo.
Jeremiah Whitton 27th. Oct.

Scouts

William Bowan   Aug. 12th
James Fowler
Thos. Maxwell 10 days   June 11th
Rees Bowan
David Ward
John Kingkeid 17 days
Wm. Priest 7 days
John Sharp 10 days
Wm. Crabtree
Samuel Hays
Robt. Davis 15 days of his time to go to Robt Moffet
   At Elk Garden 1 Sergeant 15 men
   Fort Christian 1 Ensign 1 Sergeant 15 men
   Maid. Springs Brown & Cravens & 12 men
   Whittons. 1 Ensign. Spratt & Whitten & 44 men

MUSTER ROLLS OF THE EXPEDITION

[2ZZ30.]

A List of Capt William Nalls Company [of] vallentiarrs from Augusta

September 10th day 1774

William Nalle Capt	1	William Scails	22
Martain Nalle Lieutenant	2	John Pright	23
Jacob Penee Ensign	3	Yenty jackson	24
William Bush Sergeant	1	John Owler	25
John Bush Sergeant	2	George Fuls	26
Barnod Crafford Sergeant	3	James Miller	27
Shadrick Butler	1	Gorge Harmon	28
William Feavil	2	John Chism	29
Robert Rains	3	Adam Hansburger	30
Moses Smith	4	Henry Cook	31
Steven Washburn	5	John Breden	32
Israel Meader	6	Thomas Brook (Confined)	33
Henry owler	7	Henry Miner	34
John Grigsby	8	Chesly Rogers	35
Richard Welsh	9	Sefniah Lee	36
Zacarias Lee	10	Zacarias plunkepel	37
John Goodall	11	Mecagh Smith	38
Bengaman Petty	12	William Smith	39
Michael Gurden	13	John Deek	40
Bruten Smith	14	John fy	41
James Todd	15	John Williams	42
William Spicer	16	Joseph Butler	43
James Washbun	17	James Selby	44
Charles Brown	18	James Reary	45
James Alexander	19	Abraham Rue	46
Gorge Rucker	20	Jacob Null	47
Joseph Roay	21	John Null	48

WILLIAM NALLE[32]

[32] The name of this captain in the Augusta division has been corrupted by several secondary writers. Stuart gave it as Naul, which others apparently considered a misprint for Paul, and as such this officer is mentioned in nearly all later accounts of the subject—including Roosevelt, *Winning of the West*, i, p. 221. The Nalle family was prominent in western Virginia. Capt. William Nalle served in the Revolutionary militia, and in 1781 was delegate to the Virginia assembly from Rockingham County.—ED.

[2ZZ31.]

A List of John Murray['s] Compy of Volenteers from Botetourt

Sept. 10th 1774

John Murray Capt	Danl. Simkins 31
Wm McKee Lieut.	Wm. Lyons 32
Saml. Wallace Lieut.	James Simkins 33
Adam Wallace Ensn.	Nicholas Mooney 34
Wm. Taylor Sergt. 1	Solomon Brundige 35
Moses Coiler Do. 2	Stephen Harris 36
John Larken Do. 3	Danl. Fullin 37
John Simpson Do. 4	David Wallace 38
Barney Boyls Do. 5	Moses Whitby 39
John Gilmor 1	James Gilmor 40
Hugh Logan 2	James Cunningham 41
Jas. Hall 3	John Kelsey 42
James Arnold 4	Hugh Moor 43
Stephen Arnold 5	Joseph Gibson 44
Wm. Moor 6	Wm. Cochran 45
John Nelson 7	James Logan 46
John Sedbery 8	John Logan 47
Wm. McCorkle 9	Thos. Hedden 48
Geo Milwood 10	Prisley Gill 49
Andw. Evins 11	John Coiler 50
Jos. Mc.Bride 12	Johnathan Watson 51
Thos Nail 13	Hugh Logan 52
John Lapsly 14	Wm. Neely 53
James Walker 15	James Neely 54
Ezekiel Kennedy 16	John Milican 55
John Jones 17	Petter Higans 56
John Moor 18	Wm. Connor 57
Wm. Simpson 19	Wm. Bradly 58
Thos. McClure 20	John McGee 59
John McClure 21	Wm. Brown 60
Petter Kasheday 22	James McCalister 61
Robt. Wallace 23	John Barkly 62
Thos. Peary 24	Andw. Wallace 63
John Grigs 25	Isaac Trimble 64
Geo. Cummins 26	Petter McNiel 65
John Eager 27	Wm. Johns 66
James Crawley 28	Andw. Alden 67
Danl. Blair 29	James Bambrige 68
Thos. Burny 30	John Murray [33]

[33] For Capt. John Murray, see p. 275, note 92, *ante*.—ED.

[2ZZ32, 33]

A Roll of Capt Phi[l] Love['s] Company of Volunteers[34]

Sep[r] 10th 1774

Phi Love Cap[t]
Daniel M[c]Niell Lieut
John Mills Ensign
W[m]. Ewing Serg[t] Maj[r]
Francis M[c]Elhaney Quarter M. S.
Sieltor Taylor ⎫
James Alexander ⎬ Sergeants
John Craford ⎭
1. Rob[t] Owen
2. Sam Andrews
*3. William Scott
4. Sam M[t]Gumry [Montgomery]
5. William Teasy
6. John Dodd
7. Tho[s] Perce
8. Tho[s] Armstrong
9. John Dunn
*10. Cha[s] Byrne
11. Tho[s] Gilberts
12. Abraham Demonse
*13. Will. Hooper
14. Sam Savage
15. Tho[s] Welch
16. Tho[s] Welch Ju[r]
17. Patrick Conner
18. Joseph Pain
19. Will Armstrong

20. Daniel M[c]Donald
21. James Simson
22. Tho[s] Brown
*23. James Neeley
24. Abraham Moon **Batman to** Col[o] Lewis
25. George Craig D[o]
26. Rich[d] Willson **Carpenter**
27. Rob[t] Smith **Batman**
28. John Buchanan
29. Charles Davis **Batman**
30. W[m] Franklin
31. James Franklin
32. W[m] Hanson
33. James M[c]Donald
34. [erased]
*35. Rich[d] Collins
*36. Ja[s] M Guillin
*37. John M[c]Ginness
*38. Griffin Harriss
39. John Jones **Cadet**
40. [erased]
*41. John Markes
42. John Robinson **Batman**
43. [erased]
44. John Todd **Cadet**
45. Daniel [Ormsbey] **Batman**

53 Totall

---

[34] There are two lists of the company of Capt. Philip Love. for whom see p. 273, note 89, *ante*. The second, dated Oct. 7, contains one additional name—James Neeley, cadet. The total number of the second list is but forty-two. The names marked with a star in the following list are the ones not contained in that of Oct. 7.—ED.

[2ZZ27, 28.]

A List of Capt John Lewis Company of Volunteers from Botetourt[35]

Septr 10 1774

John Henderson Lieut
Robert Alliet [Eliott] In^s
Samuel glass Sergt
William Bryans Dito
Peter Huff Dito
William Wilson Dito
Samuel Estill Dito
John Donally fife
Thomas Alsbury Drum

Privates

1 John Swoop
2 Allexander Kelley
3 Edward Egins
4 James Ellison
5 John Deniston
6 James Stuart
7 John Savage
8 Christopher Welsh
9 James Crawley [Croley]
10 James Dulin
11 Isaac Fisher
12 Peter Ellenburgh
13 Andrew Kissinger
14 Samuel Barton
15 William Clifton
16 Joseph Love
17 Leonard Huff
18 Samuel Croley
19 William Isum
20 Isaac Taylor
21 Martin Carney
22 Peter Hendrix
23 John Hundley
24 Thomas Huff
25 Thomas Edger
26 James Charlton
27 Mathew Polug
28 Thomas Canady [Kanady]
29 William Jones
30 Richard Packwood
31 John Arthur
32 William Robison
33 Samuel Huff
34 Edward Wilson
35 Robert Boyd
36 John Reburn
37 Isaac Nickels
38 Phillip Hammon
39 James Burtchfield
*40 Soloman White
41 Thomas Carpender
42 Soloman Carpender
43 Jeremiah Carpender
44 David Cook
45 John Boughman
46 Jacob Boughman
47 Robart Bowles
48 James Burnsides
49 Dennis Nail

---

[35] The Draper MSS. contain two lists of the company of Capt. John Lewis, of Botetourt, for whom see p. 274, note 91, *ante.* The second is undated, and consists of seventy-one names, in addition to the captain, lieutenant, and ensign, "5 Canoe Men, 5 Spies, 1 On Command," for whom no names are given. The names marked with a star in the following list are not in the other. The last seven names (unnumbered) are transferred from the second list, while the alternative spelling of names is derived from the same source.—ED.

*50 Henry Howard
 51 Molastin Peregin
 52 Walter Holwell
 53 James M{^c}Nitt
 54 Samuel Burcks
 55 Nathan farmer
*56 Gabriel Smithers
 57 John Carpender
 58 Thomas Burnes
 59 Adam Caperton

*60 Hugh Caperton
 61 Mathew Creed
    Matt Jewitt
    Adman Cornwell
    William Boniface
    Robert Davis
    Henry Boyer
    Mathias Kisinger
    William Man

[2ZZ36.]

A list of Capt. Bufords Company of Volunteers[86]

Thomas Dooley Lieut{^t}.
Jonathan Cundiff Ensign
Nicholas Mead ⎫
William Kenedy ⎬ Serjat{^ts}
John Fields ⎪
Thomas Fliping ⎭
 1 Abraham Sharp on Com{^d}
 2 Absalom M{^c}.clanahan on D{^o}
 3 William Bryant
 4 William M{^c}.colister
 5 James Scarbara
 6 John M{^c}.clanahan 1 Canoe
 7 James M{^c}.bride
 8 John Carter
 9 William Overstreet
10 Robert Hill
11 Samuel Davis
12 Zachariah Kennot
13 Augustine Hackworth
14 William Cook
15 Uriah Squires
16 Thomas Hall
17 William Hamrick
18 Nathaniel Cooper
19 John Cook
20 M{^r}. Waugh cadate

21 John M{^c}.Glahlen
22 John Campbell
23 William Campbell
24 Adam Lin
25 Thomas Stephens
26 William Keer
27 Gerrott Kelley
28 James Ard
29 William Deal
30 John Bozel
31 John Welch
32 Robert Boyd
33 Thomas Hamrick
34 James Boyd
35 James Dale
36 Robert Ewing
37 Francis Seed
39 William Hackworth
39 John Roberts
40 Joseph White
41 Joseph Bunch
42 Jacob Dooley
43 Thomas Owen
44 John Read
45 John Wood   Cow driving

[86] For Capt. Thomas Buford, and his company from Bed ford County, which was placed in the Botetourt line, see p. 273, note 88, *ante*.—ED.

[2ZZ40.]

Capt Stewart's [Company][37]

[MS. torn.]			John Crain	17
Charles O Haara	⎫		W^m. Dyer	18
James Donaley	⎬ Sergt.		Ed^w. Smith	19
Skid^r Harriman	⎭		[MS. torn.]	
Daniel Workman		1	John Harris	21
Samuel Williams		2	Joseph Current	22
W^m. O Harra		3	W^m. Clindining	23
Robert O Harra		4	Spencer Cooper	24
James Paulley		5	Danl. Taylor	25
James Clarke		6	Joseph Day On Com^d.	26
John Pauley*		7	Jacob Lockhart D^o	27
Archb^l. McDowell		8	George Clinding	28
W^m. Hogan		9	John Burke	29
And^w. Gardner		10	Charles Keeneson	30
Qeavy Lockhart		11	W^m. Ewing	31
Samuel Sulivan		12	John Doherty	32
Thomas Fargison		13	John McNeal	33
John McCandless		14	Joseph Campbell	34
Thomas Gillespy*		15	gon back	
Henry Lawrance*		16	2 on Com^d.	

[2ZZ39.]

A List of Capt Robert McClenachans Company of Volenteers from Botetourt[38]

1 William McCoy Leutenant   4 William Craig Sargant
2 Mathew Breken Ensine   5 Samuel Clark Sargant
3 Thomas williams Sargant   6 William Jones Drum

---

[37] The following list of Capt. John Stuart's [Stewart's] company is in his own handwriting. The upper part of the MS. is mutilated, so that the names of the subordinate officers are missing. It is believed that this is the only extant list of the company. The stars are part of the original document, and their purport does not appear. For Capt. John Stuart, of Greenbrier, see p. 104, note 151, *ante*.—ED.

[38] This list is undated; but from the context we judge that it was drafted about Sept. 10, with those of other Botetourt companies. For Capt. Robert McClenachan, and his two subordinate officers, William McCoy and Matthew Bracken, see respectively, pp. 160, note 10; 349, note 70; 120, note 78.—ED.

MUSTER ROLLS 411

7 John Harmon
8 James Kinkaid
9 Gorge Kinkaid
10 David Cutlip
11 James Morrow Senior
12 James Morrow
13 James Gilkeson
14 Even Evens
15 William Stewart
16 Edward thomas
17 Patrick Constantine
18 William Custer
19 Lewis Homes
20 William Huchisen

21 Edward Baret
22 John Williams
23 Richard Williams
24 James Burrens
25 John Patten
26 Thomas Ellias
27 Charles Howard
28 James Guffy
29 Thomas Cooper
30 William McCaslen
31 John Cunningham
32 Francis Boogs
33 John Vaun

[Captain Pauling's list of Botetourt troops. 2ZZ41.][39]

officers 3
Capt. Henry Paulling
Lieutt. Edward Gouldman
Ensign Samuel Baker

Sarjts 3
Sargt. Obediah H. Trent
Sargt. Robert Findley
Sargt. James Woods

Robert Watkins	1
Philip Hanee	2
James Dehority	3
William Thompson	4
William Holley	5
Joel Doss	6
William Ray	7
Dangerfield Harmon	8
Stephen Holston	9
James Wilson	10
Dudley Callaway Canoe	11
David Bellew Do	12
Andrew Rodgers	13
Robert Ferrill	14
Andrew Harrisson	15
George Simmerman	16
Thomas Wilson	17
Alexander Culwell on Comd	18
William Gilliss	19
Edward Ross	20
Matthew Ratliff	21
William Glass	22
John Fitzhugh	23
William Canaday	24
John Clerk	25
John Frazer	26
George Davis	27
Thomas Mecrary	28
Richd. Rollens	29
Mical Luney	30
John Gibson	31
Charles Ellisson	32
John Aggnue	33
James Dunowho	34
Thomas Reid	35
Joseph Whitticor	36
Isham Fienquay Canoe	37
David Condon Do	38
Richard Lemaster	39
James King	40
John Hutson	41
William Micalister	42
Jeremiah Jenkins	43
Edward Carther	44
Martain Baker	45
James Lyn	46
4 Canoemen	
1 Comd.	

[39] For Capt. Henry Pauling see p. 187, note 33, *ante.*—ED.

[2ZZ37, 38.]

A List of Capt. Shelby Compy Volunteers from Fincastle[40]

1 Capt.	Saml. Samples **
1 Lieut	Arthur Blackburn
1 Ensign	Robert Herrill [Handley]
4 Sergt^s	Geo. Armstrong 25
4 Canoe Men	William Casey
1 On Com	Marck Williams
James Shelby	John Stewart [wounded]
John Sayers	Conrad Nave
John Findley	Rich^d. Burck 30
Henry Shaw [Span]	John Riley
Daniel Mungle 5	Elija Robison [Robertson]
Frederick Mungle [Mongle]	Rees Price
John Williams	Richard Holliway
John Carmack	Jarrett Williams 35
Andrew Terrence [Torrence]	Julias Robison
Geo. Brooks 10	Charles Fielder
Isaac Newland	Benj^a Grayum [Graham]
Abram Newland	Andrew Goff
Geo. Ruddle [Riddle]	Hugh Ogullion [O'Gul-
Emanuel Shoatt	lion] 40
Abram Bogard 15	Barnett Ogullion
Peter Torney * [Forney]	Pat^k St. Lawrence
William Tucker	Jo^s. Hughey [James
John Fain	Hughey]
Saml. Vance *	John Bradley
Saml. Fain 20	Basilael Maxwell 45
Saml. Hensley* [Handley]	

E. SHELBY

Total 45 privates Including Six of Captⁿ. Herberts men from Fincastle
7 Octr. 74

[40] The following list of Capt. Evan Shelby's company of Fincastle troops is printed from an original in his own handwriting. As far as known, the other officers were Isaac Shelby, lieutenant, and James Robertson and Valentine Sevier, sergeants. A similar list is printed in Summers, *Southwest Virginia*, pp. 155, 156, and Ramsey, *History of Tennessee*, p. 116. The bracketed emendations in the following list are based on data in the former. The stars are found on the original MS., and their purport is uncertain. For Shelby and his sons, Robertson and Sevier, see pp. 270, 271, note 85, *ante*.—ED.

[2ZZ23.]

RETURNS OF THE TROOPS

A Return of the Bottetourt Troops in Camp Septr. 11th 1774 Under the Command of Coll⁰. Andrew Lewis. Union Camp.

Field Offrs	Companies	Commisd offrs				Staff Do	Non Com: Do			Rank and File.							
		Captns	Leutns	Ensigs	Agetent	Quartermaster	Sergts	fifes	Drums	fit for duty	Caddets	Captr	Sick	on Comd	pack H. Men	Baumen	Total
	Capt Love	1	1	1	1	1	5	.	.	26	3	1	1	.	2	5	38
	Capt Buford	1	1	1	.	.	4	.	.	42	1	.	.	.	.	.	43
	Capt Lewis	1	1	1	.	.	5	1	1	61	.	.	.	.	.	.	61
	Capt Murrey	1	2	1	.	.	5	.	.	61	.	.	5	2	.	.	68
	Capt Paulin	1	1	1	.	.	3	1	1	51	.	.	2	.	.	.	53
	Cap McClennachan	1	1	1	.	.	4	.	1	25	.	.	7	8	1	.	41
	Cap Stewart	6	7	6	1	1	26	2	3	266		1	15	10	3	5	304

Wᴍ Fleming

[*Order of March*]

4 Scouts Capt. Lewis Comy. to March in frunt he is to keep 4 a head as scouts. those followed by a Sargent & 12. who is to keep out a flanker on each side—then his Compy.

Sergt Mag^r Quarter master s'gt included in Sergts.
2 with the advanced party 1 Sergt & 5 R & F unfit for duty
The drum^r & 2 R & F unfit for duty

	327	Sergts	26
Sick	15	Fifers	2
On Com^d	10	Dr^s	3
	342		309
Effective	266	5 Capts	5
Volunteer	4	Lieut^s	7
Packhorse men	3	Ensgn	6
Batmen	5		
	278		327

[2ZZ72.]
[MS. torn] Union on the G[reat Levels] 1774[41]

[Comp]anies.	Lieut	Ensg	Sergt	Fife	Drum	Rank & file
Col^o C: Lewis						
Capt M. Dowell	2	1	4	.	.	52
Capt McClen[nechan]	2	1	5	1	1	71
C " Moffat	2	1	4	.	.	50
C " Dickinson	1	1	3	.	.	22
C " Mathews	2	1	2	1	1	60
C " Wilson	1	1	2	.	.	27
C " Harrison	1	1	4	.	.	51
C " Haynes[42]	1	1	4	.	.	48
C " Skidmore	1	1	8	.	.	32
C " Lockridge	1	.	3	.	.	26
C " Lewis	2	1	3	1	1	70
Capt Gilmore[42]	1	1	.	.	.	31
Capt Nawl	1	1	3	.	.	[48]
13	18	12	40	3		[588]

[41] The MS. of this return is damaged, but enough exists to show that it is a return of the number of Augusta County troops, made during the encampment at Camp Union—therefore before Sept. 12. Charles Lewis marched with the van Sept. 6, but it is not probable that the entire Augusta contingent accompanied him. The number for Captain Nalle's company is supplied from his muster-roll.—Ed.

[42] Capt. Joseph Haynes, and probably Capt. James Gilmore.

MILITIA RETURNS

[2ZZ20.]

A Morning Return of [the Botetourt regiment][43] Under the Command of Col. [William Fleming].

Colo William Fleming	Comd offrs			Non Comd.			Rank & file									
	Captns	Leutns	Ensigns	Sergts	fifes	Drumrs	fit for Du	Sick	on Comd	Armour	Scouts	Carpenter	Caddates	Cowherds	Batmen	
Capt Shelby	1	1	1	4	1	.	35	.	8	1	.	.	.	.	.	44
Capt Russell	1	1	1	3	.	.	39	2	.	.	1	.	.	.	.	42
Capt Love	1	1	1	5	.	.	22	1	3	.	.	.	3	1	6	36
Capt Buford	1	1	1	4	.	.	44	.	.	.	.	.	.	.	.	44
Capt Lewis	1	1	1	5	1	1	50	2	.	.	5	6	.	.	.	63
Capt Arbuckell	1	1	1	4	.	1	61	.	.	.	.	.	.	.	.	61
Capt Murrey	1	2	1	4	.	.	59	2	.	.	.	.	.	.	.	61
Capt Stewartt	1	1	.	.	.	.	34	.	.	.	.	.	.	.	.	34
Capt McClanehan	1	1	1	3	.	1	26	1	2	.	.	.	.	.	.	29
Colo Fields	1	.	1	3	.	.	37	.	.	.	.	.	.	.	.	37
Capt Pauling	1	1	1	3	.	.	46	3	.	.	.	.	.	.	.	49
Total	11	11	10	38	2	3	453	11	13	1	6	6	.	3	1	6	500

[2ZZ24.]

A general Return of the Army Incampt on Elk River Under the Comm'd of Collo. Andrew Lewis Commander in Chief Sept 27th 1774[44]

The latter was from the part of Augusta County that is now included in Rockbridge, and commanded a company at the battle of Cowpens.—ED.

[43] The date of the following return does not appear, because of mutilation of the MS. It probably was written at Camp Union.—ED.

[44] For the five captains whose names are missing, because of the mutilation of the MS., we have seven names from the two preceding returns: Captains Shelby, Love, Buford, Lewis of Botetourt, Murray, Nalle, and Gilmore. It would appear that upon this date two companies had not arrived at Elk River.—ED.

{Col}lo,s {Ch}arles Lewis {Wil}liam Fleming	Com^d offr			non comd				Rank & file						Total
	Captns	Lieutns	Ensigns	Sergts	fifes	Drummrs	Caddates	fit for Du	Sick	on Comd	Carpenters	Drovers	Batman	
	1	1	1	5	.	0	4	22	1	3	1	1	6	34
	1	1	1	3	1	0	.	26	.	.	.	.	.	40
	1	1	1	4	.	.	.	*	.	.	.	.	.	4*
	1	1	1	5	1	1	.	.	1	4	6	.	.	*
[Capt. Arbu]ckell	1	1	1	4	.	1	.	53	.	2	.	.	.	55
	1	2	1	4	.	.	.	51	1	.	10	.	.	62
[Capt McCl]anihan	1	1	1	3	.	1	.	27	1	2	.	.	.	30
Capt Russell	1	1	1	3	.	1	.	38	1	.	4	.	.	43
Capt Pauling	1	1	1	4	.	.	.	43	4	3	.	1	.	50
Capt Stewart	1	1	.	3	.	.	.	34	.	.	.	.	.	34
Capt Fields	1	1	.	3	.	.	.	39	.	.	.	.	.	39
Capt Ward	1	.	.	1	.	.	.	7	.	.	.	.	.	7
Capt Dickinson	1	1	1	2	.	1	.	19	2	.	.	.	.	21
Capt McDowell	1	1	1	4	.	1	.	44	1	.	.	.	.	45
Capt Moffett	1	1	1	4	.	1	.	51	.	.	.	.	.	51
Capt Harrison	1	1	1	4	.	.	.	40	.	.	.	.	.	40
Capt McClanehon	1	2	1	5	.	3	.	66	3	.	.	.	.	68
Capt Mathews	1	2	1	4	1	1	.	57	3	.	.	.	.	60
Capt Lockridge	1	1	.	3	.	.	.	21	3	4	.	.	.	28
Capt Skidmore	1	1	1	3	.	.	.	32	.	.	.	.	.	32
Capt Wilson	1	1	.	2	.	.	.	25	.	.	.	.	.	25
Capt Lewis	1	1	2	3	.	1	.	56	.	.	.	.	.	56
Capt Hains	1	1	1	4	.	.	.	45	3	3	.	.	.	51
Total	23	25	19	80	3	11	4	909	28	20	22	2	6	987

*[MS. torn]
twelve artificers not included in this Return

[2ZZ25.]

A Return of the Botetourt and Fincastle Troops under the Command of Colo. Andw. Lewis encamped on Point Pleasant Octobr. 7. 1774

Companies	Commissd. Officers				Non Commiss Do.			Rank & File				
	Colo.	Capts	Lieuts	Ensigns	Sergts	Fifers	Drumrs	Fit for duty	Sick	On Comd	Totall	
	1	.	.	.	.	.	.	.	.	.	.	
Capt Buford	.	1	1	1	4	.	.	44	1	.	45	1 herd 2 Canoe M: encluded & 2 on Comd
Capt Jno Lewis	.	1	1	1	5	1	1	64	.	.	64	5 Scouts encluded & 4 Canoe Men
Capt Phil. Love	.	1	1	1	5	.	.	25	9	.	34	3 Cadets & Servts encluded with the sick & Canoe M. 1 on Comd
Capt M. Arbuckles	.	1	1	1	5	.	1	59	.	.	59	Cap Ward not included 2 Canoe Men & 1 on Comd. encluded
Capt Murray	.	1	2	1	5	.	.	60	.	.	60	1 Canoe M. 1 on Comd. encluded
Capt Stewart	.	1	1	.	3	.	.	33	.	.	33	2 on Comd. encluded
Capt McClennachan	.	1	1	1	3	.	1	27	.	.	27	1 Canoe 1 on Comd encluded
Capt Pauling	.	1	1	1	3	.	.	46	.	.	46	4 Canoe men 1 on Comd encluded
Capt Shelby	.	1	1	1	4	.	.	45	.	.	45	Six of Capt Herberts Co encluded 4 Cannoe Men. 1 on Comd
Capt Russell	.	1	1	1	3	.	.	42	.	.	42	1 On Comd
Colo Fields	.	0	0	0	0	0	0	39	.	.	39	One Man sent Express to Culpepper by the Colo Field encluded in the Above
	.	10[11]	11	9	40	1	3	484	10	.	494	

[2ZZ26.]

A Morning Return of the Botetourt & Fincastle Troops Campt on Point Pleasant Under the Command of Colo. Andrew Lewis Commander in Chief

Octr. 9th 1774

Colo. William Fleming	Com^d off			non comd			Rank and file					
	Captns	Leutns	Enseigns	Sergnts	Fifes	Drums	fit for Duty	Sick	On Comd	Caddates	Spies	Batmen
Capt Shelly	1	1	1	4	1	.	44	.	.	.	.	.	44
Capt Russell	1	1	1	3	.	.	41	2	.	.	.	.	43
Capt Love	1	1	1	5	.	.	23	1	2	3	.	5	34
Capt Buford	1	1	1	4	.	.	40	.	4	.	.	.	44
Capt Lewis	1	1	1	5	1	1	58	.	.	.	5	.	63
Capt Murry	1	2	1	4	.	.	61	.	.	.	.	.	61
Capt Stewart	1	1	.	3	.	.	36	.	.	.	.	.	36
Capt Arbuckle	1	1	1	5	.	1	58	.	4	.	.	.	62
Capt McClanihon	1	1	1	3	.	1	27	.	2	.	.	.	29
Capt Pauling	1	1	1	3	.	.	45	1	.	.	.	.	46
Colo. Fields	1	.	1	3	.	.	35	.	.	.	.	.	35
Total	11	11	10	42	2	3	468	4	12	3	5	5	497

[2ZZ21.]

A Morning Return of The Troops Campt on Point Pleasant Under the Command of Colo William Fleming Octr 19th 1774[45]

---

[45] Colonel Fleming was left in command of the camp at Point Pleasant, with the care of the wounded, while the remainder of the troops advanced towards the Indian towns. The following is a return of the command left with him at the Point.—ED.

MILITIA RETURNS

	Comd offiser			non Comd		Rank and file			
	Captans	Leutnts	Ensigns	Sergnts	Drums	Fit for Duty	Sick	on Comd	Wounded
Capt Harbert	1	1	1	6	.	72	.	.	29	101
Capt Lockridge	1	1	1	6	1	60	.	.	63	123
Capt Slaughter	1	1	1	4	.	38	.	.	22	60
[Total]	3	3	3	16		170	.	.	114	284

[2ZZ35.]

A List of the Wounded men Now on my List Octr. 23 1774

Capt Shelbey Company
John Stuart
Reece Price
John Cormick

Capt Russell Company
John Basdel
William Prince

Capt Campbells Company
Thomas Baker

Capt Arbuckle Company
John McMullin
David Glascum
John Freeland
William Morris

Capt Lewis Company
Thos Hoof [Huff]
Thoms Carpenter

Capt Loves Company
James Alexander
William Franklin

Capt McKee Company
Stephen Arnold

Capt Stuart Company
Charles Kinson
Thomas Fourgeson

Major Robertson Company
Henry Bowyer

Capt Herbert Company
James Newell

[2ZZ22.]

A Morning Return of the Troops Campt at Point Pleasant Commanded by Colo. Wm Fleming

Octr 28th 1774

Companies	Com^d offrs			non Com^d			Rank and file									Total
	Captns	Leuts	Ensigs	Sergnts	Fifes	D[r]ums	Fit for Duty	Sick	Wounded	Wounded Waiters	Batmen	Pack H[orse] Men	Cowherds	Armourer	Spies and Coopers	
Capt Lockridge	1	1	1	6	.	1	62	6	43	10	5	2	2	1	.	131
Capt Herbert	1	2	2	6	1	.	63	12	20	9	.	.	.	.	5	109
Capt Slaughter	1	.	1	4	.	.	59	3	7	.	.	.	.	.	.	69
Total	3	3	4	16	1	1	184	21	70	19	5	2	2	1	5	309

[List of Harrod's Men from the McAfee Papers. 14J128.] [46]

Capt. Jas. Harrod's Party, 1774.

James Harrod.
Azariah Davis.
Arthur Campbell.
William Campbell.
John Cowan.

William Fields.
William Martin.
David Williams.
James Kerr.
Silas Harlan.

---

[46] This list was sent to Dr. Draper October, 1886, by W. D. Hixson of Maysville, Ky. These were the pioneers of Harrod's Kentucky settlement, in the spring and summer of 1774. See p. 108, note 55, *ante*. After they came in to the Virginia settlements, twenty-two of the number enlisted under Harrod, and joined Colonel Christian's division of Fincastle troops that arrived at Point Pleasant after the battle. Collins, *History of Kentucky*, ii, p. 517, gives a list that differs somewhat from the following.—Ed.

MISCELLANEOUS PARTICIPANTS

Joseph Blackford.
Patrick Doran.
James Sanders.
Davis Glenn.
James Wiley.
John Shelp.
James Davis.
Elijah Harlan.
William Crow.
William Myres.
Jared Cowan.

John Crow.
Abraham Chapline.
Henry Hogan.
John Smith.
James Brown.
Azaria Reese.
Martin Stull.
William Garrett.
John Clark.
William Venable.

OTHER PARTICIPANTS

[Additional names of those mentioned in the Draper MSS. The bracketed references are the library press-marks to documents cited.]

Dunmore's Division

Lewis Bonnet (2E8); Joseph Bowman (14J177, 196); Henry and James Brinton (3S book 5, 20); Colman Brown (14J171); John Caldwell (3S, book 2, 44); William Caldwell (17S235, 247); George Cox (6ZZ79); Jacob Drennon (14J196); Patrick Haggerty (14J199); John Hardin, Jr. (14J175); Lieut. John Harrison (3S52); Lieut. William Heath [Heth] (15J55); Silas Hedges (2E26); Leonard Helm (14J196); Capt. Peter Helphinstone (14J199); Henry Hoagland (3S7); John Hoffman (14J99); —— Kirkendall [Kuykendall] (3S5); William Linn (37J24, 2S, book 6, 53); Daniel McNeill (15J55); Captain Mitchell (14J199); John Moody (3S5); Capt. Daniel Morgan (3S5); William Morris (14J206); Samuel Murphy (3S5-17, 5S7); John and Joseph Neaville (14J176); Peter Parchment (3S, book 2, 15); James Parsons (14J171, 15J55); Thomas Ravenscroft (5S3); David Rogers [Rodgers] (9NN13); Capt. Hugh Stephenson (14J 199); James Sullivan (3S6, 5S7); Lieut. James Trabue (32S, book 3, 3); George Vallendigham (14J176); Samuel Wells (3S5); John and Martin Wetzel (2E8); David Williamson (15J123); Benjamin Wilson (15J97); Capt. James Wood (14J178, 199); Ebenezer Zane (4ZZ17).

Lewis's Division

John Bailey (3S, book 5, 50); James Barnett (37J129); Jacob Baugh (14J203); Thomas Bell (30S64); Alexander Breckinridge (8ZZ50); Low Brown (36J117, 14J204); George Carr (2DD190); William Casey (30S135); Thomas Collet (8ZZ71); John Cutright (8ZZ71); Duncan Gullion (30S54); Samuel Handley (5XX43); Thomas Hart (8ZZ53); Benjamin Haynes (3S100); Edmond Jennings (3XX18, 2DD287); Andrew Kishioner and father (30S156); John McKinney (11CC69, 13CC137); Alexander McNutt (8ZZ35); Brice Martin (3XX18); Joseph Mayse [Maze] (8CC59, 2ZZ48); William Moore (3ZZ54, 8CC59); Jacob Persinger (3S99); Andrew Reid (3ZZ54); John Steele (3ZZ55); Walter Steward (14J166); John Tipton (5XX47); James Trimble (8ZZ13); Jacob Warwick (4ZZ24, 8ZZ37); David and William White (8ZZ71); William Wilson (14J166).

Whites among Indians[47]

George Collet (8ZZ71); Tavenor Ross (3S5-17, 5S7); John Ward (9BB63).

[Additional names, mentioned in the following secondary works: (1) De Haas, *Indian Wars of Western Virginia* (Wheeling and Philadelphia, 1851); (2) Hale, *Trans-Allegheny Pioneers* (Cincinnati, 1886); (3) Kercheval, *History of Valley of Virginia* (2nd ed. Woodstock, 1850); (4) Lewis, *History of West Virginia* (Philadelphia, 1889); (5) Peyton, *History of Augusta County, Virginia* (Staunton, Va., 1882); (6) Price, *History of Pocahontas County, Virginia* (Marlinsburg, 1901); (7) Stuart, "Narrative of Indian Wars," in *Virginia Historical Collections*, i (Richmond, 1833); (8) Summers, *History of Southwest Virginia* (Richmond, 1903); (9) Thwaites, *Withers's Border Warfare* (Cincinnati, 1895); (10) *Trans-Allegheny Historical Magazine;* (11) Waddell, *Annals of Augusta County* (2nd ed. rev., Staunton, Va., 1902);

---

[47] These were whites who had been captured by Indians when children, and had grown up among them. Collet was killed, and his body recognized by his brother; Ross afterwards returned to the settlements; Ward married among the Indians, and was finally killed in a skirmish with a party of whites led by his own brother, James Ward.—ED.

MISCELLANEOUS PARTICIPANTS 423

(12) *West Virginia Historical Magazine;* (13) MSS. in possession of J. T. McAllister.][48]

Lewis's Division

John Arbuckle (12—Jan., 1902).
William Arbuckle (12—Jan., 1902).
John Bailey (9, 12).
Francis Berry (8).
—— Blair (2, 12—Jan., 1902).
Moses Bowen (8).
Rees Bowen (8).
—— Burroughs (12—Apr., 1904).
Hugh Cameron (12—Oct., 1902).
Robert Campbell (8).
Capt. William Christian (12—Jan., 1902).
—— Clay (9, 12).
Alexander Clendennin (12—July, 1904).
Charles Clendennin (12—Jan., 1902).
George Clendennin (2, 12—Jan., 1902).
Robert Clendennin (12—Jan., 1902).
William Clendennin (2, 4, 12—Jan., 1902).
Leonard Cooper (12—Jan., 1902).
—— Coward (9, 12).
Joseph Crockett (10—Oct., 1902; 12—Oct., 1902).
Lieutenant Dillon (3, 5, 7, 9).
Robert Dunlap (12—July, 1903).
William Ewing (6).[49]
William Easthorn (2, 12—Jan., 1902).
James Ellison (3).
George Findley (8).

---

[48] The figures placed after the names, indicate in which of the foregoing publications they are to be found. In the preparation of this supplementary list of participants, the Editors have had the assistance of J. T. McAllister, Esq., of Hot Springs, Va.—Ed.

[49] A letter to the Editors, dated Mar. 15, 1905, from Hon. A. E. Ewing of Grand Rapids, Mich., gives the information that William Ewing, his great-grandfather, was a settler on Swago Creek, an affluent of the Greenbrier, near Buckeye, Va., and was a member of Arbuckle's company. This rests, our correspondent states, on an assured family tradition. A similar tradition represents that William Ewing was one of the garrison at Point Pleasant when Cornstalk was massacred, and tried to prevent the deed. Our correspondent states that he is the author of the reference here cited, in Price, *History of Pocahontas.*—Ed.

Jeremiah Friel (6).
Lieut. George Gibson (13).
John Gilmore (8).
John Grim (9).
James Hamilton (11).
Philip Hammond (2, 12—Jan., 1902).
John Hayes (11).
Lieut. John Henderson (12—Jan., 1902).
—— Hickman (1, 2, 8, 12).
Ellis Hughes (2, 4, 6, 12).
John Jones (12—Oct., 1903; 13).
Charles Kennison (6).
Edward Kennison (6).
Simon Kenton (12—Jan., 1902).
Samuel Lewis (1, 12).
Thomas Lewis (1, 12).
Ensign Joseph Long (13).
John Lyle (8, 11).
William McCune (11).
William McCutcheon (13).
—— McFarland (8).
Edward McLaughlin (8).
John McNeel (6).
John Moore (8).
Captain Morrow [Murray] (2, 5, 9).
Walter Newman (10—Oct., 1902; 12—Jan., 1902).
John Prior [Pryor] (2, 12—Jan., 1902).
Alexander Reed (2, 12—Jan., 1902).
Lieut. William Robertson (13).
—— Robison (2, 7, 8).
William Saulsbury (13).
Capt. William Shelby (4, 12—Jan., 1902).
George Slaughter (12—Oct., 1902).
Conrad Smith (8).
William Stephen (12—Apr., 1904).
John Steward (8).
Lieut. T. Tate (12—Jan., 1902).
William Tate (2, 4, 8, 9, 11, 12—Jan., 1902).
Robert Thompson (13).
John Trotter (2, 12—Jan., 1902).
Richard Trotter (12—Jan., 1902).
Isaac Van Bibber (12—July, 1903).
Jesse Van Bibber (12—July, 1903).
John Van Bibber (2, 12—Jan., 1902).
Peter Van Bibber (2, 12—Jan., 1902).
Andrew Waggoner (8).
James Welch (2, 12—Jan., 1902).
Bazaleel Wells (1, 4, 9, 12—Jan., 1902).

Dunmore's Division

S. L. Barret (12—Apr., 1904).
Lieut. Gabriel Cox (12—Apr., 1904).
Joseph Cresap (12—Apr., 1904).
William Henshaw (12—Apr., 1904).
Captain Johnson (12—Apr., 1904).
Capt. Daniel Scott (12—Apr., 1904).
Isaac Williams (12—Jan., 1902).
Capt. John Wilson (12—Apr., 1904).

BIOGRAPHIES OF FIELD OFFICERS

Dunmore

[Abridged from account by Dr. Draper. 3D chap. xiii.]

John Murray, fourth earl of Dunmore, viscount Fincastle, baron of Blair, of Monlin and of Tillimet, was born in Scotland in 1732, and succeeded to the earldom at the age of twenty-four. In 1770 he was appointed governor of New York, two years later being transferred to Virginia—its last colonial governor. He was soon involved in disputes with the house of burgesses, which he twice dissolved for expressing revolutionary sentiments. His vigorous defense of the Western frontier, in which he participated personally, was the most popular event of his administration.

Early in 1775, having removed public powder to a British ship of war, he was attacked and forced to flee to the vessel, whence he carried on petty warfare along the coast, and fired Norfolk (1776). In July of that year, a brisk engagement occurred at Gwynn's Island, in which Dunmore was defeated by Gen. Andrew Lewis. Shortly afterwards, he retired to Great Britain; his later public service consisted of the governorship of the Bahamas (1787-97). He died March 5, 1809. Dunmore was a short, sturdy Scotchman, who during the campaign of 1774 shared its hardships with the privates, marching on foot and carrying his own knapsack.

Andrew Lewis

[Abridged from account by Dr. Draper. 3D chap. xvii; 21U9-39]

Andrew was the third son of John Lewis, who fled from Ireland after a dispute with his landlord, and became one of the earliest settlers of Augusta County. Born in Ireland, Oct. 9, 1720, Andrew Lewis's early life on the frontier fitted him for Indian warfare, and by 1742 he was appointed captain of militia, and ten years later colonel for his county. Upon the threatened outbreak of hostilities with the French (1754), Lewis enrolled a company and joined Maj. George Washington, being wounded at Fort Necessity. Early the following year he was sent with his rangers to build border forts, thus did not join Braddock's expedition. In 1756 he was detailed as major upon the disastrous Sandy Creek expedition, and was officer in Forbes's army (1758). Therein, he made part of Grant's detachment, so signally defeated Sept. 14, and after surrendering to a French officer was with difficulty rescued from savage fury. After a brief imprisonment at Montreal, he was exchanged in time to command a foray against the Cherokee, seeing active

service until the disbandment of the regiment in 1762.
The next year he was appointed county-lieutenant for Augusta, and equipped for Bouquet's campaign a regiment of two hundred and fifty riflemen, in which John Field, Charles Lewis, Alexander McClanaghan, and Thomas Buford, all with Lewis at Point Pleasant, were among the officers. Appointed Virginia commissioner by the governor, he treated with the Indians at Fort Stanwix (1768) and Lochaber (1770). This latter year he removed to the neighborhood of Salem, in Botetourt County, of which he was chosen lieutenant, president of the board of justice, and coroner. At the assembly in 1774, the danger of an Indian war was discussed, and measures concerted which led to the campaign resulting in the victory at Point Pleasant. Lewis was somewhat unpopular, because of his reserved manners and strict discipline, and unfounded derogatory reports were circulated, because in the battle he did not lead his troops in person. Washington, however, testified his appreciation of his military talents, by urging his appointment as commander-in-chief of the continental army (1775). Chosen brigadier-general, his Revolutionary services were wholly within the limits of Virginia, whence he drove Lord Dunmore in 1776.

The following year he resigned his commission, but continued to render public service, managing an Indian treaty at Fort Pitt (1778); and while a member of the assembly acting on the council of state. Returning homeward from the capital, he died upon his journey Sept. 25, 1781. General Lewis was tall, of commanding personality, with a full face and dark brown eyes.

His manners were austere, but his judgment was esteemed by his equals and superiors. Virginia has shown recognition of his eminence by placing his statue upon the Washington monument in the public square at Richmond.

WILLIAM FLEMING

[Abridged from account by Dr. Draper. 3D chap. xvii; 21U157]

William Fleming was born of English ancestry in Jedborough, Scotland, Feb. 18, 1729. His education was both classical and scientific. Graduating from the medical department of the University of Edinburgh, he entered the navy as a surgeon, seeing active service and being imprisoned in Spain.

Arriving in America soon after Braddock's defeat, he was commissioned by Governor Dinwiddie as ensign in Washington's regiment, wherein he also served as surgeon. On Forbes's campaign he was lieutenant, afterwards visiting the southern frontier on the Cherokee expedition of 1760–61. The next year, as captain in Col. Adam Stephen's regiment, he commanded both at Vaux's and Stalnaker's frontier forts.

In 1763, Captain Fleming married Anne Christian, and settled on a farm in Augusta County, removing in 1768 to a plantation named "Belmont," near the modern Christianburg, Montgomery County. As colonel of the Botetourt militia, he led its regiment to Point Pleasant—Colonel Lewis, the county-lieutenant, holding the command of the division.

Wounds received at Point Pleasant disabled Fleming for active Revolutionary service, but as county-lieutenant he was concerned with frontier defense, was state senator for two successive years, and served on the privy council in 1780–81. While in the latter office, he was for some months acting governor, providing against Cornwallis's invasion of 1781. Twice he served as commissioner to settle land-titles and public accounts in Kentucky (1779, 1782–83), where a county was named in his honor. Chosen member of the Virginia ratifying convention for the federal constitution (1788), he voted for the instrument, with qualifying amendments. An interesting letter in Draper MSS. (5ZZ83) is significant of his attitude and that of most Westerners at this critical time. His death, Aug. 24, 1795, was the result of the wounds received at Point Pleasant. Fleming was a man of benevolent character, much beloved by his contemporaries, and his services as surgeon and phyisician were valuable. For an extended notice of him, from original sources, see Brock, "Virginia Convention of 1788," in *Va. Hist. Colls.*, new series, xi, pp. 42–51.

William Christian

The Christians were a Manx family settled in Ireland, whence Israel migrated to America in 1740, settling near Staunton, Virginia, where his son William was born in 1742. When in his twentieth year, William commanded a company on Byrd's Cherokee expedition; and again, in 1764, headed a militia company wherein Henry Pauling and Walter Crockett were his subordinates.

Removing first to Botetourt, then to Fincastle County, Christian established his home at Dunkard

Bottom, on New River, whence he was called to represent his county in the Virginia assembly of 1774. In Colonel Preston's enforced absence, he commanded the Fincastle regiment during Dunmore's war, arriving at Point Pleasant at midnight, after the victory had been won.

In 1775, Christian acted on the Fincastle committee of safety, and the following year was chosen second in command of Patrick Henry's continental regiment. Upon hearing of the danger from the Cherokee, however, he resigned his commission, and enrolled an expedition of seventeen hundred men to advance to the Cherokee towns (1776), which were burned, and the savage uprising quelled. In 1781, Christian acted as one of the commissioners who concluded a lasting peace with this tribe.

Early in 1785, he removed to the neighborhood of Louisville, Ky., where his advent was eagerly welcomed by the harassed frontier. He did not live to secure its permanent peace, being mortally wounded by a party of marauding Indians, Apr. 9, 1786. His widow, sister of Patrick Henry, and six children, survived him. His only son John died while a youth; all of his daughters married Kentuckians.

WILLIAM PRESTON

[Abridged from account by Dr. Draper. 5Bx; 21U120.]

William Preston, son of John and Elizabeth Patton Preston, was born on Christmas, 1729, in the north of Ireland. While still a child he emigrated with his parents to Augusta County, Virginia, where he was educated under the care of a Presbyterian clergyman, John Craig. His father having died when William was seventeen, his maternal uncle, Col. James Patton, became his guardian, and appointed him secretary to the treaty-commissioners at Logstown (1752). During the French and Indian War, he led a party of rangers, serving on the Sandy Creek expedition (1756). He was deputy surveyor, magistrate, and sheriff for his county, until 1767, when he removed to Fincastle, Botetourt County, where he held similar offices of public importance. Migrating to Draper's Meadows (Smithfield), in Fincastle County (1773), he was commissioned county-lieutenant, and took charge of the defense of its extended frontier. Detained by family reasons from the Point Pleasant expedition, his services were nevertheless equally important with those of the acting officers.

During the Revolution he continued to watch the frontier, defeating a Loyalist plot in 1780, and sending efficient aid to the King's Mountain expedition. The following year he took the field in person, leading his regiment at Whitsell's Mills, Mar. 6, 1781, where his life was saved by his friend and neighbor, Joseph Cloyd. He died at a regimental muster near his home, June 28, 1783. A tall, finely-proportioned man, with fair hair and blue eyes, his manners were easy and graceful, and his intellect strong and well-cultivated. He left eleven children, from whom descended many men of prominence in American history.

Cornstalk

[Abridged from account by Dr. Draper. 3Dxviii.]

The Indian name of Cornstalk was Keigh-tugh-qua, signifying a blade (or stalk) of the maize plant. Born in the Scioto towns of the Shawnee, his earliest recorded foray was that against Carr's Creek (1759), in what is now Rockbridge County. Pursuing frontiersmen rescued the prisoners, and recovered considerable booty. Again, in Pontiac's War, Cornstalk led a marauding party into the same neighborhood. Coming in the guise of friendship, the settlers at Muddy Creek in Greenbrier were first attacked; then the Clendennins, near Lewisburg—the party penetrating with fatal effect as far as Jackson's River and Carr's Creek.

Cornstalk was one of the hostages exacted by Bouquet in 1764, but escaped from Fort Pitt the following year. Nothing more is known of him until the opening of Dunmore's War, wherein, after failing to dissuade his tribesmen from joining battle, he led the native forces with vigor and audacity. After his treaty with Lord Dunmore, the chief proved his desire to maintain peace by frequent visits to Fort Randolph to restore stolen horses, and to renew friendship with the whites. It was in the capacity of mediator that he came thither in the autumn of 1777, when, detained as a hostage, he with his son and two companions was murdered by mutinous troops, whose officers tried in vain to prevent the outrage. In the excited state of public feeling, it was impossible to convict the perpetrators of this deed, although Preston and Fleming made efforts in this direction, and attempted to pacify the Shawnee "on behalf of all the good people of Virginia" (Draper MSS., 2ZZ44). Cornstalk was a large man, of commanding appearance, oratorical ability, and intellectual grasp. At Camp Charlotte, it was reported, "When he arose, he was in nowise confused or daunted, but spoke with distinct, audible voice, without stammering or repetition and with peculiar emphasis. His look while addressing Dunmore were truly grand and majestic, yet graceful and attractive." A monument to the chief has been erected in the court-house yard, of Point Pleasant.

CONTEMPORARY VERSE[50]

[2S, book 4, 6C17; 3XX18.][51]

Brave Lewis our Colonel, an officer bold,
At the mouth of Kanhawa did the Shawnees behold.
On the tenth of October, at the rising sun
The armies did meet and the battle begun.

---

[50] The following collection of popular verse was culled by Dr. Draper from the memory-stores of several pioneers whom he visited during the first half of the nineteenth century. In our editing, no liberties have been taken with Dr. Draper's versions, save where there are variants; in such cases the best has been chosen. Compare with the following four fragments of verse, that found in Newell's Journal, pp. 361, 362, *ante*. The latter appears to be a camp-song, written to inspirit the loyalty and zeal of the army. The following are more in the nature of poetic chronicles, devised to perpetuate the battle, its participants, and the heroic deeds which it invoked.—Ed.

[51] The following appears to have been the most popular of the songs, for there are three more or less complete versions among the Draper MSS., and one or two odd verses, connected with especial names. The first was received by Dr. Draper in 1845, from Mrs. Lydia Cruger (born 1766), daughter of Capt.

One thousand, one hundred we had on Ohio,
Two thirds of this number to the battle did go,
The Shawnees nine hundred, some say many more,
We formed our battle on the Ohio shore.

Like thunder from heaven our rifles did roar,
Till twelve of the clock, or perhaps something more,
And during this time the Shawnees did fly,
Whilst many a brave man on the ground there did lie.

From twelve until sunset some shots there did fly,
By this kind of fighting great numbers did die,
But night coming on, the poor Shawnees did yield,
Being no longer able to maintain the field.

Forty brave men on the ground there did lie,
Besides forty more of our wounded did die,
Killed and wounded on the Ohio shore,
Was one hundred and forty and perhaps something more.

What the Shawnees did lose we never did hear,
The bodies of twenty did only appear.
Into the Ohio the rest they did throw,
The just number of which we never did know.

Charles Lewis our Colonel was the first in the field,
He received a ball but his life did not yield,
In the pursuit of honor he did animate,
All those that fought near him or on him did wait.

George Fleming was a Colonel, courageous and bold,
He had been a hero, a hero of old;
He received three balls but did not expire,
He animated his men and to camp did retire.

John Boggs, living near Wheeling. For a sketch of this interesting person (with portrait), see *West Va. Hist. Mag.*, July, 1903; another version was obtained in October, 1844, from Mrs. Tabitha Moore, daughter of William Bowen, at Round Lick, near Rome, Tenn.; the third was included in a letter to Dr. Draper, dated Dixon's Springs, Tenn., May 13, 1843, from Col. William Martin, son of Col. Joseph Martin. The version we present, is a conglomerate of the three.—ED.

Brave Fields was a Colonel, courageous and bold,
Who had been a hero—a hero of old;
He received a ball and but these words said,
"Fight on brother soldiers and don't be dismayed."[52]

There was good Captain Buford and old Captain Ward,
They were both in the battle and fought very hard,
They fought like two heroes, and like heroes did die,
And in a short time on the ground there did lie.

Of commanders and subalterns great many did die,
And like our brave Captains, on the ground there did lie.
There was Goldman and Allen and a great many more,
Had the honor of dying on the Ohio shore.

There was Capt. John Murray, and McClanahan,
They were both in the field when the battle was begun,
They fought like two heroes, and like heroes did die,
And in a short time on the ground they did lie.[53]

There's cowardly Haynes, I am sorry for him
His valiant Lieutenant commanded his men
While he poor soul in the brush work did lie
Like a rogue in a halter, condemned to die.

And old Andrew Lewis, in his tent he did set
With his cowards around him, alas he did sweat
His blankets spread over him, and hearing the guns roar,
Saying was I at home, I would come here no more.

There was Slaughter and Christie both valiant and kind,
Waiting for provisions, their command was behind,
The day of the battle they heard of the fight,
They made a long march and joined us that night.

The chief of the Shawnees and Mingoes so poor,
Declared with us they would never fight more,
Those words to confirm, did each hostages give
That they and their wives and children might live.

---

[52] There is some confusion about the last two stanzas, taken from different versions, and due to failure of memory on the part of the probably aged narrators. Fleming's name was William, not George.—ED.

[53] Another version gives the first two lines as follows:
"Wilson, Murray and McClanahan
Were all in the field when the battle began."—ED.

[8ZZ18.] [54]

Ye daughters ar   sons of Virginia incline
Your ears to a story of woe;
I sing of a time when your fathers and mine
Fought for us on the Ohio.

In seventeen hundred and seventy four,
The month of October, we know,
An army of Indians, two thousand or more,
Encamped on the Ohio.

The Shawnees, Wyandottes and Delawares, too,
As well as the tribes of Mingoe,
Invaded our lands, and our citizens slew,
On the south of the Ohio.

Andrew Lewis the gallant, and Charley the brave,
With Matthews and Fleming also,
Collected an army, our country to save,
On the banks of the Ohio.

With Christian, and Shelby, and Elliot, and Paul,
And Stuart and Arbuckle and Crow
And soldiers one thousand and ninety in all
They marched to the Ohio.

These sons of the mountains renowned of old
All volunteered freely to go
And conquer their foeman like patriots bold,
Or fall by the Ohio.

They marched thro' the untrodden wilds of the west,
O'er mountains and rivers also,
And pitched, at Point Pleasant, their bodies to rest,
On the banks of the Ohio.

The Army of Indians, in Battle array,
Under Cornstalk and Elnipsicow,
Was met by the forces of Lewis that day,
On the Banks of the Ohio.

---

[54] The following was sent Dr. Draper by Charles H. Lewis, in a letter dated Staunton, Va., Aug. 31, 1845. He says, "I send you a copy of the song found on one of the lids of my grandmother's Bible."—Ed.

They brought on the battle at breaking of day,
Like heroes they slaughtered the foe,
Till two hundred Indians or more, as they say,
Were slain by the Ohio.

The Army of Indians were routed, and fled,
Our heroes pursued the foe,
While seventy soldiers and Charley lay dead,
On the banks of the Ohio.

The brave Colonel Fields and the gallant Buford
Captains Wilson and Murray also,
And Allen, Mc Clenahan, Goldsby and Ward,
Were slain by the Ohio.

Col. Fleming, and Matthews, and Shelby, and Moore,
And Elliot, and Dillon, also,
And soldiers one hundred and thirty and four
Were wounded by the Ohio.

Farewell, Colonel Lewis, till pity's sweet fountains
Are dried in the hearts of the fair and the Brave,
Virginia shall weep for her Chief of the mountains
And mourn for the heroes who sleep by his grave.

As Israel mourned for Moses of old,
In the valley of Moab by Nebow
We'll mourn for Charles Lewis the hero so bold,
Who fell by the Ohio.

As Israel did mourn and her daughters did weep,
For Saul and his host on Gilbow
We'll mourn Colonel Fields and the heroes who sleep
On the banks of the Ohio.

[3XX18.][55]

The tenth day of October, the morning being clear
We spied a savage army which was approaching near,
With full intent they marched along, the white men all to slay,
But indeed they were mistaken, for we did gain the day.

---

[55] Sent to Dr. Draper by Col. William Martin, in a letter dated May 13, 1843, at Dixon's Springs, Tenn.—ED.

It was by God's kind providence, that or-der-ed it so,
That Robertson that morning, a hunting he did go,
Before that he had walk-ed far, a savage army spied
Which drove him to the camp again, "there's Indians boys he cried.

Come now brave boys" he boldly said, "to meet them let us go,
For fear these cruel savages, give us a fatal blow,
And we must ne'r give way to them, whilst we remain alive
Or else into the River, they surely will us drive."

Then marched out three hundred men, with courage stout and bold,
Commanded by Charles Lewis, who ne'r could be controll'd.
He was as bold a warrior, as ever fired a gun
We soon did meet the savages, and then began the fun.

The Indians they kept bawling, as loud as they could strain
Thinking upon that morning, the battle they would gain,
That they would kill and scalp us all, and do the thing so neat,
And in the Camp that morning, their breakfast they would eat.

From morning until evening, the guns kept constant fire,
We gave the Indians something more than what they did desire,
We like unto bold heroes, victoriously did shine
We put the Indians to the route, and stopped their bad design.

The battle being over, the Indians they did say
All this is but a trifle, that we have seen today.
But this was their impertinence, their very best had done,
They saw their own destruction, the battle being won.

Our Royal Governor Dunnmore, he being of high renown
With fifteen hundred jovial men, he marched towards their town
With a full resolution, to slay both old and young
For all the barbarous actions, the savages had done

The Indians with aching hearts, on bended knees did fall
And for his Lordship's mercy, so loudly they did call
His Lordship with compassion, forgave them from that day,
If all the costs and charges amongst them they would pay.

* * * * * * * * [56]
Now bless our bold commander, Charles Lewis by name
He has been slain in battle, but we'l record his fame
He was as noble a warrior as ever fired a gun,
Success to Old Virginia, and thus concludes my song.

[46J14.][57]

1 Mark well the 10 day of October which
causes woo the Indian savages the[y]
Cover the pleasant Banks of the Ohio

2 Judgment Calls to execution let
faim throughout all Nation goe ouer
heroes fout with Reslution on
the plasant bankes of the Ohio

3 Brave Charles Lewis and som nobal
Captains down to death the[y] did go alls[o]
there h[e]ads is bound with naptkins
benath the plasant Banks of the Ohio

4 much honar to this Valiant numbr
of Champains that did face there foose
Augusta weeping for those that slumbr
Beneath the plasant banks of the Ohio

Kings laments that dredfull falling
on the mountang of gillboah so Shall
we weep for brav Hugh allan
farre from the banks of the Ohio

---

[56] Colonel Martin states that there were one or two stanzas here, that he could not recollect.—ED.

[57] The following fragment was found among the papers of Capt. Thomas Madison. On the reverse is written : "Robert Elliott His Orderly Book Camp at Valley Forge Jany. 29th. 1778."—ED.

INDEX

ABINGDON (Va.), 78, 81, 111, 232.
Able, Jeremiah, 402.
Adair, James, 106.
Adams, George, letter by, 227, 228.
——, John, 400.
——, Samuel, 207.
Adkins, Parker, 398.
——, Willinton, 398.
Agnew (Aggnue), John, 411.
Alden, George, "New Government West of the Alleghenies before 1780," 370.
——, Andrew, 406.
Alexander, James, 405; sergeant, 407, 419.
Alexandria (Va.), 274, 317.
Allen, ——, 126, 127, 181.
——, Hugh, lieut., killed, 276, 280, 288, 289, 296, 339, 343, 346, 355, 435, 437, 439; sketch, 276.
——, Hugh, Jr., 276.
——, James, 339.
——, John, 276.
——, William, 276.
Alley, Thomas, 94.
Alsbury, Thomas, drummer, 408.
Alsup, John, 106, 189, 235.
Ambrosia (W. Va.), 357.
American Archives, 8, 12, 33, 36, 37, 56, 67, 74, 86, 97, 114, 127, 131, 133, 134, 151, 155, 161, 193, 203, 208, 241, 270, 273, 302, 307, 310, 311, 340, 368, 374-376, 383, 387, 390, 395; *Historical Magazine,* 107; *Historical Review,* 370; *Pioneer,* 131, 208, 246, 306, 374.
Amherst, Gen. Jeffrey, 393.
Ammunition, 30, 45, 49, 50, 57, 58, 64, 72, 73, 76, 77, 80, 90-92, 96, 99, 100, 105, 110, 144, 149, 173, 174, 192, 193, 195, 205, 210, 216, 219, 227, 228, 233, 235, 237, 241, 245, 252, 298, 313, 314, 316, 318, 319, 323, 328, 329, 334, 337, 339, 341, 345, 349, 350, 361, 398.
Andastes. See Mingo Indians.
Anderson, ——, 29, 244, 245, 359.
——, Andrew, 137.
——, James, 402.
——, Job, 244.
——, John, pioneer, 137; ensign, 137, 148; sketch, 137.
Andrews, Samuel, 407.
Anvil Cliff (Va.), 111.
Arbuckle, John, 423.
——, Capt. Matthew, 103, 112, 190, 274, 276, 282, 310, 314, 315, 330, 332, 334, 415-419, 423, 446; sketch, 103.
——, Gen. Matthew, Jr., 104.
——, William, 423.
Ard, James, 409.
Armstrong, ——, ensign, 251.
——, George, 412.
——, Col. Martin, sketch, 221, 222.
——, Thomas, 407.
——, William, 407.
Arnold, Gen. Benedict, 223.

Arnold, James, 406.
——, Stephen, 406, 419.
Arthur, John, 408.
Astle, Samuel, 397.
Atkins, Blackburn, 94.
——, Charles, 397.
——, Henry, 200, 397.
——, William, 99.
Augusta (Va.), 73, 160, 339, 439.

BABBITT, Ishmael, 397.
Bailey, John, 422, 423.
Baily, Campbell, 399.
Baker, ——, 15, 16, 18, 378.
——, Martin, 411.
——, Samuel, ensign, killed, 296, 411.
——, Thomas, 165, 419.
Baker's Bottom (Ohio River), 17.
Bambrige, James, 406.
Baret, Edward, 411.
Barkly, John, 406.
Barnes, ——, 188.
Barnett, James, 165, 422.
Barret, S. L., 425.
Barton, Samuel, 408.
Basdel, John, 419.
Bates, ——, 135.
Batson, Mordecai, 111.
Baugh, Jacob, 422.
Baylstone, William, 229.
Bedford (Pa.), 29.
Bell, James, pioneer, 63.
——, John, 172.
——, Thomas, 399, 422.
Bell's Meadows (Va.), 63.
Bellew, David, canoe-man, 411.
"Belmont" Fleming's Estate, 181, 182, 254, 428.
Bergman, Christian, 396, 404.
Berkeley (Va.), 191.
Berry, Francis, 423.
Bickley, George W. L., *Tazewell County*, 234.
Biddle, ——, 240.
Big Bone Lick (Ky.), 111, 121.

Big Cove (Pa.), 68.
"Big Grave," Indian Mound, 36.
Big Levels, 195, 181, 281. See also Levels of Greenbrier, and Camp Union.
Big Lick (Va.), 41, 178.
Bigelow, John, *Franklin's Works*, 368, 370.
Billey, Cherokee Indian, 38, 39.
Bird, Col. Henry, 388.
Biscoe, Dr. ——, 309.
Bishop, Levi, 403.
Blackburn, ——, 133.
——, Arthur, 412.
Blackford, Joseph, 421.
Black Hoof, a chief, 347.
Blackmore, John, 85, 88, 238, 305, 309. See also, Fort Blackmore.
Blair, ——, 423.
——, Daniel, 406.
——, William, scout, 352.
Blankenship, Richard, 200, 201.
Bledsoe, Abraham, ensign, 148; letter by, 221-224.
——, Capt. Anthony, 106, 148, 165, 166, 168, 171, 226; letters by, 169, 260, 261; sketch, 106.
——, Isaac, 148.
Bledsoe's Lick (Va.), 106.
Blesly, Jacob, 400.
——, John, 400.
Blue Jacket, a chief, 347.
Blue Licks (Ky.), 4, 82; battle of, 44, 114, 344.
Bogard, Abram, 412.
Boggs, Capt. John, 433, 434.
Boh, Adam, 400.
——, Jacob, 400.
Boles, ——, 2.
——, John, 400.
Boniface, William, 409.
Bonnet, Lewis, 421.
Boogs, Francis, 411.
Boone, Daniel, 2, 4, 49, 51, 78, 81, 84, 88, 89, 108, 168, 171-173, 209, 218, 220, 234, 240, 245, 248-251, 272, 298, 326.

INDEX

Boone, James, killed by Indians, 2, 39, 173, 220, 375, 376.
Boonesborough (Ky.), 24, 32, 51, 78, 82, 107, 174, 388.
Boughman, Jacob, 408.
——, John, 408.
Bouquet, Col. Henry, 11, 28, 75, 78, 82, 113, 276, 373, 427, 432; sketch, 373.
Bowen, Moses, 423.
——, Reese, 403, 404, 423.
——, William, 157, 158, 167, 170; scout, 404, 434; lieutenant, 396; sketch, 158.
Bowes, ——, sergeant, 335.
Bowles, Robert, 408.
Bowman, Col. John, expedition, 68, 82, 187.
Bowman (Bownam), Joseph, 303, 304, 421.
Bowyer, Henry, 419.
——, Mary (Polly), 300.
——, Prudence, 300.
——, Lieut.-Col. William, 254; letters by, 299, 300, 344; sketch, 254.
Boyd, James, 409.
——, Robert, 408, 409.
Boydstone, ——, 279.
Boyer, ——, 125.
——, Henry, 409.
Boyls, Barney, 406.
Bozel, John, 409.
Bracken, Matthew, ensign, 276, 280, 344, 410.
——, Matthew, lieutenant, 120, 288, 289, 355.
Braddock, Gen. William, 2, 25, 28, 48, 74, 191, 348, 426, 428.
Bradley, John, 412.
——, William, 406.
Bradshaw, ——, 193.
Brander, ——, 47, 77, 157, 172, 212, 219, 233.
Brandywine, battle of, 191, 197.
Branstead, Andrew, 404.
Breckenridge, ——, 76.
——, Alexander, 161, 422.
——, James, 27.
——, John, 27.
——, Preston, 27.
——, Col. Robert, sketch, 27.
——, William, 27.
Breden, John, 405.
Breeze, Richard, 401.
——, Robert, 401.
Brinton, Henry, 421.
——, James, 421.
Bristol (Tenn.), 49, 238.
British, 28, 40, 42, 125, 152, 236, 256, 270, 271, 302, 370, 373, 375, 425, 428; army, 39, 274, 393; Historical Manuscripts Commission *Report*, 151; Colonial Papers, "America and West Indies," 368.
Brock, R. A., "Virginia Convention of 1788," 429.
Bronstetter, Andrew, 399.
Brook, Thomas, 405.
Brooks, George, 412.
Brown, Charles, 405.
——, Colman, 421.
——, Jacob, 41.
——, James, 27, 421.
——, Rev. John, letters by, 26, 27, 159–161; sketch, 27.
——, John, Jr., 27.
——, Low, 422.
——, Patrick, 230.
——, Robert, sergeant, 229, 396 401–404.
——, Thomas, 407.
——, William, 406.
Brownsville (Pa.), 12, 17, 50. See also, Redstone Old Fort.
Brumfield, Humphrey, 398.
Brumley, Thomas, 401, 403.
Brundige, Solomon, 406.
Bryan, Morgan, pioneer, 220.
——, Capt. Thomas, sketch, 220.
Bryans, Shorgan, 94.
——, William, sergeant, 408.
Bryan and Rose, *Pioneer Families of Missouri*, 276.
Bryant, William, 409.

INDEX

Buchanan, —, commissariat, 195, 242, 252.
——, Archibald, 203, 231.
——, James, 198, 199.
——, Jane, 9.
——, John, colonel, 78, 199, 203, 231, 407.
——, Margaret, 78.
——, William, ensign, 52, 199; receipt by, 174; sketch, 174.
Buckeye (Va.), 423.
Buffalo Spring Lick, 320.
Buffaloes, 122, 133, 286, 367.
Buford, Col. Abraham, 273; sketch, 273.
——, Capt. Thomas, 273, 275, 276, 280, 284, 286, 288, 289, 296, 306, 315, 318, 330, 334, 344, 351, 355, 409, 413, 415, 417, 418, 427, 435, 437; sketch, 273.
Bull Town, massacre of, 377.
Bullitt, Col. —, 23, 32, 113, 125, 126, 207.
Bunch, Joseph, 409.
Bunshell, John, 399.
Burck, Richard, 412.
Burcks, Samuel, 409.
Burk, Thomas, letter by, 398.
Burke, James, 140.
——, John, 410.
Burke's Garden, (Va.), 140.
Burnes, Thomas, 409.
Burny, Thomas, 406.
Burnsides, James, 408.
Burrens, James, 411.
Burroughs, —, 423.
Burtchfield, James, 408.
Bush, John, sergeant, 405.
——, William, sergeant, 405.
Bushy Run, battle of, 373.
Bustar, David, 403.
——, William, 402.
Butler, —, 8, 234
——, Joseph, 405.
——, Richard, 67.
——, Shadrick, 405.

Butterfield, Consul W., *Expedition against Sandusky,* 103; *History of the Girtys,* 152, 285; *Washington-Crawford Letters,* 8, 10, 36, 62, 86, 155, 302, 304.
Byrd, Richard, 402.
——, Col. William, 21, 38, 52, 65, 100, 146, 205, 211, 429; sketch, 21.
Byrne, Charles, 407.

CALDWELL, John, 421.
——, William, 421.
Callaway, Dudley, canoe-man, 411.
Cameron, Alexander, 72; letter to, 40, 212; sketch, 40.
——, Charles, 275.
——, George, killed by Indians, 275, 301, 346.
——, Hugh, 423.
Camp Charlotte, 302.
Camp Union (Va.), 104, 114, 181, 183, 185, 189, 190, 195, 196, 205, 212, 222, 260, 281, 282, 284, 313-320, 327, 413-415, 433; sketch. 181.
Campbell, —, killed by Indians, 36, 272.
——, Capt. —, 22, 166, 167.
——, Dr. —, 303.
——, Maj. Arthur, 31, 56, 59, 77, 80, 84, 85, 91, 157, 158, 205, 207, 212, 231, 241, 272, 420; letters by, 38-42, 47-49, 57, 58, 72, 73, 108, 109, 134-138, 142-144, 158, 159, 162, 163, 170-172, 192-195, 202-205, 209-212, 219-222, 226, 227, 229-233, 238-240, 244-246, 250-252, 278, 279, 297, 298, 374, 377; letters to, 145, 146, 161, 164: sketch, 39; manuscripts, 270, 291.

INDEX

Campbell, David, 39.
—, James, 23.
—, John, captain, 47, 230, 234, 403, 409; sketch, 47.
—, Joseph, 410.
—, Robert, 423.
—, Samuel, 200, 397, 399.
—, Capt. William, 6, 40, 43, 52, 59, 75, 76, 84, 137, 143, 147, 148, 159, 170, 177, 178, 189, 317, 363, 399, 401, 409, 419, 420; letter by, 261-266; sketch, 43; manuscripts, 270, 291.
Canadian Archives, 394.
Canady. See Kennedy.
Caperton, Adam, 409.
—, Hugh, 409.
Carlisle, Robert, 111.
Carlisle (Pa.), 11, 66.
Carmack, John, 412.
Carney, Martin, 408.
Carolina, 165, 166, 169, 209, 212, 216, 217, 252.
Carpenter (Carpender), John, 409.
—, Jeremiah, 408.
—, Richard Willson, 407.
—, Solomon, 408.
—, Thomas, 408, 419.
Carr, —, 234.
—, George, 400, 422.
—, James, 400.
—, William, 400.
Cartain, James, 399.
—, Joel, 398.
—, John, 398.
Carter, Deal, killed by Indians, 244, 279.
—, John, 409; sketch, 221.
Carther, Edward, 411.
Cary, Jeremiah, 397.
Casey, William, 412, 422.
Cashaday, Simon, 399.
—, Thomas, 398.
Castle Hill (Va.), 242.
Castle's Woods (Va.), 2, 73, 80, 88, 173, 218, 228, 248.

Catawba Indians, 216.
Catfish, Indian Chief, 10, 15.
Catron, Adam, 400.
—, Francis, 400.
—, Jacob, 399, 400.
—, Michael, 400.
—, Peter, 400.
—, Philip, 400.
Cats, Roger, 400.
Cattes, John, 400.
Cavanaugh, Charles, 397.
—, Philemon, 397.
—, Philip, 201, 234.
—, William, Sr., 397.
Cayuga Indians, 305.
Cecil, Saul, 229.
Champ, William, 165, 400.
Chapline, Abraham, 421.
Chapman, John, 399.
—, Richard, 398.
Charleston (Ind.), 197.
—— (S. C.), 6, 111, 273, 375.
—— (W. Va.), 24, 112, 113, 325.
—— (Mass.), 340.
Charlton, James, 408.
Chenusaw (the Judge), 305.
Cherokee Indians, 5, 6, 8, 20, 26, 39-41, 43, 47, 48, 50-52, 57-59, 72, 73, 75, 81, 107, 122, 210, 216, 217, 221, 232, 239, 242, 246, 276, 278, 305, 376, 426, 430; expedition against, 38, 43, 48, 55, 59, 72, 75, 81, 84, 107, 109, 168, 225, 235, 251, 271, 273, 312, 428-430.
Chesapeake & Ohio Railway, 360.
Chickamauga expedition, against Indians, 48, 55, 107, 197, 225, 251, 252, 271.
Chickasaw Indians, 376; agents, 271.
Chillicothe (O.), 263, 292, 293, 301, 347; sketch, 292, 293.
Chism, John, 405.
Chiswell, Col. John, 52.
Chiyawee, Wyandot chief, 347.
Chota, Cherokee town, 38.

446 INDEX

Christian, —, captain, 359.
——, Anne, 206, 428.
——, Gilbert, lieutenant, 359; sketch, 251.
——, Israel, 360, 429.
——, John, 430.
——, Mary, 184.
——, Priscilla, 184.
——, Robert, 251.
——, Rose, 184.
——, Col. William, 49, 55, 79, 81, 89, 106, 107, 121, 126, 146, 158, 169, 173, 182, 184, 189, 190, 206-208, 214, 215, 223, 225, 239, 245, 251, 260, 261, 266-269, 273, 288, 292, 293, 305, 317, 331, 340, 363, 420, 423, 435, 436; letters by, 42-47, 55-57, 63-66, 75-78, 80-85, 176-179, 185-188, 196-199, 205, 206, 291, 301-307, 316; letters to, 52-55, 59-61, 73; sketch, 46, 429, 430.
Christianburg (Va.), 428.
Cincinnati (O.), 120.
Circleville (O.), 290, 292.
Clark, George Rogers, 68, 102, 155, 197, 207, 225, 303, 344; letters by, 10-12, 115.
——, John, 421.
——, Samuel, sergeant, 410.
Clarke, James, 410.
Clarksville (Tenn.), 225, 271.
Clay, —, 235, 319, 423.
——, David, 200.
——, Ezekiel, 200.
——, Mitchell, 200, 397.
Clay Lick, 203.
Clehany, James M., 403.
Clendennin (Clendinen, Clindining, Klendenning), Adam, 397.
——, Alexander, 423.
——, Charles, 347, 423.
——, George, 113, 423.
——, Robert, 423.
——, William, 410, 423.
—— family, 432.
Clerk, John, 411.

Cleveland, Col. Benjamin, 235.
Clifton, William, 397, 408.
Clinding, George, 410.
Clover Bottom, 109, 139, 140, 142.
Clover Lick (Va.), 273.
Cloyd, Capt. Joseph, 45, 76, 174, 241, 431; sketch, 45.
——, Ninian, 63, 64.
Cloyne, Nicholas, 399.
Cochran, William, 406.
Cocke, Capt. William, 77, 107, 210, 217, 227, 240, 251, 252; letter by, 208, 209; sketch, 107.
Coile, James, 402.
Coiler, John, 406.
——, Moses, sergeant, 406.
Coleman, Robert, 197.
Collet, George, Indian captive, 422.
——, Thomas, 422.
Collins, L., *History of Kentucky*, 119, 420.
——, Richard, 407.
Columbus (Miss.), 107.
—— (O.), 304.
Colville, Andrew, captain, 75; sketch, 75.
Comstock, —, 181.
Condon, David, canoe-man, 411.
Conestoga Indians, 28, 246.
Connolly, Dr. John, 35, 62, 66-68, 74, 86, 102, 125, 191, 264, 373, 380-382, 389, 392; letters by, 12, 42, 101, 102; letters to, 37, 151-154; sketch, 42.
Connor (Conner), Patrick, 407.
——, William, 406.
Constantine, Patrick, 411.
Cook, David, 408.
——, Henry, 405.
——, John, 409.
——, William, 409.
Cooper, —, 387.
——, Abraham, 402.
——, Francis, 402.

INDEX 447

Cooper, Leonard, 423.
——, Nathaniel, 409.
——, Spencer, 410.
——, Thomas, 411.
Copley, Thomas, 399.
Corder, John, 106.
Cormick, John, 419.
Cornstalk, Indian chief, 104, 181, 272, 301, 302, 308, 310, 319, 347, 423, 436; sketch, 432, 433.
Cornwallis, General Charles, 25, 196, 272, 429.
Cornwell, Adman, 409.
Coshockton (O.), 37.
Courtney, Charles, 396.
——, John, 396.
Cowan, David, 80.
——, James, killed by Indians, 131.
——, Jared, 421.
——, John, lieutenant, 109, 420; sketch, 109.
Coward, ——, 423.
Cowpens, battle of, 415.
Cox, Gabriel, lieutenant, 233, 425.
——, George, 15, 16, 19, 421.
——, Capt. John, 220, 229.
Covington (Ky.), 120, 360.
Crab Orchard (Ky.), 270.
—— (Va.), 234.
Crabtree, Isaac, 39–41, 43, 48, 73, 78, 143, 172, 240, 377.
——, William, scout, 404.
Craige, ——, 79.
——, George, 407.
——, John, 94, 431.
——, N. B., 18.
——, William, sergeant, 276, 410.
Crain, John, 410.
Cravat, Robert, 100.
Craven, Joseph, sergeant, 234, 403, 404.
Cravens, James, 403.
——, John, 403.
——, Robert, 403.
Crawford (Crafford, Craford), Alexander, 360.
——, Barnard, 405.

——, John, sergeant, 400, 404, 407.
——, Valentine, 10.
——, Major William, 14, 37, 86, 103, 152, 155, 156, 302–304; receipt by, 103; sketch, 103.
Crawley (Croley), James, 406, 408.
Creed, Mathew, 409.
Creeks: Bear, 123; Beargrass, 9, 39, 124, 125; Bell, 324; Beaver, 8; Big Sandy, 117; Bracken's, 120; Cabin, 325; Carr's, massacre, 272, 432; Cedar, 76, 88, 156; Chartier, 102; Congo, 290, 301; Copper, 41, 43, 51, 77; Cove, 85; Cripple, 163; Crooked, 343; Cross, 16; Dickerson's Branch, 325; Dunkard, 97, sketch 36; Dunlop's, 360; Dry, 325; Eighteen Mile, 337; Elk, 194; Elk-Horn, 128–130; Federal, 302; Fish, 155; Four Mile, 117; Grave, 11, 36, 108, sketch, 36; Greasy, 179; Harrod's, 124, 125; Howard, 359; Hurricane, 336, 357; Indian, 30; Kelly's, 112, 306, 307, 309, 324–326; Kinnickinnik, 290; Laurel Run, 322, 323; Lawrence, 7, 23; Lee's, 120; Lick, 324; Licking, 120; Limestone, 121; Little Sandy, 117; Locust, 120; Maiden Spring, 30; Mann's, 322; Meadow, 320, 358; Mile Branch, 325; Moccasin, 77, 220, 227; Muddy, 23, 36, 64, 103, 109, 319, 432; sketch, 319; Nashes, 119; Ohio Brush, 119; Opequon, 220; Otter, 124; Paint, 76; Peak, 46, 55; Pigeon, 17; Pine, 304; Pipe, 11, 115; Pitman's, 239; Reed, 137, 194, 217, sketch, 63; Reedy, 208, 210, 229, 240, 251, 252; Rich, 95, 112, 176, 188, 189, 199, 205, 247, 323, 324,

397; Salt Lick, 118; Scippo, 290, 301, 302; Shot Pouch, 118; Silver, 23; Sinking, 111, 112, 135, 207, massacre, 134, sketch, 111; Stony, 85, 88; Swago, 423; Sycamore, 119; Ten Mile, 37, 68, 102, 108, 202; Toms, 188; Tuscarawas, 36; Tygert's, 117; Walker's, 56, 77, 79, 85, 241, 320; Warrior's, 322; Watson's Branch, 325; Waxhaw, 273; Wheeling (Weilin), 37; Witcher, 325; Wolf, 105, 141, 247; Yellow, massacre of, 10, 11, 13, 14, 16-19, 36, 115, 246, 305.

Cresap, Joseph, 425.
——, Capt. Michael, 11, 12, 14, 16, 18, 29, 67, 155, 156, 304-306, 312, 377; letters to, 246, 247, 260, 393; sketch, 12.
——, Michael, Jr., 15, 155.
——, Col. Thomas, pioneer, 12, 185, 393.
—— family, 191.
Crinar, John, 149.
Crisman, Isaac, 402.
Crockett, Joseph, 423.
——, Capt. Walter, 44, 52, 58, 59, 73, 77, 79, 80, 84, 137, 149, 177, 179, 189, 224, 251, 429; letter to, 76, 80; sketch, 44.
Croghan, Col. George, 7, 29, 33, 66, 121; "Journals," 7, 121; sketch, 7.
Croley, Samuel, 408.
Crow, John, sergeant, 194, 421, 436.
Crouch, ——, 63, 64.
Cruger, Lydia, 433.
Crumrine, Boyd, *Washington County*, 97, 155.
Culbertson's Bottom, 76, 94, 95, 99, 103, 109, 138, 140, 145, 235, 243, 248.
Culwell, Alexander, 411.

Cumberland settlement, 3, 85, 168.
Cummings, Rev. Charles, 81, 226, 229, 230, 244, 251; sketch, 81.
Cummins, George, 406.
Cundiff, Jonathan, ensign, 276, 280, 288, 289, 296, 344, 355, 409; sketch, 276.
Cunningham, James, 406.
——, John, 411.
Current, Joseph, 410.
Custer, William, 411.
Cutlip, David, 411.
Cutright, John, 422.
Cuttenwa, Indian chief, 305.

Dale, James, 409.
Dandridge, Alexander Spottswood, 8, 25, 111, 114, 116, 126, 191; letter by, 22-24; sketch, 24.
——, Nathaniel West, 24.
Danville (Ky.), 25.
Darnell (Darnold), Lawrence, sketch, 7, 22, 116.
Dartmouth, Lord, 149, 394; letters to, 151, 368-395; letters by, 368, 372.
Davis, ——, 56.
——, Azariah, 420.
——, Charles, 407.
——, George, 411.
——, James, 23, 79; sketch, 79.
——, Patrick, 359.
——, Robert, scout, 404, 409.
——, Samuel, 409.
Davis's Bottom (Va.), 56.
Davis's Fancy (Va.), 79.
Davise, Jonathan, 94.
Day, Joseph, 410.
——, William, 106.
Deal, William, 409.
Deek, John, 405.
Delaware Indians, 28, 29, 33, 36, 37, 74, 114, 116, 121, 124, 150, 153, 156, 256, 273, 301, 346, 373, 381-384, 387, 436; sketch, 28.

INDEX

Demonse, Abraham, 407.
Deniston, John, 408.
Denton, John, 106.
Detroit, 152, 306.
Devereaux, Charles, 211.
Diamond Rocks, 18.
Dickerson, —, Indian, 123.
Dickinson, Adam, pioneer, 272.
——, Col. John, 56, 73, 272, 275, 280, 286, 288, 289, 296, 306, 331, 341, 351, 355, 356, 414, 416; sketch, 272.
Dickson, Captain, (Indian), 347.
Dillon, —, lieutenant, 423, 437.
Dingus (Dingos), Peter, 106, 397.
Dinwiddie, Gov. Robert, 276, 428.
Diver, John, 400.
Dixon's Springs (Tenn.), 434, 437.
Doack, —, 26, 217.
——, David, 79.
——, David, Jr., 399.
——, Capt. Robert, 58, 59, 135, 137, 144, 145, 162, 193, 194, 220, 241, 399; letters by, 73, 76, 78-80; sketch, 399.
——, Samuel, 399, 404.
——, William, ensign, 241, 399.
Dobler, Jacob, 399.
Dodd, John, 407.
Doddridge, —, 344.
Dollarhide, Samuel, 396.
Donald, Robert, 64, 149.
Donaley, James, sergeant, 410.
Donally, John, fifer, 408.
Donalson, Robert, 396, 401, 402.
Donelson, Col. John, 5, 122, 172, 221, 233, 239.
——, Thomas, 401, 402.
Dooley, Jacob, 409.
——, Thomas, lieutenant, 409.
Doran, Patrick, 421.
Doss, Joel, 411.
Dougherty (Dehority, Doherty, Dohorty), George, sergeant, 403.

——, Henry, 230.
——, James, 411.
——, John, 410.
——, Joseph, 230.
——, Michael, ensign, 224, 225, 241, 250.
Douglas, George, 400.
——, James, sketch, 111; surveyor, 111, 116, 121, 123-129, 131, 400, 403.
Downy, James, sergeant, 399.
——, John, 399.
Drake, —, killed by Indians, 39.
——, Ephraim, scout, 4, 163.
——, Joseph, 78, 81, 143, 159, 163-168, 170, 171, 178, 401; sketch, 78.
Draper, John, lieutenant, 64, 101, 103, 105, 109, 110, 139, 141, 179, 351; sketch, 64.
——, Lyman C., 9, 15-17, 38, 88, 110, 111, 121, 151, 291, 311, 368; manuscript collection, 10, 12, 51, 68, 71, 75, 78, 107, 111, 131, 133, 134, 153, 154, 158, 160, 168, 173, 185, 191, 206, 207, 219, 225, 230, 235, 236, 239, 271, 272, 276, 280, 285, 296, 297, 302, 305, 306, 308, 316, 317, 326, 344, 347, 351, 374, 387, 388, 402, 408, 420, 421, 425, 426, 428-431, 433, 436, 437; *King's Mountain and its Heroes*, 43.
——, Mary, captured by Indians, 101.
Draper's Meadows (Va.), 101, 431; massacre of, 45, 64.
Drennon, Jacob, 421.
Dresden (O.), 153.
Dulin, James, 408.
Duncan (Duncom, Dunken, Dunkin), John, sergeant, 28, 29, 194, 219, 234, 402.
Dunkard Bottom (Va.), 42, 429, 430.
Dunlap, Robert, 423.

INDEX

Dunmore, Lord, governor, 12, 13, 19, 29, 42, 43, 51, 52, 67, 68, 92, 103, 125, 145, 152, 153, 155, 156, 183, 185, 186, 198, 201, 236, 256, 262-264, 269, 270, 276, 281, 288-290, 292, 293, 296, 301-309, 311, 341, 361, 362, 373, 377, 387, 390, 395, 421, 425, 427, 433, 438; letters by, 33-35, 37, 61-63, 67, 86, 87, 91, 97, 98, 145, 149, 150, 177, 285, 338, 340, 348, 351, 368-395; letters to, 286, 368, 372; titles, 353, 360; sketch, 425, 426.
Dunn, John, 407.
Dunowho, James, 411.
Durrett, Reuben T., 207; "Centenary of Louisville," 125.
Dutton, Philip, 400, 403.
Dyer, William, 410.

Eager, John, 406.
Easthorn, William, 423.
Edger, Thomas, 408.
Edgington, George, 16.
Edmiston (Edmondston), William, lieutenant, 84, 402; sketch, 84.
Edwards, James, 403.
——, Jonathan, 404.
Egins, Edward, 408.
Elinipisco, Indian chief, 347, 436.
Elk Garden (Va.), 88. See also Fort Elk Garden.
Elkins, Jesse, 94.
Ellenburgh, Peter, 408.
Ellias, Thomas, 411.
Elliott, Ca'pt. Robert, 152, 408, 436, 437; orderly book, 439.
Ellison, James, 408, 423.
Ellisson, Charles, 411.
Elswick, John, 94.
Emery, Will, Cherokee, 239.
English (Inglish), Joseph, 397.
——, Joshua, 397.
——, Stephen, 175.

Estill, Samuel, sergeant, 408.
—— family, 281.
Evans (Evens, Evins), Andrew, 411.
——, Evan, 411.
Ewing, A. E., 423.
——, Alexander, 400.
——, Alexander, Jr., 400.
——, Robert, 409.
——, Samuel, 400.
——, William, sergeant major, 400, 407, 410; sketch 423.

Fain, John, 412.
——, Samuel, 412.
Falling, William, 75.
Falls, of Kanawha, 325; of Ohio, 23, 68, 81, 88, 124, 125, 245, 306, 309, 310.
Fargison, Thomas, 410.
Farley, Francis, 200, 201.
——, John, 201.
Farlor, Francis, 397.
——, John, 397.
——, Thomas, 397.
Farmer, Nathan, 409.
Fauquier, Gov. Francis, 374.
Feavil, William, 405.
Ferrill, Robert, 411.
——, William, 402.
Field, Ephraim, captured by Indians, 114.
——, Col. John, 113, 185, 186, 190, 197, 265, 274, 275, 280, 284, 287, 288, 294, 296, 301, 309, 315, 319, 322, 330, 334, 346, 349, 355, 415-418, 427, 435, 437; sketch, 113, 114.
Fielder, Charles, 412.
Fields, John, sergeant, 409.
——, William, 420.
Fienquay, Isham, canoe-man, 411.
Filson, John, geographer, 4.
—— Club *Papers*, 125, 133, 273.
Fincastle (Va.), 6, 7, 24, 27, 64, 72, 81, 164, 189, 192, 207, 259, 343, 360, 366, 412, 431.

INDEX

Findley, George, 423.
——, John, 412.
——, Robert, sergeant, 411.
Fisher, Isaac, 408.
Fitzhugh, John, 411.
Fitzpatrick, Timothy, prisoner, 328.
Fleming, Leonard Israel, 182, 184, 213, 300; sketch, 182.
——, Nancy, 307; letters to, 181-184, 205, 206, 212-214, 253, 254, 279-281, 299, 300.
——, Col. William, 146, 181, 185, 196, 205, 206, 258, 265. 266, 272-275, 279, 280, 286-289, 300, 306, 313, 315, 319. 328, 330, 341, 343, 344, 351, 355, 358, 360, 367, 413, 415, 416, 418, 420, 433, 434, 436. 437; wounded, 294, 296 ; sketch, 428, 429 ; *Journal*, 113, 114, 236, 281-291, 236, 339, 340, 344; letters by, 181-184. 191, 212-214, 236-238, 253-257, 299; Orderly-Book, 281, 313-360; papers, 313, 346 ; report, 315 ; plan of march, 283, 285, 358, 360.
—— family, 65.
Flinn, ——, killed by Indians, 325.
——, Chloe, captured by Indians 325, 326.
Flintham, John, 403.
Fliping, Thomas, sergeant, 409.
Floyd, Benjamin Rush, 316.
——, Capt. John, 32, 42, 50, 112-119, 137, 143, 144, 157, 170, 171, 188, 205, 301, 310, 342, 363; surveyor, 8, 9, 23, 24, 111, 122-127, 129-132, 137, 151 ; letters by, 7, 22, 23, 163-168, 206-208, 214, 215, 266-269 ; sketch, 9.
——, John, Jr., 9.
Fontaine, Charles D., 291.
——, Patrick H., colonel, 291.
Forbes, ——, 99.

Forbes, Gen. John, 2, 11, 48, 68, 113, 276, 373, 426, 428.
Forney, Peter. See Torney.
Forts: Bell's Meadows, 63 ; Big Crab Orchard, see Whitton's; Black, 75 ; Blackburn's, 133 ; Blackmores, 85, 157, 172, 210, 211, 217, 218, 220, 229, 232, 234, 240, 244, 245, 252, 279 ; Blair, 310, sketch, 310 ; Burke's 140 ; Byrd, 12, 85, 88, 100, see also Moore's ; Castle's Woods, 2 ; Chiswell, 52, 79, 89, 106, 163 ; Christian (Smith's), 85, 88, 194, 404 ; Clover Lick, 273 ; Cowan's, 80; Culbertson's, 100, 235 ; Dickenson, 39 ; Dunmore, 35, 37, 62, 68, 86, 97, 99, 101, 186, 197, 380, 390 ; Elk Garden, 194, 197, 229, 234, 252, 401, 404 ; English, 38 ; Fincastle, 86, 103, 155 ; Glade Hollow, 194, 234, 402 ; Gower, 191, 302, 308, 311 ; Greenbrier, 160 ; Henry, 86 ; King's, 210 ; Lexington, 344 ; Long Island (Tenn.), 75 ; Loudon, 375 ; Maiden Spring, 194, 203, 234, 401, 403, 404 ; Maxwell's Mill, 194 ; Moore's (Byrd's), 85, 209, 219, 234 ; Necessity, 426 ; Pitt, 8, 11, 29, 33, 35, 36, 50, 73, 74, 91, 104, 123, 124, 152, 154, 177, 202, 235, 302, 308, 375, 427, 432 ; Pittsburg, 373, 388 ; Preston, 80, 88, 91, 158, 250 ; Randolph, 104, 115, 310, 358, 432 ; Ruddell's, 388 ; Russells, 80, 234 ; Smith's, see Christian ; Spring, 104 ; Stalnaker's, 428 ; Stanwix, 242, 427 ; Stuart's, 189, 281, 282 ; Vause's (Vaux), 65, 428 ; Warm Springs, 273 ; Watauga, 81 ; Wheeling, 37, 62, 86, 302, sketch, 86 ; Whitton's (Big

INDEX

Crab Orchard), 234, 401, 404; Wood's, 141, 176; Young, 360, sketch 360; frontier, 29, 30, 32, 34, 42-45, 49, 57, 62, 67, 71, 79, 83, 88, 95, 105, 117, 197, 208, 216, 234, 335, 351, 352, 364, 380, 401.
Fourgeson, Thomas, 419.
Fowler, James, scout, 230, 231, 263, 333, 337, 338, 404.
——, Samuel, 403.
——, William, 165.
Fox, Nathaniel, 155.
Frankfort (O.), 292.
—— (Va.), 104.
Franklin, Benjamin, 9.
——, James, 407.
——, William, 407, 419.
Franklin, state of, 40, 48, 107, 160, 215, 221, 252.
Frazer, John, 411.
Fredericksburg (Va.), 2.
Freeland, John, 419.
French, 28, 254, 273, 305, 426.
Friel, Jeremiah, 424.
Frogg, John, lieutenant, killed by Indians, 280, 296, 301, 346; sketch, 280, 281.
Fry, George, 398.
——, George, Jr., 398.
——, John, 405.
——, Joshua, colonel, 191.
Fulkison, —, 251.
Fullen, Charles, 399.
——, James, 403.
Fullin, Daniel, 406.
Fuls, George, 405.
Fur-trade, 7, 11, 12, 29, 59, 66, 67, 72, 221, 256, 347, 374, 377, 379, 381, 391.
Fur-traders, 28, 29, 48, 58, 59, 66, 67, 72.

GAGE, Gen. Thomas, 35, 340.
Gardner, Andrew, 410.
Garrett, William, 421.
Gasper's Lick, 51, 81. See also Mansco Lick.

Gass, David, sketch, 173.
Gatliff (Gatleph), Squire, 235, 397.
Gauley (Va.), 198, 282, 318.
Georgetown (Ky.), 131.
Georgia, constitutional convention, 160.
Gekelemupechunk.. See Newcomerstown.
Genet, Edmond Charles, expedition, 225.
Germans, 36, 79.
Germantown, battle of, 160, 191, 197.
Gibson, Lieut. George, 160, 424.
——, Col. John, fur-trader, 11, 15, 17, 290, 303, 305, 356, 411; sketch, 11.
——, Joseph, 406.
Gilberts, Thomas, 407.
Gilihan, John, 399.
Gilkeson, James, 411.
Gill, Prisley, 406.
Gillespy, Thomas, 410.
Gilliss, William, 411.
Gilmer, George R., *First Settlers of Upper Georgia*, 160, 274, 281.
Gilmore, Capt. James, 224, 406, 414, 415.
——, John, 406, 424.
Girty, Simon, 152, 154, 285; sketch, 152.
Gist, Christopher, 57, 133.
Givens, —, lieutenant, 349.
Glascum, David, 419.
Glass, Samuel, sergeant, 408.
——, William, 411.
Glaves, Michael, 403.
Glen, Thomas, 7, 116.
Glenn, Davis, 421.
Goff, Andrew, 412.
Goldman, Edward, lieutenant, 276, 280, 288, 289, 306, 344, 355, 411, 435.
Goldsby, —, 437.
Goodall, John, 405.
Gordon, Moses, 399.

INDEX 453

Gormon, David, 398.
Graham (Grayum), Benjamin, 412.
Grand Rapids (Mich.), 423.
Grant, Alexander, 403.
Gray, Benjamin, 277, 297.
——, Joseph, 180.
Grayson, —, 179.
Greathouse, Daniel, 10, 15–17, 19, 378.
Great Levels of Greenbrier, 185, 190, 414. See also, Levels of Greenbrier.
Great Meadows, battle of, 191.
Green, —, 259.
——, John, 172.
Green Township (O.), 290.
Greenbrier (Va.), 23, 36, 56, 103, 104, 358, 410, 432.
Greene, Gen. Nathaniel, 25, 45, 160.
Greenwood, —, 360.
Grenadier Squaw, 308.
Grenadier Squaw's Town, 290, 301.
Griffin, Robert, 396.
Grigger, Michael, 399.
——, Peter, 399.
Grigs, John, 406.
Grigsby, John, 405.
Grim, John, 424; *Recollections*, 308.
Grinup, John, 404.
Guffy, James, 411.
Guilford Court House, battle of, 25, 43, 331.
Guillin, James M., 407.
Gullion. See Ogullion.
Gurden, Michael, 405.

HACKETT, Thomas, 397.
Hackworth, Augustine, 409.
——, William, 409.
Haggerty, Patrick, 421.
Hains, Capt. —, 331.
Haldemand, Gen. Frederick, 393; letter to, 394; sketch, 393; *Papers*, 394.

Hale, Edward, 398.
——, John P., *Trans-Allegheny Pioneers*, 46, 64, 101, 180, 270, 326, 422.
——, Thomas, 398.
——, William, 398.
Hall, James, 406.
Hamilton (Hambleton), —, 80, 188, 319.
——, Francis, 400, 404.
——, Isaiah, 400, 404.
——, Jacob, 400.
——, James, 131, 424.
——, John, 403.
——, Jonathan, 193.
——, Thomas, 400.
Hammond, Philip, 320, 358, 408, 424.
Hamrick, Thomas, 409.
——, William, 409.
Hard, Gen. Edward H., 104.
Handley (Herrill), Robert, 412.
—— (Hensley), Samuel, 399, 412, 422.
Hanee, Philip, 411.
Hannastown (Pa.), 42.
Hanover (Va.), 22, 23, 307.
Hansburger, Adam, 105.
Hanson, Thomas, 120, 129; *Journal*, 7, 32, 39, 110–133, 338.
——, William, 407.
Hardin, John, 155.
——, John, Jr., 421.
—— county (Ky.), 197.
Hardy, —, 112.
Harlan, Elijah, 421.
——, Silas, 420.
Harmon, Adam, pioneer, 70.
——, Dangerfield, 411.
——, George, 405.
——, Israel, 70, 229.
——, Jacob, 70.
——, John, 411.
Harrel, William, scout, 4.
Harriman, Skid., sergeant, 410.
Harris, Griffin, 407.
——, John, 410.
——, Stephen, 406.

INDEX

Harrison, —, 230, 231.
——, Andrew, 411.
——, Benjamin, killed by Indians, 230.
——, Capt. Benjamin, 205, 272, 286, 331, 341, 414, 416; sketch, 272.
——, Daniel, 272.
——, John, lieutenant, 421.
——, Peachy R., 272.
—— family, 230.
Harrisonburg (Va.), 272.
Harrod, Capt. James, 32, 68, 108, 109, 136, 144, 189, 317, 363, 420; sketch, 108.
——, Capt. William, 121, 12f, 201, 202; letters to, 101, 102, 395, 396; receipt by, 68; receipt to, 103; sketch, 68.
Harrodsburg (Ky.), 68, 108, 109, 111, 131, 207.
Hart, —, Indian agent, 48.
——, Thomas, 422.
Hartness, —, killed by Indians, 374.
Hatfield, Andrew, 398.
Havens, James, 399.
——, John, 399.
Hayes, John, 424.
Haynes, Benjamin, 422.
——, Capt. Joseph, 414, 416, 435.
Hays, Charles, 397.
——, Samuel, scout, 404.
Haywood, John, *Tennessee,* 377.
Head, Anthony, 252.
Heath (Heth), William, lieutenant, 421.
Heckwelder, J. G. E., *Indian Nations,* 381; *Narrative of Missions of United Brethren,* 381.
Hedden, Thomas, 406.
Hedges, Silas, 421.
Hedrick, Peter, 400.
Helm, Leonard, 421.
Helphinstone, Capt. Peter, 421.
Hempinstall, Abraham, 172.
Henderson, Alexander, 404.
——, Daniel, 400, 404.

——, John, lieutenant, 24, 48, 207, 400, 408, 424.
——, Samuel, 400.
Hendrix, Peter, 408.
Henly, George, 400.
——, William, 400.
Henry, Anne, 206.
——, John, wounded by Indians, 192, 202, 232, 233.
——, Patrick, 6, 40, 59, 86, 118, 161, 191, 206, 242, 266, 430; letter to, 291–295.
——, Susanna, 59.
——, William, 118.
Henshaw, William, 425.
Hensley. See Handley.
Herbert, Capt. William, 44, 59, 135, 137, 144, 145, 159, 162, 177, 189, 193, 194, 205, 241, 250, 316, 317, 319, 351, 352, 361, 363, 364, 366, 367, 412, 417, 419, 420; sketch, 44.
Herd, Richard, 397.
Herrill. See Handley.
Hickman, —, 424.
Higgins (Higans), Peter, 406.
——, Philemon, 400.
Hildreth, S. P., 9; *Pioneer History,* 285, 302.
Hill, Capt. —, 188.
——, James, 94.
——, Robert, 409.
—— Town, 309.
Hinkson (Hinkston), Maj. John, 387; sketch, 387, 388.
Hite, Col. Abraham, sketch, 31.
——, Abraham, Jr., letter from, 31, 32; sketch, 32.
——, Capt. Isaac, 32, 111, 116, 117, 122, 123, 125, 127, 131; sketch, 32.
——, Joist, 31.
Hixson, W. D., 111, 121, 420.
Hoagland, Capt. Henry, 155, 156, 421.
Hobbs, Vincent, 229.
Hoffman, John, 421.
Hogan, Henry, 421.

INDEX

Hogan, William, 410.
Hogg, Capt. Peter, 65.
——, Thomas, 23, 24, 114, 151, 338.
Holder, ——, defeat of (1782), 174.
Holley, William, 411.
Holloway (Holliway), Richard, 116, 412.
Holmes, George F., 111.
Holston, Stephen, 411.
—— (Va.), 3, 38, 48, 50, 59, 72, 75, 81, 82, 108, 127, 146, 194, 209, 232, 251, 270; troops from, 136, 159.
Holwell, Walter, 409.
Homes, Lewis, 411.
Hooper, William, 407.
Hopton, Stephen, 400.
——, William, 400.
Horn, ——, 165.
Horne, Joseph, 396, 402.
Horse-head Bottom, 304.
Hot Springs (Va.), 261, 284, 423.
Howard, Charles, 411.
——, Henry, 409.
Howards, ——, 27.
Howe, Henry, *Ohio*, 155.
——, John, 304.
Huchisen, William, 411.
Huff, Leonard, 408.
——, Peter, sergeant, 408.
——, Samuel, 263, 408.
——, Thomas, 408, 419.
Hughes, David, 180.
——, Ellis, 424.
Hughey, Joseph (James), 271, 412.
Humphries, John, 201, 397.
Hundley, John, 408.
Hunter, Robert, 398.
Hunters, 26, 72, 123, 376.
Hutchins, Thomas, maps, 58.
Hutson, John, 411.
Hynes, Francis, 404.

ILLINOIS campaign, 6, 8, 102, 197, 225, 304.
Indiana territory, 11, 196.

Ingles, Mary, captured by Indians, 70, 179.
——, Thomas, 179; sketch, 179, 180.
——, Col. William, 101, 146, 179, 188, 317, 318, 320, 337, 339, 340, 349, 350, 352; letter by, 257-259; sketch, 101.
Ingles's Ferry, 65, 76, 101, 149.
Inglis, Joshua, 200.
Inglish. See English.
Innes, Henry, letters, 246.
Ireland, 101, 214, 220, 225, 239, 276, 612, 348, 426, 429, 430.
Irish, 111, 160, 387.
Iroquois Indians, 28, 33. See Six Nations.
"Iroquois of the Ohio," 28.
Irvine, John, 400.
Islands: Bahamas, 426; Big, 5; Great, 217, 218, 226; Gwynn's, 425, Long, 75; Mann, 429; Moccasin, 73; Oppony, 119; West Indies, 206; Wheeling, 11.
Isum, William, 408.

JACKSON, Francis, 319.
——, Yenty, 405.
Jacob, John J., *Life of Cresap*, 7, 8, 10, 155, 306, 374.
Jameson, John, 403.
Jedborough (Scotland), 428.
Jefferson, Thomas, 242, 305; *Notes on Virginia*, 9, 10, 12, 246, 305.
Jefferson County (Ky.), 32, 124, 197.
Jeffersonville (Ky.), 234.
Jenkins, Jeremiah, 411.
Jennings, Edmond, 422.
Jewitt, Matthew, 409.
Joanes, John Litton, captain, letter to, 146, 147.
Johns, William, 406.
Johnson, Capt. ——, 425.
——, Sir William, 7.
Johnston, John, 400.

Johnston, Patrick, 399.
Jolly, Henry, judge, 9.
Jones, Capt. —, 183, 221, 310.
——, Benjamin, 396, 401, 402.
——, Gabriel, 28.
——, John, 406, 407, 424.
——, Thomas, 401.
——, William, 408, 410.

KANAWHA & Michigan Railway, 357.
Kasheday, Peter, 406.
Kaskaskia, capture of, 225, 344.
Keener, —, killed by Indians, 36.
Keeneson, Charles, 410.
Keightughqua. See Cornstalk.
Keith, Samuel, 94.
Kelley, Alexander, 408.
——, Gerrott, 409.
Kelly, Walter, killed by Indians, 104, 109, 112, 306, 309.
Kelly's Place, 181, 284, 325, 357.
Kelsey, John, 406.
Kendrick, James, 396.
Kennedy, Ezekiel, 406.
——, Thomas, 408.
—— (Canady, Kenedy), William, sergeant, 409 411.
Kennerly, William, sergeant, 160.
Kennison, Charles, 424.
——, Edward, 424.
Kennot, Zachariah, 409.
Kent, —, 180.
Kenton, Simon, 285, 424.
Kentucky, 2, 7, 25, 31, 42, 51, 64, 78, 82, 88, 107, 108, 111, 114, 120, 121, 126, 136, 164, 168, 174, 196, 206, 207, 215, 220, 225, 239, 240, 269, 272, 273, 280, 309, 344, 374, 429; military lands, 75; surveys, 7; early settlements, 4, 32, 420; pioneers, 6, 21, 23, 27, 32, 182, 276.
Kentucky County (Ky.), 44, 344.
Kercheval, Samuel, *History of the Valley of Virginia*, 374, 422.

Kerr, James, 420.
—— (Keer), William, 409.
Kinder, George, 399.
——, Jacob, 399, 404.
——, Peter, 399, 404.
Kindherook (Va.), 79.
Kinders, Gasper, sketch, 79.
King, Edward, 16.
——, James, 411.
——, John, 399.
——, William, 399, 404.
King's Meadows (Tenn.), 49.
—— Mill (Tenn.), 210, 251, 252.
—— Mountain, battle of, 39, 43, 44, 55, 70, 75, 84, 85, 107, 214, 221, 236, 252, 271, 431.
Kingsport (Tenn.), 252.
Kinkead (Kincaid, Kingkeid, Kinkaid), —, captain, 202.
——, David, 402.
——, David, Jr., 396.
——, George, 411.
——, James, 411.
——, John, sergeant, 194, 228, 229, 241, 244, 396, 402, 404.
——, Samuel, lieutenant, 37.
Kinson, Charles, 419.
Kinsor, Jacob, 399.
——, Michael, 399.
——, Walter, 399.
Kirkendall (Kuykendall), —, 421.
Kishioner, —, 422.
Kissinger, Andrew, 408.
——, Matthias, 409.
Klendenning. See Clendennin.
Knox, James, scout, 127, 267, 304; sketch, 111, 239.
Knoxville (Tenn.), 252.
Koquethagechton, Delaware chief, 29.

LAFAYETTE, Marquis de, 43, 272.
Lafayette (Va.), 65.
Lake Erie, 39.
Lammey, Andrew, 230, 231, 403.
Lancaster (Pa.), 11.

INDEX 457

Lands, surveys, 2, 3, 5, 8, 24, 79, 120, 121, 123–126, 128–131, 151, 173, 195, 205, 231; patents, 276; grants, 5, 8, 21, 22, 63, 67, 75, 152, 242, 270, 274, 368, 370, 371, 391.
Lapsly, John, 406.
Lard, —, lieutenant, 276, 280, 288, 289, 296.
Larken, John, sergeant, 406.
Lashly, John, 404.
Laughlin, James, 401.
Lawrence, Henry, 410.
Lebanon (Va.), 194.
Lee, Alfred E., *City of Columbus, Ohio*, 304.
———, Hancock, captain, 120, 122, 155.
———, Sefniah, 405.
———, Zacarias, 405.
Lemaster, Richard, 411.
Lemmey, Samuel, captured by Indians, 202.
Lesey, William, 397.
Lesly, John, 400.
Lessly, William, 94.
Levels of Allsup, 178.
Levils of Greenbrier, 104, 147, 148, 176, 181, 201, 212, 213, 222, 257, 266, 267, 306, 309, 315, 318, 335, 359.
Lewis, Agatha, 280.
———, Gen. Andrew, 19, 31, 32, 38, 51, 62, 74, 98, 112, 114, 138, 146, 149, 183, 196, 197, 199, 207, 236, 253, 254, 256, 260–263, 266, 267, 269, 270, 272–274, 281, 282, 284, 286–291, 293, 295, 297, 302, 303, 307, 308, 312, 330–332, 340, 347, 348, 350, 351, 355, 356, 361, 383–385, 413, 417, 418, 422, 425, 426, 428, 435, 436 : letters by, 38, 87, 88, 97, 149, 190–192, 223, 267 ; letters to, 86, 87, 91, 97, 98, 145 ; manuscripts, 415 ; sketch, 426–428.
———, Andrew, Jr., colonel, 310.
———, Col. Charles, 74, 98, 104, 167, 177, 181, 183, 185, 186, 188, 196, 240, 253, 255, 258, 265, 272, 274, 275, 280, 282, 284–289, 293, 296, 301, 311, 312, 314, 317, 319, 321–323, 331, 341, 343, 346, 355, 358, 385, 407, 414, 416, 427, 433, 434, 436–439 ; letter by, 73, 74 ; sketch, 74, 75, 97.
———, Charles H., 436.
———, Capt. John (of Augusta), 74, 272, 414, 416, 427 ; sketch, 272.
———, Capt. John (of Botetourt), 274, 285, 315, 330, 334, 342, 343, 408, 413, 415, 417–419 ; sketch, 274.
———, John, private, 400, 401.
———, Samuel 424.
———, Thomas, 175, 272, 280, 347, 424 ; letter by, 311, 312 ; sketch, 312.
———, V. A., *History of West Virginia*, 422.
Lewisburg (Va.), 104, 181, 432.
Lexington (Ky.), 344.
Lin, Adam, 409.
Lincoln County (Ky.), 44, 187, 270, 348.
Linn, William, 155, 421.
Lister, John, 94.
———, Samuel, 94.
Little Carpenter, Cherokee, chief, 48, 375.
Litton, Burton, 396.
———, Solomon, 402.
Litz, William, 400.
Lloyd, Dr. —, 219.
Lockhart, Jacob, 410.
———, Queavy, 410.
Lockheart, Patrick, 182, 184, 276
Lockridge, Capt. Andrew, 272, 273, 331, 351, 352, 367, 414, 416, 419, 420 ; sketch, 272, 273.
Logan, Gen. Benjamin, 81, 82, 111, 239, 251 ; sketch, 82.
———, Hugh, 406.

INDEX

Logan, James, 305, 406.
—— (Shikellimo, Indian Tachwechdorus), Capt. John, 11–16, 36, 37, 107, 153, 158, 239; letters by, 246, 249, 260; sketch, 13, 305, 306.
Logan's Station (Ky.), 82.
Logstown (Pa.), 430.
Long, David, captain, letter to, 147, 148.
——, Joseph, ensign, 424.
Long Hunters, 51, 78, 111, 239, 374.
Long Island (Tenn.), 75, 225, 226.
Long Island Flats, battle of, 47, 107.
"Long Knives." 12, 13.
Lorton, Jacob, 180, 298.
Louisville (Ky.), 39, 197, 207, 430.
Loyalists, 101, 220, 221, 375, 431.
Love, Joseph, 408.
——, Patsy, 274.
——, Capt. Philip, 149, 195, 199, 273, 286, 315, 330, 334, 341, 359, 407, 413, 415–419.
—— family, 273.
Luallen, Thomas, 94.
Lucas, Charles, 398.
——, Charles, Jr., 398.
——, John, 398.
——, Robert, lieutenant, 148.
——, William, 398.
Luney, Michael, 411.
Lybrook, Balser, killed by Indians, 134, 140, 398.
——, Henry, 398.
—— (Librough) family, massacre of, 398.
Lyhnam, Richard, 400.
Lyle, John, 424.
Lyn, James, 411.
Lynch, ——, 3.
Lyons, William, 406.

McAfee, George, pioneer, 207.
——, James, pioneer, 207.
——, Robert, pioneer, 207.
——, Samuel, 207.
——, William, 207.
—— family, 23; papers, 420.
McAfee's Station (Ky.), 207.
McAllister, J. T., 261, 423.
—— (McColister, Micalister), William, 409, 411.
McAnore, James, 263.
McBride, James, 409.
——, Joseph, 406.
McCalister, James, 406.
McCall, James, sketch, 109.
——, Joseph, 177.
McCandless, John, 410.
McCarmick (McCormack), ——, 201, 202, 277.
McCartney, John, 399.
McCarty, James, 402.
McCaslen, William, 411.
McClanahan, Absalom, 409.
——, Capt. Alexander, 160, 161, 331, 342, 414, 416, 427.
——, John, canoe-man, 409.
——, Capt. Robert, 160, 274, 275, 280, 288, 289, 296, 301, 315, 321, 330, 334, 344, 346, 349, 355, 410, 413, 415, 417, 418, 435, 437.
McClelland's Station (Ky.), 130.
McClung, William, 358.
McClure, Capt. Francis, killed by Indians, 37.
——, John, 406.
——, Thomas, 406.
McConn, James, Jr., 207.
McCorkle, William, 125, 406.
McCoy, William, 349; sketch, 349.
——, William, lieutenant, 349, 410.
McCra, Roderick, 111, 125, 126, 128, 129.
McCulloch, William, fur-trader, 119, 256; sketch, 256.
McCune, William, 424.
McCutcheon, William, 424.
McDonald, Major Angus, letters by, 151–154, 395, 396; sketch,

INDEX 459

152, 153; Wakatomica expedition, 13, 19, 87, 154, 155, 183, 184, 186, 220. 304. 382.
McDonald, Daniel, 407.
——, James, 407.
McDowell, Archibald, 410.
——, John, 25.
——, Capt. M., 414, 416.
——, Samuel, captain, 25, 26, 161, 328, 331; sketch, 25.
McElhaney, Francis, 407.
McFarland, —, 424.
——, William, 396.
McFarling, Robert, scout, 352.
McFerran, Martin, sketch, 184.
McGee. John, 406.
McGeehey, Samuel, 94.
McGinness, John, 407.
McGlahlen, John, 409.
McGriff, John, 398.
——, Patrick, 398.
McGriffs, John, 140.
McGuffin, John, 111.
McGuire, John, wounded by Indians, 186, 282.
McIlwreath, Jean, "Sir Frederick Haldimand," 393.
McIntosh, —, campaign, 272.
McKee, Alexander, 364.
——, Capt. William, 33, 74, 152. 406, 419; sketch, 348.
McKinney, John, 422.
McKinsey, Henley, 398.
——, Mordock, 398.
McLaughlin, Edward, 424.
McMullin, John, 419.
McMullen. William. 248.
McNeal (Niel), John, 410, 424.
——. Peter, 406.
McNiell. Daniel, lieutenant, 359, 407. 421.
McNitt. James. 409.
McNutt, Alexander. 422.
McRoberts. Samuel, 184.
Madison, Capt. —, 65, 179, 180, 307.
——, George. 280.
——. Gov. George, 59.
——, James, 59.
——, James, bishop, 280.
——, James, president, 59, 236, 280.
——, John, letters by, 59, 279– 281; sketch, 280.
——, Rowland, 280.
——, Thomas, 280.
——, Capt. Thomas, 59, 439; sket●h, 59.
—— County (Ky.), 23, 173.
Magazine of American History, 104, 286, 309; *of Western History,* 368.
Magee, William, 229.
Manadue, Henry, 401, 402.
Manifield, —, 179.
Mann, John, 398.
——, Thomas, killed by Indians, 374.
——, William, 263, 264, 409.
Mansco, Kasper, 51.
Mansco's Lick (Tenn.), 51.
Mares, Alexander, 106.
——, John, 229.
——, Joseph, 106, 229.
Marion (Va.), 40, 261.
Markes, John, 407.
Martin, —, killed by Indians, 155, 374.
——, Brice, 422.
——, Christian, 398.
——, George, 398.
——, George, Jr., 398, 399.
——, Capt. Joseph. 4, 234, 235; letters to, 247, 248, 298, 299, 434; sketch, 235.
——, Philip, 398.
——, Col. William, 420, 434, 437, 439.
Martinsburg (Va.), 191.
Maryland, 12. 42, 48, 84, 158, 270, 376, 377, 393. 396: *Gazette,* 8; *Journal,* 28, 155.
Mason, —, 233.
—— County (Ky.), 7, 21, 120.
Masdin (Mastin), Thomas, 100, 101, 110, 139.
Matthews. Capt. George. 160, 177, 188, 196, 223, 274, 276,

INDEX

309, 367, 414, 416, 436, 437; sketch, 160.
Matthews, Sampson, colonel, 223, 331, 342; sketch, 223.
Max Meadows (Va.), 52.
Maxwell, Bezaleel, 400, 412.
——, David, 400.
——, James, captain, 69, 70.
——, John, 399.
——, Thomas, 70, 229, 404; sketch, 70.
May, John, 21, 119; sketch, 21.
Mayer, Brantz, *Logan and Cresap*, 115, 304, 306.
May's Lick (Ky.), 21.
Mayse (Maze), Joseph, 422.
Maysville (Ky.), 21, 420.
McAdoo, William, 229.
Mead, Nicholas, sergeant, 409.
——, Thomas, 399, 404.
Meader, Israel, 405.
Mecrary, Thomas, 411.
Meek, William, sergeant, 399.
Meeks, Guy, killed by Indians, 374.
Mercer, Dr. Hugh, 121; letter by, 1; sketch, 2.
—— County (Ky.), 207.
Messersmith, Barnet, 399.
——, John, 399.
Middlesborough (Ky.), 40.
Milican, John, 406.
Miller, James, 405.
——, Robert, 400.
Mills, John, ensign, 407.
Milwood, George, 406.
Miner, Henry, 405.
Mingo (Andastes) Indians, 28, 30, 36, 37, 74, 103, 124, 149, 156, 237, 273, 302-304, 308, 309, 346, 347, 435, 436.
Mississippi, 180, 374.
Missouri, 168.
Mitchell, Capt. ——, 421.
——, James, 400, 404.
——, Thomas, 400.
Moffat (Mauford), Capt. Robert, 404, 414, 416.
——, Capt. George, sketch, 331.
Mobile, 375.
Money, Holton, 106, 229.
——, Samuel, 229.
Monroe, James, president, 270.
Montgomery, Capt. James, 65.
——, Col. James, 65.
——, John, 220, 226; letter by, 224, 225; sketch, 225.
—— (Mt. Gumry), Samuel, 407.
—— family, 65.
—— County, (Mo.), 276.
Montour, John, 302.
Montreal, 426.
Moody, John, 421.
Moon, Abraham, 407.
Mooney, James, 271, 272, 328.
——, Nicholas, 406.
Moore, Capt. ——, 437.
——, Sergt. ——, 234.
——, Frederick, 400.
——, Hendly, ensign, 402.
——, Hugh, 406.
——, John, 406, 424.
——, Moses, 399.
——, Samuel, 399.
——, Tabitha, 434.
——, William, 85, 406, 422.
Moorefield (W. Va.), 31.
Moravian missionaries, 28, 36, 153, 381.
Morgan, Gen. Daniel, 111, 155, 196, 239, 421.
Morris, William, 419, 421.
Morrison, ——, 11, 12.
Morrow, James, 411.
——, James, Jr., 411.
Moundsville (W. Va.), 36.
Mountains: Alleghany, 97, 150, 156, 242, 284, 323, 360: Blue Ridge, 24, 58, 86, 176; Chestnut Ridge, 322, 323, 358;. Clinch, 60, 226, 231; Cumberland, 53, 133, 242; Gauley, 112, 284, 323, 357, 358; Iron, 232; Muddy Creek, 319; North, 360; Powells, 158; Rich Creek, 111, 188, 397; Rocky Ridge, 241, 242; Stony Hills, 140;

INDEX 461

Toms Creek, 188; Walker's, 79; Yellow, 38.
Mounts, Ab., 106.
Mullin, Thomas, 396.
Mungle (Mongle), Daniel, 412.
——, Frederick, 412.
Murphy, Cherokee Indian, 278.
——, Samuel, 285, 421.
Murray, Capt. John, 275, 280, 288, 289, 296, 301, 315, 330, 334, 344, 346, 348, 349, 355; sketch, 275.
——, Capt. John, 406, 413, 415, 417, 418, 424, 435, 437.
Murtory, Joseph, 259.
Muster-rolls, 55, 273, 276, 352, 396-412, 420-425.
Myers, Capt. Michael, 17, 18, 19; sketch, 17.
—— (Myres), William, 421.

NAIL, Dennis, 408.
——, Thomas, 406.
Nakatomakee, destroyed, 184.
Nalle, Martin, lieutenant, 405.
—— (Nawl, Naul, Nalls), Capt. William, 405, 414, 415; sketch, 405.
Nash, William, surveyor, 7, 116, 119, 127-131.
Nashville (Tenn.), 51, 271.
Nave, Conrad, 412.
Neal, William, 106, 396.
Neaville, John, 421.
——, Joseph, 421.
Neely, James, cadet, 406, 407.
——, William, 406.
Negroes, captured by Indians, 209, 220, 232, 238, 240, 245, 274, 305, 309, 373, 375, 379.
Neil, John, 400.
Nelson, John, 406.
——, Thomas, sketch, 241.
——, Thomas, Jr., 242.
——, William, sketch, 242.
Nelsonville (O.), 302.
Newa, Indian hostage, 305.
Newbern (Va.), 55.
Newberry, Joseph, 400.

Newburgh (O), 17, 18.
Newcomerstown (Gekelemupechunk, O.), 36.
New Dublin (Va.), 46, 63.
Newell, James, 179, 316, 419; Journal, 319, 327, 339, 341, 350, 361-367, 435.
——, Samuel, lieutenant, 364; sketch, 214, 215.
New Inverness (Ga.), 375.
New Jersey, 28, 191.
Newland, Abram, 412.
——, Isaac, 412.
——, John, 403.
Newman, Walter, 424.
Newport (Ky.), 120.
New Providence (Pa.), 27.
New Orleans, 23, 42, 82, 111, 131, 207.
New York (city), 12, 160, 369, 393.
New York (state), 28, 425; Colonial Documents, 10, 11, 377.
Nicholas, John, 397.
Nicholson, Joseph, 12, 154, 285.
——, Thomas, scout, 13, 285.
Nickajack campaign, 225.
Nickels, Isaac, 408.
Niles' Register, 270.
Norfolk (Va.), 206, 425.
North Bend (O.), 121.
North Carolina, 38, 49, 65, 72, 106, 169, 220-222, 270-272.
North Mountain (Va.), 81.
Northwest Territory, 392.
Nowell, John, 399.
Nuland, John, 400.
Null, Jacob, 405.
——, John, 405.

OCONASTOTA, Cherokee chief, 38, 212, 221; sketch, 38.
Odear, James, 397.
Oglethorpe, ——, 375.
Ogullion, Barnett, 399, 412.
——, Duncan, 399, 422.
——, John, 399.
——, Hugh, 412.

O'Haara, Charles, sergeant, 410.
——, Robert, 410.
——, William, 410.
Oharron, Henry, 397.
Ohio Company, 12; expedition, 64, 78, 80, 92, 158, 172, 213, 222, 223, 281, 291, 297, 313, 315, 317, 324, 325, 368; Indians, 80, 84, 85. 101, 153, 243, 255, 256, 262, 263, 281, 315, 317, 380, 391; Arch and Hist. Soc. *Publications*, 12.
Oldtown (Md.), 185, 393.
Olverson, Joseph, 396.
Oneida Indians, 13, 305.
Onondaga Indians, 154.
Ormsbey, Daniel, 407.
Ottawa Indians, 273, 284, 346, 347.
Overstreet, William, 409.
Owen, Thomas, 409.
Owens, David, 152, 153.
Owler, Henry, 405.
——, John, 405.
Owen, Robert, 407.

PACK, George, 201, 397.
——, Samuel, 397.
Packwood, Richard, 408.
Pain, Joseph, 407.
Parchment, Peter, 285, 421.
Paris (Ky.), 388.
Parkman, Francis, *Half Century of Conflict*, 246.
Parsons, James, 421.
Pate, ——, 180.
——, Jacob, 180.
——, Jeremiah, 94.
Patten, John, 411.
Patton, David, 229.
——, Col. James, 43, 65, 139, 141, 231, 242, 431.
—— family, 65.
Pauling, Capt. Henry, 187, 274, 276, 296, 315, 321, 330, 334, 335, 340, 351, 411, 413, 415, 416, 418, 429, 436; sketch, 187.

Paulley, James, 410.
——, John, 410.
Pawlings, Moses, 396.
Paxton, Samuel, 328, 400, 403.
Peary, Thomas, 406.
Pendleton, Col. Edmund, sketch, 242.
Penee, Jacob, ensign, 405.
Penn, Capt. Abraham, 248, 252, 298, 299; letter by, 234, 235; sketch, 235.
——, Gov. John, 387, 390-393, 395.
Pennsylvania, 2, 7, 25, 28, 30, 42, 67, 81, 101, 108, 114, 115, 152, 156, 173, 202, 343, 372, 376, 382, 387, 389, 391, 392; *Archives*, 29, 37, 67, 86, 97, 153, 155, 306, 372, 381, 387, 388, 390; *Colonial Records*, 387; *Gazette*, 36, 37, 66, 87, 295.
Pensacola (Fla.), 111, 373.
Pentecost, Capt. Dorsey, 101, 102, 201, 202; letter by, 102; sketch, 101, 102.
Pepper family, 65.
Perce, Thomas, 407.
Peregin, Molastin, 409.
Persinger, Jacob, 422.
Petty, Benjamin, 405.
Peyton, John Lewis, *History of Augusta County, Virginia*, 422.
Pharis, William, 402.
Pharo, ——, 328.
Philadelphia, 242, 305, 311, 390, 391.
Philips, Capt. ——, sketch, 31.
Pickaway Plains (O.), 290, 301.
Pierce, ——, lieutenant, 194.
——, John, 399.
Piqua campaign, 197, 207.
Pittsburg, 1, 7, 8, 10, 12, 14, 28, 31, 37, 42, 51, 87, 99, 152, 156, 183, 380-382, 392.
Plain Facts, 368.
Pluggy's Town (O.), 306.
Plunkepel, Zacarias, 405.

INDEX 463

Poage, William, sergeant, 234, 250.
Point Pleasant, 245, 261, 291, 303, 304, 306–308, 310, 319, 339, 340, 345–349, 351–353, 362, 364–367, 417, 418, 420, 423, 433, 436; battle of, 6, 9, 43, 47, 48, 55, 56, 75, 78, 82, 101, 104, 106, 108, 115, 120, 158, 160, 168, 180, 223, 225, 236, 253–259, 269–277, 305, 313, 345, 363, 402, 428–431.
Polke, Edmund, 68.
Polug, Mathew, 408.
Pontiac, Ottawa chief, 273.
Pontotoc (Miss.), 291.
Poors, Peter, 64.
Port Republic (Va.), 280.
Porter, Robert, 400.
Posey, Thomas, commissary, 314–316, 318, 350; sketch, 196.
Potter, Thomas, 403.
Powell, Ambrose, 4.
Presbyterians, 27, 81, 431.
Preston, Elizabeth Patton, 430.
——, John, 174, 430.
——, Lettice, 27.
——, M. L., 261.
——, Margaret, 27, 174.
——, Robert, receipt to, 174; sketch, 174.
——, Col. William, 2, 3, 27, 32, 45, 57, 87, 110, 115, 123, 125, 134, 189, 279, 281, 235, 363, 430, 432; advertisement, 8; letters by, 24–26, 52–55, 59–61, 91–93, 95–97, 106–108, 127, 133, 145–148, 151, 161, 162, 203, 241–243, 247, 248, 270, 291–295, 298, 299; letters to, 1–3, 7, 9, 19–21, 26, 30, 31, 35, 38–51, 55–58, 61–66, 69–85, 87–91, 94, 95, 98–101, 103–106, 108–110, 135–144, 149, 156–180, 185–188, 190–212, 214–234, 238–240, 244, 246, 248–252, 257–269, 278, 279, 297, 298, 301–312, 397–399; manuscripts, 297; sketch, 430, 431.

Price, James, 396, 402.
——, Michael, 47.
——, Reese, 412, 419.
——, Richard, 396, 402.
——, Thomas, 396, 401, 402.
——, William Thomas, *History of Pocahontas County, Virginia,* 422, 423.
Pricket (Pucket), Drury, 396, 402.
Priest, David, 401, 402.
——, Samuel, 401, 402.
——, William, 401, 404.
Pright, John, 405.
Prince, William, 419.
Princeton, battle of, 2, 191.
Proctor, ——, killed by Indians, 36.
Pryor, ——, scout, 320, 358.
—— (Prior), John, 424.
Puckeshinwa, Indian chief, 347.
Purdie, Alexander, sketch, 295.
Putnam County (O.), 336, 337.

QUINNIMONT (W. Va.), 322.

RAINS, Robert, 405.
Ramsey, Eliza, 206.
——, James G., *History of Tennessee,* 412.
——, Josiah, sketch, 168, 169.
——, Thomas, 168.
Rapp, Frederick, 400.
Ratcliff, William, 94.
——, Matthew, 411.
Raven, Cherokee Indian, 72.
Ravenscroft, Thomas, 421.
Ray, William, 411.
Razor, Michael, 404.
Read, John, ensign, 177, 409.
Reagh, Archibald, 400.
——, John, 400.
Reary, James, 405.
Reburn, John, 408.
Red Hawk, 347.
Rediford, Benjamin, 404.
Redstone Old Fort (Brownsville, Pa.), 12, 37, 50, 156.

Reed, Alexander, 424.
——, James, pioneer, 63.
Reese, Azariah, 421.
Reid, Andrew, 422.
——, Thomas, 411.
Rentfrow, Capt. ——, 149.
Rich Creek (Va.), 199, 201.
Richards, ——, killed by Indians, 374.
Richardson, ——, 143.
——, Benjamin, 400.
——, William, 400.
Richfield (Va.), 149.
Richmond (Va.), 428.
Riley, John, 412.
Rivers: Big Connewagas, 32; Big Sandy, 133, 139, 142, 145; Blue Stone, 56, 57, 69, 70, 77, 99, 109, 110, 139, 140, 217; Buffalo Fork, 321; Bullpasture, 272; Capteen, 16; Catawba, 307; Clinch, 2, 3, 6, 19, 20, 25, 30, 38, 41, 51, 53, 59, 60, 64, 69, 71, 73, 76-78, 80, 82, 83, 85, 88, 89, 100, 133-135, 144, 145, 157, 161, 162, 165, 172, 173, 178, 192, 194, 195, 202, 204, 207, 209, 211, 217-219, 228, 230, 231, 241, 244, 245, 251, 252, 297, 307, 400; Cole, 24, 114, 151, 328, 332, 334, 335; Crab, 114; Cross, 142; Cumberland, 5, 26, 51, 81, 89, 225, 242, 271, 374; Detroit, 152; Dicks, 131, 240; East, 141; Elk, 112, 113, 177, 185, 187, 190, 195, 212, 214, 223, 237, 240, 258, 260, 261, 266, 267, 282, 285, 304, 306, 324, 327-334, 338, 340, 349-351, 357, 374, 415; Floyd's, 126; French Broad, 47, 215, described, 47; Gauley, 320, 324, 333, 357; Gist (Guess), 133; Great Guyandotte, 116; Great Kanawha, 5, 8, 34, 35, 86, 98, 103, 104, 112, 114, 185, 187, 266, 269-271, 284, 285, 291, 292, 295, 301, 306, 336, 337, 370, 385; Great Miami, 121; Green, 78, 239; Greenbrier, 112, 276, 313, 319, 324, 333, 423; Hickson's Fork, 388; Hockhocking, 236, 237, 256, 263, 286, 292, 302, 308, 309; Holston, 5, 20, 38, 39, 41, 43, 44, 47, 48, 53, 56, 58-61, 63, 65, 71, 75, 76, 79, 82-84, 90, 106, 108, 109, 163, 178, 193, 194, 202, 208, 209, 214, 221, 224, 226-228, 230-232, 234, 236, 241, 247, 249, 270, 277, 297, 305; Hurricane Fork, 324; Jackson, 360, 432; James, 103, 360; Kanawha, 22, 24, 42, 62, 67, 223, 237, 257, 261, 277, 322, 324, 327-329, 335, 337, 338, 346, 349, 352, 353, 357, 365, 384, 433; Kentucky, 5, 20, 53, 81, 83, 85, 89, 108, 121-123, 127-129, 132, 173, 195, 208, 242, 297; Laurel Branch, 112; Licking, 51, 88, 108, 388; Little, 149; Little Guyandotte, 7, 22, 116; Little Kanawha, 115, 191, 263; Little Miami, 120; Little Scioto, 304; Louisa, 5, 20, 26, 70, 121, 298; Mad, 306; Maiden Spring Fork, 239; Meadow, 320, 321, 358; Mississippi, 111, 124; Monongahela, 17, 36, 37, 68, 155, 202, 246, 396; Muskingum, 28, 36, 150, 153, 155, 156, 373; New, 22, 23, 26, 42, 44-46, 55, 56, 63, 65, 70, 76, 77, 81, 83, 84, 89, 99, 103, 105, 111-113, 116, 141, 147, 149, 157, 158, 161, 163, 172, 181, 194, 198, 206, 212, 232, 235, 243, 260, 261, 281, 282, 284, 288, 320, 322, 324, 325, 327, 328, 332, 333, 430; Nolichucky, 41, 47, 48, 278; Ohio, 1, 2, 7-12, 17, 21-24, 34, 37, 45, 51, 62, 82-86, 89, 91-93, 97, 98, 103, 104, 108, 110,

INDEX

111, 114, 116, 118, 119, 121, 122, 150, 187, 197, 206, 212, 213, 217, 220, 256-258, 262-265, 267, 268, 274, 275, 282, 285-289, 291, 297, 299, 301, 302, 305, 306, 308-310, 312, 333, 338-350, 353, 361-368, 376-378, 383-386, 434-437, 439; Pocotilico, 114, 328, 335, 336, 357; Potomac, 31, 75, 196; Powell, 133; Roanoke, 65, 74, 149, 301; Salt, 126, 128, 131, 207; Salt Lick, 88; Sandy, 60, 69, 70, 76-78, 80, 85, 89, 204, 232; Scioto, 4, 82-84, 117, 150, 186, 292, 304, 306; Susquehanna, 13, 305; Taylor's Fork, 23; Tellico, 38; Tennessee, 4, 38; Watauga, 38, 48, 271; Yadkin, 220, 272; Youghiogheny, 102, 103, 155.
Roads: Augusta path, 357, 358; Cumberland Gap, 4, 51, 76, 84, 88, 89, 171, 217, 242, 298; Mocassin Gap, 60, 73, 76, 77, 80, 85, 226, 229, 233, 252; Pound Gap, 133; Sandy Creek Pass, 81; Warrior's Path, 4, 89; Wood's Gap, 176.
Roay, Joseph, 405.
Roberts, —, lieutenant, 260, 349.
——, John, 409.
——, John, killed by Indians, 208, 210, 218, 219, 226, 246, 250, 305; sketch, 208.
Robertson, —, pioneer, 38, 51.
—— (Robison), Elijah, 412.
——, James, captain, 44, 76; sketch, 44.
——, James, sergeant, 412.
——, Major James, 176-179, 187, 188, 197, 363, 419; letters by, 94, 95, 99-106, 109, 110, 134, 140-142, 174, 175, 179, 180, 199-201; letter to, 95-97.
——, William, lieutenant, 160, 424, 438.
Robinson, Hugh, 399.
——, James, 271, 407; sketch, 271.
——, Thomas, 177.
——, William, 94, 135.
——, William, captured by Indians, 246; sketch, 246.
Robison, —, 424.
——, Elijah. See Robertson.
——, James, lieutenant, 276, 288, 289, 297, 344, 355.
——, Julius, 412.
——, William, 408.
Rocky Ridge (Va.), 49.
Roe, Capt. —, 349.
Rogers (Rodgers), Andrew, 411.
——, Chesly, 405.
——, David, 421.
——, James, 400, 401, 403.
——, Thomas, 400, 404.
——, William, 165.
Rollens, Richard, 411.
Rome (Tenn.), 434.
Roosevelt, Theodore, *Winning of the West*, 51, 111, 121, 155, 185, 190, 270, 291, 306, 344, 405.
Rosegill (Va.), 87.
Ross, Edward, 411.
——, Tavenor, 272, 422.
—— County (O.), 290, 292.
Round Lick (Tenn.), 434.
Rowan, Francis, 397.
Royal Oak (Va.), 40, 47, 56, 134, 136, 142, 159, 162, 163, 192, 202, 216, 226, 230, 237, 244, 278, 297.
Rucker, George, 405.
Ruddle (Riddle), George, 412.
Rue, Abraham, 405.
Russell, Henry, killed by Indians, 1, 39, 72, 173, 220, 278, 374, 376.
——, Gen. William, 2, 4, 6, 25, 80, 81, 83, 135-137, 143-145, 159, 162, 164, 171, 178, 187, 189, 196, 210, 240, 249, 270, 273, 284, 286, 292, 298, 303, 315, 317, 318, 330, 334,

341, 363, 415-419; letters by, 19-22, 49-51, 88-91, 156-158, 172, 173, 308-311; letters to, 31, 158; sketch, 6.
Russell, Gen. William, Jr., 6.
Rutherford, Benjamin, 400.
Rye Coves (Va.), 3, 133.

St. Asaph's (Ky.), 9, 187.
St. Clair, Gen. Arthur, 37, 387, 392, 393: defeat, 152; letters by, 29, 306; sketch, 392.
St. Lawrence, Patrick, 400, 412.
Salem (Va.), 74, 149, 427.
Salt Licks, 81, 126.
Saltville (W. Va.), 6.
Samples, Samuel, 412.
Sanders, Mrs. Adam, 316.
——, James, 421.
Sandusky (O.), 14, 103.
Sandy Creek expedition, 101, 297, 426, 431.
Santown. See Staunton.
Sapling Grove (Tenn.), 238.
Sappington, Daniel, 9.
——, John, 16, 17, 19.
Saratoga, battle of, 111, 239.
Saulsbury, William, 424.
Saunderson, ——, trader, 29.
Savage, John, 408.
——, Samuel, 407.
Sawyer, ——, 46.
Sawyers, Col. John, 55; sketch, 55.
Sayers, ——, 297.
——, John, 412.
——, William, deputy sheriff, 171.
Scails, William, 405.
Scarbara, James, 409.
Scard, Lieut. ——, 355.
Scioto Indians, towns, 432.
Scoppathus, Indian chief, 347.
Scotch, 40, 191, 295, 426.
Scotch-Irish, 28, 39, 81, 82, 348.
Scotland, 104, 392, 425.
Scott, Archelaus, 396.

——, Archibald, 402.
——, Capt. Daniel, 425.
——, George, 397.
——, James, 396, 402.
——, Joseph, 213.
——, William, 407.
—— County (Ky.), 130.
Scouts, 4, 19-21, 25, 47, 48, 50, 51, 61, 69-71, 78, 79, 89, 97, 98, 100, 104, 109-111, 139-141, 153, 158, 162, 168, 171, 173, 198, 201, 203, 204, 206, 212, 217, 230, 231, 234, 235, 239, 248, 256-263, 267, 278, 282, 285, 286, 299, 318, 320, 323, 327-329, 332, 333, 337-339, 341, 348-350, 352, 363, 364, 387, 404, 408, 413, 415.
Sedbery, John, 406.
Seed, Francis, 409.
Selby, James, 405.
Semple, Samuel, lawyer, 42.
Seneca Indians, 152.
Sevier, Gen. John, 40, 160, 271; sketch, 271.
——, Valentine, 271, 412; sketch, 271.
Shadrack White's Station, 239.
Shain, John, 94.
Shallow Ford, battle of, 220.
Shamokin (Pa.), 305.
Shannon, John, 106.
——, Samuel, 233, 247, 279.
——, Thomas, 106, 229.
Sharp, Abraham, 409.
——, Benjamin, 246.
——, John, scout, 404.
Sharpe, Edward, scout, 4, 403.
Shaw (Span), Henry, 412.
Shawnee Indians, 7, 11, 28-30, 33, 42, 45, 48, 54, 58, 59, 66, 72, 92, 98, 114, 124, 133, 149, 156, 186, 210, 212, 217, 237, 239, 243, 256, 260, 273, 278, 289, 292, 302, 304, 306, 310, 319, 346, 347, 361, 362, 381-

INDEX 467

384, 432–436; towns, 28, 37,
53, 82, 83, 100, 110, 152, 153,
155, 161, 175, 237, 246, 272,
277, 288–290, 292, 301, 379,
382, 384.
Shawneetown (Ill.), 196.
Shea, John G., *Historical Magazine*, 28.
Shelby, Capt. Evan, 48, 55, 77, 135–137, 143, 147, 148, 158, 159, 164, 178, 189, 196, 197, 210, 225, 226, 238, 240, 245, 271–274, 277, 278, 284, 286, 292, 315, 317, 318, 330, 334, 341, 363, 415, 417–419, 436, 437; letters to, 106–108; manuscripts, 412; sketch, 48, 270.
——, Lieut. Isaac, 49, 70, 270, 271, 412; letters by, 262, 269–277, 341; sketch, 270.
——, James, 412; sketch, 270, 271.
——, John, letter to, 269–277.
——, Thomas, 271.
——, Capt. William, 424.
—— family, 106.
—— County (Ky.), 82, 111.
Shell, Arnold, 399.
Shelp, John, 421.
Sheperdsville (Ky.), 126.
Shickalamy, murdered, 13.
Shillin, John, 94, 110.
Shikellimo, John. See Logan.
Shoat, ——, 210, 211, 239.
Shoatt, Emanuel, 412.
Simms, Capt. Charles, 188, 317; sketch, 317.
Sinclair, ——, hunter, 239.
Sinking Spring (Va.), 81.
Simkins, Daniel, 406.
——, James, 406.
Simmerman, George, 411.
Simpson (Simson), James, 407.
——, John, 406.
——, William, 406.
Six Nations (Iroquois), 5, 383.
Skaggs, ——, 94.
——, Charles, 239.
——, Henry, fur-trader, 64, 239.
——, James, 64.
——, John, 239.
——, Reuben, 94.
——, Zachariah, 94.
Skidmore, Capt. John, 275, 280, 286, 288, 289, 297, 331, 341, 355, 414, 416.
Slaughter, Capt. ——, 351, 352, 367, 419, 420, 435.
——, Col. Francis, 197; sketch, 197.
——, Col. George, 197, 261, 267, 349, 424.
——, Lawrence, 197.
Sloane, ——, 18.
Smith, ——, 63, 267, 347, 351.
——, Bruten, 405.
——, Conrad, 424.
——, Capt. Daniel, 85, 143, 157, 159, 161–163, 178, 192–194, 203, 204, 217, 219, 231, 245, 252, 254, 278, 297, 357, 359, 396, 401; letters by, 2, 3, 30, 31, 69–71, 135, 233, 248–250; letters to, 134, 241–243; sketch, 3; manuscript map, 30, 41, 76, 88, 94.
——, Devereux, 156.
——, Edward, 410.
——, Ericus, 401.
——, J., 85.
——, James, 396.
——, John, 106, 229, 421.
——, Mecagh, 405.
——, Moses, 405.
——, Robert, 407.
——, William, 405.
Smithers, Gabriel, 409.
Smithfield (Va.), 3, 26, 91, 101, 145, 146, 151, 161, 179, 224, 229, 234, 235, 249, 279, 301. See also Draper's Meadows.
Snakes town, 154.
Snodgrass, ——, 233.
Snydoes, ——, 140.

Sobe, George, 397.
Sodowsky, —, 119.
Somerset (Ky.), 215.
South Carolina, 331, 375.
Spain, 82, 160, 207, 375, 428.
Spars Ford, 359.
Spear, Benjamin, killed by Indians, 36.
Speed, Thomas, "Political Club," 273.
Spicer, William, 405.
Spratt, Isaac, sergeant, 403, 404.
Springs: Burning, 112, 133, 326, 357; Floyd's, 130; Grey Sulphur, 112; Limestone, 23; Royal, sketch, 130; Salt, 122.
Squires, Uriah, 409.
Staffy, Michael, 400.
Staily, Martin, 399.
Stalnaker, Samuel, killed by Indians, 232; sketch, 58.
Stalnaker's (Va.), 58, 76.
Stanton, Richard, scout, 4.
Starn, Jacob, 177.
Staunton (Va.), 74, 104, 149, 160, 177, 196, 223, 254, 257, 280, 295, 299, 311, 331, 339, 429, 436.
Steel, Andrew, 403.
Steele, John, 422.
Stephen, Gen. Adam, 24, 237, 238, 308, 340, 428; letter to, 236–238; sketch, 191.
Stephens, John, 399.
——, John, lieutenant, 399.
——, Thomas, 409.
——, William, 424.
Stephenson, Capt. Hugh, 421.
——, Robert, 400.
Sterns, Conrad, 400.
Stevens, —, 178.
Steward, John, 424.
——, Walter, 422.
Stewart, John, 412.
——, William, 411.
Stiffay, Peter, 95.
Stillwater, battle of, 111, 239.

Stoner, Michael, scout, 51, 81, 108; sketch, 51.
Stoner's Station (Ky.), 51.
Stony Point, capture of, 6, 196.
Strother, Miss —, 280.
Strother, James, killed by Indians, 164.
Stroud, Adam, killed by Indians, 374.
Stuart, —, 405.
——, James, 408.
—— (Stewart), Capt. John, 104, 274, 281, 286, 315, 330, 334, 344, 413, 415–419, 436; sketch, 104; "Narrative," 104, 113, 286, 309, 410, 419, 422.
——, Capt. John, Indian agent, 5, 374, 375; sketch, 375.
Stull, Martin, 421.
Stump, Michael, 106.
Sullivan. James, 421.
——, Samuel, 410.
—— County (Tenn.), 75, 208, 252.
Summers, L. P., Southwest Virginia, 194, 412, 422.
Sumner County (Tenn.), 158.
Sumter, Gen. Thomas, 235.
Sunbury (Pa.), 305.
Surveyors, 5, 7, 9, 21–23, 25, 31, 32, 43, 46, 49, 54, 78, 81, 83, 88, 89, 111, 112, 115, 118, 124, 151, 174, 195, 222, 231, 270, 312, 431.
Susquehannocks, 28.
Swiss, 373, 393.
Switzerland, 393.
Swoop, John, 408.

TACHNECHDORUS (Logan), 305.
Tarleton, Colonel, 273.
Tarrence, Big, 11.
Tate, Lieut. T., 424.
——, William, 424.
Taylor, Capt. —, 172-174.

INDEX

Taylor, Archibald, 210, 211.
——, Daniel, 410.
——, Hancock, surveyor, 1, 2, 112, 114, 116, 120, 122-125, 129, 152, 164, 195, 207; sketch, 23.
——, Isaac, 408.
——, Capt. John, 45, 47, 172-174, 188; sketch, 45.
——, Richard, 23.
——, Sieltor, sergeant, 407.
——, William, sergeant, 406.
——, Zachary, president, 23.
—— County (Ky.), 239.
Teasy, William, 407.
Tecumseh, 347.
Tennessee, 4, 41, 44, 48, 85, 107, 180, 221, 236, 273.
Terrence (Torrence), Andrew, 412.
Terry, Rev. —, 258.
Thomas, Col. —, 266.
——, Edward, 411.
Thompson, Andrew, ensign, 399.
——, Capt. James, 43, 56, 57, 59, 85, 157, 159, 161, 171, 210, 220, 226, 227, 233, 240, 247; letter by, 278; sketch, 43.
——, Henry, 99, 100, 234.
——, Richard, 402.
——, Robert, 424.
——, William, 105, 106, 143-145, 148, 173, 176, 177, 189, 403, 411.
Thwaites, R. G., *Daniel Boone*, 13, 51; *Early Western Travels*, 4, 7, 13, 65, 121, *Withers's Border Warfare*, 31, 36, 422.
Timber Ridge (Va.), 27.
Tipton, John, 422.
Todd, Charles S., 270.
——, James, 405.
——, John, 313, 340, 341, 343, 344, 350, 407; sketch, 343.
Toledo & Ohio Railway, 357.
Tomlinson, —, 10.
——, Joseph, 15.

——, Nathaniel, 15.
Topp, Roger, 277.
Torney (Forney), Peter, 412.
Town House, rendezvous, 53, 58, 60, 143, 163, 165, 169, 170, 230.
Trabue, Lieut. James, 421.
Trans-Alleghany Historical Magazine, 422.
Transylvania, 32, 111, 344; company, 9, 24, 39, 51, 207, 235.
Treaties: between English and Indians, 293, 301, 302, 304-306; between Indians and Transylvania Company, 39; Bouquet's (1764), 28, 163, 373, 374, 377; Dunmore's, 29, 304-306, 347, 356, 386, 432; Fort Pitt (1778), 427; Fort Stanwix (1768), 5, 242, 370, 427; Hopewell (1785), 236; Lochaber (1770), 5, 370, 427; Logstown (1752), 431; Mobile (1764), 375; of Paris (1763), 38; Sycamore Shoals (1775), 221.
Trent, —, canoe master, 350.
——, Obadiah H., sergeant, 340, 411.
Trigg, Daniel, 65.
——, Louise Johnston, 110, 111.
——, Capt. Stephen. 44, 49, 55, 182, 184; sketch, 44.
Trimble, —, 227.
——, Isaac, 406.
——, James, 422.
——, John, killed by Indians, 331.
Trotter, John, 424.
——, Richard, 424.
Tucker, William, 412.
Turner, Frederick Jackson, "Western State Making in the Revolutionary Era," 370.
——, John, 285.
——, Joseph, 106, 229.
Tygert, Michael, 117.

VAILS, John, 400.
Vallendigham, George, 421.
Valley Forge, 272, 439.
Valleys: Carter's, 221; Clinch, 195; Draper's, 64; Kanawha, 103, 104, 113; Kishacoquillas, 305; Ligonier, 392; Poor, 79; Powell's 2, 4, 5, 207, 220, 235, 239, sketch, 4; Rich, 79, 193, 195, 205, 230, 232; Shenandoah 374.
Van Bibber, Isaac, 424.
——, Jesse, 424.
——, John, 424.
——, Peter, 424.
Vance, ——, 143, 159, 165-168, 170, 215, 230, 231, 233, 250.
——, Edmond, 94, 140, 266.
——, Lieut. Samuel, 276, 288, 289, 296, 351, 355, 412; sketch, 276.
Vandalia, 370.
Vanhook, Samuel, 396.
Van Meter, Abraham, receipt to, 68.
——, Jacob, 68.
——, Rebecca, 31.
Vaut, Andrew, 400.
——, Christian, 400.
——, George, 400, 404.
Venable, William, 421.
Vincennes (Ind.), 344.
Vaughn (Vaun), John, 411.
Virginia, 4-6, 9, 10, 20, 21, 29, 30, 32, 39, 41, 55, 62, 69, 74, 92, 101, 150, 153, 168, 180, 206, 207, 223, 230, 271, 296, 306, 343, 360, 368, 374, 388, 392, 394-396, 425, 428, 433, 436, 437, 439; assembly, 20, 21, 25, 32-34, 39, 44, 74, 107, 187, 191, 242, 272, 280, 303, 307, 310, 344, 379, 387, 405, 427, 430; first bishop, 280; boundary line, 5, 8, 19, 20, 26, 42, 48, 67, 236, 392; committee of claims, 25; committee of safety, 242; revolutionary committee, 242; constitutional convention, 25, 184, 191, 242, 249, 312, 348; council, 20, 63, 241-243, 307, 380, 390, 391, 395; governor, 20, 21, 93, 145, 242, 260, 379; House of Burgesses, 20, 31, 92, 98, 304, 307, 312, 425; military grants, 152; settlements, 58, 225, 226, 420; troops, 2, 12, 103, 160, 161, 191, 197, 231, 273, 317; *Gazette*, 295; *Historical Collections*, 104, 191, 286, 422, 429; *Historical Magazine*, 316; *Historical Register*, 270, 303, 310; "History of Virginia Federal Convention," 191.
Virginians, 7, 13, 28, 65-67, 114, 115, 136, 373, 374, 382, 384, 391.

WADDELL, J. A., *Annals of Augusta County*, 74, 101, 137, 360, 422.
Waggoner, ——, 116, 171.
——, Andrew, 424.
——, Henry, 399.
——, Henry, Jr., 399.
Wakatomica (Wapatomica), 150, 152, 153, 155, 304, sketch, 153.
Walker, ——, 4, 252.
——, Adam, 399.
——, Henry, 397.
——, James, 406.
——, Dr. Thomas, 20, 56, 58, 109, 235, 242; sketch, 242.
Wall, Henry, killed by Indians, 36.
Wallace, Adam, ensign, 406.
——, Andrew, 406.
——, Caleb, judge, 184.
——, David, 406.
——, Robert, 406.
——, Samuel, lieutenant, 406.
Walpole, Thomas, letter by, 151; sketch, 370; land grant, 370.
Walter, Michael, 400.
Wambler, George, 400.

INDEX

Wambler, Mitchel, 400.
Ward. Charles, pioneer, 276.
——, David, ensign, 396, 403, 404.
——, Capt. James, 275, 276, 280, 296, 301, 330, 355, 416, 417, 422, 435, 437; sketch, 276.
——, James, Jr., pioneer, 276.
——, John, Indian captive, 422.
——, William, sergeant, 399.
Ware, —, 125.
Warm Springs (Va.), 74, 177, 196, 222, 223, 273, 306, 314.
Wars: Cherokee, 38, 84, 216, 218, 252, 376; French and Indian, 2, 5, 8, 11, 21, 28, 38, 48, 65, 84, 103, 113, 191, 223, 236, 242, 272, 276, 305, 360, 375, 426, 431; Indian, 29, 32, 36, 43, 47, 48, 58, 63, 69, 74, 101, 152, 196, 212, 214, 218, 247, 278, 348, 427; Northwest Indians, 152, 225, 392; of 1812-15, 6, 107, 270; Pontiac's, 11, 28, 75, 78, 103, 191, 272, 373, 432; Revolutionary, 2, 3, 6, 11, 14, 24, 25, 27, 29, 39, 40, 42-45, 55, 81, 86, 103, 152, 160, 161, 191, 196, 197, 214, 221, 223, 225, 239, 242, 272, 273, 310, 331, 375, 392, 405, 427, 428, 431.
Warwick, Jacob, 422.
Washburn, James, 405.
——, Steven, 405.
Washington, Gen. George, 8, 12, 14, 23, 24, 65, 74, 103, 112, 114, 191, 272, 426-428; letters to, 24, 151; sketch, 8; *Writings*, 114; manuscripts, 151.
——, Martha Dandridge, 24.
—— (D. C.), 107, 151, 160.
—— (Pa.), 10.
Watauga, 107, 148, 164, 165, 221, 278; massacre, 63, 72; purchase, 48; settlements, 38, 40, 58, 59, 75, 135, 232.

Watkins, —, 255, 266.
——, Robert, 411.
Watson, —, 31.
——, Jonathan, 406.
Waugh, —, cadet, 409.
Wayne, Gen. Anthony, **152, 196.**
Weaver, Christian, 399.
——, Michael, 399.
Welch, James, 424.
——, John, 409.
——, Thomas, 407.
——, Thomas, Jr., 407.
Wells, Bazaleel, 16, **424.**
——, Samuel, 421.
Welsh, Christopher, **408.**
——, Richard, 405.
Westfall (O.), 292.
West Liberty (Pa.), **16.**
Westover (Va.), 21.
West Virginia, 78, 345, 360; *Historical Magazine,* 272, 423, 434.
Wetzel, John, 421.
——, Martin, 421.
Wheeling (W. Va.), 11, **12, 16,** 19, 29, 37, 62, 102, 152, 155, 156, 304, 434.
Wheeler, Dr. Charles, 11, **12.**
Whigs, 84, 152, 191, 221, 242.
Whitby, Moses, 406.
White, David, 422.
——, Edward, 11.
——, Capt. Jacob, **12.**
——, Joseph, 409.
——, Shadrach, 239.
——, Solomon, 408.
——, William, 280, 422.
—— Eyes (Koquethagechton), Delaware chief, 29, 156, 256, 302, 384; sketch, 29.
—— Fish, Indian chief, 290, 356.
—— Sulphur Springs, 359, 360.
Whitsell's Mills, battle of, 431.
Whitticor, Joseph, 411.
Whitton, Jeremiah, 404.
——, Thomas, 234, 404.
——, Thomas, Jr., 404.

Wiley, James, 421.
———, Robert, 397.
———, Robert, Jr., 397.
———, Thomas, 397.
William, Col. William, 435.
Williams, Alden, 396.
———, David, 420.
———, Evan, 211.
———, Isaac, 425.
———, James, 200, 397.
———, Jarrett, 412.
———, John, 399, 403, 405, 411, 412.
———, Mark, 277, 412.
———, Philip, 398.
———, Richard, 411.
———, Rowland, 404.
———, Samuel, 410.
———, Thomas, sergeant, 410.
Williamsburg (Va.), 1, 19–21, 26, 33, 37, 61, 86, 87, 111, 155, 295, 304, 307, 368, 394, 395.
Williamson, Aldin, 400.
———, David, 421.
Willis, Henry, 403.
Wilmoth, William, 402.
Wilson, Capt. —, 205, 210, 217, 231, 241, 251, 414, 416.
———, Benjamin, 421.
———, Edward, 408.
———, James, 411.
———, Capt. John, 272, 425, 435, 437.
———, Col. George, sketch, 28.
———, Richard, 254.
———, Capt. Samuel, 272, 275, 288, 289, 296, 301, 331, 343, 346, 349, 355; sketch, 272.
———, Thomas, 411.
———, William, sergeant, 408, 422.

Winchester (Va.), 98, 152, 185.
Wipey, Indian, 387.
Withers, Alexander Scott, *Border Warfare*, 112, 155, 319, 344, 347, 374, 377.
Wolf Hills (Abingdon Va.), 75, 81, 232.
Wood, Dr. —, 8.
———, Capt. James, 155, 421.
———, John, 409.
Woods, —, 178.
———, Adam, 397.
———, Andrew, 200, 397.
———, Archibald, 402.
———, Billey, 100.
———, James, sergeant, 411.
———, Capt. Michael, 175, 176, 199, 201; letters by, 175, 176, 397, 398.
———, Michael, pioneer, 176.
———, Richard, 397.
Woolsey, Richard, 400.
Workman, Daniel, 410.
Wormsley, Ralph, 87.
Wright, Col. Gideon, 221; sketch, 221.
Wyandotte Indians, 103, 346, 347, 436.

XENIA (O.), 292.

YAZOO acts, 160.
Yorktown (Va.), 43, 242.
Young, John, 240, 399.

ZANE, Col. Ebenezer, 12, 421.
Zanesville (O.), 256.
Zeisberger, David, Moravian missionary, 36, 153.

www.ingramcontent.com/pod-product-compliance
Lightning Source LLC
Chambersburg PA
CBHW060313230426
43663CB00009B/1685